HEAVEN and EARTH

Volume 1: Bereishis, Shemos, Vayikra

Yerucham Reich (Raymond Reich, MD)

HEAVEN and EARTH

A Real-World View of Jewish Life through
the *Parashah* and the Holidays

Volume 1: Bereishis, Shemos, Vayikra

אשר בך ירחם

gefen
publishing house   בית הוצאה לאור
JERUSALEM ◆ NEW YORK   Est. 1981

Cover Design: Azi Creative Visuals LLC

ISBN: 978-965-229-932-1

1 3 5 7 9 8 6 4 2

Gefen Publishing House Ltd.
6 Hatzvi Street
Jerusalem 9438614, Israel
972-2-538-0247
orders@gefenpublishing.com

Gefen Books
140 Fieldcrest Ave.
Edison NJ, 08837
516-593-1234
orders@gefenpublishing.com

Library of Congress Cataloging-in-Publication Data

Names: Reich, Raymond, author.
Title: Heaven and earth : a real-world view of Jewish life through the
    Parashah and the holidays / Raymond Reich.
Description: Springfield, NJ ; Jerusalem : Gefen Publishing House, [2018]
Identifiers: LCCN 2018003360 | ISBN 9789652299321
Subjects: LCSH: Bible. Pentateuch—Commentaries. | Fasts and feasts—Judaism.
Classification: LCC BS1225.53. R45 2018 | DDC 296.7/2—dc23 LC record available at
    https://lccn.loc.gov/2018003360

www.gefenpublishing.com

Printed in Israel

הרב משה הלוי פלוטשאק

ק"ק שערי תורה בברוקלין נ.י.

אודותינו ספרו לנו והננו ראינו תלמידי חכמים מובהקים צעד ואל שאו שהדים
לראשית תורתך חייהם וזה הגן כל ימיהם

מכון המפורסמים הה הגדא כ'אינ'גל בצדקל סוחר ואיש ספקים ראון יתורה מאוש'
ספרו המפורסם שמחת כהן הי היא ואן פיעה ראשון וזה חכל הלכה . ואשרהו כדבולה הה
כדל חיי אבק ראון פוס דין ההלכה נצאת שבלשד צאון דכסריו היקרים

וה . לנו חורה פנכף ומרגלות צ' גתרה כהקרד'ב מבאווישצט דכסרו היקר פרכס יוסף צהה
תוצאה זו ציונה חדשה הרי כאה וכאה ארושונל שאלוק'פ כתלאנ'ק כהכלך' והראבן
דלבה . שכל הקך . ורוב צכר כלים לחיי הצולם הבא רוכאנים אוקהקים הי .

וצתה קד יביר הקר איש שורק מסף כולו שחמרפ לבכו מאתקיפ . רוכא נשאן
שוון כאצא אולתנו . סוקר סטורק . ודאאה שריה נהודו

הה הרקן הע"ד הה ר' ירוחס צרוק ר"ך שלשא ש"ל ל ולא שתמק ס'יותא צל'פ.ה.
וקהת הסופר קידו נאיוה זו אוסר כספפל החשוק של אחברים וקה.ג.פ.פ.
והנה קיודפו ורר'רו קא אומיע . ואני הקר ראוימיהו סקיפ רגות צלה ואתצלה כהלוש . וכל כי
ראשע סודאת לקומל . לבכ ירשעו לסקלוו היר יקוגו מר'נוער חולה . ויעררו קין סוורי סוף
ושין סוף ולא תעלה!

יצבת' רק קרב' . ולא סלצת קמאצלנ סר' הסכניאים ורוכנ הערגת . שולה צברק אני קרוא
ולנרכו צני ילבצ . ול'רה' . היקר נצוה צברק שכה יוסף וכה ירקה וכה יקר חביל צטורה ולדעודה
וסטוא לא ישול ולא יכום התמין. צך יקן צלה ולי יקהת צת ולידעל קוסמיות צרדעל

כה דקר ידיד' וחאברו כלונה
מאשג הלו' פלוטשוק

הרב אביגדור בורשטיין

רב בית הכנסת רננים ירושלים

בס"ד, יום השישי לסדר עלה נעלה התשע"ח

הנה באתי בקצירת האומר לברך את רעי וידידי, כאח לי, הרב החסיד ר'
ירוחם ברוך רייך שליט"א ביום שמחת לבו ולבנו -אנו לרגל הוצאת ספרו
היקר והחשוב *Heaven and Earth* ואכן, יאה השם למחברו ,
סולם מוצב ארצה וראשו מגיע השמימה. טוב עין הוא יבורך, ומטיב
עינים כרופא מומחה יתברך בכפלים.

שנים רבות הקדיש המחבר להעלות על הכתב מאשר רחש לבו הטהור
בדברי תורה וחכמה, דרך ארץ ומוסר, סיפורים מרגשים המחברים בין
ארץ ושמים, העושים את התורה הקדושה לתורת חיים. בעין בוחנת,
בלב הומה ובתבונת הדעת הצליח הרב המחבר לשזור ולארוג מסכת
נפלאה של דברי תורה על פרשיות השבוע, חגים ומועדים ומה שביניהם.

זכיתי להמנות עם ידידיו של המחבר, להוקיר מידותיו ויראת השמים
שהיא אוצרו, להתפעל ממסכת דרך ארץ שהנחיל למשפחתו ולסביבתו
יחד עם רעיתו החשובה שרה מנב"ת. כל אלו ויותר באים לידי ביטוי
בספרו רב האיכות. מבין קפלי הספר הכתוב בחן ובחכמת לבב בוקעת
האמונה כי "לך שמים, אף לך ארץ".

והנני לברכו שיזכה לראות בטוב ירושלים, להגדיל תורה ולהאדירה,
שיפוצו מעיינותיו החוצה מתוך בריאות הגוף וחדוות הנפש יחד עם
רעייתו וכל משפחתו.

אשרנו שזכינו!

בהוקרה מרובה ובידידות עוז

אביגדור בורשטיין

הרב אביגדור בורשטיין
ירושלים ת"ו

RABBI DR. TZVI HERSH WEINREB

Executive Vice President, Emeritus

212.613.8264 *tel*
212.613.0635 *fax*
execthw@ou.org *email*

ELEVEN BROADWAY | NEW YORK, NY 10004-1303

212.563.4000 | info@ou.org | www.ou.org

In times gone by, books written on the weekly Torah portions were limited either to textual commentary, *pshat*, or to stimulating novel interpretations of a phrase or verse, *drash* or a *gut vort*. Often, these books were collections of rabbinic sermons, delivered for specific audiences over long periods of time.

A new trend has developed, however, and it has become increasingly popular. This trend has come about as a response to an urgent need in the Jewish community. I refer to the need to make the *parashah* relevant to the daily lives of the reader.

The book before you, *Heaven and Earth*, is an example of this trend. Its major feature is its remarkable ability to address "real life" contemporary issues from the perspective of traditional texts and commentaries.

The book's subtitle says it all: *A Real-World View of Jewish Life through the Parashah and the Holidays*. The author, Dr. Raymond (Yerucham) Reich, is a prestigious physician whose "real world" credentials are impeccable. His professional training and experience combine with his humanity and erudition to form the context for his writing.

The author is thoroughly familiar with contemporary Jewish culture, its problems, challenges, and very real successes. He draws from his personal experience and from the experiences of his family and friends. There is a wealth of material here about Jewish history, particularly about the Holocaust era and the American Jewish experience. It is apparent that he comes from a pious background and that he has incorporated that piety into his very soul. *Yiras Shamayim*, fear of heaven, is to be found on every page, as is *ahavas Yisrael*, love and respect for every Jew.

Heaven and Earth is both inspiring and instructive. It is inspiring because it delivers a practical spiritual message to the reader. It is instructive not only because of its impressive scholarly content, but because of the historical, scientific, and cultural information that it conveys. The author occasionally draws upon his medical expertise, but also introduces us to men such as Alexander Rubowitz, a long-forgotten hero who deserves to be remembered.

This book will lend itself to multiple uses. The reader may peruse it for his or her own edification. The teacher can use it in the classroom. It will be a wonderful basis for talk at the Shabbos table, particularly if that table is graced by individuals of diverse backgrounds.

This is not just another book on the *parashah*. This is a book to which one can turn as a "workbook" for the integration of day-to-day routine with authentic and uplifting religious teachings.

I especially recommend this book to the many who struggle with "real world" challenges and need an intelligent but practical framework within which to deal with them.

As a fellow author of a book on the weekly *parashah*, I congratulate Dr. Reich for his contribution to the growing literature of edifying and intellectually satisfying English language Torah works.

Tzvi Hersh Weinreb

Tzvi Hersh Weinreb
Jerusalem, Israel
July 4, 2018

Founded in 1898 as the Union of Orthodox Jewish Congregations of America

איחוד קהילות האורתודוקסים באמריקה

הרב אברהם חיים פייער

Rabbi Avrohom Chaim Feuer

שערי חסד ירושלים

A breath of fresh air! Those are the words that rise in my heart when I read the lines of this masterpiece, *Heaven and Earth*, authored by my old friend, Dr. Yerucham Reich, who blends the roles of a serious *ben Torah* and an accomplished eye doctor who trained his vision to see Hashem's world through "Torah spectacles."

Somehow every line of this splendid *sefer* refreshes my soul and fills it with a new appreciation for the glory of God and the majesty of His creation. This work speaks for itself. Just open it and read any section, and you will find your mind filled with original insights and a yearning to delve even deeper.

Yasher koach, Reb Yerucham!

Rabbi Avrohom Chaim Feuer
Shaarei Chesed, Yerushalayim
July 2018

Rabbi Yehudah Yonah Rubinstein
Inwood, NY

It is interesting that Dr Yerucham (Raymond) Reich chose to call his book, "Heaven and Earth". Open it and start reading and you will soon find that he offers profound insights into both.

As he steers you towards an intriguing or exciting Torah idea, he uses his knowledge of science and human nature to set the stage for a Jewish concept which unfailingly pleases and delights.

He may introduce you to the intricacies of the structure of the Human eye. He may invite you to use your eye to look up at a cluster of stars in the constellation called Taurus and then see those wonders mirrored in the pages of the Chumash.

But don't think that this author is offering his readers heavy intellectual material that you will have to push yourself to read. Dr Reich knows precisely how to inject fascinating stories to bring his chapters to life. He also knows how to use his well known sense of humor to complement his Torah wisdom (wait until you read about the confrontation between the Rabbi and the Goat and you'll see for yourself).

In short he has penned a charming book that will enhance your understanding of the Torah's weekly Parshas as well as the Yomim Tovim. It is also guaranteed to delight the guests at your Shabbos table.

I have to admit that Dr Reich and I have been close friends for a long time. That of course would have to put my role as an unbiased voice attesting to the quality and value of his book somewhat in doubt.

But I am going to insist nevertheless that this is a really excellent work. I am also able to state that if this level of Torah Scholarship can be combined so seamlessly with insights into human nature and science as it has been here, then "Heaven and Earth" will delight you, as it did me.

Rabbi Y Y Rubinstein, Inwood, New York, 11096 yy@rabbiyy.com

Contents

Preface .... *xi*

ספר בראשית **1**
  Bereishis 3
  Noach 12
  Lech Lecha 24
  Vayera 41
  Chayei Sarah 57
  Toldos 65
  Vayetzei 77
  Vayishlach 96
  Vayeshev 111
  Miketz 127
  Vayigash 139
  Vayechi 153

ספר שמות **165**
  Shemos 167
  Va'era 185
  Bo 198
  Beshalach 210
  Yisro 225
  Mishpatim 231
  Terumah 241
  Tetzaveh 256
  Ki Sisa 267
  Vayakhel-Pekudei 281

ספר ויקרא **295**
  Vayikra 297
  Tzav 309
  Shemini 311

Tazria-Metzora 332
Acharei Mos-Kedoshim 344
Emor 357
Behar 372
Bechukosai 384

Preface

I once sat in on a *shidduch* meeting in a *yom tov* hotel catering to a reasonably well off, educated, mostly *yeshivish* crowd. Concerned parents were given advice and direction by *shidduch* professionals and *"mevinim"* on navigating their way through this fraught, often distressing challenge in life. Their children's future, happiness, and fulfillment are at stake.

Much of what I heard involved decision making and direction on *shidduch* choices by the boy's rebbe or the rebbetzin the girl consults with. After a while, I realized that I was hearing something by *not* hearing something. I was not hearing anything at all about the judgment of the parents in this weighty matter affecting their own children. It was as if the parents themselves don't have much – except perhaps a checkbook – to contribute to this process. Of course, it cannot be so, and for most people it isn't so – and yet, from what was being said at this "official," very *yeshivish* establishment forum, hard as it is to believe, so it seemed.

It was as if there are people – however wise, however experienced, however caring, even however dedicated they might be (and it's a reasonable assumption but unfortunately not an absolute certainty that they are) – who are assumed to be wiser or more caring about these children than their own parents. In fact, of course, nobody cares more, nobody worries more, nobody thinks more, nobody's life is more bound up with these children, nobody is more giving or more self-sacrificing, nobody more reliably puts the children's best interests first than their parents.

I couldn't help myself. I got up and said something about it. At first they just stared. Then I got a general response to the effect that "well, of course the parents are important, yes, yes, we didn't mean to imply...but..." I also thought I detected a bit of unspoken, dismissive "you don't really get it, and you must not really be too *frum*" as well. But the parents, I could tell, for the most part, heard me very well.

Sometimes, in this life and in this society, there is something so obvious that needs to be said, but few, if any, perhaps for fear of being perceived as outside the "norm" (yes, the *frum* PC), actually say it. This book, this *sefer*, if you will, in part, tries to say some of those things.

There is no one like a parent. Lucky and blessed is the child with the right parents, who do more than anyone else to form the person that child becomes.

And so, I proclaim before all how blessed I am to be the child of the parents I had, Shimon and Chana Reich, of blessed memory, Holocaust survivors whose love, self-sacrifice, strength, determination, bravery, and faith inspired virtually every step I have taken in life. They made sure I knew who I am, where I come from, the noble family forebears I sprang from, the kind of person I have to be, how to be a loving and well-thought-out parent, how to be a man and a husband and a father, how to be a Jew. How to be a thinker and a doer. And from my brother, Walter (זאב), הי"ו, what it means to be a loving, generous brother, how a fine and decent person behaves, and how to strive to excel. No big brother ever set a finer example in decency and goodness. These pages, this body of work and thought, is the product of my upbringing.

I proclaim before all, as well, that the wellspring of love and strength and loyalty and devotion that has, throughout my adult life, made everything else possible is embodied in my blessed wife Sue (שרה), עמו"ש, who is, has always been, and always will be my hope and my inspiration. No husband has ever had a better or more dedicated protector against the many dangers of this world. May Hashem bless her and the children in every way.

I gratefully proclaim that the children God has blessed me with – every one of them a gem, הי"ו – make me proud, always, to be their father and inspire me always to continue to strive and to make myself worthy of such children. Yael, Shlomo, Yitzchak, Yosef, Avigail, their beloved husbands and wives, and their wonderful, adored children, fill my life with sweetness and *nachas*. And they make me want to leave the words and the thoughts in this book as a legacy for them.

And I must proclaim as well, with love, gratitude, and respect, the one who pushed me more than anyone else to take the musings and the thoughts that have been for years roiling around in my head and sometimes on paper, and to *write*, my esteemed son-in-law Rabbi Akiva Eisenstadt, עמו"ש, whose remarkable weekly Torah journal, *The Shtieble*, has been the vehicle for much that I have written.

I thank my *rebbeim* over all the years, who have taught me and inspired me.

And to you, readers, those who are familiar with my work and have encouraged me in this endeavor, and those who have taken the plunge and picked up this volume, I proclaim, thank you. Join me on this journey of thought, emotion, learning, and commitment, in our lives as Jews and as human beings – those creatures who can rise so high and yet also sink so low, who can be so incredibly strong and yet also so pathetically weak, whose capacity for evil is breathtaking, even as their capacity for goodness and nobility bears eloquent testimony to man's creation in the very image of God.

The thoughts expressed in these essays are, to me, a straight-talk, commonsensical approach to life and to Judaism, to our lives as Jews, *maaminim bnei maaminim*, without regard to being "politically correct" or subservient to any "party line," other than loyalty to the Ribbono shel Olam and our holy *mesorah*. Depending on their orientation, not everyone may be entirely comfortable with everything, but that is their right (and their error, of course!). No, this book is *not* particularly controversial, but it is, I think, independent minded.

It is drawn from life, from history, from the world as it *really is*, from the world *as it ought to be*, from my lifetime experiences and observations as a Jew, as a physician, and as the son of Holocaust survivors, from the *mesorah* of my forebears, from the teachings of our *chachamim*, from elements of Jewish history and life that are critical to preserve and to share. It reflects, I hope, some measure of wisdom in life and insight into the Torah and holidays that may be beneficial to others. And so, thank you for joining.

And I thank the Zalman Aryeh Hilsenrad Keren Hachesed – an outstanding undertaking of pure tzedakah, in which every cent contributed goes to support the deserving poor of Eretz Yisrael – for its imprimatur. Mr. Hilsenrad was an uncommon man, pure and good, whose soul thirsted for the One Above.

Before all and above all, I proclaim my thanks to the Living God of Israel, our Father in Heaven, for this blessed life, for this uncommon opportunity, for being with me, for sustaining me and bringing me to this day.

Yerucham Baruch Reich
Tishrei 5778

ספר בראשית

Bereishis

Deus Ex Punctum Lacrimalis

If you look inside a human tear duct, will you find God?

And if you were to contemplate that tear duct, as you watch it, would God emerge and show Himself?

The tear duct is a fascinating bit of physiology. Everyone understands that the eye must be kept moist, and that keeping the eye open for just seconds too long causes pain, then severe pain, then damage to the eye. A cruel form of torture is to keep the victim's eyelids forcibly open. The eyelids direct the tear film across the eye, keeping it moist and healthy. We must produce tears constantly. But where do the tears go? When we weep, they run down the face as well as down the nose. Hence, we need to wipe the tears away and blow our noses when we cry.

What happens when we're not crying? Each eyelid has a little opening in it, a few millimeters from the nose. This opening, the punctum lacrimalis, leads to a tiny canal in the eyelid, running just under the skin to the corner of the eye near the nose. There the canal from the upper lid meets the canal from the lower lid, and the two together lead into the tear sac, which sits in a little depression in the bone, that fits just right and cradles it, where the eye meets the nose. The sac then gives rise to another canal that runs down through the bone into the nose, emerging in the nostril under a small bony structure called the turbinate, which protects it. The tiny amounts of fluid in the system at any time thus disappear into the nose and throat, undetected by the person under normal circumstances. It is when we cry, producing tears in large quantity, that the system is overwhelmed, and tears flood the nose and run down the face.

But it's actually a lot more sophisticated than that. In order to get the fluid down into the nose, the eyelids function as a pump. Closing the eyes creates positive pressure to push the fluid down. Opening the eyes creates negative pressure to draw the fluid further down and to make room for the next bit of fluid.

But it's actually even more sophisticated than that. The opening to the tear duct, the lacrimal punctum, is situated on the inner aspect of the margin of the eyelid; for a lower lid, this is the top edge of the lid. But the tear lake, sitting in the corner of the eye and waiting to be drained, will not so readily find its way into the punctum if the punctum is sitting on the top of the lid, out of the tear lake. So just at this spot, just where it's needed, the lid turns inward a little, just enough to have the punctum sit in the tear lake, so the whole pump mechanism can work more efficiently.

This lacrimal drainage system, as sophisticated and as complex as it is, is itself infinitely simpler than most basic biological functions.

There are those to whom evolution is not just a way of understanding and explaining observed natural phenomena (as it indeed is). Driven by an atheistic secularist social agenda, they have made a veritable religion out of it, and, in a desperate attempt not to have to answer to God, will twist logic every which way to conjure up accident after accident to explain why the world works the way it does. And still they cannot explain how life itself came to be, except that, as a matter of dogmatic faith, it cannot be by intelligent design. That is, to them, heresy, and not to be tolerated. It is, indeed, routinely ridiculed as unscientific, even if logic screams that it is the most obvious – and thus far, the only – explanation. It is the ABG theory of the world: anything but God.

This essay is not a scientific statement, or a treatment of the broad subject of evolution, or the "Big Bang," or the specifics of how the Creator put things in place. It is about the willful, dogma-driven denial of the obvious: the obvious Hand of God in the creation and design of life. Aside from the insane improbability of life itself, utterly inexplicably, somehow, arising out of inert chemicals that happened to be lying around, they would have you believe that every impossibly, incredibly complex life process in the world – every cell, veritable factories of life, every organ system, and every living thing, as well as the interaction of all of them together in a functioning world – came about utterly by accident. Just don't say it was designed by divine intelligence!

Because then they would have to answer to God for how they live, and for their actions – and that they desperately do not wish to do. And so they ridicule people of faith as primitive. Even as scientists, they would readily accept any other explanation for life with far weaker obviousness, as long as it does not involve God.

We, the children of the Covenant, understand otherwise.

In the beginning, God created the heavens and the earth.

He created life as we know it, with its infinitely complicated plan.

It makes sense. It is so obvious.

Where can you find God? Everywhere. In everything.

In an inturning punctum lacrimalis.

Shabbos Bereishis 5771

How I Became More Religious by Becoming Less Religious

What would the world be like today if man had not fallen, if Adam and Chavah in the Garden of Eden, had remained true, and had not sinned?

Civilization, and all of history, would be utterly different. But God, Who created the world and put it in place before the fall, also knew full well that mankind would, in fact, fall, and He created it anyway. Being the omniscient God, and having created the very nature of man in such a way as to make that fall likely, if not inevitable, clearly the Ribbono shel Olam designed the world with the anticipated fall in mind. We (through our ancestors Adam and Chavah) had to have the *choice*, but fall we would. God is not capricious. There is a plan, a divine purpose in this.

So what does God really want? What does He get out of creation, with so much that's so nasty in the world He created? What does He expect of man, who, in fact, has a choice, who *should* hold true and not fall, but who, of course, tends to fall, and to fall quite badly?

We have just observed that period and that special day of heightened introspection culminating in Yom Kippur. We seek forgiveness and kindness from God in His judgment of us. He Who created us knows exactly what we are capable of and what to expect of us.

What would Yom Kippur be about if man had not fallen? God created Yom Kippur before He set man in place, before man even faced the choice of whether to sin. God created His expectations of the fallen man before man ever fell, and He built His system of the universe around that reality.

I suggest that some insight into this plan may be gained from a profound piece of the Yom Kippur liturgy we have recently recited on that holy day, when the very basics of creation and existence come to the fore.

There are two parallel pieces, apparently two segments of one whole, one recited in Shacharis and one in Musaf. They present a stark contrast. From where does God always receive praise? From the army of angels whose job that is. From where does He *seek* praise? From weak, downtrodden, sinful man.

Asher ometz tehillasecha – the powerful praise of God is rendered, routinely, by the heavenly angels who glow like lightning, by the flaming legions of *keruvim*, by the celestial beings whose names are unknowable, by those who guide the clouds, by those with wings and four faces who call out, in the high heavens, "Holy, Holy, Holy!" By their very nature, they have God's holiness in their mouths, and His awe is upon them.

But God's *desired* praise, we are told, *v'ratzisa shevach, v'avisa tehillah*, is from a very different source, and in *that* He finds (*k'v'yachol*) His glory. From limited, miserable man, with his limited life, that life filled with rage and frustration, toil and trouble, grief and pain, fashioned from the very clods of earth to which he is destined soon to return, whose youth and energy quickly fade, who accomplishes little, who struggles for his sustenance, who is of limited intelligence, who is indelibly stained by sin, whose deeds are putrid, who is devoid of truth or righteousness, who amounts to nothing, who is filled with vanity, who is but a passing shadow, who lives only through God's mercy, and inevitably is judged by God and dies.

It is when these miserable, limited creatures (us!), with all their faults and limitations, turn to God, pray to Him, cry out to Him, seek His graciousness, seek His forgiveness, and proclaim His glory that God finds the praise that He seeks, in that He finds the glory and the *kavod* He desires, and it is upon those very miserable creatures that He bestows His glory.

After their sin, Adam and Chavah were expelled from the Garden of Eden, the paradise that was the only world they knew. Created on the sixth day, they had never even seen night. Having so quickly besmirched themselves (the Talmudic word used in *Sanhedrin* 38b to describe their sin is *sarchu* [סרחו], denoting a dirty stench), expelled and left out on their own, broken and ashamed, they witnessed the world go dark – the first night of their lives. What conclusion could they come to other than that their actions had now brought an end to the world? And so they spent the night in bitter regret and repentance.

Eventually there came the dawn, a new day and a new opportunity, and the realization that in the world they now found themselves in, it was possible to rise up from misery, from sin, from guilt, to return to God and to go on, to try again. That they could still stay with Him and He would still stay with them. That given what they had done and what they had come to, this was now what God expected of them, and what He offered them. Life, rebirth. The possibility of reaching out to Him, no matter how far one has fallen, no matter how badly they had messed things up, no matter what perfect paradise they had foolishly tossed away. Turn to God, or return to God: the nobility, the humility, the honesty, the goodness, the sincerity in doing that is just what God, in His great goodness, wants of us, and indeed is what He seeks in the handiwork of His creation.

The very essence of goodness, God teaches us that not only is it possible to be good and avoid sin, and thereby serve Him, it is also possible to be bad, to be lowly and miserable, to be limited and to feel impotent, to feel lost and helpless, and yet still to remake ourselves, to turn to Him, and in doing so, to serve Him as well, indeed to fulfill one of the very purposes of creation.

Those of us who have been privileged to live a very sheltered Jewish life don't always realize what the reality is out there in the world. People – even people of whom you would never expect any such thing – sometimes mess up so badly, create such a stench of sin, that not only is it unimaginable to us, it seems beyond redemption. And yet, with the world as it is, life as it is, human nature as it is, people do things. That does not excuse it. But that's reality.

I did not always fully realize this. I may have been, in the past, somewhat harsher in my judgment of others. The wisdom and the experience that those who have seen it all and dealt with it all have shared with me have helped me temper my own judgment of others – not to approve, God forbid, their bad behavior, but to recognize it for what it is. And to understand that even for them there is usually a way back. And God designed that way back for them, knowing they would need it, and "hoping," as it were, that they would take it. And that way back is not only a part of His plan of creation, it is central to it.

I am grateful to those wise people who helped me understand this. By being more understanding, even as God is understanding, by being more tolerant – not of bad behavior, but of human nature – by being, in this narrow sense, *less* "*religious*," I can aspire to be, in actuality, *more* "*religious*."

How good and giving is our God. In our purity and goodness, in our avoiding evil and sin, He finds celestial pleasure. And in our reaching above the degrading limitations of human nature and of the human experience, in reaching out to Him, even from the depths of our own disgrace, He finds celestial pleasure. Indeed, it is His desire.

Better than any human being, the God who designed life in this world understands it.

And, it seems, our God-given capacity to break out beyond the shackles of our weaknesses, to reach out toward the sublime from the grit and the grime of this world is one of the reasons for creation itself.

In the bright plenty of paradise, it's easy to appreciate but not *really* appreciate what one has. In the darkness of the pit, in the desperate struggle for existence, it's easy to lose perspective altogether. But even in its darkest recess, God is waiting hopefully, as it were, for us to reach out to Him.

People aren't perfect. We have no right to expect them to be. And sometimes those imperfections are the very vehicle of their potential strengths, or highlight those strengths. And the wisdom to see that in others is also a gift from God.

Seeing the goodness and the wisdom in others, seeing – and appreciating – in others the strength and the spirit to raise themselves up, allows us, in a limited way, to see people the way God sees them. And what a gift that is.

On the yahrzeit of my father, Reb Shimon ben Reb Shlomo Z'ev, of blessed memory, who saw and appreciated the goodness in other people, and whom I never heard speak ill of any other person.

17 Tishrei, Sukkos 5777

DNA

The Torah does not spell out everything we might like to know, but it does tell us things we need to know. The first example of this, cited in the first Rashi in Bereishis, is that one reason the Torah begins with the story of creation is to make clear that the Creator apportions the world according to His will, and accordingly, the Land of Israel belongs, by right and in perpetuity, to the People of Israel.

Adam and Chavah. There are about *seven billion* people in the world today, and *every one* of *us* is a descendant of those two original people. And while those two were fashioned directly by the Hand of God, all of us since then are products of the same biological process, and we all carry some combination of that original DNA. And that, I submit, is one reason the Torah spells out the story of Adam and Chavah.

The entire Adam and Chavah saga, of course, has many lessons for humanity. This biological fact – that we all share one common DNA source, that we are all derived from the same biological *shoresh* – is a particular lesson of great importance to us as Jews.

Let's not confuse biology with sociology. It is certainly clear that not all societies and cultures are of equal value and accomplishment, contrary to the foolishness of the PC crowd, who, I doubt, really believe their own posturing.

Every human being derives from the same source as every other human being, and by making that plain in the Torah, God clearly wants us to be aware of it.

And so, it seems, the more religious you are, the more *frum* you are, the more you should be aware of it. And the less excuse you have for being a bigot.

Bigotry refers to being hateful toward others simply because they belong to a different racial or sociological group. There is no justification other than that they are "Other." Prejudice (literally, "prejudging") refers to an attitude, usually negative, toward another sociological group that may or may not be justified. Prejudice may be the result of baseless bigotry (hating Asians because they look different) or the result of some belief that may, in fact, be reasonable (prejudice about buying a German car) or unreasonable (prejudice against all Finns because you once read about a Finn who wasn't nice, or who cheated; perhaps something similar about Jews).

My parents suffered greatly in their lives as a result of bigotry and baseless prejudice. But I never heard a racist or bigoted word cross their lips. They were too decent for that, and too inherently Jewish. The Jewish culture in which they were raised had no room in it for that depravity, that corruption of Jewish values.

That does not mean that they held no prejudice toward the Germans, or their accomplices the Polish antisemites, whose crimes are beyond description. But there was nothing inherently bigoted or racist about their reaction to those crimes. And they remained perfectly capable, after all the loss and suffering inflicted upon them, of viewing human relations in a rational and decent way, and relating with kindliness and friendliness and respect to all people. In fact, I would think their experiences made them more sensitive to this issue. Lucky me.

We can rejoice in our own elevated, holy Torah culture, and appreciate this gift that God has given us, appreciate the difference between our Torah-filled lives and the life of the street, or of distant, alien cultures, without bigoted contempt for others who are not like us, just *because* they are different, or look different. It is unbecoming for a *ben Torah*, or a *bas Torah*, to do so.

No one is perfect. Sometimes you may hear a bigoted word emerge from the mouth of someone who should not speak that way, and who, in doing so, discredits the "uniform" (yes, the Jewish uniform) in which he presents himself to the world.

Some of us, in the Torah world, do use external uniforms to help us behave the way we should. Some of us do not (except, perhaps, a yarmulke). But we all have an internal uniform, a way of thinking and behaving that is, or ought to be, governed not by human foolishness, but by the divine will. It is that divine will that requires us to approach all people with kindness and decency and respect, simply because they are human beings created in God's image. And that includes those who may sometimes be referred to thoughtlessly by some unpleasant epithet, without regard to who that person just denigrated really is.

God is certainly not a bigot. He may have prejudices – based on people's behavior and therefore deserved – but His Torah, which teaches us the specialness of Am Yisrael, also teaches us the commonality of all humankind. He Who created Adam and Chavah, and authored the Torah, made sure to include in the Torah the information that the *physical* DNA within us and all other human beings in this world derives from the same divine source.

God is certainly not a bigot. Nor should any of us who serve Him and accept the Torah ever be.

Parashas Bereishis 5773

The Night Primeval

The scene: After their sin, Adam and Chavah are expelled from Gan Eden.

Before long, the sun sets, and darkness descends upon the world.

They have never seen night, and so they reach the obvious, logical, and terrible conclusion: the world is coming to an end. Having sinned and ruined the original plan of creation, they have now brought about the end of the world.

Adam sits and mourns, contrite, the first *baal teshuvah*. Thus he sits all night, filled with regret, remorse, despair.

And then something incredible happens: the sun rises. A new day dawns.

The world is not over after all. Life goes on.

In relief and thanksgiving, Adam is moved. In praise of God and the new day He created, Adam sings out: *Mizmor shir l'yom haShabbos!* A prayerful song in praise of Shabbos.

And what a unique day it is: the Midrash, in describing their sin, says *sarchu* (סרחו) rather than *chatu* (חטאו). That word denotes a foul odor. They *fouled things up* – they fouled the perfection of the six days of creation until that point with their sin. Shabbos, which had not yet occurred for the first time when they sinned, was the one day in the week whose essential quality was not affected or altered by their sin. Shabbos remained untainted.

The late Lubavitcher Rebbe points out that several valuable lessons are learned by Adam.

Teshuvah is possible.

Life can continue after tragedy and error.

New days provide new opportunities.

There is an order of creation and a system for life: *Va'yehi erev, va'yehi boker.* Darkness gives rise to light. Chaos gives rise to order.

At birth, as we leave the womb and enter the world, we proceed from darkness to light; from ignorance, incomprehension, and a bare awareness of our surroundings to a slow and gradual process of awareness, recognition, and understanding the world. We find the light. Ultimately, we bring our own light into the world.

In Torah too, a similar process applies.

In Torah She'b'chsav, much is hidden.

In Torah She'b'al Peh, there is a process of elucidation and illumination, an arduous, laborious process that sheds light on the meaning and the message of the Torah.

God could have made the world bright all the time.

We could have been born mature, fully formed, fully developed.

The Torah could have been given to us all spelled out.

But God taught us a *derech* with His plan for creation, one that we need in order to make it in this world, which Adam came to understand as that terrible first night turned to day:

Darkness can give rise to light.

Chaos can coalesce into order.

Ignorance can be supplanted by knowledge.

Toil and struggle can result in achievement and merit.

And on yet a different level, Adam discovered something else as that first dark and terrifying night gave way to a new day. He found, in it, an additional lesson, a priceless gift: *Mizmor shir l'yom haShabbos, l'haggid ba'boker chasdecha, v'emunascha ba'leilos.*

In the bright light of day, it's easy, if you allow yourself, to see *chasdei Hashem.*

Adam saw Gan Eden and all its bounty.

But what happens when the fearful night descends?

And, we have come to learn, what dark and fearful nights are possible!

How can we deal with – how can we survive – those terrible nights?

By means of the great gift: *emunascha ba'leilos.* Our faith, even in the dark of night.

By our *faith* do we survive, through our faith do we find the strength to hold on, when the terrible darkness of night reigns.

We pray that we never be tested. But sometimes, in fact, we may be sorely tested. Even then, to the man or woman of faith, the darkest night is but a prelude to the dawn.

Parashas Bereishis 5770

Noach

Tzaddik

It doesn't take long for the Torah, in its narrative of how the world came to be, to bring us to the concept of good and bad, tzaddik and *rasha*. I suppose that's because God wants to make it clear to us that a major point, indeed an obligation, of life, is to choose – that is our duty – between good and bad, all the time.

And so the creation story itself quickly comes to the first critical moral choice humans had to make, and the negative consequences of their poor choice. We soon discover, as the generations pass and mankind finds its way in the world, that people indeed have a choice, but they have quite a penchant for choosing the wrong way. *La'pesach chatas rovetz*: sin is lurking, always, at the very door (Bereishis 4:7). We are challenged to overcome it: *v'ata timshol bo* (ibid.). You, mankind, are expected to rule over your impulses, rather than be ruled by them.

And so by the time the first *parashah*, Bereishis, ends, mankind has spoiled everything, and God is ready to take drastic action.

With the introduction of Noach, we are introduced also to the concept of a tzaddik. Before that, Chanoch is described as one who "walked with God" (Bereishis 5:24). He is not specifically referred to as a tzaddik, but we understand that he was indeed righteous. But as a tzaddik, he was on the weak side, so God took him prematurely to prevent him from falling into sin.

Noach was a bona fide tzaddik. But wait! The Torah (in Bereishis 6:9) attaches a qualifier to that description: *b'dorosav*. He was a tzaddik *in his generation*. Chazal waste no time before disagreeing whether that is a good thing or not such a good thing. Was Noach a tzaddik only when considered relative to his wicked contemporaries, or was he such a tzaddik that even in a thoroughly evil generation, one of universal depravity, he was truly righteous, and all the more so in any other generation? That is the classic question.

There is always a point to such revelations and the questions they raise. I think one lesson we are being taught is that we cannot always tell on our own who is a true tzaddik, who is righteous, and who is not.

We live in an age (and "we" have probably *always* lived in an age) when too many judgments are made about people (and why indeed are we so busy making judgments about people?) based on external, visible factors that may not be truly revelatory of who they really are. We all know that.

To label someone *"charedi,"* for example (literally one who lives in fear of God), based on a costume alone is silly, but it's done all the time. Sure, there is a role in life for a uniform, and we all know that. But defining someone – his character and his piety, his morality and his fear of God – based on a uniform alone is ridiculous, and we all know that too.

What's the lesson of the question of Noach's *tzidkus*? Of course he was a tzaddik. God Himself tells us so, and it was in his merit that mankind was saved. And yet we are deliberately offered the portrait of Noach with that subtle question mark attached to it.

Don't rush to judgment about people. Don't make assumptions. In fact, you just don't know what's in there unless you actually know what's in there.

Yesterday, early Shabbos morning, on a quiet residential street in Jerusalem, on my way to shul, I passed a woman walking her dog. Fiftyish, wearing pants and a T-shirt, her dog on a leash, she certainly didn't look too religious. Except for the beautiful Shabbos morning singing of the birds, absent traffic, the street was silent. And so I heard, quite clearly, the softly spoken words the woman was saying.

She wasn't talking to her dog. She wasn't talking to me. Very quietly, but very clearly, slowly, with utter clarity and obvious concentration, she was reciting *birchos hashachar.*

I don't know who this woman is, or what her story is. I don't know if she is even *shomer Shabbos* in the conventional way. I don't know. Her presentation in the street was certainly unconventional for...well, a conventional *frum* person. And yet, when I heard her proclaim *"Baruch Ata...oter Yisrael b'tifarah,"* it was quite clear to me that it would be a rare person who would make that *berachah* with greater concentration, clarity, or *kavanah* than she did. Even with the dog leash in her hand. I'll leave the rest of the judgment up to God, the only One Who knows what's in this woman's heart.

Last week someone in Israel told me about the time he bought a piece of wood and needed it sawed to a certain size and shape. The fellow in the lumberyard who does the cutting looked very much like a typical non-*frum* Israeli. He placed the wood in position, turned on the power saw, and said, quietly but clearly, *"Elokim, azor li"* (God, please help me) as he cut the wood. Astounded, my friend stood away a bit and watched the man work for a while. Indeed, the man invoked God's help every time he cut a piece of wood.

Yes, of course we have Torah formulas according to which a Jew is expected, and required, to live. It is the Law. It is usually apparent, on some level, who lives that way and who does not. But apparent as it may be, it is not always obvious. *Habochen kelayos*, He Who knows the true heart of man, knows who is a tzaddik and who is not, who is righteous and who is not, who is a *yerei Shamayim* and who is not, who really means it and who does not, who is sincere and who is not, who is a hypocrite and who is not, who is true to his uniform and who is not, and indeed, for whom is that uniform irrelevant.

It is not for us to be judgmental. The ambiguity about the extent and the nature of Noach's *tzidkus*, that concept presented to us early on in the Torah, is a lesson to prepare us for how to learn the rest of the Torah, which is, after all, a blueprint not only of how we are to relate to God through His mitzvos, but how we are to relate to Him through our fellow human beings, and especially our closest family, our fellow Jews, who have all been imbued by God with the holy *neshamos* created and set aside for us.

That special *neshamah* may be quite obvious in some, and far from obvious in others.

God and God alone judges *neshamos* and what people have done with theirs. Our job is to learn from the tzaddikim, be repelled by the *resha'im*, and to look for the *tzidkus* in every person.

Parashas Noach 5777

Who by Fire and Who by Water

So, now that nearly a year has passed since the flood (the devastation of Hurricane Sandy), and 4,118 years since the Flood, what do you think? Is a flood necessarily a bad thing?

For the people of Noach's generation, it was a very bad thing. For Noach, one can argue that it was a good thing. It immortalized him. God wrought miracles for him. Now he is the granddaddy of everyone on earth. On the other hand, he must have lost a whole lot of relatives. But then, maybe he didn't care too much for them.

The Sandy flood was terrible for us. Absolutely devastating. But it was great for the pumpers-out of basements, the builders and contractors and electricians and plumbers and carpenters and landscapers and sellers of appliances and of furniture.

It wasn't so good for the few decent insurance companies. It wasn't so bad for the many evil ones who refused to do what they were supposed to.

On the whole, it was horrible, horrible, horrible for everyone who lived through it (and certainly for those who died in it, and for their survivors). It wasn't supposed to happen here. We're accustomed to seeing terrible images of monsoon flooding in Bangladesh or such places, or even in America when the Mississippi or other rivers overflow their banks. Just not here.

And yet, go look at a satellite image of the Nile River Basin in Egypt.

Egypt is a big, brown, dry, desiccated land mass, incapable of supporting its population, except for the thin ribbon of land on either side of the Nile, which is lush and green and feeds all of Egypt and supplies much of the world's finer cotton. It runs from its mysterious source in deepest Africa, the Blue Nile meeting the White Nile and continuing north to the incredibly lush, broad Nile Delta as it empties into the Mediterranean. That rich land is identified with the land of Goshen, where Yosef settled his father and brothers.

It doesn't rain much in Egypt – certainly not enough to support its agriculture. *It is the annual flooding of the Nile, when the water rises greatly and overflows its banks, spreading for miles, that irrigates the land.* All of Egyptian history, culture, and power depended on this annual flood. Its absence was a catastrophe that resulted in starvation. So it has been from the beginning of time – until the opening of the Aswan High Dam in 1970, designed to exert some measure of control over the process.

But the floodwater must rise for the dam to accomplish its task.

So a flood – an overflowing – can be good, too.

And when we fill our cups with wine for Havdalah, we overfill the cup a bit, so that it overflows, as a sign of plenty and of blessing. *Kosi revayah.*

So, can blessing carry with it a component of curse, and curse be accompanied by blessing? You know they can. But we must be careful not to confuse or conflate the two. And in order to do that, we must distinguish between God's perspective and our own.

It is a principle of our faith that *kol d'avid Rachmana l'tav avid.* God is altogether good and what He does is, somehow, in some manner well beyond our comprehension, in His inscrutable wisdom, for the ultimate good. But there is no way we can understand that good, unless it is specifically revealed to us.

And so while an individual may accept some calamity that befalls him as *yissurim shel ahavah,* that is a noble personal statement of faith, but it does not in any way reveal the actual good in his predicament. And it can, under no circumstances, be applied to individuals other than himself. The calamities that he may lovingly and faithfully accept when visited upon himself, he must abhor and object to when they befall others. God doesn't want us to lovingly accept the pain and suffering of others. He expects us to cry out and object, to pray and to beg for the relief of others. And He wants us to pray and to beg for our own relief as well.

If, on some supernal level, if somehow, in the Grand Design, this suffering serves some higher purpose, if it fulfills some overarching plan that will somehow result in ultimate good, *well, that's God's business how He works things out*. Our business is to cry out when there is pain and suffering, to object, to pray, and to merit that He bless us in a way that's *obvious* blessing, and that He not have to test our faith in this terrible way.

While we never cease to mourn the unspeakable tragedies that have befallen – that have plagued and pursued – our people throughout history, Tisha b'Av in particular is set aside as an especially sad day in commemoration. We mourn the Destruction, and again the Destruction, the exiles, the expulsions, the burnings, the enslavements, the forced conversions, the loss of independence, the mass murders, the degradations, the mutilations and the violations, the hatred, the gassings and the starvation and the shootings and the torture, the whole miserable story.

And yet, we are told, upon the final Redemption, Tisha b'Av will be transformed into a great, jubilant *yom tov*.

How wonderful that will be. And may it come speedily, in our days. And yet…

And yet: Will the arrival of the Moshiach, the Ingathering of the Exiles, the rebuilding of the Beis Hamikdash, the reestablishment of God's palpable Presence among us – as good as that will be, as liberating and great and as exultant as that will be, as facilitated or made possible by all the weighted and freighted history that precedes it as it may be – will that, in any way, cause the immeasurable suffering and the loss, the unspeakable pain, the tragedy upon tragedy, the torture and death of innumerable innocents *not to have happened*? Of course, it cannot. That pain and that tragedy and that loss is indelibly inscribed upon this world. It may be, in some way, mitigated, but it can never be negated. It happened. We may find solace, we may find comfort in the new reality, but what happened did happen. What hurt and what devastated did hurt and did devastate. The innocents who suffered terribly did suffer terribly.

The happy new reality cannot be separated altogether from the old reality, for that is the very nature of reality.

And yet, Tisha b'Av will be the ultimate, permanent *yom tov* of our permanent Redemption. That is God's plan and His promise. It is His recompense to us for all that has happened, and, in some way knowable only to Him, made possible by all that has happened.

God is telling us, it seems, that this is the way of the world. This is life. There are times and places in which life is better and easier than in other times and places. There are people who have better lives and better circumstances and better *mazal* than other people. There is, in fact, a bigger, God-driven picture that is unknowable to us. We, the children of faith, trust God, our Father in Heaven, to run His plan according to His wisdom. In the context of our own lives, we pray that our lot, our roles in that larger plan, be experienced by us as peaceful, prosperous, and healthy, as good and blessed, and not hard.

My father, a"h, was born at the beginning of the twentieth century and passed away as it drew to a close. For a while I believed – or at least I hoped – that having witnessed and experienced all of its upheaval and unspeakable tragedy, he would merit, as well, to see the Redemption. He did not. I do not know if we who are alive today will, or if our children or grandchildren will. Sometime, hopefully in the not-too-distant future, our people certainly will.

And as we contemplate that, we recall what we recently read in Koheles, that there is a time for all things under the heavens. There is tragedy and there is joy, there is a time to weep and a time to rejoice. There is blessing and there is the opposite of blessing.

Even so, the good and the bad may coexist, to serve different purposes. In the end, *sof davar*, when all has been considered, *es ha'Elokim yera v'es mitzvosav shemor, ki zeh kol ha'adam*: that is what the life of man is about, that is his duty, his hope, and his best recourse in this world.

Says the Psalmist (Tehillim 66:12): "*Banu va'esh u'va'mayim*" (We have come through fire and through water), "*va'totzienu la'revayah*" (and You [our God] have carried us through, *to a place of overflowing*).

Sometimes, in this life, the oceans or the rivers or the other tides of life overflow, and they carry some of us away, *lo aleinu*. Some survive, and some do not; some revive, and some do not.

Other times, in this life, the goodness and the blessing overflow, and if we are wise enough to recognize it and to appreciate it, the very joy of it carries us away.

Sometimes the same calamity brings tragedy to some and apparent blessing to others.

And those who do survive and can become whole again may recognize that there is blessing in that, too.

Noach, identified as a *tzaddik tamim b'dorosav*, survived the Flood. He planted a vineyard, overflowed his cup – and himself – with wine, and sadly, experienced degradation.

We, identified not as Bnei Noach but as Bnei Yisrael, also relate to an over-flowing cup, a metaphoric one: *Dishanta va'shemen roshi, kosi revayah*. God, Father in Heaven, how I recognize and appreciate Your many blessings! *My cup runneth over!*

Even now, even after so much suffering, even after all the fires and the floods of this world, we are Yours, and we thank You for everything.

Banu va'esh u'va'mayim, va'totzienu la'revayah. We have come through fire and through water, and You, our loving God, have carried us through to a place of overflowing.

Parashas Noach 5774

Passacaglia and Fugue in C Minor

The cycle of the year brings us again to the beginning, beginning with *in the beginning*.

For us as Jews, how different was the beginning? If we could travel in time, and survey Jewish belief and practice through the ages, how different would it be from the way we experience it today?

Core beliefs, of course, have not changed at all for the past thirty-seven hundred years. The way Avraham Avinu understood God – the way he transmitted that to the other Avos and to the Children of Israel after them – has remained our constant core of faith. It was at Har Sinai that our ancestors experienced God personally, so that those beliefs and those understandings were etched permanently into our identity as a nation – specifically as God's special, treasured nation – and were given form in the *taryag* (613) mitzvos.

Jewish practice, at its core, has, of course, also remained constant, with regard to the specific requirements outlined in the Torah. But that which can be described as broader Jewish practice has developed and evolved through the ages, as the experience of our people – their circumstances and their conditions – dictated.

Thus, the Siddur, central to Jewish life today, did not exist in the beginning.

No doubt Jews prayed, but the form of that prayer has been developing for thousands of years. Anshei Kenesses Hagedolah established the basic form of prayer we employ today, forms that may have supplemented the service in the Beis Hamikdash when it existed, but that now have replaced that service for a nation bereft of its holy place, with its direct connection to the Eternal.

The Siddur itself has, of course, also evolved. From time to time, it grew and developed in size and scope, as the practices *ba'kodesh* of various *kehillos* and *chachmei Yisrael* were incorporated into and became the basics of Jewish worship.

These developments are not random or haphazard. God operates in history.

He directs history and He certainly directs Klal Yisrael. With all the storms and the tribulations of our existence – and our persistence – throughout the Galus, we needed the tools to stay alive as Hashem's people, and, as promised, He has stayed with us and has guided us. So the right leaders arise at the times needed, the right achievements in scholarship and study, social and religious development. And so we had Tannaim and Amoraim, a Rashi, a Rambam, a Mechaber and a Rema, Rishonim and Acharonim, a Vilna Gaon and a Baal Shem Tov, a Chofetz Chaim.

The "music" of Judaism is one of ever-growing complexity and beauty. This complexity, it would appear, this method of growth and development, is part of God's plan as we move toward the fulfillment of His ultimate plan for us. Every addition to our rites, over the ages, is another step upon which our people can climb to bring us closer to our ultimate fulfillment. Thus, these steps are also necessary. They are a gift from God.

Now listen to J. S. Bach's *Passacaglia and Fugue* in C minor.

You will hear a theme, quite simple and only a few phrases long, played by one instrument. It is a theme that is repeated over and over as the piece develops, each time expanded, broadened, built upon. It grows in power and complexity; it takes the listener over as it moves toward its thundering crescendo.

L'havdil elef alfei havdalos, the "music" of our history and our development grows in power and complexity. Each step, each addition to the Siddur, each minhag, once accepted, becomes a solid basis for the next step in our march to Redemption.

This is apparently how Hakadosh Baruch Hu wants us to proceed. The various minhagim among Klal Yisrael are part of the beauty and the complexity of that music.

I have encountered learned people – far more learned than me – whom I thoroughly respect, who, in their erudition, feel that they can, for whatever reason, skip this or that in the daily service because those parts are not so ancient, or are not so critical, and they have a valid halachic basis for doing so. In all respect and deference, however, I feel this interferes with the beautiful, heavenly symphony that our forebears have presented us. The best thing we can do, I submit, for the sake of Heaven and of Klal Yisrael, is to pick our feet up high and to march enthusiastically, together, to that divine music.

Parashas Noach 5771

Leadership

Noach, a tzaddik, is contrasted with Avraham, a far different kind of tzaddik.

Avraham Avinu, together with Sarah Imenu, spent his life in purity, seeking God.

In large measure, that search for God was expressed through *chesed*. Entirely unselfish, he could not keep his knowledge of God to himself. He and his wife spent a lifetime – and risked their lives – teaching others and elevating their souls: *es hanefesh asher asu b'Charan* (Bereishis 12:5).

Noach also spent his life in purity, a *tzaddik tamim*. But he spent 120 years building the ark in full public view, and did not succeed (did he try?) in turning even one person around.

Leadership is not easy. Spiritual leadership, especially for Jews, is especially not easy.

It's not enough just to look the part. It's not enough just to have the knowledge. It's not enough just to impart knowledge. To be successful, to be effective, leadership of a *kehillah* requires extraordinary giving of oneself, often to the detriment of family. It requires leading by example. It requires carrying the burdens of others, burdens that can be so heavy that the strongest shoulders stoop under their weight. And sadly, it is sometimes a reality that this giving, and the carrying of these burdens, is grossly – and sometimes obscenely – underappreciated.

Ashreinu that there are such dedicated leaders among us.

We have just concluded a seven-week period of heightened and intense spiritual activity.

We are all very involved in the Yamim Noraim, the buildup and preparation in Chodesh Elul, Rosh Hashanah, Aseres Yemei Teshuvah, Shabbos Shuvah, the spiritual climax of Yom Kippur, and then the sustained activity and halachic complexity of the *chag*.

It is a challenging and draining period for our spiritual leaders.

Thank you so much, Rabbi.

Thank you, *manhigei Yisrael* everywhere.

May Hashem bless you and your families in every way.

Parashas Noach 5772

Saving the World

Their favorite time of the week, by far, was the Friday night Shabbos *seudah*.

All the family gathered around the table, Shabbos candles glowing, the workaday week and school worries put away somewhere else. In their Shabbos finery, singing Shalom Aleichem, Kiddush, *zemiros*, great and comforting food, *divrei Torah*, family conversation, catching up on each one's news – it was beautiful and unhurried. The Shabbos *tish*. Sure, as in any family with children, there were occasional squabbles. But what did they "fight" about? Whose turn is it to sit next to Abba this week. The joys of life.

"*Vus iz di parshah di voch?*"

"Noach!" the girls cried out.

"Noyach!" the boys said. It's all good, *baruch Hashem*.

We delve into the Torah portion of the week.

Was Noach a tzaddik? Of course he was. The Torah clearly says so.

But what kind of tzaddik? A really great tzaddik or a not-so-great tzaddik?

The children provide all the answers they learned in school. All great answers, all correct, Abba tells them. *But why the question?* What would be the point of letting us know that he might *not* have been such a great tzaddik? What would be the purpose of such a revelation? We delve into it because we want to know, to understand, as well as we possibly can, the meaning of every word and letter in the Torah, which is the revealed word of God. And it is also clear, from the very question, from the subtle way the language of the Torah raises the question, that there is indeed a purpose to the question itself.

With the Flood, a holocaust befell the world, destroying all in its path. Noach and family were saved, and ultimately the world went on. But it didn't have to be that way. The same God Who created the world ex nihilo could have wiped it all out and started all over again, just as easily. There are, after all, midrashic sources that tell us that God had, in fact, created many worlds before ours and destroyed them. Why save this world through Noach, identifying his *tzidkus*, and then identify him further as an apparently *flawed* tzaddik?

So, children, Abba continued, let's think about another holocaust, the Holocaust of our own time, and all the holocausts throughout the ages, of which there has been no shortage. Some survived even when so many others perished. Why were they chosen to survive? Were they super tzaddikim and the others not? That is very far from the actual reality. What happened – in terms of the *tzidkus* or the opposite of *tzidkus*, and everything in between, of the saved individuals – is utterly unknowable, except that being a tzaddik did not alone clearly save anyone. And yet we know that God is the True Judge, Whose every act is Justice itself – even as we are utterly unable to fathom it.

There is a concept of a holocaust consuming everyone and everything in its path, regardless of individual merits (*androlomosia*; see *Bereishis Rabbah* and *Tanchuma*), but that phenomenon, as we limited mortals view it, is even more incomprehensible. And so we must cling to what we might be able to understand, on some level.

And so, children, what are the lessons of Noach, for the purposes of this discussion a flawed tzaddik (and, in fairness, there are those who maintain that he was, in fact, a great tzaddik), being the vehicle for the saving of mankind and indeed of the world?

Well, *kinderlach*, for one thing, it certainly pays to be good. If Noach weren't a tzaddik, it appears that the Ribbono shel Olam would have let the whole thing go. Kaput. And clearly the merit of *one* tzaddik alone may suffice to save the whole world. But why *davka* a *flawed* tzaddik? To teach us that you don't have to be a perfect tzaddik for God to be aware of you and to watch out for you. To respond to you. To relate to you. To save the world for you. To make miracles for you. A person should try to be a tzaddik because that's his job in serving his Creator. The Ribbono shel Olam does His "job," *k'v'yachol*, by looking at each of us, knowing who we are even better than we know who we are, and doing according to His *chesed* and His Judgment, even plucking us from a world-destroying holocaust because He is our Father in Heaven, He has a world to run, His perspective transcends time, and this is His plan.

Which brings us, *kinderlach*, to an even more fundamental question, and it's about each and every one of you.

Noach's *tzidkus*, as it was, was not only about Noach himself, but also about Avraham and all that emerged from Avraham. It was about every good and worthwhile thing that has happened in the world since Noach.

Your grandparents, *kinderlach*, my parents, were two twigs saved from a terrible fire, while almost everyone else in their world perished, burned in that terrible conflagration. Why? Why them? Why not others instead of them? *Why them? Because of YOU!* The lives that they were given are the lives that *you* were given. When they were spared, *you* were spared. Just as the Avos – and Klal Yisrael at Har Sinai crying out *"naaseh v'nishma!"* – justified, in a real way, the saving of Noach, aside from his own merits, so too, children, it is for you, with the way you live your lives, to "justify" not only the saving of your grandparents, but the survivors of every persecuted generation that came before, the stalwarts of every generation that resisted the temptation to fall away and seek a seemingly easier path in life.

God may save someone not just on his own merit, but because of what his future generations might be. And that means you. Hashem saved Bubby and Zaydie not just for themselves but for *you*. His challenge to me and to you is to justify that. In saving them He has told us that the existence of the world is in *our* hands, that what we do in this world really counts, that our lives have purpose, and our being here is testimony to the purpose we have been given, to keep the world going. It means me, and it means you, as individuals.

It means every one of us. Noach was a tzaddik, but that little question mark that hovers over him comes to teach us that we, each of us, can be the Noachs of our own little worlds. And we should live as if we are.

Parashas Noach 5778

Lech Lecha

Asher Yutzarlech

If you're old enough, you may remember President Lyndon Johnson running around the White House in his pajamas late at night, turning off lights. No one else bothered. He grew up poor in a farmhouse with no electricity, and although he was now wealthy, at the pinnacle of success and power, he hated waste.

I admired him for it. I understood him. During my own fellowship training, in the fanciest of medical academic ivory towers in the academic ivory tower-filled towns of Boston and Cambridge, I was impressed with – and somewhat appalled by – some of the excess and waste I saw. Part of the culture and the mystique and the medical luxury of the ivory tower was that anything and everything was readily available. A byproduct of that ready availability was that there were also lots of resources wasted.

I recently visited somewhere for Shabbos, a very nice house in a very nice location, and I found, in preparation for Shabbos, hand-cut sheets of toilet paper. I haven't seen that in a very long time. I understood immediately something about the hosts' history, even in the comfort of their very upscale house. These days, thank God, such preparation usually entails an open box of tissues, and the light switch left on. It wasn't always that way.

Luxury, of course, is relative. When a cold water flat in an ancient tenement building, with a communal toilet in the hallway (as opposed to an outhouse or an open ditch) and a potbellied stove in the kitchen providing the possibility of heat and hot food (assuming one buys coal or wood to burn in it) is considered a luxurious step up in the world, one can imagine what these "luxuries" compare to.

We live in a time, and a place, and in circumstances, where, thank God, it's hard to relate to that, except as something in the history books. Except that I remember it very well from my early childhood. To my parents, however, and later my grandparents, it was an appreciated safe haven. And my parents understood that in the Land of Opportunity, they too would, with God's help, eventually move up in the world. And they did.

We moved into a larger, much better apartment in a nicer neighborhood that had its own toilet, a refrigerator instead of an icebox, and steam heat, but which had…well…seen better days. But it was a marked step up. And affordable. By the time we got there, the rent was actually lower than it had been years before.

The refugees left behind the cold water flat, and the Displaced Persons camp in Germany before that, and the…*terrible* before that. They settled into a normal life. But, as any armchair psychologist can tell you, the refugee does not readily lose the habits that made his survival possible, even when conditions improve.

And so, we prepared cut pieces of toilet paper for Shabbos. (My father called them *"asher yutzarlech,"* referring to the *berachah* one makes after their use.) Who, except for people raised in America, would use expensive tissues for that? And don't think a full-wattage light bulb would be left burning for twenty-five or twenty-six hours. That's the way it was.

Which brings us, oddly, to Avraham Avinu. Actually, to exactly that: Avraham's oddity.

"Va'yavo hapalit va'yaged l'Avram Ha'ivri" (14:13). Avraham is identified as the Ivri.

While the word is commonly rendered in English as "Hebrew," Chazal tell us that there are three main understandings of what Ivri (עברי) derives from.

In response to God's command, Avraham crossed (עבר) from the east bank of the Euphrates to come to the land of Canaan, which would subsequently be the eternal heritage of his children, the Nation of Israel.

A descendant of the righteous Ever (עבר), Avraham carried on his legacy and thus deserved to be called the Ivri.

And most profoundly, Avraham lived in a time when no one knew God, indeed when no one wanted to know God. He had to fight the whole world, to stand apart from them, to face the terrible trials that he did, the ridicule and the accusations that he did, in order to be true to his Creator, come what may. He had to be different. He paid the price, and apart from the whole world he stood, knowing that he stood with God. They were all on one side of this profound divide (מעבר אחד), and he was steadfastly on the other (מעבר השני). Hence, the Ivri (עברי). He was, for the world, uncomfortably different, even odd. And so has it been for us, Avraham's children, ever since.

In a fundamental way, the Jews have always been apart from the rest of humanity. Viewed – and treated – as uncomfortably different. It is our history and it is our destiny. And when we forget to keep it that way, the rest of the world tends to remind us. One need only pick up a newspaper these days to see how obvious this is, even from our "friends."

That discomfort is not ours, in general, but theirs, the others'. Sadly, there are those of our own tribe who – lacking a well-formed sense of self-worth, not "getting" what God has given us, never having learned to appreciate or too often even experience the true nature of that difference – are themselves uncomfortable in their own skin, or with the actions, the habits, the self-assertion of their "too obvious" fellow Jews.

Even for those of us whose lives, outwardly, mesh with those of our neighbors – those of us who are out there in the world in business, in the professions, in every sphere of life – we remain, at our core, different, sometimes indeed uncomfortably different. It is, in God's inscrutable plan, for some reason central to the plan itself. There is a wide chasm that separates us from the rest, a chasm that is often beyond the understanding or the explanation of the very people who find us uncomfortably different.

Avraham set himself apart in his quest for God and paid for it with the many tests that he faced; he experienced the *kivshan ha'esh*, the fiery furnace he was thrown into for his faith. Avraham miraculously survived that. Untold numbers of his descendants, in their travails, did not, but the nation as a whole did, and always will. That is God's end of the bargain.

It is the legacy of Avraham that makes it possible for us to cling to Him in an unbreakable bond. It's what makes us different. It's what empowers us to relate to everything in life as a function of our relationship with our God. It's what gives us the strength to *be* different, however uncomfortable that is for our neighbors – and, as a result, for us. It's what motivates us to infuse the most mundane things with sanctity, so that even a simple Jew might refer to a piece of *toilet paper*, not by the function it serves, but by the blessing one makes after its use, thanking the Creator for a normal, healthy life function. *Asher yutzarlech.*

Avraham set himself apart from a corrupt world, but he was not a hermit. He shared his knowledge and his spirit with all who would listen. God chose him because he had chosen God. We, the descendants, the *inheritors* of the original Ivri, the one who had the will and the faith and the courage to stand apart from the rest of humanity, if need be, draw upon that will and that faith and that courage to be who we need to be, no matter how difficult it may be, no matter how awkward it may be, no matter the price, no matter how inconveniently different it makes us.

Those, over the thousands of years and hundreds of generations since Avraham Ha'ivri, who have had that fortitude are still here today, an unbroken chain of Ivrim. Like our forefather, we find ourselves regularly on one side of a yawning chasm, seemingly alone. But we also believe, with perfect faith, that God has privileged us with this role, and, indeed like our forefather, God has chosen us because we have chosen Him.

Parashas Lech Lecha 5776

Avraham, M. J., and Me

What was the weather like before the Flood? How was the physical world different?

I don't know. We do know that God declared, after the flood, that from then on there would always be seasons and regular, cyclical natural phenomena.

We also know that God acknowledged that mankind has a nasty streak, *ki yetzer lev ha'adam ra mi'ne'urav*, that people are tempted, from early life, to do bad, and they often do, despite their God-given potential for good. Having destroyed the world once, He will now accommodate that reality and run the world accordingly, rather than destroy it again.

Man's failure to live up to God's initial expectations of him resulted in the destruction of the world, and its being, in a sense, recreated afterward, through Noach.

In the ten generations from creation until Noach, human beings failed to develop an essential quality upon which the world's continued existence depends, and so that world ceased to exist. After the Flood, Noach should have initiated the necessary change, but it took another ten generations, until Avraham, for it to properly manifest itself. God said He would wait it out, and then Avraham came along, and taught the world forever after about *chesed*.

Olam chesed yibaneh (Tehillim 89:3). The rebuilt world merited rebuilding because *chesed* was to be a part of it. And *chesed* continues to be a force that creates and builds worlds within the World. Avraham Avinu brought *chesed* into the world, and that *middah*, which he personified, is most closely associated with him.

One criticism of Noach is that he worked on the ark for 120 years, and although he told anyone who asked why he was doing so, and what was going to happen, nowhere are we told that he actually went out and urged the people to repent, to mend their wicked ways, and thus avert tragedy. *Va'yaas Noach k'chol asher tzivah oso Elokim ken asah*: Noach did precisely what God commanded him to do. Nothing more. God could have saved Noach without an ark, but He wanted him to be engaged in building one over a long period of years precisely so people could see what he was doing, find out why, and, like the sinners of Nineveh centuries later, do *teshuvah* and save themselves. Noach could have tried to convince them; he could have pleaded; he might have moved them. He did not.

Avraham, on the other hand, was busy all the time – even when he was in dire pain from his *milah* – with *chesed*. *Es hanefesh asher asu b'Charan.*

Avraham and Sarah dedicated their lives and their energies to helping people and bringing them *tachas kanfei haShechinah.* And when he heard that God was planning to destroy Sedom, a consummately evil society that deserved destruction, he begged God to find a way to spare them.

Chesed saves worlds and builds worlds.

Most of us, if we are lucky enough, learn the important things in life from our parents and our teachers. And if we are especially lucky – and smart enough to find wisdom and goodness when it is presented to us – we also manage to learn from others whom we encounter in life. But we need to be awake and alert to catch the lessons God arranges for us.

I once was sitting in the front office of a man I had an appointment with, waiting to meet with him. The secretary was on the phone, regaling a friend with a distressing story about her personal life. She did not keep her voice down, so my awareness of her personal details can hardly be called eavesdropping. She described a situation in which someone created a great deal of painful unpleasantness for her. And then she described her own reaction and judgment of that person. It left me stunned and humbled. The generosity of spirit, the *chesed*, displayed by this young girl in judging that person was almost beyond imagining. And I understood that witnessing that moment and learning from that girl was the real reason I was in that office that day.

And so to the real story I want to share today. God indeed has many messengers. Usually, good people are the ones who serve as His unwitting messengers for good. They are not unwitting in their goodness, but they have no way of realizing how what they say and do might impact on others – sometimes countless others, as worlds are built as a result.

The power of *chesed* is unfathomable. And so is the power of those unwitting heroes who teach us *chesed*.

I grew up in Crown Heights, back when it was a very large and diverse Jewish community (of which Lubavitch was but one component). It was a really beautiful community, with lots of different kinds of shuls and schools, large and small. One of the premier institutions back then was the Yeshivah of Crown Heights, with a large elementary school and a shul. There were hundreds of seats in the very large and beautiful synagogue, which was usually filled to capacity on Shabbos morning. We often davened there.

During much of my childhood, one of the chief *parnassim* of the shul was Mr. Morris J. (Moishe) Golombeck, often referred to as "M. J." He was a successful spice merchant who had started out with a horse and wagon, a colorful character, and a rather friendly fellow, even to a kid like me. He spoke with a heavy Poilishe Yiddish accent. He lived on Crown Street, with his elegant wife, a real lady, and his excellent children.

One Shabbos, when I was perhaps eight or ten years old, he got up to make an appeal.

I don't remember what the tzedakah was for. Now, what little kid sits and listens to an appeal speech in shul from an "old" man with a funny accent when the other kids are outside playing ringalevio, red light/green light, or "three feet off to Germany"? I don't know. Maybe I got stuck. Maybe I liked his accent. Maybe because I respected him. But I sat there.

He was frustrated. People were not responding to the appeal. He broke stride and said, "*Rabboisai*, listen to me! I know what I'm talking about! I've been poor and I've been rich. I know. *Don't be afraid to give. I know: you'll never miss it in your life!*"

It was as if a kind of arrow had pierced my awareness and my being. When he said those words, I heard him.

I heard him. "*Don't be afraid to give. You'll never miss it in your life.*"

How often in life are we lucky enough to really hear something we really need to hear?

Mr. Golombeck understood that for most people, it takes a certain amount of courage to give tzedakah seriously, whatever one's economic level. It goes to human nature, *ki yetzer lev ha'adam ra mi'ne'urav*. But our father Avraham taught us that the power of *chesed* to build worlds can be far greater and more enduring than the power of *ra*, or even indifference, to tear them down.

I believe that because in life I would need to hear and to absorb that lesson, *I would need that courage*, God kept me in that room to hear that remarkable man utter those simple yet profound words, and then, having heard them, *to really hear them*.

Olam chesed yibaneh. I wish I were a remarkably charitable person. Like most of us, I try, and I still have a long way to go. But I do know that but for that lesson, but for that enabling, liberating lesson, I would be a far lesser person in the *chesed* department. And in what ways the world has been affected by it – how many worlds within the World have been affected by it, have been built by it, because of it, over all these years – only the Creator can know. And I am so grateful for it.

I expressed this sentiment to the late Mrs. Golombeck and to a few family members over the years. He earned, and deserves, that his descendants know this about him.

What he said is absolutely true. Don't be afraid to give generously. You'll get along just fine. You'll never miss it in your life. Have the strength of purpose and the courage to give.

Lack of *chesed* in the time of Noach cost the world its life. A life of *chesed*, that of Avraham Avinu, gave the world the possibility and the promise of life. God, in His own *chesed*, waited ten generations for Avraham to come along and accomplish that.

And, in His infinite *chesed*, He sends each of us messengers and messages to teach us what we need to know in life, to make life meaningful and purposeful, if we will only remain alert to and aware of those lessons wherever we find them. When He speaks to us, we need to be listening, and we need to hear it.

Parashas Lech Lecha 5773

The Eye of God upon Us

After the Babylonian conquest, with the destruction of the Beis Hamikdash and the mass exile of the people to Babylonia, the Babylonians themselves were in turn defeated by the Persians, to whom passed power and hegemony over the land. The Persian king Cyrus invited the Jews to return to Israel. Only about forty-two thousand heeded his call. It was extremely difficult for them, but they persevered, and eventually the great Second Commonwealth of Israel developed and flourished.

Alexander the Great's epic march out of Greece defeated the Persians and brought the Holy Land under Greek dominion. When the Seleucid Greeks interfered with the practice of Judaism, the Maccabean revolt resulted, after a long and costly series of wars, in the independent Hasmonean kingdom.

Rife with corruption and internecine battles, the Hasmoneans degenerated. The civil-warring Hasmonean brothers Hyrcanus and Aristobulus each tried to enlist Rome to his side. The inevitable result was Rome's conquest of Israel by Pompey in 63 BCE, the dissolution of the Hasmonean kingdom, and the incorporation of Israel into the Roman Empire as a province of Syria.

Rome's heavy hand resulted in the Great Jewish War, which culminated in the destruction of the Second Beis Hamikdash in 70 CE and the exile and enslavement of a large segment of the population. The Bar Kochba revolt, defeated in 135 CE, was utterly catastrophic, with huge loss of life, further exile, and repression. Large areas of Israel were closed to Jewish habitation, including Jerusalem itself, which was renamed Aelia Capitolina to remove from it any vestige of Jewish identity. For a time, some Jews were permitted in on Tisha b'Av to mourn their destroyed Temple.

But Jews in significant numbers persevered in the land, most notably in the Galilee.

It was here that Rabbi Yehudah Hanasi and his colleagues the Tannaim put together the Mishnah. Subsequent generations of Amoraim continued their work, alongside their brethren who engaged in agriculture and commerce, and the Jewish presence in the land went on.

Over the centuries, Roman, then Byzantine Roman dominion maintained law and order, allowing for relatively normal life and commerce, although always under suppression, and later, Roman Christian subjugation. There were, over those centuries, periodic Jewish uprisings. In 613 a Jewish revolt against the Byzantine emperor Heraclius led to the conquest of Jerusalem by a Jewish army, aided by Persian forces, and, for the first time in centuries, an autonomous Jewish entity. This was crushed in 629, and the Jews were massacred.

It was only after the Muslim conquest of Jerusalem in 637 that the ruling authorities permitted Jews to live and practice their religion in Jerusalem, five hundred years after their expulsion from that city. The wars, and the breakdown of law and order in that period, however, when Islamic jihad spread across the region, created the conditions in which Jews in large numbers were forced to abandon the Holy Land, after so many centuries of tenacious holding on.

A major Amora in the third century CE was Rav Shmuel bar Nachman (sometimes rendered Nachmani). It was in his troubled time that multiple catastrophes, including four major earthquakes, befell the land. *Taanis* 8b relates that a double calamity struck, with simultaneous famine and plague. In times of trouble, Jews naturally turn in prayer to their Father in Heaven for relief. And here they faced a dilemma: What to pray for?

There was an established custom that special prayers are not instituted for two different things, but must be directed at one specific request. The Gemara offers explanations and scriptural hints why this might be so. Hence, their dilemma. It was suggested that special prayers be said for the elimination of the plague, as it had a higher and faster death rate, and that they would endure the famine as best they could. Rabbi Shmuel bar Nachmani replied that they should rather pray for relief from the famine, for when God sends plenty, He does so for the living. *"Pose'ach es yadecha u'masbia l'chol chai ratzon"* (God opens His hand to satisfy the desire of every living thing). Thus, Rabbi Shmuel reasoned, once God hears their prayers and relieves the famine, the plague will cease as well.

It was this same Rabbi Shmuel bar Nachman, a master aggadist and a product of his turbulent times, who taught a remarkable Midrash (*Eichah, pesichta* 24) regarding the destruction of the Beis Hamikdash.

When the Mikdash was destroyed, Avraham Avinu came before the Ribbono shel Olam, weeping and tearing at his beard, pulling out the hairs of his head, hitting himself in the face, tearing his clothes, ashes on his head, wandering in the burnt ruins of that holy place, inconsolable, lamenting and crying before God: *How can such a calamitous shame fall upon me and my children?* Seeing his despair, the angels cried out, *Ribbono shel Olam! How could the many roads that brought the Jews joyously to Jerusalem now be desolate? How could Your covenant with Avraham and his children now be discarded? How could the Jerusalem that You have chosen now be cast off? How can You let Your chosen Avraham weep and lament so, and go unanswered?*

Avraham continued: *Ribbono shel Olam! How can You have exiled my children, giving them over to their foreign oppressors, who murder them in every cruel and torturous way, and You have destroyed the Beis Hamikdash, built on the very spot where I offered my son Yitzchak to You?*

Because your children have sinned, God told Avraham. *They transgressed every mitzvah in the Torah, and violated every one of the twenty-two letters with which it is written.*

Who will testify against them? Avraham asked. The Torah itself began to testify. *Stop!* countered Avraham. *Are you not ashamed to testify against my children? Do you not remember when God offered you to the whole world, all of whom rejected you, while my children cried out "naaseh v'nishma!" and honored you? Now you come to testify against them at the moment of their tragedy?*

The Torah stood aside and would testify no more. *Let the twenty-two letters come and testify,* God said. The *aleph* began to testify. Avraham stopped it in its tracks. *Aleph! The world rejected God's Law, and you began His Revelation to my willing children with "Anochi Hashem Elokecha." How are you not ashamed to testify against them?*

The *aleph* stepped aside and would testify no more.

The *beis* stood to testify. *Beis! You are the first letter in the Torah, in the scholarship of which my children excel. Are you not ashamed to testify against them?* And the *beis* stepped aside and would not testify.

And so it went with the *gimmel*, which Avraham's children honor with *gedilim* (tzitzis).

At this point all the letters with which the Torah is written would not testify against the Children of Israel.

Avraham continued: *Ribbono shel Olam, You blessed me with a son when I was a hundred years old. When You asked me to bring him, at age thirty-seven, as a sacrifice, both he and I went willingly. I put pity aside – and chesed is the guidepost of my life – and bound him as a sacrifice for Your sake. Will You now not have pity on my children?*

The remarkable Midrash goes on to describe the pleadings of Yitzchak, Yaakov, Moshe, and Rachel. Ultimately, it is Rachel's plea that works: *I had pity on my sister,* she declares, *and helped her to become the wife of my beloved Yaakov instead of me. I was not jealous of her. Why, God, should You be jealous of false and empty gods of wood and stone, regarding which You exiled my children and brought death and calamity upon them?*

God is moved by Rachel's plea, and declares: *Rachel, hold your voice back from crying and your eyes from tears! Your efforts are rewarded, and there is hope in the end: your children shall return. V'shavu banim li'gevulam.*

Prefaced by the *chesed* of Avraham, the *chesed* of Rachel moves God to "relent" and to soften the punishment.

We are a people with a long and tragic history of suffering, well acquainted with pleading and praying. It is said of us that our power, as a people, is vested in our mouths – in prayer, in Torah. And yet we know, from our experience, that that power, however great, is limited. In Rabbi Shmuel bar Nachmani's time of plague and famine, they could not even organize prayers against both tragedies. What, indeed, can we do?

The Maggid of Kozhnitz tells us that there is, in fact, a path to power even greater than prayer alone, revealed to us by God, and in fact, personified by Avraham Avinu and Rachel Imenu.

Avraham, God's faithful servant, followed Him to the land of Canaan, where he dealt with many tests and difficulties while waiting for Him to fulfill His promise of children. He and his wife had grown old, yet they remained barren. How would he fulfill the destiny God promised him?

God showed him the innumerable stars in the heavens. *As many as these will be your offspring. Do not be afraid. I am with you. Believe.*

And Avraham believed God, Who considered that faith righteous: *va'yachsheveha lo tzedakah.* Literally, He reckoned that as an act of tzedakah.

Why that choice of words? *Va'yachsheveha lo tzedakah.*

Va'yachsheveha denotes not just thinking, but calculation, as in *l'chashev es haketz,* to calculate the "End of Days." Tzedakah, "righteousness," is inseparable from its far more common translation, "charity." Goodness. *Chesed.*

Avraham Avinu personifies *chesed.* That is his special and particular *middah.*

Clearly, that was his nature. But perhaps God was giving him something here, a calculated reward for his faith, an extra dose of power connected to his *chesed.*

Let me digress. Years ago, I attended a *hachnasas sefer Torah,* the inauguration of a new Torah scroll, always a festive event. Traditionally, people are afforded the opportunity to actually write the final letters completing the Torah. I had the good fortune to be chosen to write the letter *ayin*, ע, which also is the word for "eye" – a nice coup for an ophthalmologist, especially if that letter *ayin* is in the very word for eyes, *eini*, in the final phrase of the Torah, *eini kol Yisrael* (the eyes of all Israel).

Now look at Tehillim 33:18–19: הנה עין ה' אל יראיו למיחלים לחסדו. להציל ממות נפשם ולחיותם ברעב. (The eye of Hashem is upon those who fear Him, who await His *chesed*, to rescue their lives from death, to sustain them in times of famine).

The *ayin* of God is given to those who fear Him. The *ayin* is an eye, but it is also a letter, ע. That letter, as well as God's watchful eye, is given to His servants.

God has calculated the power of the letter ע and has gifted it to us, the children of Avraham, as a powerful tool to save our lives from *maves* (death) – be it plague or *raav* (famine), or any other *tzarah*.

Take that ע and place it in the word for death, מות, and you will have undone that word, מות, you will have undone death, and turned it into מעות, literally money, meaning tzedakah. And צדקה תציל ממות (tzedakah rescues us from death).

To Avraham, on the strength of his faith and his chesed, was given the power, passed on to us, to transform that *chesed*, that tzedakah, into a powerful tool for acquiring life. *Va'yachsheveha lo tzedakah*. With it we might undo death.

Rachel Imenu, always especially dear to the Jewish heart, as well epitomized that power of selfless *chesed*, which not only saved her sister from utter humiliation, but served as the catalyst for God's declaration: *You, Rachel, your prayers, offered with the power of your unparalleled* chesed, *I will listen to, I will heed. Cease your weeping. Your children will come home.*

God, in His infinite wisdom, runs the world according to His celestial judgment, *cheshbonei Shamayim*. But He has also made room, in His system, for input from human beings. Hence, the role – and the critical need for – prayer and good deeds, to affect that judgment.

הנה עין ה' אל יראיו למיחלים לחסדו. להציל ממות נפשם ולחיותם...

We can, if we are *zocheh*, do away with death by turning מות into מעות, *maves* into *ma'os*, transforming death and destruction into life and recovery, through the power of tzedakah and *chesed*. Avraham Avinu's profound faith and *chesed*, at a time when there was no precedent for it, is a legacy that has served, and saved, his children through the ages, in peace and in their times of trouble.

And the loving *chesed* of Rachel Imenu, her own tragic, short life highlighted by her incredible generosity of spirit, earned for her not only God's resolve to salvage her wayward children, but a special warm, yearning place like no other in the heart of every one of us.

Parashas Lech Lecha 5777

Va'yachsheveha Lo Tzedakah

Are you jealous of your children and resentful of their accomplishments and rewards?

Not if you're normal. Most of us have been raised by dedicated parents who only hope that we surpass them in every way, and we tend to do the same. So it has always been.

This makes Rashi's explanation of *ve'heyeh berachah* in Lech Lecha seem a little obscure.

Hashem promises Avraham Avinu greatness in his future generations. *V'e'escha l'goy gadol* – that, Rashi explains, refers to the language of *tefillah*, "*Elokei Avraham*." "*Va'avarechecha*," Rashi continues, refers to "*Elokei Yitzchak*." And "*va'agadla shemecha*" refers to "*Elokei Yaakov*." But, Hashem promises Avraham, don't worry, *ve'heyeh berachah: b'cha chosmin v'lo bahen* – the *chasimah*, the finalization of the *berachah*, will refer only to you, Avraham, and not to your children.

Doesn't sound right, does it? Was Avraham jealous of his as yet unborn offspring, Yitzchak and Yaakov, and did he begrudge them greatness on a par with his own?

Not likely.

One explanation that has always appealed to me I saw in Rabbi Moshe Bogomilsky's *Vedibarta Bam*, in which he quotes his grandfather, Rav Tzvi Kaplan. There are others who offer parallel insight.

The Mishnah in *Avos* (1:2) teaches that the world stands on three pillars: Torah (Torah study), *avodah* (prayer and the service of God), and *gemilus chasadim* (tzedakah and acts of kindness).

We also have been taught that the three Avos each represented one of those pillars in particular. Avraham personified *chesed*, Yitzchak personified *avodah*, and Yaakov personified Torah. There are various *pesukim* that demonstrate and document this.

In Jewish history, there have been various periods when one or another of these attributes was dominant in Jewish life. Sometimes it was Torah scholarship (as represented by Yaakov). Sometimes it was religious devotion (Yitzchak). And sometimes the *middah* of *chesed* (Avraham) was strongest.

Hashem is telling Avraham here, says Rav Kaplan, that while they are all vital for the life and the continuity of Klal Yisrael, the *chasimas haberachah*, the conclusion of our long and bitter *galus* and our ultimate Redemption, will be through the strength of *chesed*, personified by Avraham Avinu.

This, I believe, adds significance to a simple yet profound *pasuk* in the Bris bein Habesarim. Hashem made great promises to Avraham, but had not yet delivered on them. And Avraham believed. He had no teacher, no role model, no positive influence in his life. But he believed with perfect faith. And the Torah attests to that faith by using the very word that represents Avraham's special attribute: *V'he'emin ba'Shem va'yachsheveha lo tzedakah*. The strength of Avraham's tzedakah is an attribute that works in multiple ways.

The Ateres Yeshuah picks up on this language. *"Va'yachsheveha"* appears three times in Scripture: here, *va'yachsheveha l'zonah* (Yehudah and Tamar) and *va'yachsheveha Eli l'shikorah* (Chana, mother of Shmuel Hanavi).

Va'yachsheveha lo tzedakah. The mitzvah of tzedakah is so great, says the Ateres Yeshuah, that in its merit lies the key to our ultimate Redemption: *Tzion ba'mishpat tipadeh v'shaveha b'tzedakah.* But the commonality of language (*va'yachsheveha*) also teaches us that not all tzedakah giving is equal, even if it superficially looks alike.

Va'yachsheveha l'zonah. There are people who violate the Torah, sometimes very seriously, and try to "clean it up" by giving some of their ill-gotten gains to tzedakah.

Midrash Rabbah (Mishpatim), in discussing those who violate the Torah by lending money to Jews and charging them interest, even if some of that interest winds up as charity in the hands of poor people, compares them to the *zonah* who receives beautiful apples in payment for her sin and then gives some to the sick, thus posing as a righteous person. Hashem rejects that kind of charity (*esnan zonah!*). The Midrash goes further and describes the evil government that confiscates honest people's money in the guise of taxes (excessive) and then gives some out to poor people, cloaking their confiscatory *geneivah* – their legal robbery – in pseudo virtue. (Attention, Washington and Albany!)

I will digress to share a true story, told to me by my great uncle, my grandfather's brother Reb Berish Nussbaum, *a"h*. (For part of his life he was known as Berish Geldzahler, using his mother's maiden name. That's a story for another time.)

A Jew who had emigrated to America and made money returned for a visit to Galitzia. The son of pious parents, he dressed right, he "talked the talk" and proudly showed that it is possible to remain a good Jew in America. He visited the Dzhikover Rebbe and asked for a *berachah*. As was customary, he put a *pidyon* of tzedakah money on the table. The Rebbe took one look at it and demanded to know where he got it. "I own real estate," he replied. The Rebbe would not touch the money. He insisted until the man finally admitted that his "real estate" interests included a building where *va'yachsheveha l'zonah* was no metaphor and required no resorting to deep *machshavah* to understand what that place was for. The Rebbe sent him packing, along with his dirty money.

As important and as potent as tzedakah is, one cannot cleanse himself by being *tovel v'sheretz b'yado*.

And then there's *va'yachsheveha l'shikorah*. Shmuel's mother Chana prayed, but no sound was heard. Her devotion was real, it was intense, it was unostentatious. This represents the ideal of tzedakah. Avraham Avinu says to the king of Sedom, "*v'harimosi es yadi el Hashem Keil Elyon*." The lying, cheating, nefarious, and promiscuous wife of Potiphar also uses the term *harimosi*: "*Harimosi koli v'ekra*."

The Ateres Yeshuah concludes that if one raises one's hand to distribute tzedakah for the sake of Heaven, without fanfare, without noise, without publicity, without *gaavah* – silently, like the prayer of Chana (*va'yachsheveha l'shikorah*), that's true tzedakah, the fulfillment of *va'yachsheveha lo tzedakah*. Tzedakah given "noisily" as a vehicle for publicity and *kavod* is not true tzedakah, but "*harimosi koli*" – reminiscent of *eishes Potiphar*.

Do you want to really be blessed? Do you want to realize the full potential reward of tzedakah? Do you want to give, and really do so *l'shem Shamayim?* Of course. We all do. We must do so generously and do so quietly. The real audience, the One Whose applause really matters, will know it.

Ve'heyeh berachah. The ultimate source of merit, stamped with the identity of our forefather Avraham Avinu, who bequeathed to all of us this most precious *middah* of tzedakah v'chesed is not limited to those with *gemara kep* (as important as that is), is not limited to those who can pray and sway and worship with great fervor (as important as that is). It is something we must teach our children by example. It is learned behavior, but something any one of us can do, if we want. And it has the singular power of *chasimas haberachah*: the power to bring the ultimate Redemption, *bimherah v'yameinu*.

Amen.

Parashas Lech Lecha 5772

Honor Your Father and Your Mother

There is a very beautiful place in the Galil of Eretz Yisrael called Beit She'arim, which, eighteen hundred years ago, was one of the places where the Sanhedrin survived and thrived after its exile from the ruined Jerusalem.

It was where, for a number of years, the great Rabbi Yehudah Hanasi, Rabbenu Hakadosh, lived and presided over the great assembly of Torah scholars as they codified the Mishnah. Based on Talmudic references, it is even discernible today where they sat in assembly and learned Torah.

It is also particularly remarkable for the multiple large burial caves where many of those great scholars were laid to rest. For many years, as well, deceased wealthy Jews from the Diaspora were brought there for burial. Jerusalem and Har Hazeisim were no longer options in those oppressive times, and the importance in Jewish life and history of this place made it the obvious place in Eretz Yisrael for one to desire as his last resting place.

The point, of course, is not so much Jerusalem or Beit She'arim, but the Land of Israel.

To be buried there, after 120, was the dream of every Jew, but it was, for nearly everyone, not a practical possibility. And later on that became a virtual impossibility for nearly everyone not actually living there. During the long years of exile, especially in the far-flung places Jews found themselves, a very rare and prized possession was a little bag of earth from the Land of Israel, which would be placed in the grave of the deceased, under his head, so that his remains could, in some small measure, be integrated into the soil of the Holy Land. To actually be buried there was an impossible dream.

In our day, the miraculous rebirth of Jewish presence and hegemony in the Land of Israel, and jet flight, make the historic impossibility of that dream seem less obvious than the depressing reality it actually was for most of history. But the ideal of coming to one's final rest in the holy soil of Eretz Yisrael, something Yaakov Avinu and Yosef Hatzaddik urgently desired and begged their descendants to do for them, remained forever as a high ideal for every Jew.

And so the *haftarah* for Shabbos Chol Hamoed Sukkos, the prophecy of Yechezkel Hanavi, is most interesting, and utterly surprising, in this regard. He foretells the march of the armies of Gog against Israel, with murder and mayhem in their hearts, destruction of the Jews their battle plan. In his gracious love for us, God will, instead, rain destruction down upon Gog.

And then the *navi* makes a point of saying that the Children of Israel will come out and bury the dead of Gog *in the Land of Israel*. In its soil. The area of the battle, it appears, is not that far from the border, but the burials will take place, intentionally, *within* Israel. By design. It does not say why. But it does say quite clearly that God Himself *promises* it.

We can find an answer in Parashas Noach, a lesson so profound that we should all take notice and act on it, if we are so fortunate, while we can, as well as we can, as long as we can.

Noach emerges from the Ark, plants a vineyard, gets drunk, and in this state, becomes degraded, and is further degraded, abused, and mocked by his son Cham. The Torah tells us that his other two sons, Shem and Yafes, respectfully take a cloak, put it on their shoulders, walk backward into their father's tent so as not to see him in his degraded state, and cover him up. An early lesson in *kibbud av*. And we understand that such lessons are recorded in the Torah because they speak to us for all the ages.

The Torah records what Noach's reaction to his sons' actions was, what his blessings for Shem and Yafes and his curse for Cham were. The *Midrash Rabbah* tells us what God's rewards and punishments for these actions were.

Middah k'neged middah, measure for measure, indecent exposure and redeeming covering will follow for the descendants of these brothers. Cham's descendants will suffer degrading nakedness in their history. Shem's descendants, at a time when they need it the most, will be rewarded through their raiment: Chananiah, Mishael, and Azariah will emerge from the fiery furnace of Nevuchadnezzar, at a time when Israel is at an all-time low, the nation and the faith of Israel apparently utterly defeated. They are, for all to see, not only personally unscathed by the fire, but even their clothing remarkably, miraculously, bears not even a faint smell of smoke from the smoky furnace into which they had been cast, giving a great and desperately needed boost, credibility, and honor to the Jews and to Judaism itself.

The dead of Gog lay strewn about in the land they came to conquer and despoil. One of the worst "pains" one can endure, after death itself, we are told, is to lie unburied and degraded. Military history is rife with stories of the dead lying unburied, decomposing, food for scavenging animals, rotting and stinking things that were once actual people, human beings who had thought and felt, who had been created *b'tzelem Elokim*, in the "image of God." It is the worst degradation. But the ancestor of these dead soldiers of Gog, Yefes ben Noach, had shown reverential and sensitive respect for his father, who was lying there drunk, exposed, and degraded. The reward of Yefes was that his children, the army of Gog, would, in honor of their *zeide* Yefes, not only be spared that cruel fate, but would be buried *davka* in the Land of Israel, their bodies covered and sheltered in its holy soil, something that most generations of Jews did not merit to receive. And their buriers would be their cousins, the descendants of Shem, the People of Israel, who would go out, as God promised, to gather and to put their bodies to rest in Israel's own holy soil.

Noach was saved from the Flood, and the world went on. All of mankind sprang from his children, whose totipotentiality gave rise to all the different nations and their various characteristics. *Ashreinu*, we are the children of Avraham, the descendant of Shem, whose best characteristics were, in Avraham, refined to the point that he became a perfect man, unique in discerning the Ribbono shel Olam, the Creator of all. The others went their own way, and like people everywhere, there is good and there is bad.

And God does not miss a thing, nor does He forget. Shem and Yefes ran to do what, one would think, any respectful son would do. But how would we really know that, except that the Torah makes a major point in telling us. In honoring one's parents, one honors his human creators. And in so doing, one honors as well the Creator of all, Who sees, in the *middah* of *kibbud av va'em*, the expression of goodness and decency that the world was created for.

Our forefather, Avraham Ha'ivri, was the first to take it to the next step, to show that goodness and decency can be so refined, so elevated, so far beyond just the justification of mere existence, that he showed mankind that it can reach, through its spirit and its actions, the very heights of existence, an existence so exalted and so rarefied that the very angels of Heaven, those purely spiritual beings, can only stand in awe and praise the Creator of such a creature.

And it is to that, oh blessed children of Avraham, that we must aspire. For the potential to do so is implanted within each and every one of us.

Parashas Lech Lecha 5778

Vayera

Akeidah

It came to pass, *after all these things*, that God tested Avraham, and said to him, *take your son, your solitary, special son, whom you love, Yitzchak, go to Moriah, and offer him up there as a wholly burnt offering, on the mountain which I will specify.*

Avraham rose early in the morning and set out to do God's bidding. He did not inform his wife Sarah what his purpose in leaving was, lest she kill herself in her grief. Yitzchak too did not inform his mother, out of the same concern. The irony is that although in the end Yitzchak survived, Sarah did not. Informed by the Satan what the expedition was about, *although not that it was only a test and that Yitzchak was safe*, she expired in her shock and horror.

It was on the third day that they reached Mount Moriah. It was not a three-day journey, but it lasted three days to ensure that Avraham had time to reflect and that he not appear to have acted hastily or to have been rushed into it by an urgently demanding God.

Avraham did not want to sacrifice his beloved son. It made no sense, yet God demanded it, and so, perfect servant of God, Avraham sprang to do God's bidding.

Yitzchak did not want to die. But, perfect servant of God, he bade his father bind his hands and feet, lest, shaking in fear, he cause an imperfection in the *shechitah*, rendering him a *baal mum* and ruining the sacrifice offering.

We recite the entire Torah portion of the Akeidah every day, invoking the *tzidkus* of our forefathers and their total devotion to God as currency in our beseeching God for our own lives and the lives of our children. I suspect, however, that we have been doing this throughout our long and tortured history also *because we have had to.*

How else can we have endured?

O God, O God Almighty, how else can we have endured?

The iconic photo above was taken in Warsaw. It stands alone in the annals of terror.

Look at that little boy's terrified face. And look at that German soldier with his submachine gun trained on the child. The situation depicted is, sadly, hardly unique. As a photo document, it has become emblematic and is known virtually everywhere the Holocaust is not denied.

One looks at that scene and understands that it would not be long afterward that all those people were murdered. In fact, however, that may not be the case for all of them. No one can be entirely sure, but that child has been tentatively identified as Tsvi Nussbaum, born in Tel Aviv but brought back to Sandomierz, Poland, for safety with his little brother Ilan, at the urging of his grandparents, upon the wild Arab rioting of 1939. In the end, in the way that God works these things, he was a child survivor, who went on to study medicine at the Albert Einstein College of

Medicine in New York, a war orphan on a Tootsie Roll scholarship. He married, raised a beautiful family, and had a fulfilling career as a doctor. His parents were murdered, as was his little brother, who was together with his great-grandmother Genendel (Geldzahler) Nussbaum, who was also my maternal great-grandmother. Our grandparents were siblings.

I had another cousin Tzvi, a little boy who was called Hershele, the son of my father's older sister Henia (Reich) Kuhl. His mother managed to hide him in a cellar in Ulanow, Poland, when the Germans dragged her and her daughter Chana off to be murdered. Not wanting to be bothered to search, and for their cruel amusement, the Germans simply cemented the cellar shut, as they did countless similar cellars and bunkers, leaving the mostly child inhabitants of those hiding places to die of thirst, alone in the darkness, in terror. A classmate of mine in yeshiva elementary school told me back then, in third grade, that he had an older brother whom he never knew: the Germans cemented him into the cellar in which he was hidden.

And I have, over the years, encountered many of my contemporaries who knew, as children, that they had older siblings whom they never knew, who were cruelly murdered before the younger children were born, whose parents somehow survived not only the murder of their children and the rest of their families, but survived, as well, the horror of having survived their murdered children.

And it came to pass, *after all these things,* that God tested Avraham, and said to him, *Take your son, your solitary, special son, whom you love, and offer him up as a burnt offering.*

We recite the entire Torah portion of the Akeidah every day, invoking the *tzidkus* of our forefathers and their total devotion to God as currency in beseeching God for our own lives and the lives of our children. I suspect, however, that we have been doing this throughout our long and tortured history also *because we have had to.*

How else can we have endured?

O God, O God Almighty, O Merciful God, how else can we have endured? How?

How else can we have possibly had the strength to go on? How is it possible?

And, if I may be so bold, let me suggest the possibility as well, playing history forward, that Avraham Avinu drew the strength that he needed not just from his own reserves of faith, but also from the faith and the strength and the sacrifice and the unspeakable, unimaginable burden that his descendants would in the future be called upon to bear, *because they were his descendants,* time and again, and again and again, tests so terrible and so numerous that Avraham's own test, terrible as that was, objectively, seems almost to pale in comparison.

And so, we draw strength and invoke protection from the Akeidah of Yitzchak, Avraham's child. In the way such things work in God's divine plan, it seems, Avraham also drew strength from the Akeidah of an infinite number of future Yitzchaks, of Chanales, from an endless, endless army of little Hersheles.

Parashas Vayera 5776

I Once Was Lost but Now I'm Found; Was Blind but Now I See

Avraham Avinu famously arrived at knowledge of God on his own. He had no teacher, no role model, no positive influence in his life. But his sensitive spirit and deductive mind, his endless quest for holiness and goodness, led him to the inescapable conclusion that there is a Ribbono shel Olam, a Creator by Whose will the world came into being and all things are governed and ordained.

How lonely it must have been for the young Avraham in the house of his father Terach, a trafficker in idols. With his talk of the One God, and the goodness He mandated, Avraham was such a disappointment to Terach that he found himself turned in by his own father to the wicked king of idolaters, Nimrod, for punishment: the fiery furnace.

Avraham was different from everyone else in his world. What bravery and determination he needed to stand up to the ridicule, the abuse, the rejection of his loved ones, the utter loneliness! But he was Avraham. It was upon him that the world we know was ultimately built. He was pure and he was good and he survived the alienation of his entire society. And he persevered until God finally revealed Himself to him, and our nation – and the world of the Torah – came into being. The lonely man of faith built an entire world.

He became Avraham Ha'ivri, Avraham who was separate from the rest of the world he came from.

Despite all his greatness, his achievements, his sacrifice, and his successes, he had his share of trials and travails, as we well know. His *nisyonos* (tests) are well documented. And finally, after the most difficult test of all, the Akeidah, he asked of God, belief in Whom was his life's work, to test him no more.

The lonely man of faith. What faith is required for that lonely man to survive his loneliness!

When Avraham arrived in Gerar, the local king, Avimelech, tried to take Sarah for himself. As he had in Egypt, Avraham found that he had to pose as Sarah's brother rather than her husband, in order to avoid being slain. It was only God's intervention to save Sarah from Avimelech, as it was with Pharaoh in Egypt, that brought the facts to light. Avimelech reprimands Avraham for having put him in that position. Avraham responds that there was no fear of Heaven in Gerar: when he arrived in town they asked him not about his needs to survive there, but about the woman who was with him and her availability. He understood what they were about.

And so he tells Avimelech that he has been a wanderer, and in the various places he goes, it has been safer for him to portray Sarah as his sister, lest he be murdered.

Bereishis 20:13: "*Va'yehi ka'asher his'u osi Elokim mi'beis avi*" (When God caused me to wander from my father's house), "*va'omar lah, zeh chasdech asher taasi imadi*" (I said to her, this is the *chesed* that you should do for me), "*el kol hamakom asher navo shamah, imri li achi hu*" (in every place to which we arrive, say of me, "He is my brother").

Onkelos's rendition of this *pasuk* is strikingly unusual. Whereas his is usually a straightforward translation, with the occasional added word to lend insight, here his "translation" is not a translation at all, but the presentation of a concept in totally different words. He must have been driven by a unique imperative.

Onkelos, whose Targum appears in virtually every Chumash right alongside the Hebrew text, was a high-born gentile, nephew to the Roman emperor. Some believe it was the evil Titus, and others believe it was the wicked Hadrian. Needless to say, his upbringing in that corrupt, cruel, and dissolute society in no way contributed to the saintly, immortal tzaddik he became, Onkelos the Ger, author of the Targum on the Chumash.

How lonely this sensitive and spiritual person must have been, searching and striving for the sublime while yet physically mired in the filth of depraved Roman society.

What a disappointment he was to his patrician Roman family! Shamed by his actions, they threatened to kill him.

Onkelos was different from everyone else in his world. What bravery and determination he needed to stand up to the ridicule, the abuse, the rejection of his loved ones, the loneliness. But he was pure and he was good and he survived the alienation of his native society. And he became the great Onkelos.

And so, in light of this remarkable parallel with Avraham, Onkelos's rendition of the above *pasuk* becomes particularly striking. I wish I remember where I first saw this described. The sentiment evoked is haunting.

Rashi alludes cryptically to it: "*Onkelos tirgem mah she'tirgem*" (Onkelos rendered what he rendered).

How did Onkelos, in fact, translate this *pasuk* (20:13)? "When the nations erred, when they wandered from the Truth, worshiping gods that they themselves built with their own hands [*and I was among them, among the lost!*], God [*in His mercy*] brought me near to Him, to the fear of Him, away from my father's house [*He saved me from the terrible, corrupt world I was brought up in!*]. I said to her then [*I said to God then*], let this be the *chesed* you do for me: in every place that we go, say of me, 'He is My brother!'"

Seeing his own dramatic and turbulent history mirrored in that of Avraham Avinu, Onkelos, in this *pasuk*, gives thanks to God for separating him from the rest of the world he came from (*ha'Ivri!*), for bringing him *tachas kanfei haShechinah*, and prays that in his wanderings from his father's house, God will do him the *chesed* of identifying him, always, as His "brother," as it were, His protected ward.

The lonely man of faith. What faith is required for that lonely man to survive his loneliness!

In the many generations since Avraham Avinu showed the way, countless people of spirit have, by the grace of God and by the courage borne of that spirit, found their way from the darkness – the darkness of Ur Kasdim, the darkness of pagan Rome, the darkness of empty materialism, the darkness of a world without values – to the light of goodness, of *chesed*, of Godliness. It is often a lonely odyssey and a difficult one. It is often marked by the scorn and ridicule of the spiritually blind and lost.

Those who have no hope – and no ambition – to achieve grandeur of the spirit often do not want others to achieve that either, and seek to hinder them. That journey, for those who are raised among such people – and this is, sadly, so common – is often a long, lonely, and arduous one.

But what can be dearer, and for what can one be more grateful, what sweeter song for the human spirit can there be, than to thank God Almighty for His help in emerging from that darkness, to declare (borrowing a beautifully expressed sentiment from our neighbors), "I once was lost, but now I'm found; was blind, but now I see."

Thank you, Ribbono shel Olam, dear Father in Heaven, for bestowing Your supernal light upon us, that we may indeed see, and that we may nestle, secure and *found*, in your loving embrace. And thank You for sending us those heroes, those brave, often lonely, struggling, yearning souls, who, in every generation, inspire us and show us the way.

Parashas Vayera 5774

How Could Something So Lost Be So Found?

To the lost children of Israel: God will find you.

If there is even one Jew to be found in an entire city, or two Jews lost in an entire nation of gentiles (*echad me'ir u'shnayim mi'mishpachah*), Hashem will find you and bring you back to Zion (Yirmiyahu 3:14). *Return to Me, wayward children, for you are Mine, and I will provide you with shepherds according to My heart; they will feed you knowledge and understanding.*

This concept of Hashem "finding" us is a powerful and recurrent theme.

David Hamelech refers to this when he portrays the Ribbono shel Olam saying "*Matzasi David avdi…*," I found My servant David, and anointed him with My holy oil (Tehillim 89:21).

Midrash Rabbah (Bereishis 29:3) quotes Rabbi Shimon: *Shalosh metzios matza Hakadosh Baruch Hu.* Avraham (*matzasa es levavo ne'eman l'fanecha*), David (*Matzasi David avdi*), and Yisrael (*k'anavim ba'midbar matzasi Yisrael*).

Honing in on David, the Midrash goes further: *Matzasi David avdi. Heichan?* Where? In Sedom. How so?

The Torah tells us that Lot also had much wealth when he parted ways with Avraham.

He had cattle and tents. The Midrash expounds: two *special* tents. He had within him two special future offspring, women who would be "tents," *houses*, of everlasting significance: Rus Hamoaviah, who would marry Boaz and be the great-grandmother of David Hamelech, and Naamah Ha'amonis, who would marry Shlomo Hamelech and, as the mother of Rechavam, be matriarch to Malchus Beis David.

It should be obvious to you now where this is heading. If David Hamelech was "found" in Sedom, because his ancestor Lot was there, then we are reminded just how it came about that those forebears of David begat him: through the vilest possible form of interaction between a father and his daughters. Shocking, but openly revealed by the Torah. There was some kind of excuse, but it's no less shocking.

The Imrei Noam brings this discussion back to *echad me'ir u'shnayim mi'mishpachah*, quoted above from Yirmiyahu. The Redemption, through Moshiach ben David, will be traced back to *echad me'ir* (Lot, one man saved from an entire city) and to *shnayim mi'mishpachah* (Lot's two daughters, who raised two nations, Amon and Moav).

They found wine in that cave, waiting there for them, in order to facilitate the birth of two nations, so that, in God's inscrutable wisdom, Moshiach should emerge from them.

The Imrei Noam further quotes a strange Midrash (*Bereishis Rabbah* 51:9): *Ein kol Shabbos v'Shabbos she'ein korin bah parshaso shel Lot*. There is no Shabbos that we do not read the *parashah* of Lot.

Really? When? Where?

Many ask this obvious question. The Imrei Noam has a wonderful response.

The Torah tells us that after the argument between their shepherds, Avraham and Lot decided to part ways. They did so on good terms. *Anashim achim anachnu*, they declared. They were closely related. They even looked alike. Avraham took Lot with him when he left Charan, and when he traveled to Canaan and then to Egypt and back. Lot threw his lot in with Avraham. He had learned many good things from him. And indeed, later, when Lot was captured, Avraham went to war to retrieve him.

It seems strange, then, that when Avraham prays so hard, arguing with God and risking His good graces in an effort to spare Sedom, not once does he mention Lot, who deserved to be saved, nor does he ask God to spare him!

The *Zohar* says, "Come see the modesty and humility of Avraham Avinu," who did not pray that Lot be saved. Rather, Hakadosh Baruch Hu Himself remembered the righteousness of Avraham, in whose merit Lot was saved: *Va'yehi b'shaches Elokim es arei hakikar va'yizkor Elokim es Avraham va'yishalach es Lot mi'toch hahafecha*.

In the merit of Avraham Avinu, the *yeshuah* came without any need for prayer, similar to the concept of *terem yikra'u va'ani e'eneh* (Yeshayahu 65:24).

On Shabbos we don't ask for our personal needs. And so the Gemara (*Shabbos* 12b) advises one who visits the sick on Shabbos to say, "*Shabbos hi mi'lizok u'refuah kerovah lavo*." That too is the *nusach* for a Mi She'berach on Shabbos. The power of Shabbos is such that *yeshuah* can come without specific prayer.

The saving of Lot, says the Imrei Noam, was a *yeshuah* that affected all of the world, for all time, because the *neshamah* of Moshiach was to be released via Lot. The highest form of *yeshuah* is that which is bestowed without the need for prayer. We do pray for Moshiach to come, but ultimately he will be sent by God as a free gift, a function of His infinite love and mercy: *L'maani, l'maani aaseh* (Yeshayahu 48:11).

This is somewhat akin to our prayer on Erev Rosh Hashanah, in the Selichos of Zechor Bris Avraham: *Go'el chazak l'maancha pedeinu, re'eh ki ozlas yadeinu, shur ki avdu chasideinu, u'mafgia ein ba'adeinu* (there is no one to pray for us) – but rather, let God's *middah* of *rachamim* take over completely.

By not praying for the saving of Lot – in effect, not praying for the saving of Moshiach – Avraham Avinu was redirecting the ultimate *yeshuah* to be totally in God's hands, totally a function of His divine mercy.

Hashem found David in Sedom.

Sedom was the lowest of the low. Lot was essentially good, but he was drawn to Sedom.

Through his flaw, he eventually came to cohabit with his own daughters. They were non-Jews living in a bad environment. You would think that these people and everything about them would be lost among the long history of iniquities in the world. Instead, we discover that the spark of holiness that would give rise to David Hamelech, Malchus Beis David, and Melech Hamoshiach, the very fulfillment of God's promise of ultimate Redemption for all time, derived from them, and they were saved for this very purpose.

God has no shortage of candidates or resources for His will to be expressed.

Why *davka* through Sedom? Why from that filth?

Perhaps the lesson derives from the very name God bestowed upon human beings. *Adam*, deriving from the low earth (*adamah*). Adam, *adameh l'Elyon* (I will resemble the Most High). A person, in his behavior, can be reminiscent of the lowest of the low, the dirt, or the highest of the high – *adameh l'Elyon*. He can be high, and God forbid fall down low, even to the depths of Sedom. He can be low – as low as Sedom – do *teshuvah*, and raise himself high, even to the point of *adameh l'Elyon*.

In which guise we make this journey through life is our choice.

"There is no Shabbos that we do not read the *parashah* of Lot."

Lot was saved, and thus Moshiach was saved, not through prayer but through the virtue and merit of Avraham Avinu. So too, the merit of Shabbos heals the sick on Shabbos more effectively than prayer. Because the ultimate source of salvation, of healing, of blessing, is God's *middah* of *rachamim*. And that *rachamim* is, in turn, evoked by who we are and what we make of ourselves.

Hashem "found" David in Sedom. He "found" Moshiach in Sedom.

That priceless lesson teaches us that there is virtually no limit to how high we can raise ourselves, to what we can achieve, if we only want to, if we are truly determined.

And in the process, the whole world can be saved.

Parashas Vayera 5772

Testing, Testing, 1, 2, 3

Early in my career, I came to realize that my oldest patients were also among my healthiest. That doesn't mean they weren't weakened by age, but they weren't sick. By and large they weren't fat and they weren't hypertensive and they weren't diabetic. I suppose that's how they got to be old. It pays to have good genes, as well as good health habits.

We know that in early biblical times, there were people who lived hundreds of years. By the time of Avraham and Sarah, the lifespan had come down to something much closer to today's standard. Avraham did live 175 years, and Sarah 127, but we also know that well before that, they had become biologically old, so that it was a miracle for them to have a child when they did. Sarah, at eighty-nine, was called old, no longer capable of bearing a child. So too for Avraham at ninety-nine, when the *malachim* visited.

So we encounter Avraham at age 137, having traveled for three days, trudging up the mountain, preparing to offer his beloved son as a sacrifice, for that is what God had commanded.

The climb itself must have been physical torture, let alone the horrific purpose of that climb. But that is what the aged Avraham did, along with his thirty-seven-year-old son who was heir not just to his earthly fortune but to the spiritual enterprise of his entire life's work, which was his real fortune. And Yitzchak was the promised medium of the ultimate fulfillment of that enterprise.

But if Yitzchak were to die that day, could Avraham start over? At age 137?

Who could have the *koach* – *physically as well as spiritually* – for that?

We all know what actually happened. And Chazal tell us that afterward something else happened. This was not Avraham's first test. It was his tenth, and had to be his most difficult test, even tougher than being thrown into the fiery furnace in his youth.

Avraham had no reason to think that this was to be his last test, or even his most difficult. The God Whom he had followed – Whose existence he discerned intellectually long before God actually revealed Himself to him, and for Whom even then he was prepared to give his life – evidently had chosen to repeatedly test him, *and presumably would continue to do so as long as he lived.*

But now he was old and, one can assume, quite shaken. His beloved wife Sarah died in the immediate aftermath of this *nisayon,* and indeed that loss can be seen as part of the *nisayon,* testing whether he would come to regret doing what God asked at the cost of his wife's life.

In fact, it would never occur to that tzaddik not to obey God's will; he would do whatever God asked, no matter what. But the iron will to serve God does not make it automatically easy to do so. What test would it be if it were easy? And the greater the tzaddik, the more challenging the test has to be in order to be a true test.

And how terrible would the next test be? What could be more difficult, more wrenching, than the Akeidah? And so old Avraham turned to God and said,

Ribbono shel Olam, *enough*! Please, please, do not test me any more. *Ich hob shoyn nisht kein koach* for any more tests. I am Yours. Test me if You must, but please – *don't!*

And God didn't.

We Jews have a Yiddish expression: "*M'zol nisht geprivt veren*" (May we not be tested).

It is a prayer, really, for a test is a terrible thing. We ask that Hashem bless us *b'chesed* and *b'rachamim*, essentially as a free gift, or because we live according to His mandates, but we pray that doing so should not be too difficult or too painful, as it has so much been in our tortured history. It is certainly an appropriate prayer, and please God, so may it be. But it isn't always so in life. And Avraham Avinu did not become Avraham Avinu without being sorely tested, repeatedly.

And so, it does seem odd that Avraham, who succeeded so greatly in all his *nisyonos*, is portrayed by *Midrash Tanchuma* in the beginning of Vayera in a most puzzling way.

Va'yera elav Hashem b'Elonei Mamre. Sore and sick three days after his circumcision at age ninety-nine, Avraham is sitting at the door of his tent in the heat of the day, resolutely looking to greet and host wayfarers, to show them kindness and perhaps to introduce them to the concept of God and His kindly ways. Why does the Torah spell out that he was sitting in Mamre's grove of trees, thereby immortalizing that fact forever?

We know that Avraham was friendly with the magnates Aner, Eshkol, and Mamre.

He had good relations with them, yes, but they were hardly his religious mentors.

And yet *Tanchuma* tells us a strange thing. God told Avraham at age ninety-nine to circumcise himself. In fact, Avraham knew all about this mitzvah for a long time, and although he kept all the mitzvos, he refrained from this one until he was actually commanded to do it. It is far greater, and more meritorious, to perform a mitzvah in response to God's specific command than to just do so voluntarily. *Gadol hametzuveh v'oseh mi'mi she'eino metzuveh v'oseh.* He must have wanted to circumcise himself for a long time, but he waited until he was commanded to do so, the better to position himself as God's servant who does as God commands.

And yet *Tanchuma* tells us that before he actually did it, Avraham asked the advice of Aner, Eshkol, and Mamre! *Should I do it?* Huh? Avraham asked those three *goyim* if he should do what God commanded? Our Avraham did that? The same Avraham Avinu who submitted to the burning furnace rather than renounce the One God?

Tanchuma relates that Aner advised him not to do it, lest, in his weakened state, the survivors and the successors of the kings he defeated come and slay him in revenge.

Eshkol advised him not to do it, as he was old and he might bleed and not survive it.

Mamre's response was quite different: Avraham! How can you even consider not doing it? The God Who saved you from the fiery furnace, Who saved you from the kings you warred with, Who protected every one of your organs and body parts from harm – now that He asks you to do something to a small part of one body part, will you consider not doing what He asks of you? What sense would that make?

God's response to Mamre's advice was everlasting reward: "When I appear to Avraham now, I will only do so in *your* domain, and your name will forever be associated with it in the eternal Torah."

But why would Avraham even ask them? If they said don't do it, would he listen to them? The Kesav Sofer suggests that Avraham, having waited to do his bris until actually commanded to do so in order that his *sechar mitzvah* would be greater, now asked his friends so that when the majority advised him not to do it, doing it anyway would garner him even greater *sechar*.

I would like to suggest an alternate explanation.

As one who was thoroughly tested, Avraham knew very well about being tested. And who says the testee cannot also be the tester? How do you know, until the crunch comes, who is a real, reliable friend, and whose judgment and advice are sound?

Avraham was close to Aner, Eshkol, and Mamre. Even as he influenced them, they apparently also influenced him. He needed to understand in a very critical way who among them was an appropriate influence for someone with Avraham's critical historic mission. He too had to be a tester. That was part of his mission.

All of us, in life, need to be so careful whom and what we allow to influence us. Chazal make that clear. We too need to test very carefully and to judge, for ourselves and for our families, which influences are appropriate for us, for our growth, for our *kedushah*, for the fulfillment of the divine mission God has ordained for each and every one of us.

That too is part of our mission.

If Avraham Avinu needed to do it, and the Torah informs us that he did, is it not obvious that each of us must do so as well? Like our Father Avraham, our destiny demands that we do.

Parashas Vayera 5773

Note: Since this was written, all of us in our community (Manhattan Beach and other shore communities) have been, and continue to be, sorely tested. The devastation of Hurricane Sandy has been beyond belief. May Hashem strengthen us all, and may we all find within ourselves the strength and the fortitude and the faith to rebuild our lives. *Hashem Hu Ha'Elokim. Hashem Hu Ha'Elokim.* His judgments and actions are altogether just, even if it requires a great deal of faith to understand that.

צדיק אתה ה' וישר משפטיך. צוית צדק עדתיך ואמונה מאד (תהלים קי"ט).

May we find that faith. And may we no longer be tested. May the God Who heeded Avraham's prayer – and tested him no longer – bless us and do the same for us.

Zei Gezint

It was a summer afternoon, and I was somewhere in Midtown Manhattan. It was not a common excursion for me, a twenty-year-old yeshiva and college student. Perhaps that's why I remember it so well. I was wearing a lightweight summer suit. A panhandler, a middle-aged black man, stopped me – maybe because I was wearing a suit – and asked for a handout. It was his lucky day: I gave him a dollar.

In parting, I wished him good health. He reacted with a puzzled look on his face. He hadn't complained of being sick. Then he smiled broadly, with a look of friendly recognition.

"I know!" he said. "I used to work with Jewish people. I remember! That's how they talk. *Zei gezunt!* Good health!"

Clearly, it was not, for him, in the context of usual conversation, or in the routine parting from someone, to do so with a blessing or wishes of good health. Don't get me wrong. He seemed like a pleasant, well-meaning fellow. This is a sociological observation. It was simply not what was done in his circles.

And so I am reminded of Schenectady Avenue. When I was growing up in Crown Heights, there was a commercial strip of stores, many selling produce, for several blocks north and south of Eastern Parkway. The ladies would go there with their shopping wagons to see what *metziahs* they could find.

Tante Rivka had names for most of those merchants, although those names bore no relationship to their actual names, which I am sure she did not know. The names were more like titles or descriptives.

Tante Rivka was no rube, but she did have a charming small-town quality to her, having grown up in a small town in Poland. Thus, one of the fruit sellers was named "Der Rozivdiver" – not because he was from Rozivdiv. He was not. But he had a relative who had lived for a while in a village not too far from Rozivdiv, which was, in turn, not all that far from Rivka's home town of Kolbesov. And so that fruit merchant became, and remains for all eternity, "Der Rozivdiver."

It was on Schenectady Avenue, in those years of my childhood, that I became aware of something striking that was a routine part of the world I lived in, but which, on one most fortunate occasion, made clear to me how special and how precious that world and the society that peopled it was.

I witnessed a serious argument between two people about some business matter. They strenuously disagreed and could come to no resolution. They were clearly very unhappy with each other. When there was no point to any further discussion, they parted company, one of the men clearly indicating to the other that he'd had it. It was the words he used in telling the other fellow, in effect, to get lost, that struck me profoundly.

"OK, *gei gezinterheit.*" Go in good health.

In that very Jewish world, even an argument that is not resolved well ends with a word of blessing for the person one is arguing with.

Avraham Avinu, weakened and in pain from his recent *bris milah*, but unwilling to forgo the mitzvah of *hachnasas orchim* and the opportunities to build on that, sits in his tent in the heat of the day, looking for guests to serve, and behold, three "men" stand before him. They are angels of God in human form. He welcomes them, offering them hospitality, food and drink. Please let me do this for you, he asks of them. They accept: *"Ken, taaseh ka'asher dibarta"* (You will do as you have said).

Literally, that means they accept Avraham's invitation. *Yes, Avraham, you may prepare the food and drink, the festive meal, as you have said.*

The *Midrash Rabbah* looks at their words literally: "So will you do [*future tense*], as you have said." *Ken taaseh.* The Angels gave Avraham a *berachah*: May it be Hashem's will that you make another *seudah*, another festive meal, in the future, when a son (Yitzchak) is born to you.

Avraham Avinu was so dedicated to *chesed*, to acts of kindness, that even on the most painful postoperative day for this ninety-nine-year-old man, he persisted, on a day of uncommon, debilitating heat, looking out hopefully for someone to help. *Chesed* is the *middah* identified primarily with Avraham, the first Jew, who was its very personification. It is a *middah* passed down to his children for all generations. It is, in fact, an identifier for a Jew. We are told that a purported Jew who exhibits no trait of *chesed* may well be of suspicious lineage. We are taught, as well, that in the end, *chesed* will be the key to our final Redemption.

One of the greatest rewards of possessing the *middah* of *chesed* is the very joy of *performing* acts of *chesed*, pronouncing words of *chesed*. Giving tzedakah is an act of *chesed*. Giving tzedakah accompanied by a kind word and showing a kind face is an infinitely greater act of *chesed*. Speaking kindly to others, wishing them well, raising their spirits, blessing them with the good things we need in life are all acts of *chesed*. This is not derived from logic; it is *moreshes avos*, a loving legacy from our forebears that is part of what defines us as a nation apart, Am Segulah.

Avraham's angelic visitors gave him a *berachah*, and in so doing they also imbued him with the attribute, and the power, to confer *berachos*. And to this day, thirty-eight hundred years later, we, his children, still are in the habit of giving each other *berachos* as a routine part of our speech, in how we relate to and speak to each other, even in casual conversation, indeed, even when we are annoyed, squabbling over some business matter on Schenectady Avenue.

Parashas Vayera 5777

Va'tesa ba'Midbar

With regard to Hagar and *va'tesa ba'midbar* (ותתע במדבר): this is not the only use of this word – not a rare word in Tanach, but rare in this form – indicating painful, lost wandering, in the *parashah*. Avraham used it when he described his own history to Avimelech.

I will digress with a true anecdote.

Reuven and Shimon were wrangling over a business matter, unable to agree, and each looking for a way to resolve the impasse to his benefit. Reuven went to Chacham Rabbi X for an *eitzah*.

The wise rabbi gave him a great strategy to help him win.

Shimon also went to a *chacham* for an *eitzah*. Of course, unbeknownst to Reuven, and not knowing that Reuven had consulted Rabbi X, Shimon also went to the same Chacham Rabbi X for advice on how to defeat Reuven. Rabbi X gave Shimon a great strategy to help him win.

The rabbi's people asked him how he could give such conflicting advice.

"What's the problem?" he asked. "I gave Reuven the advice that was good for him, and I gave Shimon the advice that was good for him. Sure, they should compromise, and if they want me to be a *sholish*, I will do it. But as things are, I will give my best advice to each of them."

Sarah wanted Avraham to banish Yishmael and Hagar. For her, it was the right thing.

God told Avraham to do it, divinely understanding that it was for the best.

But from Abraham's moral perspective, there was no reason to so "cruelly" send his wife Hagar and their son off into the desert, possibly to perish there. *Va'yera hadavar me'od b'einei Avraham* (21:11). He did it because Sarah urged him to, and because God told him to listen to her, despite his misgivings. But for him it was, in a sense, *wrong*, even if it was, in a broad strategic sense, the right thing to do.

Back with Avimelech, Avraham had explained himself by describing his difficulties in life, having left his father's house and set himself apart from the rest of the world, the Ivri, wandering in the world until his own safe refuge could be established. *Va'yehi ka'asher his'u osi Elokim mi'beis avi* (20:13). It was hard for him, with many trials along the way. Sometimes he had to resort to unusual stratagems to stay alive, such as presenting his wife as his sister. He did what he had to do, but he suffered.

The very word Avraham used to denote his painful wandering, *his'u* (התעו), is used to describe what he did to Hagar and Yishmael. Sure, he had to do it. But he caused them pain, and from his *own* perspective, not considering Sarah's wisdom and God's command, he should not have. And so the Torah describes Hagar and Yishmael's travail with that very word. Avraham's payback.

A fascinating parallel, lending support to this hypothesis: Yaakov fools his father and "steals" the *berachah* from his brother. It could not have been easy for him, the *ish tam yoshev ohalim*, to do this, but, at his mother's insistence, he does so. We understand that in fact, he had to do so. But in doing so he caused his brother terrible pain, which Esav found unbearable: *Va'yitzak tze'akah gedolah u'marah ad me'od* (27:34).

Yaakov did what he was supposed to do. He did what Rivkah wanted, and indeed what God wanted. But God also keeps a *cheshbon*. Nothing is lost, and nothing is forgotten. And so when Yaakov was down, when his children were exiled from their land, when Haman arranged a massacre of the Jews, Mordechai tore his garments, and in sackcloth and ashes he went out into the city and "*va'yizak zaakah gedolah u'marah*" (Esther 4:1; see *Midrash Rabbah*). Payback.

God's justice is exquisitely fine tuned. Everything we do in life, from every perspective – every way our actions affect other people – is taken into account. For every bit of good that we do, and for every bit of harm, that is what we should expect: payback.

Parashas Vayera 5777

Chayei Sarah

Sarah

When Yitzchak Avinu married Rivkah Imenu, he was already Yitzchak Avinu. When Yaakov Avinu married, he was already well established, fully formed, as the founding father who would be known to us as Yaakov Avinu. They still needed to marry those very women in order to develop fully and to accomplish their missions, but they were, essentially, who they were to be, when they married.

But when did Avraham become fully formed as Avraham Avinu? Chazal tell us that by the time he was five he had developed, entirely on his own, a realization of God. But we are introduced to him qua Avraham Avinu when he was already married to Sarah Imenu. They developed, it seems, in partnership with each other. Together, they became the Avraham and Sarah who started it all, the couple who, in holiness and in Godliness, founded our nation.

Did he become who he became because *she* was who she was?

The Torah tells us the least, of all the Avos, about how they married, and the most about her death and burial. (We are told, tersely, of Rachel's untimely death in childbirth, and where she was buried. Not much narrative there.) Of all the Avos and Imahos, it is really only Avraham and Sarah who are portrayed, in the *meforshim* at least, as a *team*: *Avraham megayer es ha'anashim v'Sarah megayeres es hanashim*. Avraham concentrated on the men and Sarah on the women. And together they produced *hanefesh asher asu b'Charan*, the community of souls brought *tachas kanfei haShechinah*.

Their descendants, their successors, to this day, in far-flung communities, continue in those roles as rabbis and rebbetzins, as teachers, as Chabad *shluchim* couples, as dedicated lay couples.

Given the typical life expectancy in her generation, Sarah was not very old when she died. True, she was old, at ninety, to give birth, but relatively young, at 127, to die. Avraham outlived her by thirty-eight years, and that would have been forty-three years had he not died five years early to spare him seeing Esav go bad.

Yitzchak, having lost his mother, found solace and comfort in his wife, Rivkah. That is as it should be. Chazal tell us (*Bereishis Rabbah* 60:16) that while Sarah was alive, a protective heavenly cloud (akin to that which would protect her descendants in the *midbar*), the presence of which also attested to her *tznius*, did not budge from above her tent. While Sarah was alive, the doors to her tent were constantly open on all four sides in order to find and welcome guests. While Sarah was alive, God's blessing was manifest in her breadbasket. While Sarah was alive, the lights she kindled every Erev Shabbos remained miraculously unextinguished until the next Erev Shabbos. All these things ceased when she died. Upon Rivkah's arrival, they again became manifest. And thus her husband knew that she was a worthy successor to his mother. For Yitzchak, Sarah, beloved as she had been, as foundational as she had been, as miraculous as she had been, was replaced. It was now Rivkah's turn.

But what about Avraham? It is true that he eventually married Keturah and even had children with her. But the setting of Sarah's sun, coinciding with the rise of Rivkah's, also marked his own eclipse, in a sense. Nothing more is heard of him until his own death.

Without Sarah, without his *founding partner*, one can speculate, he could not quite fully be the Avraham he had been. And so the stage passed to Yitzchak.

We are well aware of one of the functions of the *parashiyos* in the Torah that relate the history and the experiences of our forebears. *Maaseh avos siman la'banim.* Many of the scenarios have been played out, in various forms, over and over again throughout the ages. They are lessons for every generation.

One of those lessons, I believe, that can be derived from the history of Avraham and Sarah relates to the empowerment of each by the other. By convention, we will often refer to Avraham, Yitzchak, and Yaakov, when we really understand it to be shorthand for the whole group, the Imahos included, and what they brought to the equation – similar to use of the simple term *mankind*, which refers to females as well as to males. Yitzchak and Yaakov needed their wives to be the Imahos and to complete the "picture" of the Avos for each of them and for subsequent generations.

Avraham, I suggest, was unique among the Avos in this respect. His mission – to *initiate, sustain, and perpetuate the Whole Thing* – required his own special *kochos*, and those of his wife, to make it "get off the ground." He and she presumably married early and formed each other, even as together they formed a new world.

There is a midrash (*Tanchuma*, Chayei Sarah 2) that relates that there are four circumstances that pounce upon a man to make him old: fear and worry, anguish from wayward children, war, and a bad wife. Avraham, in contrast, of whose wife it was written "*eishes chayil ateres baalah*" (Mishlei 12:4), reached old age so blessed by having made his life and his mission with Sarah that even after her death, the *pasuk* says of him, in his old age, that *with regard to Sarah, "Hashem berach es Avraham ba'kol"* (Bereishis 24:1) – God blessed Avraham with *everything*: his wife Sarah.

There are exceptions, of course – but in this life, in general, a man with a mission cannot readily accomplish that mission unless he is empowered by his wife. It is her reach, along with his, that helps him reach high. And conversely, she can be his greatest hindrance. One lesson to be learned from *chayei Sarah*, the life of Sarah, is that even Avraham Avinu depended upon the right wife in order to become Avraham Avinu. The greatest blessing in life, which often makes possible everything else, is to be blessed in this way. This blessed way.

Thank you, Sarah.

Thank you to all the great and noble Sarahs, by any name, with whom our nation has been blessed. We are, in large measure, the fruit of their efforts and their dedication.

Yerucham Baruch Reich, husband of Sarah Reich
Parashas Chayei Sarah 5774

But for the Grace of God

When I still had my parents, I would slink out of shul before Yizkor, hoping that nobody who was staying for Yizkor would look at me with envy, however innocently.

Most of us tend to look upon those less fortunate than we are with compassion, but also with relief, as if there is bound to be a certain measure of misfortune in the world, and if it strikes others, then hopefully it will not strike us. If we are so lucky, so blessed, as to have the things in life that we want and need, well, then we are *not* among those we see around us who are not blessed that way. Sorry for them, people tend to think, but better *they* should be in that state than, God forbid, us.

One can speculate on how those others see themselves. Do they know they are unlucky? Probably. Do they similarly view themselves as luckily better off than those who are even worse off? Probably, as well. Do those who are better off than most appreciate that they are, in fact, better off than most? Hopefully. There is no end to the possible gradations of good fortune, and lack of it, in the various spheres of life. May we not be tested. We have to do what we have to do to get by in life, though the end result is not necessarily up to us. But we are given guidelines on maximizing our chances of good fortune.

The life and death of Sarah Imenu, who together with Avraham Avinu was the foundation of *chesed* in this world, serve as a powerful lesson in what it is possible for a person to *choose* to do, which may affect what the Creator, in turn, chooses to do for us.

The Ateres Yeshuah, on Chayei Sarah, presents this case. *Chayei ha'adam* (the life of man) can be seen to fall into two categories: those whose lives are generally calm, peaceful, blessed with plenty, and those whose lot is need, sorrow, and anguish, no matter how hard they try. *Lo aleinu.*

We all see those people, we feel for them, but we do not want to share their lives.

It is well known that the Torah tells us what to do to maximize our chances of being saved: *"Aser taaser"* (You shall surely tithe), which Chazal tell us hints at *aser bishvil she'tisasher*, give *maaser*, give tzedakah, so that you will be blessed with wealth. Give. How many times? If you gave to someone already, do you have to give again? *Nason titen*: you must keep on giving, even to the same person *a hundred times* (*Sifrei* on Re'eh, Devarim 16:10).

Now, *how* to give? We know, of course, that there are better and lower forms of giving. One's attitude, of course, when approached by the poor person for help, is extremely important in the quality of that giving. But there is yet another dimension to tzedakah that puts it on a higher plane altogether.

We all have stories about pushy schnorrers. We are all familiar with people who are in fact needy, but who are so assertive in their demands that we are turned off, even as we help them as graciously as we can. There are the needy who do behave well, but driven by their need, make sure to make the rounds and find ways to reach out to the people who are likely to help them.

And then there are those who are too fine, too shy, too hurt by life, too full of shame to approach anyone for help, as much as they need it. Those are people whom we, the givers, must pursue. *We must run after them, seek them out, to make sure they receive what they need.* Imagine that: going to the poor man's home rather than his having to go to yours. The pain of running after you is too great for him to bear. You, therefore, run after him.

When do Chazal tell us is the age of running? *Ben esrim lirdof* (*Avos* 5). *Esrim* (twenty) represents this exalted *middah* of pursuing the poor person, *running* after him in order to help him.

And what are the various appellations in Tanach for the poor? There are *seven* (see *Tanchuma*, Behar 3): עני, רש, תככים, מסכן, מך, אביון, דל.

Tzedakah – the mandate to give, *"even one hundred times,"* in its finest form, by pursuing, running after (as in *"ben esrim,"* *twenty*) the needy, who are known by *seven* descriptive names.

Va'yihyu chayei Sarah. The *lives* that relate to Sarah. The life of anguish, and the life of peace and plenty. Chazal have taught us that the word *va'yehi* typically alludes to times of trouble, *tzar* (*Megillah* 10b). Thus, *Va'yihyu chayei Sarah* alludes to the potential in life for *tzar*, while *chayei Sarah* alludes to the potential in life for peace, contentment, and plenty. Thus, *shnei chayei Sarah*, those two possible roads in life.

The Ateres Yeshuah teaches that the life of our founding mother Sarah, whose life was utterly devoted to *chesed*, to goodness in its highest form, and her death at 127, a life that culminated in achieving that high ideal which is represented by one hundred, twenty, and seven, provides us with the path and the means to merit a life of goodness, peace, and plenty.

The power of tzedakah and *chesed*, and especially tzedakah framed by *chesed*, is very great indeed. God has His own *cheshbonos* in how He apportions the good things in this world. But, He has also informed us, He wants us to try, by our actions and by our hearts, to influence Him, *k'v'yachol*, to bless our lives with peace and prosperity. He has given us the tools and the role models.

As Rashi expounds on Sarah's 127 years, *kulan shavin l'tovah*, they are all equal in goodness, and they all *result* in goodness for those who learn the noble lesson of her life.

Parashas Chayei Sarah 5775

Blessed with a Wife, Blessed in Life

The movie scene is in an airport in California. An Asian woman buys some food for herself and her husband while they are waiting for their flight. She spreads some napkins on the table and unwraps and places a sandwich before her husband, along with a drink. She then does the same for herself.

A few feet away sits an American couple, clearly a very contemporary, sophisticated, West Coast "smart set" kind of couple, who observe the Koreans. The woman says to her husband, "If I ever do that for you, please shoot me."

The writer of that scene was on to something.

Does it really surprise anyone that the soaring divorce rate and the breakdown of the American family coincides with the rise of hard-core political feminism?

This is not about fairness and equality of opportunity for women. That is such an obvious requirement of decency and law as to be a no-brainer. To the extent that women may have been held back in the past, there is no excuse for it in modern society, just as for any group that has suffered from bias in the past. Anything else is, frankly, stupid and indecent.

But, as we all know, there is a radical feminist agenda out there that is part of a larger "movement" that seeks, really, to tear down much of traditional society, to do away with traditional notions of decency, to undo many of the moral accomplishments of six thousand years of civilization. They will smear any other point of view as "oppression," anti–human rights, and part of the "war on women" by knuckle-dragging apes in male form. And the media by and large smugly and self-righteously supports and propagates this agenda.

And, as we all also know, it is often in the power of a woman to make her husband – or to break him. No thinking person can underestimate the power and the value of a wife in a man's life.

When they are good to each other, and mutually supportive, life is as good as it can be for them. And when they are not, life is bad for both of them.

Avraham Avinu lived with his life partner and fellow builder of Klal Yisrael, our matriarch, Sarah Imenu, until she died at age 127. She left him bereft, but with a son to carry on and a legacy that will last for eternity. It is after she dies that the Torah declares that Avraham has grown old, although God has blessed him *ba'kol*, with *everything*. He was rich, but the meaning here is that that richness was not just about money and things. It was about the quality of the life he led. It was about his wife.

The Midrash (*Tanchuma*, Chayei Sarah) lists four circumstances that cause a man to prematurely age – fear and worry, war, heartbreak from wayward children, and a bad wife.

Sarah was Avraham's equal partner in everything and his superior in prophecy. But she refers to him as "*Adoni*," my master. She was a good and proper wife, who, knowing her power and influence, which she wielded as she needed, also understood how to treat her husband with the respect and deference that allowed him to be a proper husband and leader.

It worked so well that an entire civilization and a world of holiness was built upon it. It worked so well that we are here to talk about it all these years later. It worked so well that the darkest forces in the culture wars target it in their struggle to bring ruin upon our civilization.

It works so well that the decent people in the world – the Jewish descendants of Avraham and Sarah as well as the world at large whose traditional societies were formed as a result of their efforts – will, in the end, preserve and protect it.

Parashas Chayei Sarah 5777

That Our Prayers Be Heard

Eliezer, loyal servant of Avraham, is dispatched to far-off Aram Naharayim with a daunting mission: to find a wife worthy of Yitzchak. How can he find the precious little needle in the big, foul haystack? And then he finds, upon his arrival, everything as if prepared for him. He thanks God: ברוך ה' אלקי אדני אברהם אשר לא עזב חסדו ואמתו מעם אדני (Praised is the God of my master Avraham, Who did not withhold His *chesed* and His true devotion from my master).

It would be difficult to argue that the language of this verse is only coincidentally reminiscent of a verse in Tehillim (66:20): ברוך אלקים אשר לא הסיר תפילתי וחסדו מאתי (Praised is God, Who has not turned away my prayer, nor His mercy from me). One would have to assume that David Hamelech drew upon the content and the structure of Eliezer's prayer in expressing his own sentiment and grateful acknowledgement of Hashem's relationship with him and His ongoing acceptance of David's prayers.

What is the meaning of *lo hesir tefillasi…me'iti* (לא הסיר תפילתי...מאתי)?

There are prayers that are, for various reasons, not *mekubalim* (accepted) by God, but are, rather, *nidachim* (put off). That one's prayers are *nidachim* is disheartening in the extreme, and weakens one's resolve to pray. The perception that Hashem welcomes one's prayers, that He hears them, is, on the other hand, heartening in the extreme, and encourages the individual to grow in prayer and in his connection to the Ribbono shel Olam. David Hamelech is teaching us the power and the value of prayer in our own development and for our spiritual well-being.

The ability to pray, the sense that there is purpose to one's prayer, is a source of great hope and strength. It makes carrying on possible, no matter how difficult the struggle. For this, David Hamelech is grateful, and this verse is an expression of his gratitude.

A closer analysis of the specific wording reveals a clearer understanding of what may have been David's thinking in drawing from the prayer of Eliezer.

Eliezer says "Baruch Hashem (י–ה)," suggestive of *middas harachamim*. David says "Baruch Elokim (א–ם)," suggestive of *middas hadin*. Eliezer speaks of *chasdo v'amito*, that God, in His *chesed*, had already made His promises to Avraham come true (*emes*) by the time Eliezer arrived in Aram Naharayim – the promises of *lo yirashcha zeh* (that Eliezer will not be Avraham's heir), but his own son will (*ki b'Yitzchak yikareh lecha zera*) and Hashem blessed Avraham "*ba'kol*," with everything.

Eliezer, his own personal hopes thwarted (to be Avraham's successor, or, barring that, for his own daughter to marry Yitzchak), was in a unique position to recognize God's promises fulfilled. David, on the other hand, speaks of *tefilasi v'chasdo*. The emphasis here is different. David is still struggling, but with hope, even confidence. He is aware of his own shortcomings, but he believes that Hashem will lovingly overlook them: אָוֶן אִם רָאִיתִי בְלִבִּי לֹא יִשְׁמַע אֲדֹנָ-י (If I had seen iniquity in my heart, the Lord would not hear).

He has the strength to carry on, the hope to carry on, and therefore the ability to carry on. Look, he says, what Hashem has done for me: לְכוּ שִׁמְעוּ וַאֲסַפְּרָה כָּל יִרְאֵי אֱלֹקִים אֲשֶׁר עָשָׂה לְנַפְשִׁי (Come and hear, all who fear God, and I will declare what He has done for my soul).

It is as if David Hamelech were proclaiming joyfully, thankfully, hopefully:

> לֹא צֵרֵף הקב"ה מחשבה למעשה
> ולֹא דחה תפילתי
> וגם לֹא ידחה – זה חסדו
> ויש תקוה לאחריתי –
> גם לי, כמו לאברהם אבינו, יאמת הבתחתו לי
> אברהם האמין בה' ויחשבה לו צדקה
> גם לי, שגם אני מאמין, יעשה לי צדקה וחסד

And just as Hashem promised Avraham (Bereishis 17:19) regarding Yitzchak, even before he was born, that וַהֲקִמֹתִי אֶת בְּרִיתִי אִתּוֹ לִבְרִית עוֹלָם לְזַרְעוֹ אַחֲרָיו (I will establish My covenant with him for an everlasting covenant for his seed after him), and Eliezer recognized, in the wondrous finding of Rivkah, that the promise was being fulfilled, and he expressed thankful recognition of that fulfillment in proclaiming בָּרוּךְ ה' אֱלֹקֵי אֲדֹנִי אַבְרָהָם אֲשֶׁר לֹא עָזַב חַסְדּוֹ וַאֲמִתּוֹ מֵעִם אֲדֹנִי, so too David Hamelech thanks Hashem for the continued opportunity and the hope of fulfillment embodied in his prayer, בָּרוּךְ אֱלֹקִים אֲשֶׁר לֹא הֵסִיר תְּפִלָּתִי וְחַסְדּוֹ מֵאִתִּי.

And the strength of this hope – enshrined in the words of David Hamelech, who remains *chai v' kayam* through these Tehillim – continues to sustain us from generation to generation.

Parashas Chayei Sarah 5767

Toldos

What Yitzchak Saw in Esav

Among my family and friends, it is common knowledge that I am something of a naïve Pollyanna, while my wise wife, *ad meah v'esrim*, is the hard-eyed realist who sees things as they really are, whose better and wiser judgment keeps us out of trouble.

Maybe.

And maybe it's not so *pashut*.

It all goes back to the story of Yitzchak and Rivkah, Yaakov and Esav, and all the history generated by their complex relationships. Who had a better grip on reality, and who had a better sense of what was the right course of action? The apparent answer, that Rivkah was the better maven on who her children were, is, I submit, a bit simplistic, even if true. To suggest otherwise would be to brand Yitzchak Avinu an easily fooled naïf, *chalilah*, which he certainly was not.

Indeed, how is it possible that a perfect tzaddik like Yitzchak could father a perfect *rasha* like Esav? Avraham fathered Yishmael, who was bad as well as wild. But in the end, Yishmael did *teshuvah* and died a tzaddik. Not so Esav, who was rotten to the core and bad to his dying day. So how did Esav come from Yitzchak Avinu?

The simple answer, as most would understand it, is that Esav derived from Rivkah's side of the family, an expression of Lavan and Besuel's bad genes. It can be said, however, that Yitzchak Avinu did not see it quite that way.

Yitzchak understood that no one is born a ready-made tzaddik or *rasha*. One can certainly be born with a predisposition to be good, only to have that potential goodness suppressed and converted to evil by bad circumstances or bad choices. And one can be born with a predisposition to be bad, only to have that potential evil suppressed, overcome by the desire, the choice, the expression of free will to be good.

Such a person serves the Ribbono shel Olam by doing just that: by over-coming his powerful yetzer hara and choosing to be good. Chazal tell us that

65

Moshe Rabbenu did that. Esav could have done so as well, but he squandered the opportunity – he grew up, after all, in the home of Avraham Avinu, Yitzchak, and Rivkah – and he failed. His obligation was to meet his personal challenge and overcome it. For a while he kept up appearances, leading his father to believe, and to hope, that he would make it. In the end, however, he chose not to, and he became Esav Harasha.

In Parashas Vayera we cited the Midrash that Hashem "found" David Hamelech (and by extension Malchus Beis David and Moshiach) in Sedom – which represents all that can be rotten in human nature – to demonstrate this point exactly. It is possible to overcome even the legacy of Sedom and to achieve eternal greatness.

Perhaps that is what Yitzchak hoped for, or even expected, with regard to Esav, especially as Esav was *tzayid b'fiv*. Esav put on a good show for his father.

That one of the boys was prone to be bad from conception is clear to us from the *pasuk* (25:22): *Va'yisrotzetzu habanim b'kirbah, va'tomer im ken lamah zeh anochi, va'telech lidrosh es Hashem.*

We're all familiar with the midrashim about what stimulated which boy in utero. The *meforshim* explain that Rivkah had an excellent question: "Why me?" *Lamah zeh anochi?* She reasoned that the "bad seed" came from her, through her side of the family. Avraham sent Eliezer to Aram Naharayim to find her, because it was impossible for Yitzchak to father worthy offspring with the local girls. But why?

If Yitzchak "contributed" Yaakov the tzaddik, and Rivkah "contributed" Esav the *rasha*, why was she necessary at all? Any local girl could have carried a tzaddik from Yitzchak, and a *rasha* from her side of the family!

The reply she received explained it. *Shnei goyim b'vitneich*, two nations are in your womb, actually written as *gei'im*, two great ones, alluding to outstanding descendants such as Antoninus, a great gentile, and Rebbi, a great Jew (*Avodah Zarah* 11a). Many great and righteous people would, in fact, emerge from Esav – but only if Esav were born to the *tzaddekes* Rivkah. It would not have been possible with any of the local girls.

And so, what about Yitzchak? The Ateres Yeshuah asks, what did Yitzchak see in Esav that made him want to bestow his *berachah davka* upon Esav rather than upon Yaakov? Was he simply mistaken? And further, why did Yitzchak make the process of bestowing the *berachah* – an act of such cosmic spiritual significance that it would determine the course of human history – dependent upon Esav's preparing a banquet of foods that Yaakov enjoyed? Does that apparent appeal to *gashmius* sound like the spiritual stimulus of a tzaddik?

If anything, tzaddikim distance themselves from such things.

Further, asks the Imrei Noam (the Ateres Yeshuah's father), why did Yitzchak love Esav more than Yaakov?

He certainly was aware of Esav's earthy nature and pursuits, and he knew just as well that Yaakov was a *talmid chacham* – *ish tam yoshev ohalim* – engaged in full-time Torah study. Wouldn't it be obvious for Yitzchak to prefer Yaakov over Esav?

In essays of different emphasis but complementary perspective, the Dzhikover *admorim* portray a far subtler than usual picture of Yitzchak and Rivkah's understanding of who Yaakov and Esav were, who they could be, and who they should be.

The name Esav was apt, Rashi tells us, because he emerged fully developed, *naasah* (done). Similarly, the name suggests *asiyah* (doing). Esav was a doer, a man of action. He was a hunter, a man of the field, who brought home food. He brought in *parnassah*.

The Avos set the pattern for future Jewish life. Everywhere one looks in the Torah, especially in Bereishis and Shemos, one sees patterns of behavior – between Jew and Jew as well as between Jew and gentile – that have been historically repeated over and over.

Throughout the generations, from the earliest days of our nation until today, one such pattern has been what we commonly call the Yissachar/Zevulun relationship. Yissachar learns full-time, or practically full-time, while Zevulun ideally learns part-time, is a *ben Torah*, but goes out to work, to do business, to trade, to farm, to hunt – whatever the economy of a particular time and place dictates – so that both can exist and fulfill their roles, *l'shem Shamayim*.

Chazal refer to this as *"Torah u'gedulah b'makom echad,"* as illustrated by the *keruvim*, representing the enablers, who struggle for *parnassah* and then share it with the scholars, spreading their protective wings over the *luchos*, representing pure Torah. Together, it is indeed *Torah u'gedulah b'makom echad*. It is one unit.

Thus, when Yaakov blessed his twelve sons before his death, he generally followed the order of their birth, but he blessed Zevulun *before* Yissachar, even though Yissachar was older. So too when Moshe blessed the tribes of Israel before his own death, he also placed Zevulun first. As the Midrash teaches (*Vayikra Rabbah* 25:2), *"Machzikei talmidei chachamim notlin chelkam b'olam haba b'yachad im talmidei chachamim atzman, ki chelek hayoshev al hakelim k'chelek hayotzei l'milchamah"* (see I Shmuel 30:24).

Thus, Rabbi Akiva says of his wife, whose self-sacrifice made it possible for him to become who he was, *Sheli v'shelachem shelah hi* – my Torah and my students' Torah is really her Torah. There is compelling reason to want to bless the enablers with the continued ability to enable – indeed, to give them primacy of place in such a blessing.

Yitzchak and Rivkah did not set out to raise one son a Jew and the other a non-Jew. They had two little boys who were raised *al taharas hakodesh*, not only by Yitzchak and Rivkah, but by Avraham Avinu until his death when they were fifteen years old.

Yitzchak saw Esav, the doer, as the enabler of his brother, the *ish tam yoshev ohalim*. We know after the fact that Esav was fooling Yitzchak. Esav famously asks his father, how much *maaser* does one give on salt? That was the point exactly. Esav was, in fact, giving *maaser*, contributing to his brother's support.

Yitzchak's request that Esav bring him food, tied in with the *berachah*, was not a *gashmiusdik* request for food goodies. *Havia li tzayid* – you're out working, he told Esav, go out and make *parnassah*, and make sure to set aside a percentage for tzedakah and support of Torah for those who learn full-time, and who need you to help make that possible. But also *v'aseh li matamim* – we'll discuss *pilpulei Torah* together. Make sure you remain a *ben Torah* while you're at it.

Yitzchak knew, of course, that Yaakov was superior to Esav. Yaakov was the *ish tam* who spent his life *b'ohelah shel Torah*. But it was Esav, for whom Yitzchak still harbored high hopes, who really needed the *berachah* if he was to fulfill the role Yitzchak saw for him, and who would indeed deserve the *berachah* if he did so. And he would certainly deserve Yitzchak's extra measure of love for overcoming his problematic nature and powerful yetzer hara and living the life Yitzchak envisioned for him.

Rivkah, however, knew that for Yaakov to become who he had to be, for all future generations, he could not and should not look to Esav for support. The entire *berachah* – *Torah u'gedulah b'makom echad* – had to be his alone.

As usual, it was the woman – Rivkah Imenu – who saw Esav with steely-eyed realism. She knew he was lying to his father, she knew that whatever he did was for his own aggrandizement and not *l'shem Shamayim*, she knew that he was corrupt, she knew well before her husband did that Esav was rotten to the core.

Perhaps she understood this better than her husband because Yitzchak was blind. Perhaps she understood it as no one else could because she alone had felt his nastiness in the kicking she endured from him in utero.

Perhaps she simply understood it better than Yitzchak because...well, ok, because she was a woman.

To me that makes a lot of sense, because it's entirely consistent with my own experience in life.

Parashas Toldos 5772

Why Me?

Im ken, lamah zeh anochi?

Avraham sent Eliezer to Aram Naharayim to find a proper wife for Yitzchak. On his journey, Eliezer bypassed thousands of young ladies who lived a lot closer, perhaps even some of good character, but who were, by definition, not good enough, not special enough, not perfect enough, to be the wife of the tzaddik Yitzchak and the mother of Klal Yisrael. There was no one else worthy of producing the appropriate offspring.

When she finally conceived, after twenty years of marriage, Rivkah was tormented by the roiling motions in her belly. Chazal tell us that when she passed a place of Torah, Yaakov would kick, as if eager to emerge. When she passed a place of *avodah zarah*, Esav would kick, as if eager to emerge. Furthermore, the brothers fought in utero, already at war with each other.

Rivkah understood that the little tzaddik growing within her, Yaakov, was the product of her saintly husband the tzaddik Yitzchak's influence. And, sadly, the little *rasha* growing within her, Esav, was the product of the legacy she carried with her from the home of Besuel and Lavan. Thus, *im ken, lamah zeh anochi?*

As Rav Shlomo Kluger teaches, she was given to understand that she too was a necessary part of the equation. The greatness to be found among all her future descendants, Jew and non-Jew, depended not just upon Yitzchak, but upon her as well.

There would be great people, even righteous people, who would emerge from Esav too, *but only if Rivkah were their progenitor*. She was, in fact, necessary, for history to unfold as it had to: without Rivkah, the pure, the pious, Yaakov could not have been Yaakov, and whatever good would need to emerge from Esav could not have happened.

But still, how is it possible for a perfect tzaddik like Yitzchak to father a child like Esav, a רשע מבטן אמו, rotten to the core?

Here emerges an important principle and reality of life. A person can be born with a predisposition for good, but the circumstances of life can pervert him and bring about the opposite. And a person can be born with a predisposition for bad, but he can work on himself and make himself into a tzaddik. He has *bechirah chofshis*, free will. Moshe Rabbenu faced this challenge and emerged as Moshe Rabbenu. Esav faced this challenge and emerged as Esav Harasha. He had the opportunity to turn himself around, to absorb the lessons of his righteous parents and serve the Ribbono shel Olam by doing so. But Esav failed.

And for that too, for that possibility, Rivkah the *tzaddekes*, daughter of Besuel and sister of Lavan the *resha'im*, was the necessary partner to Yitzchak.

The Torah tells us this story, I believe, not just to help us understand who we are and where we came from, not just to put our historic and ongoing struggle with Esav in perspective, but also to send each of us a personal message: You count. Everything you do counts. Everything you do has meaning. Everything you do affects the world.

The course of history will be determined, in some way, by the choices each of us makes, by the imprint each of us leaves on the world. That is our privilege, and that is our historic burden, each and every one of us.

And there is yet another dimension to this story, a lesson that is well to remember in orienting our lives.

Yitzchak and Rivkah were, by God's design, initially unable to have children. We don't know how many wives Besuel might have had, but we do know that Avraham had a child before Yitzchak, from another wife, and he had more children later, also from other wives. Such was the way of the world then, and such is the reality of life today for many people.

Midrash Rabbah tells us that not only did Yitzchak and Rivkah pray for children, they also so valued and so cherished each other that they also prayed and begged the Ribbono shel Olam with all their hearts, Yitzchak that he have children *only* with the *tzaddekes* Rivkah, and Rivkah that she have children *only* with the tzaddik Yitzchak.

And that too is a lesson in goodness, in devotion, in marital commitment, in the total, utter appreciation of each other that makes marriage work, that makes married life so sweet for those so blessed.

Parashas Toldos 5776

On the Equilibrium of Heterogeneous Substances

Die Energie der Welt ist konstant; die Entropie strebt einem Maximum zu.

It must have been very hard for that tzaddik Yaakov Avinu, so perfect a tzaddik that, in a metaphysical sense, his face is engraved on the very throne of God, to pull such a nasty fast one on his brother Esav and, while he was at it, on his saintly, blind old father. Sure, he had to do it. Sure, his equally saintly mother talked him into doing it. But for that *ish tam yoshev ohalim*, that pious *talmid chacham*, it had to go against his grain. And the irony is that as a result of his fooling them, he himself wound up in the clutches of that arch fooler, Lavan.

There is no question, of course, that the *berachah* had to fall to him rather than to the wicked and dissolute Esav. There could never have arisen, otherwise, the nation that stood at Sinai and declared *"naaseh v'nishma."* And there is no question that when it came to the crunch, he was quite capable of doing what he had to do in order to make that happen. And so are his descendants, as we all know. And his mother (no surprise) was a *mavente*: she knew her son's capabilities.

When you look at the text, it's hard not to have some sympathy for Esav. When he finds out what happened, having lost his father's blessing, having cried out in pain, he begs Yitzchak, "Bless me too, Father! Did you not save me a blessing? Do you not have even one blessing for me, Father? Bless me too, Father!" And he wept.

Esav wept over the loss of his father's *berachah*. God does not miss a thing. The fact that that lowlife Esav wept and was inconsolable over the loss of the tzaddik's *berachah* was itself reason to reward him with the *berachah* he did get, *v'haya ka'asher tarid*, that he will become ascendant when Yaakov's children fail to perform, and the rest of his *berachah* (Kesav Sofer).

From my own relatives I heard tell of Polish gentiles who, seeking God's blessing, seeking relief from the *tzaros* in their lives, would, on occasion, visit Rebbes and tzaddikim so that they too might be blessed. They discerned the holiness and the power of the tzaddik. This they inherited from their spiritual *"zeide,"* Esav. Who knows? On other occasions these same Poles might have participated in, or perhaps abetted, pogroms. But that's Esav.

Berachos and pogroms. The main subtext of Esav's *berachah* was that when Yaakov is low (i.e., when the Jews let go of Torah observance), Esav will have dominion over them.

On this concept the Imrei Noam quotes a remarkable Midrash (*Tanchuma*, Terumah and Bamidbar). *If the nations (our enemies, who seek to harm us) only knew how much good the Beis Hamikdash did for them, they would not only not have destroyed it, they would have placed guards all around it to protect it. For from it, and from Israel's service of God there, flows good and bounty into the world, for all its people.*

And so Esav, ascendant, smites and torments Yaakov, but in so doing, he spites and harms himself. It's reminiscent of the story of the peasant who delivers eggs from his farm to the egg merchant in town. As he counts out each twelve dozen, the merchant places a coin in a bowl, for them to keep count of how many gross were delivered. The clever merchant, knowing the peasant's penchant for thievery and his dim-wittedness, intentionally goes into the back room for a moment. Sure enough, seeing a bowl full of coins, the peasant can't help himself, and helps himself to a nice handful of coins. He foolishly trades in payment for 144 eggs for each coin – worth far less – that he steals.

People and their foolish behavior. *Berachos* and pogroms. The ironies of this life.

When Yaakov Avinu slipped away, just before Esav arrived at his father's tent, was he lurking somewhere, watching or listening to the events of the denouement? I have to believe that he was too fine and too sensitive to want to witness it. And probably too frightened. How did he feel, having succeeded in defeating his brother and filching the *berachah*? Indeed, how did he feel when he "defeated" his brother years before, and got him to yield the *bechorah*?

The wisest of men, Shlomo Hamelech, famously declared (Mishlei 24:17–18), "*Bi'nefol oyivcha al tismach, u'vi'kashlo al yagel libecha*" (When your enemy falls, do not rejoice, and when he stumbles, let not your heart exult). It is not a good character trait. And God doesn't like it. "*Pen yireh Hashem v'ra b'einav, v'heshiv me'alav apo*" (Lest God see and be displeased, and [as a result!] turn His wrath away from him [the enemy]). Because you enjoyed your enemy's downfall too much, God, in His displeasure with you, reassessed the situation and turned to help your enemy.

Yaakov undoubtedly felt terrible, even as he did what he had to do. I think we can safely say the same about his mother, Rivkah.

But there is a darker – a far darker – side to the story, and to the system of justice God has emplaced in the world.

Midrash Rabbah, on "*v'es achicha taavod*" (You [Esav] will serve your brother; 27:40), has Yitzchak telling Esav, *If you see your brother Yaakov throwing off the yoke of Torah, go ahead and rule over him, degrade him, declare a gezeras shmad* (!) *upon him.* This serves to console Esav and to goad Yaakov into doing *teshuvah*. In the never-ending circle, when Yaakov has fallen low, the ascendant Esav harming Yaakov brings Esav back down, as Yaakov repents. And when Esav's depredations harm Yaakov's ability to do good, this also results in the loss of blessing in the world – blessing that Esav could have shared in. And when Yaakov brings himself down, it is Esav's invitation to torment him.

But it gets more frightening.

God indeed does not miss a thing. *Ki'shmoa Esav es divrei aviv, va'yitzak tzaakah gedolah u'marah ad me'od*, when Esav found out what happened, he cried out an exceedingly great, bitter cry. God does not overlook an exceedingly great, bitter cry, even from Esav Harasha.

On Yom Kippur, we appeal to God to bless us and to forgive us, hopefully as a free gift and not by virtue of our suffering, ר"ל. God is kind and forgiving, but He is also the Omniscient Great Keeper of the *Cheshbon*. He does not miss a thing, nor does He forget a thing.

Rabbi Chaninah teaches (*Bava Kama* 50a and *Bereishis Rabbah* 67:4), on this *pasuk*, that whoever says that God is a "*vatran*," that He disregards sin, that He just lets it go, in the absence of *teshuvah*, without asserting divine justice, himself will have his life "disregarded"; he will be subject to terrible punishments. For to say so – to suggest that one can sin or behave in a callous manner and just expect to be freely forgiven – invites more sin.

Rather, as the Torah says (Devarim 32:4), "*Hatzur tamim paalo, ki kol derachav mishpat*" (The Rock, His work is perfect; for all His ways are justice). God is compassionate and lovingly patient, delaying punishment to allow the transgressor the opportunity to repent and hopefully avoid punishment. But in the end, He does not *disregard* sin and evil, even as He does not disregard good deeds.

This, for *bein adam la'Makom*, sins against just God. But for sins against other people, for cruelty to others, for causing pain and suffering to other human beings, *for callousness toward other human beings*, in the absence of forgiveness by those other human beings, God will not relent, and He will not forgive. A price will be paid, be it sooner or later.

Yaakov caused Esav such pain that the Torah records "*Va'yitzak tze'akah gedolah u'marah ad me'od*" (Esav cried out an exceedingly great, bitter cry; Bereishis 27:34). There is one other place in Scripture where this language is used: "*va'yizak zaakah gedolah u'marah*" (and he cried with a loud and a bitter cry; Esther 4:1). That is written of Mordechai in Shushan, nearly two thousand years later. God gave Haman (the Amalekite, grandson of Esav!) dominion over the Jews, and he condemned them to destruction. And that decree elicited from Mordechai and all the Jews an exceedingly great, bitter cry.

Even though Yaakov was justified in doing what he did, even though he *had* to do what he did, even though he was such a tzaddik, he caused Esav tremendous pain. Remember, the very fact that it bothered Esav so much, that he valued Yitzchak Avinu's *berachah* so much, was to his credit, evil though he was. And God does not miss a thing, nor does He forget a thing. He held it in abeyance for so many years. And then, when it fell due (when the actions of the Jews made it fall due), he dispensed His divine judgment. Pain for pain. *Tzar* for *tzar*. Bitter cry for bitter cry. *Rachmana litzlan!*

That odd German sentence above? From the classic works on physical chemistry and the universal laws of thermodynamics by Josiah Willard Gibbs and his contemporary, Hermann von Helmholtz. The second law of thermodynamics has no known exceptions. The energy in the world, and apparently in the universe, is constant. Entropy (the tendency to randomness) in the physical world is increasing. The Creator set the world into motion, utilizing these immutable physical laws of nature that He created for this world.

Die Energie der Welt ist konstant – a physical analogue to the metaphysical yet very real and concrete constant of divine justice. God is compassionate and merciful; He waits, even thousands of years, for repentance, so that He can forgive, mercifully. But in the end, God does not miss a thing, nor does He forget. In some form, for good or for bad, there is always an accounting. Even for Yaakov, who obeyed his mother's command, and, *no doubt with divine approval*, fooled his father and brother to get the *berachah* that rightfully went to him.

But if, in the physical world, entropy is ever increasing, in the *metaphysical* world, the *antidote* to randomness reigns. Randomness is what we limited mortals perceive.

In the much larger picture, Almighty God, the Merciful, the Compassionate, and the Just Judge, to Whom past, present, and future are one, conducts this world He created in perfect order. Whether in this world or the next, His *middas hadin* and His *middas harachamim* together make His will manifest.

And we, His children, people of faith, can absorb the lesson that even the wicked Esav's bitter cry is not lost before God, that we must be sensitive to all of God's creatures, that we must seek, wherever possible, never to hurt or to harm. For God does not miss a thing, nor does He forget.

Parashas Toldos 5774

Temimus and *Temimus*

When famine struck the land, Avraham went down to Egypt to escape its ravages, even though God had commanded him to live in Canaan. He understood that in the emergency, it was OK with God for him to leave, and then to return when the emergency was over. When famine struck again in Yitzchak's time, and he too wanted to find temporary refuge in Egypt, God told him not to go. He had been an *olah temimah* on Mount Moriah, and in his heightened state of perfect holiness, it was inappropriate for him to leave the land. He went instead to Gerar, in Philistia, but never in his life did he step foot outside the Holy Land. Yitzchak was *tamim*, pure and perfect.

Of Yitzchak's sons, Esav was a bad guy – a *yodeah tzayid*, a predator, but Yaakov was *ish tam*, refined, pure, perfect. A pious scholar.

So Yitzchak and Yaakov were both *temimim*, but there was apparently a difference between them in this regard, and the Torah, it appears, hints at an invaluable practical lesson in that difference.

Yitzchak, in his *temimus*, allowed Esav to fool him. Yitzchak loved Esav because Esav was *tzayid b'fiv*. Literally, this phrase, meaning "he had game in his mouth," refers to Esav the hunter bringing home food for the family. Homiletically, we understand it to mean that Esav the predator habitually fooled his father, sweet-talking him into thinking he was a good guy. He used his mouth to snare Yitzchak. But perhaps Yitzchak should have known better. Rivkah surely did.

As my father used to teach, we must be good – but there can be such a thing as *too* good. Paradoxically, being excessively good can be destructive. For this reason, the Torah sometimes requires us to act strictly when we might perhaps do otherwise, but God knows that in these circumstances doing otherwise would ultimately be self-destructive. History is filled with examples of this.

Rivkah understood that her *temimusdik* husband and her *temimusdik* son had different roles to play in the development of Klal Yisrael and had to be different in their *temimus*.

In order to instill the *middah* of *temimus* into Klal Yisrael for all the generations to come, Yitzchak had to be so perfectly *temimusdik* that he could not see through Esav's charade. Yaakov had to be a perfect tzaddik, but the struggles of his life required him to be clever enough in the world – indeed, manipulative enough – to gain the *bechorah* that he had to gain in order to get the *berachos* that he had to get, to deal with Esav and with Lavan and with all manner of adversity, so as to set up Klal Yisrael to survive and thrive in a hostile world.

And so, it seems to me, the Torah carefully sets up the lesson, for those who would discern it, in describing how Yitzchak favored Esav because Esav was *tzayid b'fiv*.

Esav fooled him, but perhaps that was because, in his love and his goodness, he allowed himself to be fooled by that *rasha*, Esav. And Esav fooled him *b'fiv*, with his words. Later, in a kind of *middah k'neged middah*, for all the world to know, Yitzchak was fooled by words again – "*anochi Esav bechorecha*" – this time by Yaakov, when he came to snatch the *berachah*. Yitzchak discerned the voice of Yaakov, but in his *temimus*, he accepted as truth the words, and the ruse.

Temimus is a high ideal indeed. It is our precious legacy. But there is a time for Yitzchak's and a time for Yaakov's. Both are needed.

If I may be so bold as to speculate, I would venture that Yitzchak would have been constitutionally incapable of pulling off Yaakov's ruse. Yaakov's reservation, when his mother suggested it, was not that it was wrong, but fear that he might be caught and lose his father's respect. Rivkah, whose idea it was, interestingly, is identified as *Lavan's sister*. Lavan was infamous for using his wiles for evil trickery. The *tzaddekes* Rivkah, who was pure and good, used those same powers for the good, a trait she passed on to her son Yaakov.

Yitzchak, realizing what happened, actually spelled it out for Esav, telling him outright that Yaakov had tricked him out of the *berachah*. In his *temimus*, Yitzchak may not have imagined that this revelation would not only endanger Yaakov's life, but would set up a hatred and a legacy of persecution that would last through the millennia. Rivkah, the savvy, practical realist, told Yaakov to get out of town, pronto.

Of course, the reality may be that so great a man as Yitzchak Avinu was actually fooled by no one – not by Esav and not by Yaakov. He did as he did because that was his role, his lesson, and his legacy. And thus his children, who were also Yaakov's children, came to stand, in a state of high spiritual purity, at Sinai, to declare *"naaseh v'nishma"* and to experience Revelation, hearing the very voice of God, hearing His words, to cling to Him and to His words, and yet, subject to all the vicissitudes of our history, strong enough and determined enough and clever enough to survive, by the grace of God, as His people until this day.

Parashas Toldos 5778

Vayetzei

Jacob's Ladder: The Double Helix

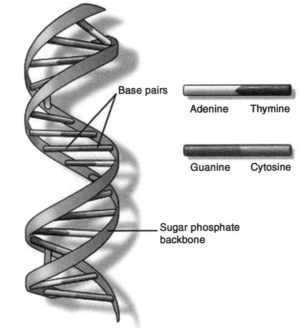

Base pairs

Adenine   Thymine

Guanine   Cytosine

Sugar phosphate backbone

U.S. National Library of Medicine

In his flight from his brother Esav, having been robbed of all his possessions by his nephew Elifaz, Yaakov arrives at Mount Moriah and lays his head down to sleep.

He dreams. He sees a ladder, with its base planted in the ground, reaching upward into the heavens. And behold, angels are climbing and descending. God speaks to him, promising him that He will watch over him in his exile, that his offspring will be as plentiful as the dust of the earth, and that this land is given to him and to his offspring forever.

Rashi, who always stresses the straightforward explanation, here quotes the Midrash that the activity of these angels was a changing of the guard. The angels accompanying Yaakov in the Land of Israel do not leave the land, so they ascended heavenward, while the angels assigned for outside the land descended to join him in his exile.

The Torah does not tell us all the details of the lives of the Avos. It reveals what we need to know. That God promised Yaakov His protection, that He promised the Land of Israel to him and to his descendants, we certainly have to know. That there was a changing of the guard of angels, that Yaakov dreamed about a ladder and angels, must also carry with it some lesson for all generations.

Various *meforshim* offer deep, meaningful insights and lessons derived from this story.

Allow me to cite an insight of the Kesav Sofer, with my own humble commentary.

Human beings are born utterly instinctual, with no self-control or self-discipline.

Psychologists speak of the *id*, describing this aspect of human behavior, with the *super-ego* playing a critical and moralizing role, while the *ego* mediates between the two. The Kesav Sofer simply describes the psychology and the actions of a baby as a *pere adam*, wild and undisciplined. This is exactly the way the Torah describes Yishmael.

It is the duty of a human being, and the mark of a developed human being, to make the transition from something wild to a self-controlled, rational, moral person, seeking to do good in the world. This is all the more expected of a Jew. And in so doing, he can raise himself higher than the angels, even those on the high rungs of that ladder.

And so let's look at another Rashi, remarkable not just for its message but for the fact that the great *pashtan* Rashi, who always aims for the straightforward explanation of a verse, waxes lyrical, as he will occasionally do for a special subject.

The evil Bilaam tries to curse the Jews as they travel toward the Land of Israel, but he cannot. What emerges from his mouth are the most beautiful blessings and praises, undoubtedly causing him no small measure of agita, even as his failure to muster a curse drives his employer Balak crazy. *"Ki lo nachash b'Yaakov v'lo kesem b'Yisrael,"* he declares. There is no sorcery in Israel; to them it will be told what God has brought about, *mah paal Kel* (Bamidbar 23:23).

Rashi explains this obscure-sounding statement with a quote from Yeshayahu Hanavi (30:20). *It shall come to pass,* declares the prophet, that *the nation will dwell in Zion, in Jerusalem. You will not have to weep; God will show you grace and provide for you. Your Teacher will no longer be hidden: your eyes will behold your Teacher.*

Israel will merit a degree of intimacy with God that even His highest angels cannot achieve. Ultimately, the source of that merit is our being wholeheartedly His: "*Tamim tihyeh im Hashem Elokecha*" (Devarim 18:13). Rashi explains: Walk with God with a pure and whole heart; look only to Him; do not try to divine the future, but whatever comes upon you accept wholeheartedly, and then you will surely be His.

We cannot ignore the historical fact that Rashi himself wrote these lines during the terrible times of the Crusades.

Rabbi Yitzchak said (*Nedarim* 32a): "One who trusts Hashem completely and gives himself completely and wholeheartedly to Him will merit that God acts wholeheartedly with him." He cites the prayer of David Hamelech (II Shmuel 22), which David composed in thanksgiving upon being saved from his enemies:

> God is my Rock, my Fortress, Who rescues me....
> I have been wholehearted [תמים] with Him....
> He has repaid me according to my righteousness...
> With the devout [חסיד], You act devoutly [תתחסד].
> With the wholehearted [גבור תמים], You act wholeheartedly [תתמם].
> With the pure [נבר], You act purely [תתבר]....
> You save the humble; Your eyes are upon the haughty to cast them down.
> You are my lamp, Hashem, You illuminate my darkness.
> The way of Hashem is perfect and pure.
> The word of Hashem is pure.
> He is a shield for all who take refuge in Him.

Ahavah ben Rabbi Zeira taught (*Nedarim* 32a): One who does not seek to divine the future (one who is wholehearted [*tamim*] with Hashem his God) merits being brought so close to Him that he enters heavenly precincts that even the ministering angels cannot enter. And so the angels will be forced to ask them, *Mah paal Kel?* What is God saying and doing?

See as well Yerushalmi, *Shabbos* 6:9. Rav Brechiah taught in the name of Rabbi Abba bar Kahana: God will, in the future, place the tzaddikim close to Him, where even the ministering angels cannot go. The angels will be forced to ask the tzaddikim, *Mah paal Kel?* What has Hashem taught you?

God will show you grace.

Your Teacher will no longer be hidden; your eyes will behold your Teacher.

The human being, made of flesh and blood, subject to all the wild and bad impulses that are inherent in human nature, indeed starts life as a *pere adam*, wild and uncontrolled, pure id. He is on the bottom of that celestial ladder, where it is rooted, embedded in the clods of earth of which man is made. The angels are far above him. But mankind, and especially the children of Yaakov Avinu, Am Yisrael, are imbued as well with the capacity to rise so high that they reach the very highest rungs of that ladder, so high that even the angels cannot reach.

V'hineh Malachei Elokim olim v'yordim bo (And behold, the Angels of God were ascending and descending). The fiery, pure heavenly beings that we refer to as angels, who are created solely to do God's bidding, and who do only God's bidding, who exist to sing His praises and to comprise the *Famalya shel Maalah* (Heavenly Hosts), are purely spiritual beings. They possess no corpus, no inclination to do good or bad, no free will. They have no needs or desires. They have no DNA.

God created man with that celestial ladder *built into him*. Physically, the rungs of that ladder are comprised of adenine and thymine, of guanine and cytosine, the base pairs that are held in place by a sugar phosphate backbone. All living things on earth are built of DNA, and ours appears not all that different from many other species. But only man's is so refined and so specialized that it carries with it, instilled by the Creator, the capacity to *choose* to be the lowest of the low or the highest of the high.

In the complex laws of *tumah* and *taharah* (ritual purity and impurity), a general rule is that the entities that can carry the most intense forms of ritual impurity are also those that are otherwise capable of the greatest holiness.

A human being, and in the context of our lives, especially a Jew, made of flesh and blood and imbued with a soul, can choose to walk so wholeheartedly with God, to so make himself His, to use the free will he was given to choose good over evil, to harness his very *humanness*, to climb the rungs of the ladder made possible by the fact that he is *not* an angel, but a human being built of DNA like other creatures, but blessed with a soul, to climb so high, to reach a place so lofty, that the very Angels of Heaven cannot follow, to come so close to God, to behold his Teacher, that those fiery Angels of Heaven will be forced to ask him, *Mah paal Kel, what has God wrought, what has He taught?*

Parashas Vayetzei 5777

The Road to Recovery

On the day we got up from *shivah*, my father and I – he bereft of his beloved wife and lifelong partner, I now motherless, facing this ordeal together – walked into shul a few minutes early for Minchah. There we encountered three people: the rabbi, my friend Elliot, who himself had just gotten up from *shivah*, and a man I did not know but whom I immediately recognized, from the stricken look on his face, to be, like me, in early and deep mourning. He and Elliot and my father and I all looked different, and all looked fundamentally alike, at least to each other. We all recognized that stricken look, the look of grief and loss, on each other's faces, the look we recognized from our own mirrors.

Sometimes it takes one to recognize one. People may be sensitive to another person's grief, but the brotherhood of grief and loss creates a bond and a connection like none other.

My father told me that in the war, and afterward, those who had suffered were immediately recognizable to their colleagues in suffering. The DP camps were filled with people who looked alike, even as they had their own individual appearances.

He told me as well that because not only Jews had suffered, it was not a safe assumption that an obvious fellow sufferer was harmless. Incredibly, many of those gentiles who themselves were victims of the Germans emulated those same Germans in their treatment of the Jews. And so a softly spoken, barely noticeable *"amcha"* became a signal to a fellow sufferer that one was a brother Jew. A brotherhood within a brotherhood.

What a world.

When I returned to Manhattan Beach after the storm (Hurricane Sandy and its devastating flood), I encountered a shell-shocked society with many of the same, readily identifiable features, etched by suffering and loss. Not only did the formerly beautiful neighborhood look like a war zone, its people stood in the streets looking lost and shocked and helpless and desperate. I very quickly became one of them.

I won't go into the multitude of calamities, but we were all marked and, I believe, recognizable to each other as being so marked.

When I walked into shul for the first time upon returning after the storm, I saw that look on every face in shul. It was eerily reminiscent of the opening story above.

Certainly, our experiences and our losses cannot in any serious way be compared to what our predecessors had to suffer a generation ago, and over many previous generations. No one, in this community, was killed or seriously injured, as far as I know. But suffering and loss do take a toll and do mark a person.

Our rabbi, ever encouraging, has told us that we are being tested, not punished. It's so interesting that there was a story in the news that some popular, Jew-hating Muslim cleric in Egypt has been preaching that this storm was a punishment and not a test! Allah, he maintains, has no interest in testing infidels, only in punishing them.

What shall we make of this test? We know that when God tests those He loves, in the end the poor testee is, hopefully, in a much more exalted position than before. I suppose that part of the test is the ability to recognize that, for it is not always obvious.

Yaakov Avinu had to flee his parents' home, where he had his *ohel*, his "tent of Torah," and fend for himself in the wicked world. There were no other Jews out there to help him. There was no one to softly and hopefully drop the word *amcha* to. He was alone as he set out, but not for long. Elifaz ran after him on his father Esav's orders to kill him.

He was headed to Lavan's den of wickedness. Alone, as far as he could tell, he surrounded himself with some rocks for safety and lay down on the bare ground.

He learned that the reality of his situation differed greatly from what he must have thought it was. He saw, in his dream, his God-sent vision, the *malachim* that were accompanying him to protect him. God Himself then spoke to him, confirming his mission, his mandate in this world and God's promise of His safekeeping.

It took a prophetic vision to make him realize it, but Yaakov awoke to a totally altered awareness and perception of reality. Things were not as they had earlier appeared to be. God had a plan. God was with him. He was not alone.

Yaakov awoke from his "slumber," *va'yikatz Yaakov mi'shenaso*, and he came to a realization: God *is* here! *He is here*, and *I did not know! I didn't see it! Achen yesh Hashem ba'makom hazeh v'anochi lo yadati! Mah norah hamakom hazeh! Ein zeh ki im beis Elokim v'zeh shaar haShamayim. How awesome is this place! This is none other than the abode of God, and this is the gate of the Heavens!*

What Yaakov thought was a dark and dreary and dangerous place turned out to be the very gates of Heaven.

And so, as the Torah tells us, Yaakov "lifted his feet" and went to the land of his destiny, the future that the God Who loved him ordained for him. He lifted his feet, with vigor and enthusiasm, with energy and with optimism, for the God Who was testing him was also with him.

Yaakov was blessed, in his trouble, with a direct message from God not to be afraid.

God does not speak to us directly, the way He spoke to Yaakov. But He *has* spoken to us *through* Yaakov. We, the inheritors of Yaakov's legacy, know what God said to him in his time of trouble, because He is, in all generations, speaking to us too in our time of trouble.

We pray that our mutually discernible troubled faces turn, by the grace of our loving God, to mutually and universally recognizable faces of joy and redemption. In this trial, we have, thank God, suffered so much less than most of our predecessors did routinely.

And so, we try to put on a brave face, we say, "thank God for that," and we soldier on.

The lesson, in this week's *Va'yetzei Yaakov mi'Beer Sheva va'yelech Charanah*, is that a Jew must always understand that when you walk with God, the darkest and most frightening road, fraught with danger and with unspeakable difficulty, can by His grace lead to the most glorious destiny.

So, please God, may it be for us.

Parashas Vayetzei 5773

Unenviably Enviable

What a profoundly complex set of relationships our forebears mentioned in Parashas Vayetzei had. The Torah, in Vayetzei, refers to love, to love that was not really love, to hatred, to hatred that was not really hatred, to jealousy, to jealousy that may or may not have been real jealousy, to desire, to desire that may or may not have been desire in the way we usually think of desire, to anger, to anger that was not really anger, to selflessness and to greed, to truth and to falsehood, to honesty and to deception, to hope and to despair, to kindness and to cruelty, to cruelty that was undoubtedly not really cruelty, to war and to peace, to triumph and to tragedy.

It's all there. Learn the *parashah* and sort it out yourself.

The sisters Rachel and Leah are both very sympathetic figures, but each in a rather different way. The Torah is clear on Rachel's beauty and Yaakov's preference for her. The Torah is ambiguous on Leah's looks and is opaque on Yaakov's true feelings for her. He certainly did *not* hate her, as a superficial reading might suggest: if that were so, he could not have lived with her – he would have been *forbidden* to live with her – and fathered with her six *shevatim* of Am Yisrael.

And yet the Torah clearly writes, in connection with the children she bore Yaakov, that God saw that Leah was *hated*, and so He opened her womb. She was fertile. Her sister, the beloved Rachel, was barren.

Yaakov's preference for Rachel apparently so poisoned the well that Leah could not enjoy her wifely triumphs, and she remained, despite her central place in the building of the Nation of Israel, a sad figure. Just look at the names she gave her children. They reflect the desperate sadness with which she saw her role in her husband's life, and her hope, with their births, that he would come to appreciate her.

And look what being loved, being preferred, did to Rachel. The dynamic of her life was sad and tragic. When she was barren, she was desperate and *ashamed*. She quarreled, at least this once, with her husband, and was, apparently, angrily rebuffed. It was only in her desperation, in her misery, when her sister had given Yaakov six sons and a daughter, that God "remembered" her, and "opened her womb" as well, with the birth of Yosef. And then she died, tragically young, in the childbirth of her second son.

God "*saw*" Leah, in her suffering, and "opened her womb" (Bereishis 29:31).

God "*remembered*" Rachel, in her suffering, and "opened her womb" (Bereishis 30:22).

It is interesting to note that several generations later, when the descendants of these mothers of Israel were in bitter bondage in Egypt, bondage so terrible and so bitter that at their lowest point of desperate misery, in their desperate cries, God "remembered" them ("*va'yizkor Elokim*"; Shemos 2:24) and He "saw" them ("*va'yar Elokim*"; Shemos 2:25).

In Yaakov's exile in the House of Lavan, his wives, who were so privileged to be his wives and the mothers of the nation, and who were undoubtedly so happy to be in that position, and who undoubtedly loved their husband greatly, but who were at the same time so personally unhappy regarding that love, each, in her misery, called out to God. First, God "saw" (Leah), and later, God "remembered" (Rachel).

In Egypt, God first "remembered" and then He "saw."

The enslavement of our forefathers in Egypt was part of God's plan in forging our nation. Bitter as that slavery was, it was a necessary passage to becoming the people who would stand at Sinai and proclaim "*naaseh v'nishma*," we are God's, forever. At their lowest point, He "remembered" the pledge He made to their forefathers, and thus He "saw" their plight, and He "knew" (*va'yeda Elokim*), He would no longer turn His Face from them, but, reckoning all the evils, public and private, that the oppressors had visited upon them, He "saw" them, He turned His benign attention to them, and the Egyptians would now be called to account. The Children of Israel would be redeemed. The time had come.

God first saw Leah's broken heart. Even if Yaakov actually loved her and cherished her and honored her, as he undoubtedly did, Leah's perception that her precious and cherished husband, Yaakov Avinu, the Father of Klal Yisrael, *whose face is enshrined on the very Throne of God*, loved her less than he did Rachel, broke her heart, and made her feel hated. It resulted in her getting to bear a disproportionately large percentage of the tribes of Israel, a triumph, but one in which the fruits of that triumph could not be fully sweet in her mouth.

Her situation was certainly enviable, but in a sense, unenviably so.

Rachel was so good and so sweet – in order to spare her sister humiliation, she helped in the deception that caused Yaakov, her intended bridegroom to whom she had pledged her love and her future, to marry Leah when he thought he was marrying Rachel – but the overwhelming love that Yaakov bore her, to the point that Leah felt hated in comparison, cost her dearly. She was barren a long time, for years, when Yaakov's other wives were giving birth to the tribes of Israel while she could only look on in hurt and humiliation. And only then, when the full measure of her sadness and her misery, her shame, weighed down her heart to the point that she preferred death over her continued barren existence, God "remembered" her. He "remembered" her incredible selflessness in substituting her sister for herself on what was to have been her wedding night, and He also chose to "remember" His divine plan in creating her sons Yosef and Binyamin and the key role they would play in bringing about the descent into Egypt that would result, ultimately, in *maamad Har Sinai*, in *naaseh v'nishma*.

Her situation was certainly enviable, but, in a sense, unenviably so.

And so, a lesson. Even Yaakov Avinu, even Rachel and Leah, figures so great and so holy and so righteous, so pure and so good, the very founders of our nation, chosen by God for those roles, paid a terrible price for the roles they played in hurt feelings, for the *perception* of a slight, even if it was unintended.

We – who are so mundane, so this-worldly, so much more prone to sin, so weak, so susceptible in our everyday lives to the possibility of hurting the feelings of others – can never know what terrible consequences may result, *Rachmana litzlan*. How careful we have to be never to be the cause of hurt, or heartache, of pain, of shame or humiliation, to others. For they are created in God's image, and to senselessly hurt another human being is an affront to God, and to the Godliness that resides within every human being.

How much more so this applies to those who are closest to us – to our husbands and wives, to our children, to our parents, to those who are near and dear – those who need us and depend on us for the loving structure upon which their lives are built. How much more sensitive they are to every nuance, how much more vulnerable they are to every perceived slight, how much more they depend upon us to make their lives sweet. It's easy to forget, in the daily grind of life, but the price of forgetting can be unbearably high.

Our holy Avos and Imahos gave us so much, the very legacy that defines who we are.

In showing us, sometimes, their more human side, and its consequences, the Ribbono shel Olam gave them the opportunity to give us even more: lessons in life that allow us to take that part of us which is the most human, and, in serving God through sensitivity and kindness to our fellow human beings, to elevate and dedicate that part to the Most High.

Parashas Vayetzei 5776

Sakmar

There's a man in our area who is a bad neighbor. He lets his dog do its "business" in the backyard, and then, using a hose, washes the filth out onto the street for his neighbors to walk on. Not only is it filthy and disgusting, but in the cold weather the water soon freezes, and people slip and fall on the resulting ice. He has been asked to stop, but he responds only with an arrogant snarl.

What makes it worse is that he himself is an immigrant, having been allowed to enter this country by people who did not know him, but whose essential goodness and good neighborliness allowed him to settle among them and to thrive. It appears that he has done very well here indeed, and he now repays those good neighbors by being himself a bad and irresponsible neighbor.

The Gemara (in the Mishnah in *Bava Kama* 30a) teaches that one who pours out water in the public thoroughfare and, as a result, causes damage to someone, is responsible for that damage and must make restitution. The Gemara then goes on to discuss related cases, such as the proper disposal of dangerous thorns or glass shards. It relates that Chassidim Harishonim used to go to great lengths not to harm anyone with such dangerous refuse.

The Gemara then concludes: Rav Yehudah says, one who wishes to be a *chassid*, to be truly righteous, should study and scrupulously observe the dictates of *Nezikin* (Bava Kama, Bava Metzia, Bava Basra), for thus he will not come to harm others, physically or financially. Rava says he should study and follow the dictates of *Avos*, and he will thus know how to relate to God and to his fellow human beings. Rashba adds here that the *middah* taught in *Avos* (5:13), *sheli shelach v'shelcha shelach*, is that of a true *chassid*, because he will thereby not come to harm his neighbor in any way. And others say he should study and follow the dictates of *Berachos* because it will help him understand his place in this world;

recognizing Hashem as the Master of all will properly develop his behavior and his *yiras Shamayim*.

Thus, we are taught, one who masters all three will be good with God (*Berachos*), good with his fellow man (*Nezikin*), and good with himself – i.e., his personal development (*Avos*).

Yaakov Avinu, who had spent his entire life thus far as *ish tam yoshev ohalim*, sitting in the sheltered environment of the *beis medrash*, is now, in Parashas Vayetzei, about to enter the rough-and-tumble outside world. He will face situations he has never had to face. He will be tested in ways he was never tested. Tzaddik that he was, he worried about his ability to be the same tzaddik in the outside world that he was in *ohelah shel Torah*. Indeed, years later, he was able to say *im Lavan garti*, I kept the entire Torah despite my proximity to that *rasha*. But beforehand he was justifiably concerned.

Indeed, that tzaddik wanted not only to remain free of sin in the outside world, he wanted to be a *chassid*. He wanted to serve Hashem in the fullest and most profound way possible. He wanted – he was driven – to be a *chassid*.

The *meforshim* tell us that this was the point of the *even* (stone) that Yaakov placed around his head as a protection. *Even* is an acronym: *aleph* for *Avos*, *beis* for *Berachos*, and *nun* for *Nezikin*. Armed with these, Yaakov Avinu succeeded in remaining a true *chassid* despite all the bad influences and difficult circumstances of life. He made of himself a *chassid*. And being a *chassid* kept him a pure child of God.

I was born in New York a few years after the war. The adults who comprised much of the world I grew up in were Holocaust survivors, the battered remnants of a destroyed world – destroyed families, destroyed communities, a destroyed way of life, a destroyed civilization, destroyed expectations, destroyed illusions, destroyed health, destroyed sanity, robbed of parents, robbed of children, robbed of brothers and sisters, robbed of normalcy, robbed of peace, robbed of the possibility of sleep without nightmares, robbed of everything that a human being would expect in a normal life.

Most of those I knew were able to rebuild their lives and cope, somehow, with the haunted memories that doubtlessly crowded their minds. Incredibly, they even thrived. Some survived but then found life unbearable; they could not survive having survived. Those died young of broken hearts. I remember them.

Most of those in my immediate world remained true to God, true to the Torah, and clung to the ways of their fathers and mothers. We knew that there were those with a similar history who did not. I don't remember hearing any judgmental words about them from those who had suffered and lost as they did. I do remember, however, a profound sense of the preciousness of each remaining Jew, no matter who he was.

And I remember the preciousness, in the eyes of that generation, of the nascent State of Israel and its repository of precious Jews. To them, it was as unbelievable in a positive way as the Holocaust was in a negative way. And to them, the two were clearly and surely tied together.

And so, the society that I grew up in, mostly Polish Jews who had survived six years of brutality, enslavement, murder, and annihilation, by and large did not take well or kindly to the attacks, mostly by Hungarian Jews of Satmar persuasion – who had also suffered terribly, but over a considerably shorter period of time – on Israel, and what it might represent.

I remember my uncle who would get red in the face with anger and bitterness over those attacks. And although I was a child at the time, I remember as well that those who were so angry were careful to distinguish between the Satmar Rebbe himself and his followers, some of whom were deemed to be overzealous, mindless fanatics. Think of that group of insane fools in heavy-duty Jewish attire who in recent times traveled to Teheran to make loud and public common cause with Ahmadinejad. That's how they were viewed.

In fact, the Rebbe himself got something of a pass. They disagreed with his religious politics on this issue, in the strongest possible terms. Having been brought up largely in the Chassidic world of Poland and Galitzia, they understood very well the Satmar Rebbe's objection, on religious grounds, to secular, political Zionism, which destroyed the Yiddishkeit of large masses of Jewish youth by promoting Zionism not as an expression of the Jewish religion, but as an alternative to it, a kind of successor secular religion that had no place for authentic Torah. There was, and is, in fact, a great deal in secular Zionism to complain about.

But there were many Torah-true Jews who were *chovevei Tzion* and who did identify with the basic idea and sentiment of Zionism, from a religious perspective. And whereas in Hungary the rigorous religious establishment left no room at all for political Zionism and viewed it as entirely bad, the mindset in Poland, at least in some fervently religious circles, was different, with room for a broader view.

And so they understood the Rebbe and his theology. Many of their own parents had opposed political Zionism. But they felt that the Rebbe should have controlled his followers better. In the post-Holocaust world, they could not abide the strident words and deeds of some members of the Satmar camp, which they saw as hurtful attacks on the remnant of the Jews, in a miraculously emergent Jewish state in the Land of Israel, which clearly, to them, God had given the Jewish People as a *nechamah*.

What was it, then, about the Satmar Rebbe who created the very community that so aroused the ire of so many others, but who, as a Rebbe and a tzaddik, personally retained so much respect among those same people?

A preeminent leader of Hungarian Jewry before the Destruction, the Rebbe arrived in America at the end of 1946 virtually alone. The large and powerful institutions that in later years became known as Satmar did not exist at all. In the beginning he could barely put together a minyan.

Rav Yoel Teitelbaum was an uncommonly focused and determined man. The America he found was sadly deficient as a home for Torah Yiddishkeit in general, and for real, fervent, especially Chassidic Yiddishkeit in particular. There were stalwart, loyal Jews, genuinely pious and committed, there were shuls and schools and *rabbonim*, but these were little islands, and often very weak, meager islands, in an overwhelming sea of assimilation and watered-down standards. The spiritual climate was not conducive to real, old-time Yiddishkeit.

The Rebbe saw that only by accepting no compromise and by recreating, as well as he could, the religious life and devotion of prewar Europe – and for his particular group, that of prewar Hungary – could he hope to salvage Yiddishkeit for his *kehillah*, as he understood it needed to be, in America.

And so, as his little flock grew, dressed as of old, beards and flowing *peyos* as of old, learning Torah devotedly in the old manner, utterly and uncompromisingly devoted to *kedushah* in every way, as of old, the community became recognizable and made its presence felt. The Rebbe taught them to do so proudly and unselfconsciously, unashamed, despite the ridicule they were subjected to, especially early on.

And when nearly everyone was quite poor, the Rebbe insisted that tzedakah and *chesed* be a major emphasis in the life of each member of the community, that they give even when they had very little themselves, an attribute that to this day is a major and well-known characteristic of that community.

The Rebbe insisted on spiritual purity in every aspect of life. He himself never even referred to his community as "Satmar," as that name derived from a religious entity (a "saint") associated with *avodah zarah*. And so he used to say "Sakmar," to avoid even pronouncing anything even remotely "unclean."

In short, in order to make sure that real, intense Yiddishkeit survive on these shores, the Rebbe did as Yaakov Avinu did when he left his father's house and set out for Charan and Lavan's bastion of iniquity. He placed an *"even"* around his head and that of his kehillah: *Avos, Berachos, Nezikin.* He insisted that his Chassidim be real, genuine *chassidim*, in every sense of the word. And in so doing, he affected the Yiddishkeit of every Jew in America.

Many disagreed with him, on many fronts, sometimes to a profound degree. Many resented some of his positions. Many called him and his followers fanatics. Many could not accept his position on Israel. Many complained that some of his followers did not fully absorb the lesson of *"even"* he set for them. No one could deny his greatness in Torah, and his championing of Torah, as he understood it needed to be.

Rav Yosef Dov Soloveitchik was asked, after the 1967 war, what he thought of the Satmar Rebbe and his positions. He replied, "After the Satmar Rebbe came to America, everyone became more religious, including myself."

Yaakov Avinu survived Lavan's house because he fortified himself with *"even."*

Thus, Klal Yisrael became possible, Matan Torah became possible, and all the rest of history became possible.

What would Torah Yiddishkeit look like in America today if not for the Satmar Rebbe's *"even"*? I am certain it would be far poorer, less well developed, and far more timid.

He was not the only great Jewish leader in town, he was not the only Torah giant, he was not the only Chassidic Rebbe, his was not the only *"even,"* he had many who disagreed with him, who resented some of Satmar's core positions, but he was, in fact, a giant, who took Yaakov Avinu's lesson to heart, and who wielded what was arguably the heaviest *"even"* in town, and with it, he built a civilization for his followers and facilitated our own.

Parashas Vayetzei 5772

Shmendriks

A guy walks into a bar. (This is not a joke; it's a true story.) He is about fifty-five years old, and he looks it. The bartender, a young woman, "cards" him: he must produce proof that he is at least twenty-one years old before she will serve him. He is incredulous. She must be kidding. She is serious. He goes ballistic. He makes a big deal of this idiocy. I learn about it as the relative merits of her position, and his, are discussed on public radio. A real intellectual analysis.

To the young woman bartender (speaking for her colleagues) and to the very PC interviewer, the merits of her position are obvious. Only a Neanderthal, or a fascist, wouldn't get it.

Try to imagine her saying this in a Valley Girl accent: "I can't ask younger people to show proof of age and not older people. That would be, like, *profiling?!* And profiling is, like, *wrong?!*"

Gevalt geshriggen. These are the people who are now running the world. Or so it seems.

I have seen "Granny Rabinowitz" picked apart by security at the airport, while Arafat lookalikes skip right through. Was that a bandolier of bullets under their jackets? No matter. Profiling is, like, *wrong?!*

I suppose if a lady asks you where the bathroom is, you should not *profile* her by gender (that would be, like, *wrong?!*), but politely ask if she is seeking the men's room or the lady's room. Then duck.

There has been a lot of noise lately about New York City's "stop and frisk" policing technique, in areas rife with violent crime, where people are attacked with guns and knives and other implements of violent death by vicious street thugs. Spotting likely candidates, based on police experience and techniques, or by recognizing known miscreants, police stop and frisk them for such weapons. It has resulted in a massive decline in these crimes. Opponents, in the name of "civil liberty" (I do believe for the sake of political posturing), label that as "profiling," *and profiling is, like, wrong?!*

Yes, of course we all understand, in light of the long, nasty history of racism and bigotry, that sensitivity is needed. But to foolishly throw out a good, proven, and inherently non-racist police tactic that protects citizens – the first duty of government being to ensure the safety of its citizens – because somebody wants to make a political point, to stir up the public, to keep his name in the news, is terribly irresponsible. Where is the sense, where is the simple *sechel*, where is the *decency* in that allegation? Where is *normalcy*? Where is the consideration for the victims of violent crimes in the beleaguered communities? The very communities that are helped the most are in the inner-city neighborhoods.

And so, when New York City Police Commissioner Ray Kelly was booed off the stage at Brown University before he could say even one word of his scheduled address on Proactive Policing in America's Biggest City, by ignorant *shmendrik* students exulting in their imagined virtue, it was that same mindset at work. The *Wall Street Journal* published an editorial on that event, entitled "The Children of Brown" (October 31, 2013).

The editorial cites the dramatic drop in serious crime in New York, especially in minority neighborhoods, upon the institution of Mr. Kelly's anti-crime strategies. The students at Brown raged against the very police tactics that keep the vulnerable residents safe, "stop and frisk" in inner city areas, and "community policing" in Muslim hotspots. "We realize that most Brown students have only a faint acquaintance with real life," it says, "and none of them know what New York City was like in the 1970's and 80's. But it is revealing to see where the Constitutional right to free speech stands in the esteem of students at one of the most liberal campuses in America." At "a better school," the editorial concludes, "the children who acted out at Brown would be expelled."

Never in history, I believe, have the *shmendriks* had such power over society. Knaves and fools certainly have. But this is the age when the *shmendrik* mentality, with its silliness and immaturity, perversely holds sway. This incident at Brown is but the tip of the proverbial iceberg.

And so it is interesting to note the role a group of *shmendriks* played in Parashas Vayetzei, and in the formative narrative of our nation. And, as usual in these *parashiyos*, the story is indicative of a pattern that will be repeated in our history.

When Yaakov Avinu arrived in Lavan's house, he brought blessing and prosperity with him, similar to his arrival in Egypt years later, when the water rose and the famine stopped. Lavan became wealthy due to Yaakov's presence.

And then there was another, fundamental dimension to Yaakov's arrival: until then, Lavan had no sons, only daughters. Chazal deduce from the first mention of Lavan's sons at the end of Yaakov's tenure in Charan, and the fact that his daughter (Rachel) was shepherding Lavan's flock upon Yaakov's arrival there, that there were, in fact, no sons at that time, or they would have been the shepherds rather than the daughter, as was the custom of the time. Yaakov was seventy-seven years old upon his arrival, and Lavan was his mother's considerably older brother. If he had sons, he would undoubtedly have had them by then. Part of the *berachah* of Yaakov's presence was the birth of sons to Lavan, late in life.

Now, how old were these sons, then, at this juncture? Teenagers. (Yaakov was there altogether twenty years.) And now these arrogant *shmendriks* said of this ninety-seven-year-old tzaddik, technically their cousin but more like their great-uncle, whose presence had brought only blessing to their father, that he was an interloper who had ripped off their father of all his wealth. And they refer to wealth not as "money," but as "*kavod*" (honor), by which they *mean* money, which for them, constitutes *kavod*.

How many times over the centuries have Jews been accused of somehow rapaciously sucking the lifeblood out of victim communities of gentiles? Over and over again. Think of the Sharpton charlatans and the other demagogues who rile up crowds with accusations of "Jewish interlopers" as they incite against Jewish businessmen, whose only crime is that they have brought commerce and business to poor areas?

In 1334, Poland was a shambles. Poor, underpopulated, undeveloped, ruined by three successive Mongol invasions, it had no economy to speak of. The new king, a wise and enterprising man, Kazimierz Wielki (Casimir the Great), invited the Jews of western Europe, who at that time were reeling from persecutions, burnings, expulsions, forced baptisms, blamed for poisoning the wells and inflict-ing the Black Death on the Christian population, to come settle in Poland, where they would be free to practice their religion and to pursue a livelihood. The pur-pose was to have them create a working economy for Poland. There were Jews there already, but now they arrived in large numbers, and by their enterprise they brought new life to the country. The Jews of Poland always held Kazimierz Wielki in high esteem.

When I was a little boy, my father told me about him, and how Poland eventu-ally became the major center of Jewish life in Europe. Constantly on the run from their tormentors in Germany, France, Moravia, and other places further west, they found refuge in Poland. It was said of Poland (in Hebrew פּוֹלִין), "פֹּה לִין" (rest here). And with their talents and their enterprise, they built up the country.

Of course, once Poland was rebuilt, the old patterns of Jew hatred reappeared.

Fast-forward to the 1930s, when antisemitism was the *official policy* of the Pol-ish government. There was even a major political party (Endecja) whose *sole plat-form* was the pursuit of antisemitism.

A common ditty, a catchy saying of the time, might have been written by those ungrateful, shallow sons of Lavan: "*Polska ulica, żydowska kamienica*" (The street is Polish, but the houses all belong to the Jews). Those Jew interlopers are ripping us off and taking everything, *our stuff*, for themselves. Jews sometimes used that same line to stick it back to the Poles who hated them.

There is, of course, always a lesson to be learned from these nasty encounters. They serve God's purpose for the Jewish People, and they serve the Jews' purpose in rectifying their service of God. And if the Jew does not learn, he pays a price.

So what can we, as individuals and as a people, as "God's Chosen People," learn from *shmendriks*? From shallow, arrogant, clueless punks? Or from outright *resha'im*? From Lavan's sons. And from Lavan himself.

The Ropshitzer Rebbe, in *Zera Kodesh* (Vayishlach 1) cites Rashi's famous com-mentary on *im Lavan garti*. Yaakov tells Esav that he dwelt with the evil Lavan for all those years, but he did not learn evil from him. Instead, he kept the *taryag* mitz-vos. Further, Tehillim 119: *Mi'kol melamdai hiskalti* (I have learned, become clever, from all who have taught me). Learn from all? How do we learn from evil people? Indeed, we can learn important lessons from them.

Watch those, like Lavan, who are driven by greed and licentiousness, who strive and go sleepless in the pursuit of their *taavos*, their base desires. Yaakov indeed did learn from Lavan. Lavan was so dedicated to his low purposes, so clever in his pursuit of them, so single-minded in his quest for pleasure and wealth and *avodah zarah* and every low thing, that Yaakov learned from him that such powers of determination and dedication within a person can be called upon to pursue Godliness and holiness instead. *Im Lavan garti*, but what I learned from him was not to do what he did, but to use that kind of energy and willpower *l'shem Shamayim* (for the sake of Heaven).

And this, the Ateres Yeshuah says, is the reason the Torah quotes the sons of Lavan, the arrogant, ungrateful young *shmendriks* and their lies (Bereishis 31:1): *u'me'asher l'avinu asah es kol hakavod hazeh*. All this wealth, they said, Yaakov usurped from their father Lavan. That is how *they* meant it.

The Torah quotes it to us because there is another way *we* should understand it. All this *kavod*, this holiness, this pursuit of Godliness, this striving for perfection, Yaakov Avinu continuing to grow and to reach ever higher, was facilitated, however paradoxically, by his exposure to Lavan's relentless and unremitting pursuit of base pleasure.

Tehillim 1: *Ashrei ha'ish asher lo halach b'atzas resha'im*. In life we cannot always avoid exposure to *derech resha'im*, the ways of the wicked. But even from them, from the energy they bring to their wickedness, we can learn to turn away from their path, and to harness our own energies in dedicating our lives to goodness and to holiness.

Everything we encounter in this world has a purpose and a lesson, if we are smart enough to learn it. Even from the wicked, even from the fools. Even from the *shmendriks*.

Parashas Vayetzei 5774

Lavan's Defense

Yaakov Avinu woke up on the morning after his wedding and behold, the woman he had married was Leah rather than his fiancée, her younger sister Rachel. He did not intend to marry Leah. But there she was. And there Rachel wasn't.

Unbelievable! He was outraged. He confronted Lavan: *"Mah zos asisa li?"* What did you do to me? How can you do this to me? Who in his right mind does things like this? *"Lamah zeh rimisani?"* Why did you fool me? You are a *rama'i*, a trickster!

Lavan was prepared. He waxed indignant, even outraged.

"You, Yaakov, *of all people* complain to *me* about this kind of behavior? Do you think I don't know why you had to come here? Do you think I don't know why you had to run away? Do you think I don't know why Esav wants to kill you?

"It may well be that where *you* come from, people (you! you! you!) do this kind of thing, disenfranchising the elder sibling in favor of the younger, by means of trickery or otherwise. But not here! We don't do that: *Lo yaaseh ken bi'mkomenu, lases hatze'irah lifnei habechirah*…around here we don't do such trickery, to put the younger sibling before the older. That's what YOU do! Who are you to call me a *rama'i*, a trickster? Aren't you the one of whom your own father, Yitzchak said (to the defrauded Esav) *ba achicha b'mirmah va'yikach es birchasecha*, your brother Yaakov came to me with trickery and snatched your *berachah*?

"And while we're on the subject, didn't you also trick your older brother years ago too, into 'selling' you his birthright, the *bechorah*, at a time when he was exhausted, famished, and not competent to make such a decision?

"And when you bamboozled him (and your father!) a second time, when you stole the *berachah*, wasn't Esav right to say of you, *hachi kara shemo Yaakov, va'yaakveni zeh paamayim! He's tricked me twice!*

"And furthermore! As long as you claim to have taken over the *bechorah* in that tricky transaction with Esav years ago, it is only fitting that you marry Leah, as you know that as the older daughter, the *bechorah*, she was destined to marry the *bechor* in your family, as your chicanery purports you to be!

"You have reaped what you have sown!"

Not a bad argument, eh?

And yet it is clear from the Torah that Yaakov was a perfect tzaddik, and Lavan was a *rama'i*, a trickster, and a *rasha*. The Torah hides nothing about Yaakov's activities in these matters. He did what was, in that circumstance, the right thing. He could not do otherwise, as his wise mother Rivkah saw so clearly. He was not passive, and he could not foolishly yield our holy birthright for all generations to his wicked and dissolute brother, who would only abuse it. It could not have been easy for this *ish tam*, this pure man, but he did what he had to do.

These *parashiyos* not only tell a tale, they set a pattern for the interaction of our people, for all time, with Esav, with Lavan, with Yishmael, with Mitzrayim, with every nation, as well as with each other (Yosef and his brothers). It is a very complex pattern, repeated over and over in history. Careful study of how Chazal understood all these actions and interactions can help guide us now and in the future in how we can relate, and react, to those who seek our harm.

Parashas Vayetzei 5771

Vayishlach

The Nation That Dwells Alone

Of all the Avos, Yaakov Avinu seems the most closely identified with the development of Klal Yisrael. It is his name, Yisrael, that is the name of our nation. He was the father of the twelve tribes. His story is the most dwelt upon in the Torah. And it was his story that led directly to our descent into Egypt, our bondage there, and our emergence from that bondage as the nation we are today.

Much of Yaakov's life was fraught with difficulty and conflict. And it is Yaakov's story, most of all, that portends what we, his children and successors, would contend with throughout history.

Indeed, the stories of the Avos are events that happened to them personally, but they are related to us in the Torah not just that we may understand how we came to be who we are, but to help us understand the flow of history, as our own stories are mirrored in theirs.

And so one of the most cryptic, mysterious stories related about Yaakov, in which he becomes Israel, is also the most poignant, and the most frightening. Yaakov's struggle with the mysterious "man" (whom we understand to be not just an angel, but specifically the angel of Esav), as a result of which he becomes Israel, is indeed a metaphor and a prelude to the ongoing, never-ending struggle of Israel with Esav, and indeed with the rest of the world.

In light of our long, tortured, and tortuous journey through the ages, it is hard to think of a more poignant, indeed disturbing *pasuk* in all of the Torah (32:25): *Va'yivaser Yaakov levado; va'ye'avek ish imo, ad alos hashachar* (Yaakov remained alone, and a man struggled [or wrestled] with him, until the dawn).

The story of Yaakov – the story of Israel – is that of a man, a nation, standing alone, apart, forever struggling with the rest (or much of the rest) of mankind. And that struggle, that unremitting wrestling match, will go on and on, repeated over and over, throughout history, until, finally, the "dawn" arrives. And in its light, the nations of the world who are driven by gratuitous hatred, *the angel of Esav*, will finally fail and remain in Yaakov's thrall. When "Yaakov" becomes fully who he needs to be, when he becomes "Yisrael."

And even at such times that he lives at peace and harmony with his neighbors, to remain Yisrael, he must remain spiritually apart. He is – and must remain – different. Apart.

Yisrael: *ki sarisa im Elokim v'im anashim, va'tuchal.* You, Yaakov, after all your struggle, have managed to overcome, *with God and with man.* You are *Yisrael. Sarisa.*

But that struggle, that violent, exhausting, seemingly endless wrestling match, that debilitating battle, even in eventual victory, is not without a terrible price. It leaves Yaakov damaged and limping.

Think of it. Think of what we have, so far, endured in history. And it is not over. To be left limping seems, I submit, but a weak metaphor for the terrible reality.

We struggle, always, with man. Just look at the UN, the EU today, and all the rest of them, the vicious, murdering lot, through the ages. But what about the struggle with *God*? What is that about?

Historically, Jews have struggled with God by serving Him…and by not serving Him.

In every such struggle, there have been those who have, *nebech*, fallen away. They could not withstand the test, the incessant pressure, and have opted out, or were taken out by forces that defeated them. They are lost. And in every such struggle, others have risen to the challenge, have understood who they are, where they come from, and with Whom, even as they struggle and wrestle, they are eternally bound. And they cling to Him so mightily that *k'v'yachol* the dust that covers them both (*va'ye'avek*: the *avak*, the dust, was raised by their mighty struggle) also binds them together. *Af al pi chen.* Even so. *No matter what.*

Every one of us, every Jew alive today, is the child of those who, covered with that dust, battered from that struggle even as we continue to be formed by it, have held on. It is a difficult and a precious legacy. Because it is not normal. Because it surpasses anything and everything in nature. Because it is who we are. Because that is how God made Yaakov, how Yaakov made himself, and the capacity he passed down to us.

And in the end, the bruised and battered Yaakov/Yisrael, damaged and limping even in victory, will not eat *gid hanasheh* (the sinew of the damaged leg) because of the pain of all that has happened. And in the end, God brought out the healing rays of sunshine, especially for Yaakov, *va'yizrach lo hashemesh*, to make him whole.

And so, please God, may it be for us. For the nation that dwells alone for His sake, for the nation that struggles in every generation, with God and with man, that is forever covered with the dust of that struggle, that will not let go of Him, *no matter what*, so may it be, very soon, for us.

Parashas Vayishlach 5774

In Yaakov's Camp

I can easily think of several families, very fine people and good Jews, whose children turned out not as they wanted, most apparently because when it was time to choose a school for them, they were utterly clueless.

It seems they assumed, somehow, that because some Jewish subjects were there, the vibrancy, the intensity, and the fervor that are the sustaining force of Yiddishkeit would also be there, *the yiras Shamayim* would be there, and they allowed considerations other than what really counts – politics, style, externals, what their friends are doing, *what their friends will say*, the availability of other subjects, language considerations, and so on to drive what is arguably the most important decision parents can make for their children, rather than the likely outcome, which should have been obvious, but to them was not. (Sometimes they do get it much later, when they can no longer do much about it.)

Why should there be Jewish schools that produce young, generally observant Jews whose Yiddishkeit seems to be but a veneer, however important, or but one dimension of their lives, however important, among many, rather than the defining dimension of their lives? Why are there Jewish schools that produce young Jews, from *shomer Shabbos* families, who, simply put, don't know too much about Judaism? Incredibly, there are.

And that's for *shomer Torah* and mitzvos families. How much more tragic for the masses of Jews who don't educate their children as Jews at all, and then wonder – or, at least in prior generations, used to wonder (or care) why there was nothing remotely Jewish about their children and how it came to be that their grandchildren were in fact not even Jews (!). And when it was pointed out to them that it's because they did not educate their children as Jews, they could only respond with a clueless blank stare. *Kelbene oygen.*

It's interesting, then, that our enemies have historically often understood this about the education of young Jews to a remarkable degree. Typically, oppressors seeking to de-Judaize the Jews would start in the obvious place – undo Jewish education for the young.

Which brings us to the question of the week. Why was Yaakov Avinu attacked by the *malach* of Esav? Why *davka* Yaakov, rather than Avraham and Yitzchak?

Va'yivaser Yaakov levado va'ye'avek ish imo ad alos hashachar.

Yaakov remained alone, and he was attacked. Familiar pattern in this world, isn't it?

Rav Elchanan Wasserman, *H"yd*, offers a profoundly insightful explanation.

Let's preface that explanation with the well-known principle that each of the Avos established and individually personified the fundamental bases of Jewish practice that, in turn, uphold the world: Torah (Yaakov), *avodah* (Yitzchak), and *gemilus chasadim* (Avraham).

The individual strength and significance of each one of those fundamentals, as compared to the others, is quite interesting.

Torah and *avodah* are of the utmost importance, but Hashem signals Avraham that it will be *his middah, gemilus chasadim*, that will provide the ultimate *zechus* for the final Redemption.

Torah is of the utmost importance, but historically there have been those who pursue it with great intellectual fervor, to the exclusion of real *avodah* – heartfelt prayer, true, fervent service of God. Such Torah is not what Hashem wants. He wants our hearts.

Torah without *avodah* and without *chesed iz nisht kein Torah.*

Avodah and *gemilus chasadim* are of the utmost importance, but Torah is the key to our being, and remaining, Jews. It is no accident that we are identified as Bnei Yisrael – we remain identifiable as a people because of the *middah* identified with Yisrael/Yaakov Avinu: Torah.

Charity and prayer are wonderful *middos*, but they are not unique to the Jewish People, and alone cannot sustain us as a people. Rav Elchanan Wasserman emphasizes that it is only with intense Torah *chinuch*, starting early in life and then never ending, that we can perpetuate ourselves as God's unique Torah nation. Only thus can there continue to be Jews.

Thus, the "person" who attacked Yaakov – the angel of Esav – attacked him in the particular manner that he did for this very reason. *Va'yiga b'chaf yerecho* is a metaphor for Yaakov's future generations (*yotzei yerecho*). The future *doros* were the real target of Esav's interest. His attack on Yaakov's "thigh" represents his quest, from generation to generation, to dominate Yaakov (i.e., *us*) by separating us from the ultimate source of our strength and survival, the Torah.

Yerucham's Dictum Number 21: The good things that we do, *if we are lucky*, our children will also do. The bad things that we do, our children will very likely also do.

The energy, the fervor, the dedication, the intensity, the emotion, the primacy of place of the Jewishness of our lives is the most effective weapon we have in the struggle to invest that Jewishness in our children.

Rabbi Yisrael Bergstein, a"h, founder of our shul in Manhattan Beach, used to say that one of the greatest acts of *chesed* a father can do for his children is to let them see him learning Torah. How we educate our children, how they see us behave, where we send them to school, by and large determines who our children will be.

And that, in turn, will determine if we – our children, their children, and all our future generations – will have the spiritual fortitude to remain in Yaakov's camp, or if they will, *chalilah*, be vulnerable to Esav's ongoing attacks upon our viability as Jews.

This battle with the forces of Esav is a struggle that will never end, until the final Redemption. And it is only with the strength of the Torah that we can harness *avodah* and *gemilus chasadim* as well in the uniquely Jewish way that makes us who we need to be, the children of Avraham, Yitzchak, and Yaakov. The children of Sarah, Rivkah, Rachel, and Leah. The children of the Living God of Israel.

Parashas Vayishlach 5772

Back to Esav – Gevalt!

Having suffered with Esav for so many years, forced to outwit and outmaneuver him, and then having to run away, forced to put up with another *rasha*, Lavan, forced to try to outmaneuver him as well, Yaakov Avinu finally heads home, with his family, back to his father. Whom does he encounter along the way? Esav and his posse of four hundred thugs, headed his way. The same Esav who was a total *rasha* and who had sworn to kill him.

Fearing for his life and that of his family, and fearing as well lest he be forced to take life in his own defense, Yaakov famously strategizes and prepares for the coming encounter.

He must put on a good face and present his family to his violent and rapacious brother.

The Torah tells us about his various preparations. There was one maneuver, however, that is only hinted at. Rashi clues us in, based on a *Midrash Rabbah*: He prepares his wives and eleven children, the Torah says. But wait! He already has *twelve* children – eleven sons, so far, and his daughter. Dinah is missing from this encounter.

The Midrash tells us that fearing especially for his daughter's safety, knowing well what a *menuval* Esav was, Yaakov hid her in a box. And he was punished for this! Saved from Esav, she wound up in the hands of Shechem instead. (It wasn't easy to be Yaakov, was it?) The reason given for this punishment is that by hiding her from Esav, Yaakov deprived Esav of a possibility of straightening out his miserable life under the influence of a good woman, the *tzaddekes* Dinah. To quote Rashi, *shema tachzirenu l'mutav*, commonly understood to mean that she might have turned him to goodness, away from sin.

After all, such is the power of a good woman. Any man who is not stupid and who is lucky enough knows that to be true.

Stop! Wait! Are you kidding? Let that murdering, thieving, lecherous *menuval* have his little girl, because *maybe* he'll turn out OK as a result?! Is it possible that Yaakov Avinu can be faulted, and punished, for not letting Esav rape and carry off his daughter? What person can be expected to do that? And even if he did, who's to say that Esav wouldn't influence *her*, instead? No, it's got to make more sense than that. The Torah Temimah provides an insightful explanation, quite consistent with the whole history of the interaction of Yaakov with Esav, and with Lavan: Yaakov, in fact, had no doubt about the potential power of Dinah over Esav.

He knew that she would, in fact, straighten him out. But that was just the problem.

Shema tachzirenu l'mutav, commonly understood as *maybe* she'll make him good, is more clearly understood as *lest* she make him good. That was just what Yaakov needed to avoid. He'd gone to a lot of trouble and vilification by the nations of the world for all the generations to make sure the *bechorah* and its attendant *berachos*, the rightful birthright of the Jewish people as a holy nation for all time, remain with us.

Now remember a key aspect of Yitzchak's *berachah*. For all time, there is an inverse relationship between the brothers and the nations that will descend from them.

When Yaakov is up, Esav is down. And when Esav is up, Yaakov is down. That's how it will always be. If Dinah were to straighten Esav out, raising him up, if Esav were ascendant, what would happen to Yaakov and his destiny? What would happen to the legacy of Avraham and Yitzchak? Where would Klal Yisrael be, and how would it ever achieve what it needs to achieve? Yaakov resolved to keep Dinah's good influence away from Esav.

And so Yaakov did what he had to do, as he had famously done on several previous occasions, to safeguard the destiny of Klal Yisrael as a holy nation, indeed, to fulfill the purpose of creation. Each time it cost him, and in this instance it cost him in a very personal and painful way, when Dinah fell into the hands of Shechem.

But just as his mother Rivkah's vision was focused on the lofty and eternal goal, leading to Sinai and eternity, so too, at all times, was Yaakov's.

Parashas Vayishlach 5771

Yaakov Limping

Mendel, healthy and vigorous at age twenty-five, came down with the flu. It hit him hard, and he was out of sorts for a few weeks. Eventually he was back to his old self. In fact, it was as if he had never gotten sick. That's part of the miracle of the power to heal that the Creator put into our bodies.

Mike lost part of his foot in an industrial accident. With time, lots of pain, rehab, physical therapy, and special shoes, he was able to walk again. He functioned. But it could never be like it was before. That would be impossible.

Ivan and Igor were in a desperate fight. Past knives, past clubs, past even fists, they were clenched in a deadly embrace, trying to squeeze the very life out of each other. It was a fight to the death. Their faces were contorted with the strain and the emotion of their desperate struggle.

Jack and Joe were as close as friends could be. War buddies, they had each sacrificed a great deal for the other. There was a deep bond of love between them. Circumstances in life forced them apart, and only with great struggle, and after much time and pain, did they manage to reconnect. Their reunion was deeply emotional. Crying freely, intensely, they embraced one another fiercely.

A photographer who captured a single moment of that loving embrace, and who had also photographed Igor and Ivan, capturing a single moment of their deathly embrace, later looked at the two photographs and could not readily discern which was which.

The intensity was obvious, the extremity of feeling and effort was plain, but the nature of the emotion driving that intensity was, in that captured instant, not that easy to distinguish. A closer look, of course, reveals that the similarities are really superficial. Love or hate. They may both be intense. They may both be all consuming. They may both lead to extreme action. And pithy sayings on the subject notwithstanding, they arise from different worlds altogether and are worlds apart. *But to the undiscerning eye, they may, at least initially, look alike.*

Whom, or what, did Yaakov Avinu encounter that fateful night when he met a stranger and then found himself caught up in a desperate wrestling match? What did he see, or think he saw?

Chullin 91a relates the opinion of Rabbi Shmuel bar Nachmani: He (the angel of Esav) appeared to Yaakov as a (wild) heathen. Rabbi Shmuel bar Acha says: He appeared to Yaakov as a (refined) Torah scholar.

The Torah tells us that they grappled with each other. Rashi offers two scenarios: The Torah grammarian Menachem ben Saruk's understanding of *va'ye'avek* (ויאבק), that in their struggle they raised a cloud of dust or *avak* (אבק), and Rashi's, that their limbs were intertwined or *ibek* (אבק), suggesting even an embrace, indeed even a loving one.

Both? We know it was a terrible struggle, and we know about it because *all these parashiyos tell us things about our forefathers that presage what will happen to us, over and over through the generations. Maaseh avos siman la'banim.* We know of Esav's implacable hatred for us. Why the imagery of an embrace?

Because, says the Kesav Sofer, in their strategy for our defeat, for bringing us down, they may appear to us as wild heathens, wreaking murder, mayhem, and *shmad*, or, if it suits them, they may appear as "scholars," gentle, kindly people who reach out to us in sham liberal-minded brotherhood for the purpose of ensnaring us in their ways. Over the millennia, both have been tried. And, in different times and places, both approaches have had their successes (and, thank God, their failures).

Esav seeks one thing for Yaakov – that he be downtrodden, so that Esav may be ascendant. The rest is just a matter of strategy. That may be a violent struggle, a no-holds-barred attack. And at times that may be in the guise of an embrace, but which, in intent, is no less of an attack.

And sometimes it requires a highly discerning eye to tell the difference between an embrace that is truly well intentioned and one that is aimed, *chalilah*, at our undoing.

The long, bitter struggle with Esav (and Yishmael!) is, sadly, not over, and indeed appears to be far from over. As our forefather Yaakov was left limping, even after he bested his opponent, so too even as we remain standing today, we remain also limping, damaged but standing.

But, thus far in our long history, there is a great difference. When the sun shone on Yaakov, he was made whole again. It was as if he was never injured. But what of us?

Oh, what of us? After all that has happened to us, we can stand. We can walk.

We survive the pain and the loss. We suffer through the difficult process of "rehabilitation," the spiritual as well as the physical "therapy" that makes continued existence possible for us, the "special shoes" that allow us to walk again.

But so much of us has been chopped away, burned and beaten, shot and starved and tortured and gassed. It is hard to understand how, like Yaakov Avinu, we can ever be made whole again.

We take it as a matter of faith that somehow, it will be. We are believers, the children of believers, a thousand generations of stalwarts who have held on.

When God finally explains the great mysteries of the universe to us, this will surely be one of those mysteries explained. Until then, we hold on and we struggle. We wrestle, in every generation, that macabre dance that is sometimes with the violent heathen and sometimes with the masquerading "scholar" seeking our destruction.

But always we hold on, waiting for that day of peace and enlightenment when we must struggle no more, when Yaakov need no longer wrestle with Esav or with anyone.

Let it be, dear Father in Heaven. Make us whole. Let Your healing sunshine somehow make us whole. Let it be.

Parashas Vayishlach 5775

Lavankisses

We are told, after Yaakov Avinu's encounter with Esav, that he arrived in the Holy Land "*shalem*" – whole, complete, intact. Rashi, citing the Gemara (*Shabbos* 31a), tells us that this refers to three specific things: his body was whole, his limp having healed from the injury by Esav's *malach*, with whom he had wrestled; his fortune was whole, despite what went to Esav; and his Torah was whole, despite his years in Lavan's house.

There is another reference to Yaakov's wholeness later, in Vayechi, that offers another possible explanation. Just before his *petirah*, Yaakov, in considering his children, bows in gratitude to the Ribbono shel Olam, "*va'yishtachu Yisrael al rosh hamitah*." Rashi explains that the reference to the bed refers to the fact that *all* of his children were tzaddikim, "*she'haisa mitaso shleimah*," that his bed was whole, as it were, complete, righteous, as all his offspring, without exception, were righteous. While this is certainly important for any Jew, it is particularly important for Yaakov, whose father Yitzchak and whose grandfather Avraham, despite their greatness, each had a son who was a *rasha*.

It was Yaakov's mandate to have only pure and righteous children, so that Klal Yisrael could be established.

Yaakov understood that Yishmael's and Esav's character was not due to bad parenting or bad role models by the earlier Avos and Imahos. Rather, it was a cleansing process that produced Yishmael in addition to Yitzchak, and Esav in addition to Yaakov.

Avraham, despite his greatness, carried Terach's genetic material, spiritual as well as physical. That all went to Yishmael. Yitzchak was then pure, but his wife Rivkah, despite her greatness, carried Besuel's genetic material, spiritual as well as physical. That found its outlet in Esav, while Yaakov was pure. But Yaakov's wives, Leah and Rachel, despite their own greatness, still carried the genetic material, spiritual as well as physical, of their wicked father Lavan. And that had to disappear before Yaakov could actually return to Israel to establish God's holy nation. He *had* to have *mitaso shleimah*.

Let us then review the final interaction between Yaakov and Lavan.

Learning of Yaakov's abrupt departure, Lavan chases after him, angrily. The night before their encounter, Hashem appears to Lavan in a dream and warns him not to harm Yaakov in any way. Did Lavan really merit *nevuah* (prophecy)? That bum? Does God have no other way to thwart him other than to miraculously appear to him in a prophetic vision? He could have gotten Lavan's wagon stuck in the mud or given him a flat tire or acute appendicitis, or used any of a million other ways to stop him. That's how it usually works. Why did God appear to him in this way? What did God *really* want Lavan to do? By not stopping him, Hashem was actually sending Lavan to Yaakov with a mission.

The Imrei Noam, in Parashas Vayetzei, tells us what this mission was. It was, in fact, an all-important mission. He had to kiss his children and grandchildren. *Lavankisses*. Citing various midrashic sources, The Imrei Noam explains that there are several types of *neshikos* (kisses). One in particular is *neshikah shel prishus*, a kiss associated with separation that does more than just say goodbye. It's a kind of absorptive kiss, a kiss in which there is a transfer of spiritual material. Thus, Orpah, turning her back on Yiddishkeit, kisses her mother-in-law Naomi, and whatever holy *nitzotzos* she had are transferred to Naomi and thus to Klal Yisrael. Orpah, now devoid of any spark of holiness, then goes on to her infamous career of degeneracy. Ruth, meanwhile, "*davkah bah*," clung to her holiness.

Va'yashkem Lavan ba'boker va'yinashek l'vanav v'li'vnosav...upon his departure, Lavan fulfilled his mission in chasing after Yaakov and his family. He kissed his grandchildren and his daughters. It was that type of kiss: he absorbed any residual "*zuhama*" (a particular type of foundational *tumah*) that might have been within them, *of which he himself was the original source*.

He in fact resorbed what he had imparted to them at birth. In this way they were totally cleansed of Lavan's nasty spiritual heritage. Thus, *va'yashav Lavan li'mkomo* – Lavan returned to his "place" (i.e., the repository of *tumah*) and *v'Yaakov halach l'darko*. Yaakov was now able to go on his way, to reenter the land, *shalem*, whole, complete, pure (*va'yavo Yaakov shalem*), *mitaso shleimah*, and to fulfill his destiny.

Our destiny.

Parashas Vayishlach 5771

Polska Ulica...

My father's bar mitzvah Shabbos, in the spring of 1919, was on Parashas Emor. A few weeks before, he put on tefillin for the first time, always a joyous celebration. For him this event took place in a bunker. Upstairs a terrible pogrom was raging. The patriots of Poland were celebrating their new national independence, a wonderful occasion for an old-fashioned Jew smashing.

What went wrong? Jews had been in the country for a thousand years, and together with the ethnic Poles had built the country. There were about three million of them, 10 percent of the population. Their lives were interwoven. But still they were seen as "Other," foreign, alien, sinister, oppressive, exploiters, interlopers, rapacious, disloyal. Foreigners who don't belong there, who take advantage of the innocent locals.

Christ killers.

In the end, the persecutions and the hatred, the violations and the murders that had been the norm all throughout the tragic history of European Jewry came to Poland too, and became an embedded part of its civilization.

Certainly, as elsewhere, there was a strong religious basis to the enmity. As elsewhere, the Jews' nonacceptance of their own son who had become the Christian deity was as unacceptable as it was, to them, inexplicable. Indeed, as elsewhere, the only way to explain it was the willful, stubborn perfidy of evil people, who deserved the punishment that was thrown their way.

As elsewhere, as well, jealousy played its role. The masses of desperately poor Jews were invisible to those jealous eyes, who saw only the prosperous Jews among them. Somehow, those Jews had taken their wealth from its rightful owners, the Poles. (Remember race huckster Reverend Al's infamous rallying cry of "white interlopers" to whip up violent action against white business owners in Harlem?)

These patterns, in all their variations, are to be found all over the Western world, throughout history. Libraries have been filled with histories of antisemitism, with a multitude of theories to explain this persistent, utterly illogical social malady.

The complex and troubled relationship between Yaakov and Esav was set long before.

Rashi explains on Bereishis 33:4: *Halachah hi b'yadua, Esav soneh l'Yaakov.* Our Sages understood the reality, established so many years and generations ago. Esav hates Yaakov. There may be periods and places of cooperation, coexistence, even friendly relations. But at his core, Esav cannot forgive Yaakov for being the good, moral son; he is murderously enraged over Yaakov's grasping their father's *berachah*; he sees whatever Yaakov has as rightfully his; he is forever clenched with Yaakov in that violent, wrenching wrestling match in that dark, lonely, frightening night so long ago, the dust of which rose to Heaven and filled the world, an enduring, debilitating storm whose end is still nowhere in sight.

Parashas Vayishlach 5777

Saved by Whom?

The Torah gives us a lot of detail about Yaakov's encounter with Esav. We learn from Yaakov how to prepare for possibly violent confrontation with hostile enemies: diplomacy, a hand extended in peace, and simultaneous preparation for war, complete with strategies that take into account the various possibilities and exigencies of war. And, while the human factor is a practical necessity, the larger picture is taken into account and addressed: prayer. God of my fathers, Yaakov prayed, Who directed me to return to my homeland, and Who has blessed me so, unworthy as I am, please save me from my brother Esav, lest he come and smite us all, mothers and children.

Yaakov knew what Esav was capable of. And so he was justifiably fearful. He prayed for God's salvation, he prepared his camps for war, and he extended the olive branch.

There is, famously, a strange inverse relationship between Yaakov and Esav, one that began as the two babies wrestled in their mother's belly and was determined for all time by Yitzchak's *berachah*. When Yaakov is up, Esav will be down. When Yaakov is down, Esav will be ascendant.

Esav has been ascendant for a very long time.

And so, I saw something striking in the aftermath of the terrible November 2015 terrorist murders in Paris.

I wondered then how long it would take for some prominent political figure or commentator to lay the blame for those murders on the Jews, who have stirred up the Muslims with "occupation," "oppression," and "humiliation." It took less than a week before the Swedish foreign minister went public with that sentiment. They understand why Muslims attack Jews ("They are desperate and using the only means available to them!"). But why attack innocent Europeans, who sympathize with them?

A young woman who miraculously survived the murders, as others all around her were killed, was being interviewed. She was, several days afterward, still visibly shaken and highly emotional. It was obvious to her that a higher power had saved her. But what she actually said was quite telling, indicative of where Europe (Esav, by the way) is.

After a momentary pause, she said, "The Universe saved me."

That's right. In another time, even not long ago, she would have said, "Thank God," and perhaps speculated on why God chose to save her while those around her died. She did so speculate, but could not bring herself to say "God." Perhaps she feared ridicule from her Godless friends. Perhaps she is too vested in the Godlessness of what is, essentially, a post-Christian Europe that is, as a result, easy pickings for the Muslim invasion we have been witnessing for the past generation, the same period during which Europeans have been busy shedding their religion.

"The Universe saved me." At first I was shocked and horrified. And then I remembered our forefather Yitzchak's *berachah* that places Yaakov and Esav at such opposite poles, and it gave me hope that with Esav's fulfilling *ka'asher tarid*, when you, Esav, descend, Yaakov will ascend.

We can use some ascending now. I know of no such inverse relationship with Yishmael. Yishmael seems stronger, and wilder, than he has ever been since he swept out of the Arabian Peninsula thirteen hundred years ago.

In this time of our fear and concern, we can learn the lesson of our forefather Yaakov and prepare ourselves by all means necessary, with the practical preparations for armed conflict if need be, with peace and diplomacy if possible, and above all, with prayer and turning to our Father in Heaven to protect us. *Halevai* that *all* of our people take Yaakov's lesson to heart, that we turn our hearts to the only real and omnipotent power in the universe, the Creator of that universe, and, thus truly well armed, we will be ascendant not only against Esav, but against Yishmael as well.

And so, in the merit of our forefathers, may it be God's will.

Parashas Vayishlach 5776

What Counts

In New Orleans, of all places, at a medical meeting, the *frum* doctor in the next seat revealed to me the chip (or one of the chips) on his shoulder. In his shul back home, there were some who wanted to install tables in the small side shul/*beis medrash*. He didn't quite sneer, but I could readily discern the sneer in his voice. "They think that having tables instead of just benches makes you more *frum*."

If I hadn't heard stuff like this before, coming especially from an otherwise intelligent person, I would have been dumbfounded. People harbor notions and resentments, of whatever origin, and express them in the oddest way, thinking they make sense. I was once in a shul – a nice, conventional large shul, with rows of seats – on Shabbos morning when someone wearing a *bekeshe* (not the usual form of dress in that shul) was asked to be the chazan for Shacharis.

As he walked to the *amud*, I could hear the sneering comment, "They're turning this place into a *shtiebel*!" That he davened very nicely, Nusach Ashkenaz, with his words pronounced just as they do, with the melodies and style they were accustomed to, made no difference.

And speaking of *nusach*, I recently heard a new one: "When they want to show how frum they are, they daven Sefard." Huh? The speaker obviously never davened in a major mainstream yeshiva, the vast majority of which, non-Chassidic, daven Ashkenaz. But the nonsensical dismissive put-downs, whatever their motivations, do not require logic or reason.

The Torah does not tell us whether Yaakov Avinu davened Ashkenaz or Sefard (*for sure Sefard!…or maybe not*), whether his shul had pews or chairs and tables (*for sure tables!…or maybe not*) or how he dressed (for sure a *silk bekeshe!…or maybe not*). It doesn't tell us things we don't need to know. Matters of style, which may be useful but are not central to our faith and not a specific parameter of our piety, are left up to us. All sincere Torah paths lead to God. Different tools work for different people as they seek that path.

The things the Torah does tell us, we do indeed need to know. The Torah does tell us that Yaakov was sorely injured by a "man" we understand to be the *malach* of Esav, and that as a result he walked with a limp, until God healed him. You can imagine for yourself, and dwell upon, the various symbolic meanings and the lessons – historic, national, and personal – of that fact. It runs very deep. But let me share with you a related personal lesson.

I was visiting somewhere for Shabbos and I sat in shul at a table with a nice white tablecloth, davening Nusach Sefard, wearing a *Shabbosdike bekeshe* and *gartel*, a big black *samet* (velvet) yarmulke and a tallis over my head. Wow, I thought, bearing the above in mind, in a very superficial and mindless world, this would go far to broadcast how very *frum* I must really be, or think I am. Can any serious person really take such notions seriously? And yet posturing is so common a human trait.

I had just finished davening Shemoneh Esrei, ending with the requisite stepping back three paces that symbolizes our subservience to the Ribbono shel Olam as we withdraw from our encounter with our Master in the Amidah prayer. The *parashah* of the week described Yaakov Avinu's riveting story and his many struggles, which include the injury that left him lame.

Out of the corner of my eye I noticed movement next to me. It was a young man in his twenties, who had davened a longer Shemoneh Esrei than I did, moving back those three steps. But they were not exactly steps. His Amidah, the term we use for Shemoneh Esrei that means, literally, *to stand*, was done not standing at all, but sitting in his wheelchair. I later learned that some years before, he had suffered a terrible injury that left him paralyzed. And when he finished davening Shemoneh Esrei, he dutifully and reverently rolled his wheelchair back the equivalent of three steps. Subservience to and worship of his Master.

Anybody with sense understands that our connection with God, in the context of Torah and mitzvos, does not depend on superficialities or matters of style, even as that style may indeed be a useful and even powerful aid that helps us in that connection. And anyone with sense and perspective understands, as well, if he stops to think about it, and to notice, how much greater that challenge, and indeed all the challenges of life – sometimes such terrible challenges – must be for others.

And indeed after that brief encounter, if there is any sense in my head, if I have any religious sensibility, if there is any sensitivity in my soul, if I have even a smidgeon of humility, if there is any measure of sincerity in my mode of worship, if I have any awareness of the myriad lessons in life that surround us, if I have any appreciation of what I am blessed with, if I understand something of the profound lessons the Torah teaches us from the lives of our Avos, if I have any ability to learn from the greatness and the quiet bravery of others, I will, I pray, never step back those three paces at the end of Shemoneh Esrei in quite the same way again.

Parashas Vayishlach 5778

Vayeshev

Ubi Sunt Qui Ante Nos Fuerunt?

The first time they crossed the river no one shot at them.

The Jews of Poland, and many non-Jews, faced a terrible dilemma when the Germans invaded from the west. To flee eastward toward the Soviets, and place themselves under that evil regime, or stay put and face the certain but as yet not fully understood evils of Nazi occupation?

Families with small children most often could not pick up and leave their homes for the unknown. They by and large stayed, and virtually all of them were subsequently murdered. Many young people without children did run. Many family men fled as well, alone, expecting to be pressed into slave labor by the Germans if they stayed. Similarly, people of substance felt vulnerable and, expecting to be targeted, tried to get away if they could. Most Jewish people, of course, just remained in their homes and became the Six Million.

My assistant did not understand the Yiddish words being spoken, but she had witnessed this scene enough times that she understood why I sat there with tears streaming down my cheeks, unable to speak, as the elderly gentleman in the exam chair recounted how, as a youth of sixteen, he wanted to run eastward as the Germans approached, but his mother feared for him and urged him to stay home with the family. "Whatever happens to the rest of us will happen to you too," she told him. Many took comfort, of sorts, from that idea. In the end he did run, and, despite the difficulties and the horrors he faced in the East, he did remain alive, the only remnant of his large family to survive the war.

That was the last time he ever saw his mother, or anyone else of his family, or of his town.

Shimon and Chana married in February 1938, and as yet were childless. They had gone to Reb Alter'l, the Dzhikover Rebbe, in late 1938 or perhaps early 1939, for a *berachah*, a blessing that they have children. The Rebbe stood up, agitated, strode to the window, and pointed at the heavens. "The skies are so overcast, and you want children now? Better not. This is not the time for children."

111

On Friday, September 1, 1939, as the bombs fell in Reishe (Rzeszow) as Shimon was returning home from Shacharis, the Rebbe's inspired foresight proved fatefully accurate.

A strong young man, as well as a man of means and property, Shimon knew he would be a target. They had to run.

Some thought the war would be over soon. After all, England and France, under a treaty of mutual defense with Poland, would step in, and Germany would undoubtedly back down. In fact, there were those who took with them, as they fled, their *machzorim* for Rosh Hashanah, but not for Yom Kippur. The war would surely be over by then, they thought. Others took a more realistic, hard-eyed view.

With the Germans advancing rapidly, Panzer divisions of tanks running down the incredibly brave Polish cavalry charging those tanks on horseback with swords drawn, quick decision and quick action were needed. Panic set in everywhere.

Shimon bade goodbye to his elderly widowed mother, who could not flee, and to his sisters, who had small children. He bought an automobile at a wildly inflated price and loaded it with whatever portable valuables he could and some food, and he and Chana set off, headed eastward, away from the advancing Germans.

Before they got out of town, they were stopped by Polish military, who, at gunpoint, commandeered the car "for the war effort." Incredulously, Shimon and Chana surrendered the car to the Polish military heroes, who promptly fled eastward in it, *away* from the fighting. Who knows what happened to those "heroes" of the Polish Republic? Maybe they melted into the crowds of refugees. Maybe they were among the twenty-one thousand-plus Polish officers and soldiers murdered in the Katyn Forest by the Soviets a few weeks later.

On foot, with what little they could carry, Chana and Shimon joined the long line of refugees headed east, facing the unknown and hoping to survive. Their incredible travails over the next six years could and should be the subject of volumes, and perhaps one day will be. What will be recounted here relates to the business at hand in this forum, Parashas Vayeshev.

Eventually, surviving much, including bombing and strafing along the way, they reached Lemberg (Lwow), where there was no bombing. The Germans had made a deal with the Soviets to divide Poland between them, and Lemberg was to be on the Russian side.

The Russians invaded Poland from the east sixteen days after the Germans invaded from the west. (It's interesting to note that students in Soviet schools were *not* taught, in history class, that Russia had, in fact, invaded Poland [ostensibly to "protect" the Ukrainian and Russian ethnic minorities in these regions]; members of my family here in Brooklyn have been harshly and angrily called liars by their

Russian neighbors when they matter-of-factly referred to the Soviet invasion of Poland on September 17, 1939. Mind boggling.)

At some point, things appeared to have quieted down. Conditions were harsh, however, under the Soviets, and some people, unaware of how bad it was in the German areas, considered going back. Shimon and Chana now had to consider how they would sustain themselves, and were very concerned about the welfare of Shimon's mother. Shimon could not go back, for the very reasons that drove him to flee in the first place. And, being a man, he could not hide the fact that he was a Jew, the physical evidence being imprinted on his flesh. Chana undertook to go back, check on Mother, and to return with whatever valuables she could carry, to keep them alive.

She smuggled back into Reishe. She looked after her mother-in-law, gathered whatever valuables she could sew into the lining of her clothing, filled a rucksack with dollars and other items, and set out to return to Lemberg. This time there was no bombing or strafing. This time there was the Gestapo.

She trudged down the road with other refugees, a shifting mass of struggling humanity.

Alongside her walked two Jewish boys trying to make it to the other side. One of them, seeing her straining to carry her things, kindly offered to carry her rucksack for a while. Gratefully, she accepted. He was still carrying it when the three of them were arrested by the Gestapo. After that she did not see him at all.

The story of what happened at Gestapo headquarters, of her interrogation, of the bloodcurdling screams she heard from every room, itself could fill a book. A brief rendition appeared in the *Family First* supplement of *Mishpacha* magazine, authored by Yael Schuster, her granddaughter. For our purposes here, it suffices to say that by the grace of God and her incredible strength of will and personality, she lived to walk out of that building and continued walking until she reached the river separating the German zone from the Russian.

This time she and others attempting to cross were shot at. From both sides, at the same time. But she did get across, and eventually rejoined her husband in Lemberg.

Without her life-sustaining rucksack, and the valuables in it. That was gone.

Life was very difficult there. It wasn't like the German occupation, but it was bad enough. There was not much to eat. She learned how to make candies from sugar, which they could sell to the lucky few who had some money. The problem was getting sugar. Shimon had to find ways to buy and sell whatever he could – all strictly, and potentially lethally, illegal – in order to be able to acquire sugar. It was a constant struggle.

Months passed. People were going hungry. Having arrived well fed, many were now looking gaunt and hollow eyed. Not knowing the future, they didn't realize that before long it would be much worse. Deportation, Siberia, prison, disease, and slavery awaited them. But at that moment, they were desperate.

In the street one day, Chana spied a gaunt, haggard figure who looked familiar. He was rail thin, and in tatters. And he was missing an ear. The Gestapo had taken it as a memento of his interrogation; he had been picked up on the road and arrested, together with another fellow and with Chana, whose rucksack he had been carrying. Yes, somehow, miraculously, that young Jewish boy was alive, and he had somehow made it beyond the German lines.

He gave my mother a big smile (if you hadn't guessed yet: yes, Chana was my mother). "I'm so happy to see you!" he exclaimed. Some teeth were missing. "I have your rucksack! I was hoping I would find you!" Somehow, he had managed to hold on to it.

He went to his place and returned with the rucksack. Full of money and valuables, it had not been opened or tampered with in any way. As hungry and as desperate as he was, and not even sure she was alive, he would not touch what was not his, what he knew would keep her and her husband alive if he should ever find them. That young boy whose name and fate I do not know, that son of Avraham, Yitzchak, and Yaakov, of Sarah, Rivkah, Rachel, and Leah, whose *neshamah* was present at Mount Sinai, whose God-fearing parents instilled in him the *yiras Shamayim* that would sustain us as a people through all the tortured millennia of our national travails, understood that even in hell, his calling was to do the will of God. And he did so joyfully.

The Gemara (*Pesachim* 113a) and similarly the Midrash (*Tanchuma*, Vayeshev 5) teach that God Himself testifies to the honesty and the integrity of three people: one who tithes completely honestly, a young bachelor who lives in the vicinity of freely available vice but holds himself pure, and a poor man who finds, or is holding, someone else's property, and makes sure to return it, untouched.

Tanchuma paints a picture of Yosef's moral predicament. He was a very lonely seventeen-year-old fellow, in the full thrall of his youth and natural hormonal drive, who knew he was very handsome, who knew that the Egyptian women wanted him, in a land full of vice, a society given over to licentiousness. And Mrs. Potiphar did everything she could, used every feminine wile and enticement, to get him to sin. But he would not sin. He saw the image of his father Yaakov before his eyes, and presumably that of his grandfather Yitzchak, who in turn bore the visage of his own father, Avraham. He knew who he was, where he came from, who he had to be, what he needed to do, and what, no matter the circumstances, he could not permit himself to do.

In truth, people are presented with temptation of every kind, every day. For us, it is expected that we defy that devil the yetzer hara and behave as a Jew should.

Hopefully, we do. But sometimes it's harder than at other times. Sometimes circumstances are so difficult, so unusual, so trying, so unnatural, that it's easy to think that this time it's OK to bend the rules. It would be so easy to rationalize.

And then we think of the heroes of our Jewish world. With the greatest respect due to our Torah leadership, I am referring here to the *amcha Yidden*, the Chaims and the Hershels, the Brandels and the Devorahs and the Mendels, the Chanas and the Shimons who comprise the nation of God's Chosen People, in whom is imprinted the goodness and the nobility of their holy forebears, and who, with steely determination, fulfill and propagate their holy mission in this world from generation to generation.

How are they able to do that? By drawing strength from those who came before, just as Yosef did. *Shivisi Hashem l'negdi samid*: the Jew sees God before him at all times.

He does so because his father did so, and his mother, and their parents before them. These are the *amcha Yidden* who comprise Klal Yisrael, whose dogged determination makes it all work.

Ubi sunt qui ante nos fuerunt? Where are those who came before us? Where are the Avos? Where are the prophets and the wise men? Where are Rabbi Akiva and Rebbe?

Where are the two million plus souls who, with utter faith in God, babies in their arms, walked into the scorching desert to follow Him, and who declared at Sinai, with one voice, *naaseh v'nishma*, we will do and we will listen? Where are those who, in nearly every generation, offered their lives for His sake?

They are here. They are all around us. They are us. They are in Egypt and in Spain and in Russia and in Germany. *They are in Lemberg*. They are past, present, and future.

All our generations are bound up as one.

What Yosef Hatzaddik saw in his father's face as it appeared in his mind's eye is what Yaakov saw in Yitzchak's face and in Avraham's. It is what the good and loyal and dedicated Jews in every generation have seen: who they were, where they came from, and where they had to go. They saw the spirit of God bestowed upon them through their faith and through their upbringing.

Ubi sunt qui ante nos fuerunt? The philosophers of old, who posed that question in classical Latin, were thinking of the ethereal nature of life. Here today, gone tomorrow.

What was the point of all the fuss? Gone, over, done.

For the Jew, those who came before are very much still here, and always will be. For what we have from them, *the very key to life*, is, for us, life itself.

Parashas Vayeshev 5775

Jacob Dwelt in the Land of His Fathers

There is a nice, leafy street in a lovely, upscale section of Jerusalem named Balfour, in honor of Arthur James Balfour, the World War I English foreign secretary who sent a letter to Zionist leaders in 1917, stating that "His Majesty's Government view with favour" the establishment of a Jewish homeland in Palestine.

There are many other towns in Israel, such as Haifa, Petach Tikvah, Bat Yam, Ashkelon, and Tel Aviv, with Balfour Streets. He is, in historical political Zionism, a very big deal. Of course, to virtually everyone else in the world, he is totally irrelevant. And, with all due credit to this diplomat who was trying to curry Jewish support for England in the desperate struggle of world war, sadly, he really is – except to the delusional Jews who think that this non-Jew, however well-intentioned he might have been, somehow owned the Land of Israel and had the power and the legitimacy to bestow it upon the Jewish People. In their view, he was more powerful than God Himself.

It's a rather flimsy claim, especially in the face of a world largely united in its view that Israel is guilty of "occupying" Arab Palestine, denying the "Palestinians" their historic national rights. And if the *umos ha'olam*, the nations of the world (the UN!), "gave" us the Land of Israel, as if it were theirs to give, they could also, by the same consensus, take it away.

Those secular political Zionists have a fundamental problem. By what right have they participated in transforming a Muslim-dominated, Arab-inhabited province into a state of the Jews? They can't say that the God Who created it also gave it to us. They refuse to admit that they believe that, and if they did, they would also have to take seriously everything else in the Torah, such as the 613 commandments. And besides, they don't want to appear ridiculous, backward, tribal, or as primitive fanatics. The gentiles, they fear, or their sophisticated Jewish friends, or the secularist media, would laugh at them.

And so they look to Arthur Balfour, English patrician and politician, whose brief note to Chaim Weizmann and his associates has, in their construct, more power and greater legitimacy than God's Torah.

But they are, of course, wrong – dead wrong, not just in what they say, but in their vain hope that it will carry more weight with the rest of the world, the world of Esav and Yishmael and all who hate us, than does the word of God. Our enemies care not a fig for Balfour or for history, of which they are largely ignorant and about which, like the truth itself, they are indifferent.

And so every time there is a terrorist outrage somewhere else in the world, there are always Jewish fools who declare, "Now the world will understand what we are up against and they will start to sympathize with us!"

Baloney. Sure, there are good and decent people out there (most of whom, I think, are in America) who get it. But the powers that be around the world – political, academic, journalistic – just don't see it that way, and never will.

The 2015 terror attacks in Paris shocked the world. Those same Jewish voices started again to say that now the world will understand, and so on. But the fact is that they don't. They do not equate what happens in Paris with what happens in Jerusalem. In fact, an attempt recently to do so in France was greeted with Gallic indignation and anger. The French people, you see, are *innocent*. How dare you compare them with the Jews, who have brought their troubles on themselves?

Our enemies don't care about Lord Arthur James Balfour, who lived and died a century ago and who merely did what politicians and diplomats do: they blow air and say what they need to say. The Jews are occupiers and oppressors. That is what they believe, because that is what they want to believe. And they believe that, in part, because the best the public relations of the secular Zionists can come up with is Balfour, the UN, flowers in the desert, and computer chips. And that means nothing to them.

Unfortunately, those who hate us will hate us no matter what, as long as the world is as it is. But our ability to stand up to the world is not rooted in Balfour, the UN, flowers in the desert, or in computer chips. Our strength, our justification, our very deed to the land, is vested in the word of God. That is our only weapon, our only ammunition, our only justification. Without that we have no legitimacy. Without that we are indeed a conquering, occupying power. And without that we have no real strength.

Before the Arabs, before the Muslim world, before the Christian world (and it is a profound embarrassment that the good Christians of America see this while so many Jews do not), before the Eurotrash of the EU, before the United Nations and its disgusting longtime secretary general, Ban Ki Moon (who pointedly omitted Israel, time and time again, from the list of nations suffering from terrorism, even as its citizens lay stabbed and run over in the streets), before the academics, before the boycotters, before the Democratic left that tried to de-Judaize Jerusalem at the Democratic Convention (and nearly did), before President Barack Obama, before John (*oy vey*) Kerry, before the Swedish and the Norwegian sanctimonious hypocrites, before the hateful British media, before the whole world: stand up and declare, without reservation and without embarrassment, that the Land of Israel belongs to the People of Israel, because their Father in Heaven has bestowed it upon them for time everlasting.

That will certainly not be less effective or convincing than the Balfour thing. But it will, I pray, and expect, convince the very One in Whose power it is, and Whose will may it be, *to set us and keep us safely established in our Holy Land forever.*

The Torah spells out that our forefather Yaakov, also known as Israel, settled in the land of his fathers, for a reason. (It wasn't easy for him either.) It is something that all his descendants need to understand and to appreciate, to internalize and to *externalize*, before all the world: This is my God, and this is my relationship with Him. Before all the world, this is my God, and this is my land.

Unabashed, unashamed, unselfconscious, unambiguous, unapologetic: this is my land.

Parashas Vayeshev 5776

Shining Through

During his time in Egypt, Yosef was a slave, a prisoner in the deepest pit for twelve years, and ultimately the viceroy of Egypt. The pressures and the temptations were enormous. And yet he held firm, remaining Yosef Hatzaddik. He even raised two holy and righteous sons in that milieu, whose names and example are evoked to this day by Jewish parents blessing their children.

Holding firm, desperately but doggedly, has been a sad but requisite attribute in the survival of our people through millennia of oppression. Here now is the story of one such pure and holy soul, who held on to the God and the faith of her people with a dreadful determination, and who was, sadly, but one of many.

In 1834, a seventeen-year-old Jewish girl, Sol ("sun") Hachuel lived in the Moroccan city of Tangier. She was befriended by a local Muslim woman who became determined to get Sol to convert. Sol would not. There were tremendous pressures in society upon Jews to convert, and it was considered very meritorious for a Muslim to get a Jew to do so.

The woman persisted, and Sol persisted in her refusal. Thwarted and resentful, the woman denounced Sol to the authorities as one who had adopted Islam and then recanted.

Under Islamic law (as it was elsewhere under Christian law), this was a "crime" punishable by death. Arrested and brought before the governor, she explained that she had never undertaken to convert, nor had she ever indicated that she would, despite the accuser's insistence that she do so.

As was typical, Sol's statement was given no credence whatsoever, and she was assumed guilty. The governor told her that she could still set things right by accepting Islam, for which she would be rewarded with riches and honor. Otherwise she would be terribly tortured and then killed. Her reply (in Ladino) became her epitaph: "*Hebrea naci y Hebrea quero morir*" (A Jewess I was born, a Jewess I wish to die). She was imprisoned and shackled, with an iron collar around her neck and chains on her hands and feet. She was transported to Fez (her parents were forced to pay the cost of the transfer), where the cadi condemned her to death by beheading in the main market square. Along the way to her death, she was reviled by the local populace. "Death!" they screamed. "Death to the blaspheming, impious wretch!"

Upon the scaffold she begged for, and was given, water to wash her hands so she could say Shema Yisrael, which she recited. The executioner placed her in position for beheading, but instead of cutting off her head, he initially just cut her neck with the scimitar, to frighten her into a last-minute conversion to save her life. Upon seeing her blood, she turned to the executioner and said, "Do not make me linger. Dying as I do, innocent of any crime, the God of Avraham will avenge my death!" She was then beheaded.

The Jewish community of Fez had to pay to have Sol Hachuel's body, her head, and the blood-soaked earth given to them for Jewish burial. She was buried in the old Jewish cemetery in Fez next to one of the great sages of Moroccan Jewry.

Our Avos and Imahos, Yosef Hatzaddik, our forefathers, as chronicled in the Torah, passed their elevated spiritual DNA to us, enabling our people, under the most trying circumstances, to survive and to continue as Hashem's people, with a strength that defies the imagination. May we never be tested. Seventeen-year-old Sol Hachuel, *H"yd*, was tested. She lost her life. But her *neshamah* came shining through. May her memory be a blessing and her merit a protection for Klal Yisrael. And may the lessons of our holy forebears serve us well, always.

Parashas Vayeshev 5771

On Their Faces

I had a friend, Bill Sullivan, who was a very smart man, with a lot of insight into human behavior and motivation. A Boston Irishman, he was a devout Roman Catholic. I do not believe he was an antisemite. He certainly gave me no reason to think so. In fact, quite the opposite.

Bill once told me a story that was to him amusing, and to me disturbing. Away on vacation once, he attended church services on Sunday morning. The other congregants were, like him, vacationers, unfamiliar with that particular church. A clever and observant fellow, he discerned that there was something odd about the priest. He said to his wife, "That priest is a Jew." She looked at him in surprise; it would never have occurred to her.

The priest began the sermon. "I know what you're thinking," he said. "You see it on my face. Yes, I *am* a Jew." He then went on to tell them how he had come to where he was.

Not a good story, from our perspective. As we all know, many of us have faces that are typically Jewish, a biological fact. We are, after all, a tribe, with common biological roots. Given the flow of history, and life, however, it isn't always so. It isn't always obvious from one's physical facial features alone.

And so, we often can recognize each other for who we are, and often we cannot. Non-Jews who are interested – often for bad reasons – sometimes can as well. And often they are just oblivious.

But there is another dimension entirely to the recognition of the face of a Jew. And while that is a spiritual one, it will reflect itself physically in that Jew's physiognomy.

On Erev Yom Kippur we bless our children with a beautiful *berachah* that includes the prayer and the hope that *yiras Hashem tihyeh al panecha kol yemei chayecha* – the fear of God should be "written on your face" all the days of your life. A beautiful *berachah* indeed. The spirituality that is within – in a Jew, the spirituality that is unique to the Jew, that of Torah and *yiras Shamayim* from the Torah perspective, the constant awareness of God's presence – should so fill a person that its presence within him is also obvious upon his face.

Yaakov sent Yosef from Chevron to Shechem, a considerable distance, to see how his brothers and their flocks were faring. Searching for them, Yosef wandered through the fields, all but lost. A man found him there and asked him, "What are you seeking?" Yosef replied, "It is my brothers that I seek. Tell me, please, where are they shepherding?"

The Torah does not say who the man was, or that Yosef told him who he himself was, who his father was, or who his brothers were. Why would Yosef assume that this man would have any knowledge at all about what he sought? *Tell me where my brothers are?* How should he know?

Let's put the question aside for the moment. Later on, when Yosef is the major-domo in the house of Potiphar, Mrs. Potiphar has designs on the handsome and clever young Jew. A God-fearing youth, he rebuffs her time and again. She keeps up the pressure and the enticement. The denouement arrives when Yosef returns to the house one day when no one but the lady in question is home, *laasos melachto,* to do his work. The Gemara (*Sotah* 37b) relates two interpretations, those of Rav and Shmuel. One says this means, literally, his actual work. The other says "work" here is a metaphor. He was preparing to succumb to her entreaties.

The Torah Temimah explains that this latter explanation is deduced from the fact that he knowingly entered the house at a time when no one but the temptress was there, indicating that he was headed her way. And then the Torah Temimah cites the Gemara in *Shabbos* (97a) regarding the incident in Parashas Behaaloscha, in which Miriam speaks ill of Moshe and is punished with *tzaraas.* But the Torah says that God was angry with Aharon too. Rabbi Akiva learns from this that Aharon was also stricken with *tzaraas,* although the Torah does not say so. For this teaching, Rabbi Yehudah ben Beseirah says to Rabbi Akiva, "You will, in the future, be punished, for you have revealed publicly what the Torah intentionally kept hidden. Your *derush* shamed Aharon when the Torah 'chose' not to." And tragically, Rabbi Akiva's end was a terrible one indeed.

If so, asks the Torah Temimah, why was it OK here to make a *derush* to the shame of Yosef, that he came home to be alone with the seductress, when the Torah intentionally kept that hidden?

Especially when there was room to interpret the *pasuk* literally, in its plain sense, that he came home, in all innocence, simply to do his household tasks?

One can answer that in the end, it was all to Yosef's credit, not his shame. That the temptress tempted him is human nature. That in the end he rejected her and ran away from her, that he withstood the test, was to his great credit.

And how was he saved? *Nireis lo demus dyukno shel aviv,* Yosef saw before his eyes the image of his father, the saintly Yaakov. That reminded him who he was, whose son he was, who he had to be, and what he had to do: get out of there.

This brings us back to something the Torah tells us in the beginning of Vayeshev about Yosef.

V'hu naar. Rashi explains, he was busy with youthful, childish actions. He was occupied with his looks. He curled his hair, he made his eyes nice, to look handsome. And so later, in describing Yosef's arrival and success in Potiphar's house, the Torah tells us, seemingly in a grand non sequitur, that he was *yefeh to'ar vi'yfeh mar'eh*, very beautiful (the same language used earlier to describe his late mother, Rachel). Immediately, in the next *pasuk*, we are told of Mrs. Potiphar's unhealthy interest in him.

Not unlike children and their parents since time immemorial, Yaakov and Yosef had a fundamental difference in outlook. Yaakov was the *ish tam yoshev ohalim*. He was quiet and conservative and reserved. He stuck close to his tent, the *ohel* of Torah, in order to avoid temptation and sin, to keep them far from him. His way was *hatzne'a leches*, the way of quiet modesty. That was his philosophy and his strategy in life.

Yosef, on the other hand, was not afraid to curl his hair and to occupy himself, at least to a degree, with his looks. Perhaps because Yaakov grew up with Esav, he learned to fear sin more. Yosef grew up only with tzaddikim. He may have been less fearful of the power of the yetzer hara. He believed not only that his free will to remain good would be stronger than the inclination to sin, but that some degree of exposure to the yetzer hara would, in fact, redound to his credit for being stronger than it, for resisting it. Such is youth!

And so, in the end, *va'yavo habaisa laasos melachto*. As a result of his *shittah*, his philosophical position on temptation, he came so, so close to falling down altogether. But then, at the last moment, he saw *demus dyukno*, the image of his father, the *ish tam yoshev ohalim*, the Jew in the Jewish uniform, Yaakov Avinu dressed as a *talmid chacham*, Yaakov in flowing beard and *peyos*, wearing a *Shabbosdike bekeshe*, so to speak, who confined himself to the *ohel shel Torah*, who held himself apart, who did everything he could to avoid temptation, while he, Yosef, who had held a different point of view, who thought that he would be stronger and smarter than the yetzer hara, who thought he could make himself attractive to the Mrs. Potiphars of the world, but then resist their powerful attraction, found himself at the very edge of losing it all, of betraying his father, his people, his God and himself, teetering at the edge of the pit. But being the tzaddik that he was, being Yosef Hatzaddik, he recovered, he ran out, and went on to his great destiny.

Ultimately it was his father who saved him. It was the image of the tzaddik. It was the realization that his father's position had been the correct one all along, and that he, Yosef, had been wrong. Allowing that *menuval* the yetzer hara anywhere near him had been a terrible mistake. Its power is greater, and more insidious, than one can imagine, and even Yosef Hatzaddik is not immune.

And so, as Rav Meir Shapiro teaches, with this in mind, let us return to the original question. How did the "man" whom Yosef encountered when he wandered, lost, in the fields around Shechem, know whom and what Yosef was talking about, who he was and who his brothers were?

Yeshayahu 61:9 says, "*Kol ro'eihem yakirum, ki hem zera berach Hashem*" (All who see them will recognize that they are the holy seed that God has blessed). The fear of Heaven is on their faces. Who they are is obvious to all. It is obvious on their faces, it is obvious in the way they dress, the way they comport themselves, the way they speak, the way they deal with people, in their way of *hatzne'a leches*, in the modesty and the quiet dignity by which they live their lives.

And so whoever sees them, even a strange man who encounters them in the fields of Shechem, recognizes immediately, in their uprightness, in their decency, in their goodness, in their inner holiness made manifest on their faces, who they are, whose sons they are, and Who their God is.

Parashas Vayeshev 5774

He's Not Heavy, He's My Brother (1)

This year I had to spend a great deal of money on new medical equipment and new technology. A lot. Hopefully, it's a good investment. But I had to do it anyway.

One small but pleasant benefit is that with all the credit card points I accrued, I was able to garner enough points to transform a coach ticket to Eretz Yisrael into a seat in business class. And that's where I am sitting right now, as I write.

As I passed the people on the long lines waiting to squeeze into the proverbial "sardine class," with which I am quite familiar, I saw a number of people whom I took to be *melamdim*, teachers of small children. The thought occurred to me that dedicating one's life to be a *melamed*, or similar servant of the Jewish People, usually also means never, or virtually never, escaping from sardine class. Sounds superficial, but think of it: that's part of their self-sacrificing dedication.

In the *parashiyos* we read this time of the year, the Avos and their fellow players in the drama of the founding of our unique nation not only set the pattern for all future generations, but also, by their dedicated actions, empower them to follow their lead. And so those who lead us and inspire us, each one of us who plays our role in the ongoing life of Klal Yisrael, draws upon the *koach* and the example and the lessons of those who came before us, back to Avraham Avinu. And in Vayeshev, especially to Yosef Hatzaddik.

Let's talk about angels. We're introduced to them in the Torah in Parashas Vayera, when the three *malachim* appear before the ninety-nine-year-old Avraham, on the third, painful day after his *bris*.

We know that *malachim* have but one mission at a time. Refael came to heal Avraham. (Later, his mission was to save Lot.) Michael came to announce Sarah's impending pregnancy and giving birth to a son at age ninety. And Gavriel came to destroy Sedom.

Upon leaving Avraham, the remaining two *malachim*, Gavriel and Refael, turn and *va'yashkifu al pnei Sedom*. Literally, they cast their gaze upon Sedom. Rashi tells us that typically, in Scripture, use of the word *va'yashkifu* (or a derivative) is associated with something bad, with anger, with punishment (as it is here: they looked upon Sedom to target it for destruction), except in one place: the prayer of one who brings *maaser* to be distributed to the poor includes the entreaty *"hashkifah mi'me'on kodshecha, min haShamayim, u'varech es amcha, es Yisrael"* (Devarim 26:15). Gaze upon us from Your Heavenly abode and bless Your people, Israel.

Says Rashi, great is the power of tzedakah; it transforms *rogez* (anger), usually associated with that word, *va'yashkifu*, to *rachamim*.

Now we are introduced to the youthful Yosef, aged seventeen. We are told (37:2): *v'hu naar es bnei Bilhah v'es bnei Zilpah neshei aviv, va'yavei Yosef es dibasam raah el avihem*.

This *pasuk* tells us three things about Yosef. *V'hu naar*: he was busy with the childishly youthful activity of making himself look pretty. *Es bnei Bilhah*: he stood up for, and especially associated with, the sons of Bilhah and Zilpah, whom the sons of Leah abused by calling them "servants." *Va'yavei Yosef es dibasam raah el avihem*: he tattled to his father about his brothers' activities that he judged to be wrong, suspecting them of various misdeeds, including inappropriate interest in the local Canaanite girls.

As the story unfolds, Yosef is dispatched to find his brothers, somewhere in the vicinity of Shechem, and he is found by a "man," wandering in the fields. *Tanchuma* identifies this "man" as none other than Gavriel, the *malach*. Gavriel asks him, *"Mah tevakesh?"* (What do you seek?). Actually, literally, it says, "What *will* you seek?" It is a challenge. Yosef replies, *"Es achai anochi mevakesh"* (I am seeking my brothers).

Yosef, the pretty boy, the *"naar,"* is *"to'eh."* Literally, he is lost; he is wandering. What direction will he take in life? The time has now come to declare himself.

Some of his *naar* actions were those of youth. But what motivated the rest of his behavior? Who is he really?

And who challenges him? The *malach* Gavriel. The same *malach* whose mission it was to destroy Sedom and every person in it.

Now, while it is the nature of a *malach* to have only one *shlichus*, one purpose at a time, the same Gavriel who was *mashkif* on Sedom with an eye to destroy it utterly is also associated with the blessing of *hashkifah mi'me'on kodshecha*.

Every night during Krias Shema al Hamitah, we recite the famous verse *"mi'yemini Michael, mi'smoli Gavriel…"* The angel Michael is to my right, and Gavriel is to my left. But wait! We also have a *maamar*, *"Yemino mechabek, smolo dochek"* (The right hand embraces, the left pushes away)! Watch out for that Gavriel, whose *shlichus* can be to destroy. He is not a "wimpy" *malach*. He is a *gavra* (a strong figure) – alluded to in his very name. But, as Rashi taught us, that very power to destroy can be transformed to the limitless power and blessing associated with *chesed*: *hashkifah mi'me'on kodshecha*.

Mah tevakesh? Gavriel asks Yosef: What's your choice? What's your motive? What in your nature underlies your actions with your brothers? What made you hang out with the sons of Bilhah and Zilpah, and "stick it" to the sons of Leah? What made you tattle on them to your father?

Yosef replies (37:16), *es achai anochi mevakesh!* Yes, I held the sons of Leah accountable, but out of love! I'm their brother! I care so much about them. They are *shivtei Kah*. Their standards must be the highest, their actions pure.

Gavriel, with the potential power to destroy, then points Yosef in the direction of his destiny. Yosef is put to the test. Sorely. He is enslaved (payback for telling his father that the sons of Leah looked upon the sons of the *shefachos* as servants themselves), and he faces the scorching test of *eishes Potiphar* (payback for accusing them of *arayos* with the Canaanite girls).

In the end, Yosef proves himself to be the Yosef Hatzaddik that he has been known as for all time. In prison, in enslavement, he remains a man of God. With *eishes Potiphar*, he remains a man of God.

And so, from the depths of prison, from the pit, Yosef is brought up for his encounter with Pharaoh. The Gemara tells us that because Yosef was *mekadesh Shem Shamayim* when he fled from *eishes Potiphar*, he was rewarded with a letter from God's name.

A *heh* was added (see Tehillim 81:6, *eidus bi'Yhosef samo*). And the Gemara (*Sotah* 36b) goes further: Yosef, who could not have stood before or succeeded with Pharaoh unless he knew all seventy languages, was taught those languages the night before his encounter with Pharaoh. And he was enabled to learn those languages only by the strength of having the *heh* from Hashem's name added to his own.

And who was it that taught Yosef those seventy languages? The *malach* Gavriel.

No coincidence. Gavriel sent Yosef down this pathway. Gavriel set him up to be tested. Gavriel set him up for his potential undoing – *va'yashkef*. And Gavriel was also the agent of his ascent to power. Because Yosef was Yosef Hatzaddik, because his actions with his brothers were actually all driven by love and *chesed*, the potential *va'yashkef* of punishment became the actual *va'yashkef* of *berachah*.

Yosef suffered for his brothers. One of my pet theses is that Yosef merited being the only person in Tanach – which is filled with the names and the accomplishments of the Avos and so many great tzaddikim – to whose name is appended the title Hatzaddik, because of his unique propensity to empathize with and feel the pain of others. A capable man, who could rule all Egypt in a time of crisis, he was also soft-natured and a *baal bechi*: he was prone to tears, as the Torah attests. And his tears typically welled up upon the discomfiture of others.

Perhaps this somewhat dual nature of Yosef, the firm ruler and the soft-hearted tzaddik, had something to do with the dual nature of the *malach* Gavriel, with whom his destiny was so bound up.

Those who suffer for us and carry the burden for us (among them those whose consciously made choices predetermine that if they can afford a ticket to Israel at all, they will have to squeeze into sardine class!) also possess the power, by virtue of their *chesed* – and this is a power we can *all* tap into – to turn the harshness of *va'yashkifu al pnei Sedom* into the *berachah* of "*Hashkifah mi'me'on kodshecha u'varech es amcha, es Yisrael, v'es ha'adamah asher nasata lanu, ka'asher nishbata la'avoseinu, eretz zavas chalav u'dvash*" (Devarim 26:15).

Parashas Vayeshev 5772

Miketz

173

I was on a ship this past year, and, thinking of ships, my thoughts turned to the vessel that brought my parents and brother to America in January 1947. They came on the *Marine Marlin*, an old bucket that had served as a troopship during the war, in a crossing that had virtually everyone vomiting with sea sickness the entire voyage. Still, it was far better than where they had been before, including the Displaced Persons camp in Berlin, at Schlachtensee.

Curious about what happened to the *Marine Marlin* afterward, I Googled it. In a flash, an image came up that included a small picture of the ship on a later Atlantic crossing. And in a flash, I recognized the image of my grandfather, Shlomo Nussbaum, and my grandmother, Brandel, sitting on the deck, together with a few other elderly survivors.

I had had no idea that they had come, a year or so later, on the same ship. They all looked thoroughly beaten up.

My grandfather looked much the same as I knew him afterward, a quiet, dignified, and laconic man with a full white beard, in a double-breasted suit he must have gotten in his DP camp in Munich, and a round, Chassidic black hat. His hands were gripping his knees. Born eight years after the end of the American Civil War, he was about seventy-five years old at the time. He did not seem to have changed much between then and when he passed away at age ninety, in good health, in his sleep, apparently *b'neshikas Hashem*, his noble soul reclaimed by God with a divine kiss.

My grandmother, in the picture, was about seventy-three, but she looked 173. She lived in America for only a couple of years. (I was less than three when she died, but I do remember her. She was extremely sweet.) The cause of death, according to her death certificate, was "starvation." I always assumed that meant health sequelae subsequent to years of deprivation. When I saw that picture, however, I realized that something else was going on.

The look on my *bubbe*'s face in that picture told me that the real cause of her death was a broken heart.

Brandel Hoffert was born in Kolbesov (Kolbuszowa) to Hersh (Tzvi Yaakov) and Feige Hoffert, a highly respected family, in 1875. At age fifteen she was betrothed to Shlomo Nussbaum, age seventeen, of Dzhikov (Tarnobzeg). The Dzhikover Rebbe, the Ateres Yeshuah, was the *shadchan*. They were married two years later and settled in Kolbesov, where Shlomo became a successful lumber merchant.

A very *frum* young Chassid, Shlomo was reluctant even to see her before they were married. The Rebbe's word that this was "*a gitte zach*," his perfect match, was good enough for him. Once married, the two were widely known as lovebirds who doted on each other. Shlomo provided for her very well and gave her as good a life as one lived in that time and place.

God blessed them with nine children. The youngest, Nechama, died in childhood, a sadly common occurrence in those times. The family always suspected that the town pharmacist, drunk when he filled the doctor's prescription, played a role in her death.

The other children thrived and did very well. The family was well off and respected. Life was good (if you discount that they lived in pogrom-prone Poland).

We all know what happened. The "seven good years" were followed by the seven worst years in history.

Because of my grandfather's prominence in town, he understood, as the Germans approached, that he would be a target. Indeed he was: the Germans, well informed by the Polish neighbors, knew his name and came looking for him almost immediately upon their arrival, as well as for the other notables. But he and his wife had already escaped eastward, just ahead of the Wehrmacht, along with many thousands of others. No longer young, they endured, in Siberia and other far-flung lands, years of privation, starvation, squalor, forced labor, disease, freezing cold, and choking heat, but they remained alive. Many of their fellow escapees, including close relatives, did not. Those who did not flee, the mass of Jews who had young children, or who did not have the means or the drive to run, perished at the hands of the German mass murderers.

Of their children, Yossel was in America (with sons serving in the US Army), and Liebe was in Eretz Yisrael. Leizer, Chana (my mother), and Sheindel survived, having fled eastward as well, and, as well, suffering those same miseries. But they lived.

Frimit, the oldest, remained in Poland with her children, and with them, and her husband, was murdered, except for her teenaged daughter Genia, who did manage to escape, and ultimately reached Eretz Yisrael as one of the Yaldei Teheran.

Rochma remained in Poland with her children, and with them, and her husband, was murdered.

Pinye, a *gaon*, remained in Poland with his children, and with them, and his wife, was murdered.

When that photo was taken on the deck of the *Marine Marlin*, in late 1947 or 1948, Shlomo and Brandel Nussbaum, elderly survivors of the horrors that befell them, had lost the majority of their offspring, killed in the cruelest ways, to the genocidal Germans and their Polish and Ukrainian helpers.

When that photo was taken on the deck of the *Marine Marlin*, as that elderly couple was headed toward a new life, to the extent that a new life was possible, all the good years that came before had been swallowed up by the seven bad years. The fat cows on the banks of the Nile had been consumed by the gaunt cows, and nothing of the fat cows remained showing. The thin, sick stalks had consumed the robust ones, and nothing of the good stalks remained showing.

How could it?

Seventy-three-year-old Brandel (not really old these days, is it?) looked 173. She was alive, she was sweet and loving, but the good years of her life had been cruelly consumed by the bad years, and virtually nothing of the good years remained showing.

There were those who remained alive after the Holocaust, but did not really survive it.

I believe my *bubbe* was one of them. Even surrounded by a loving remaining family, a doting husband and surviving children, even a new grandchild (me) or two, in the end, the gaunt cows, the sick stalks, prevailed. She probably did die of the sequelae of starvation, but I am certain it was not just about physical nutrition. The goodness of life that she had enjoyed before had been sucked out of her, leaving no sign of those good years on her worn face.

Yosef's sudden rise to prominence was prompted by Pharaoh's great agitation over his dream. We understand that Pharaoh was cruel, but we have no reason to think that this mighty king was stupid. He clearly saw that he was being sent a message, a terrible one, but he did not know its practical meaning, or what to do about it.

Life, and history, have taught us that the fat cows can be consumed by the gaunt ones, leaving nothing showing; that the robust stalks can be consumed by the sick ones, leaving nothing showing; that the seven good years can be undone by seven bad ones, leaving nothing of the good years showing; that life, and the world, can be turned upside down, even in a second.

Pharaoh wanted Yosef to interpret his dream, but also to control it, to make it good, to mitigate its frightening message. Yosef replied that it was not up to him, but to God.

And then he told Pharaoh how to manage the situation, how to make the best of it, and that also was from God.

Yosef was telling us, as well, that there will be troubles in life, sometimes terrible ones. That is up to God, although God has also told us that His judgment is affected by our behavior. But we cannot know the mind of God, we cannot see the big picture, we cannot expect guaranteed results as viewed from our limited perspective, we cannot understand all the consuming gaunt cows that appear to leave no trace of the good.

We might, God forbid, have to suffer. We might, God forbid, have to look 173 at age seventy-three.

But even then, we can remain sweet, and loving, and loyal, and faithful, and good, as did Bubbe, who went to her grave a loyal child of God, blessed to have been the wife of Shloime Nussbaum, worthy daughter of Hershele Hoffert, mother of surviving generations of Klal Yisrael.

Perhaps that was the only way to somehow mitigate what happened.

With every deep line in her face, she bought the rest of us life. And I remember, as a very young child, as I gazed into that lined face, I also saw, in her soft eyes, eyes that retained the warmth of her earlier life, an early lesson in love, devotion, faith, loyalty, and hope.

Parashas Miketz 5776, Yerushalayim Ir Hakodesh

How Mighty Is the Rock of My Salvation

The little boy peered out the window for a moment and then quickly hunkered down on the floor of the cable car. That one look made him aware that he was in a little tin can hanging by a wire, suspended over an abyss that was at least a thousand feet high, and seemingly miles on either side from safe, solid ground. He announced that he had changed his mind about becoming an Israeli Air Force pilot when he grew up.

The young woman stood on the Alpine mountain, overlooking incredibly beautiful vistas of snow-capped mountains and verdant valleys. At least fifty or perhaps a hundred feet from the edge, she threw herself down in the cow plop where she stood, out of fear of falling off the edge. This normal, intelligent woman, no coward, had been seized by an irrational, yet really normal (if somewhat exaggerated at that point) fear of heights.

Some of us do not experience this sensation at all. But it is common to have it, to at least some degree. Ask anyone who has ever stood on a narrow, high ledge. I have.

And so I did not relish the prospect of climbing into a cherry picker basket that was about to lift me up to a ridiculous height, in the freezing, howling wind. I had been asked to recite the *berachos* and to light one of those wonderful Chabad Chanukah menorahs in a public ceremony. In truth, it scared me. But I had no choice. I was committed.

A memory flashed through my mind. Many years ago, I was with some boys who were out on a Shabbos afternoon doing boyish things. I found myself on a narrow, high ledge behind an apartment house near the shul, at least thirty feet above the concrete pavement, sweaty palms holding on to a chain-link fence for dear life as I inched my way to safety, which was perhaps fifty feet away, fifty feet that looked like a mile. How did I get myself into this? What would my parents say if they saw me up here, foolishly and pointlessly putting my life at risk? The other boys did it, and I could not back down.

Well, I had gotten myself into this current situation by agreeing to the seemingly innocuous honor of being the reciter of the *berachos* and the lighter of the menorah.

Shivering in the icy wind, I forced myself into the little bucket that was supposed to suspend me safely way up in the air. What if I fell out? Would I tip over as I leaned to light the menorah? Why weren't the other two people in the little bucket scared? At least they didn't look scared. Their presence helped.

Up we went. It was freezing cold. The bucket was surprisingly steady, but still swayed somewhat in the wind. Below me I saw the crowd looking up expectantly. I was handed the lighting implements and began to recite. I opened the glass receptacles and lit the candles. Someone started singing Maoz Tzur, and those in the crowd who could joined in. The cold and the wind and the fear all disappeared, replaced by a warmth that was far greater than the negatives it had dispelled. The scene below me, in the light of those candles, was beautiful and moving and endearing. I actually regretted it when the mechanism went into action and brought me back down to earth.

We celebrate Chanukah in the winter primarily because that is the anniversary of the miracle of our deliverance. So too with Purim. But, I submit, in the great scheme of God's plan and His Providence, there is a reason for that, and a lesson. And, seasonally speaking, those days are a prelude to the holiday of our formative, definitive great deliverance, Pesach, the holiday that is always in the spring, Chag Ha'aviv.

Yosef Hatzaddik (the only person in Tanach given that title) was a little boy when life betrayed him with the death of his mother. He was further betrayed when his brothers resented him, and his father apparently did not help straighten that out. He was betrayed by his brothers when they threw him in the pit and sold him into slavery. He was betrayed by his boss's wife and was again thrown in the pit, this time an Egyptian prison pit, languishing there for *ten years*, only to be betrayed again by the *sar hamashkim*, causing him to sit there for yet another two years.

We all know people who, as children, were betrayed in some manner, by a parent, a teacher, a sibling, and who, as a result, ultimately went spinning off the reservation, they and their descendants lost to the nation. And the nation, with its God, its Torah, and its community, lost to them.

Yosef Hatzaddik, obviously incredibly strong from his earliest youth, held on. He was steady, and true, and resolute, a young man of faith and of resolve, who knew who he was, who he had to be, and Whose Providence guides the events of life and of the world. He understood that whatever his destiny was, he was in God's hands, and that wherever he was, whether in the pit or at the pinnacle of power, that consideration alone would be his guide.

And so this much-betrayed little boy, this tzaddik, went on to save his people from hunger and set into motion the chain of events that led to Sinai, and ultimately, to the final Redemption.

Along the way to Sinai, they emerged from the "pit" that was cruel slavery, and the dark "winter" of enduring that bondage in corrupt Egyptian society, to ascend, triumphant, in the miraculous Exodus, the holiday known as Chag Ha'aviv, Pesach, which *always* follows soon after the dark winter and heralds the spring.

In the dark, cold winter of oppression, it is sometimes hard to see or to believe that the light and the warmth of springtime will eventually arrive. And so we begin the winter with the lights of Chanukah and remembrance of its triumphs and miracles of redemption, and as winter drags on, we are reinforced with Purim and remembrance of its own triumphs and miracles of redemption, that we never lose faith, and never lose hope, and never lose sight of Who keeps us always close to Him, even in the pit, even in the darkest and coldest winter.

It is only normal and natural to have fear. It is part of the instincts that keep us alive. In some of us, some of those fears may be somewhat exaggerated. In life, though, sometimes that cable car wire does snap, sometimes that high ledge does give way.

We pray that for us, those things do not happen. And sometimes we do find ourselves high up in that cable car, up on that ledge, in that cherry picker. Sometimes we are suspended in the cold and the wind. And sometimes we are sunk low in the pit.

The lesson of Chanukah coming to light up the cold, dark winter night, the lesson of Purim coming to cheer up the lingering winter, the lesson of Pesach following, ushering in the springtime with its message of redemption, rebirth, and our very *chosenness*, the lesson of Yosef Hatzaddik, the youth who held on to his *tzidkus* in the most trying of circumstances, is that the warmth and the light, and the promise in God's hovering Presence, always close, even if hidden, even if at times impossibly hard to imagine, can dissolve any fear, can warm up any cold, can dispel any darkness.

Parashas Miketz, Chanukah 5774

Not in Their Faces

The tiles on the bathroom floor were a jarring mismatch. The patch job, done who knows when, made no attempt to hide itself. There was really no reason to. Nothing else in the room, or in the rest of the apartment, looked great either.

The plumber, a middle-aged non-Jew, looked up from the floor where he was patching the ancient pipes under the sink. "Why," he asked my mother, "do you people live in a dump like this?"

"It's what we can afford," my mother replied.

"Come on!" he said, with an incredulous look and irony in his voice. "Everybody knows that *you people* have money."

Why do you suppose that everybody "knows" that Jews have money?

Is ostentation a Jewish trait? Certainly not. But that's not to say that there aren't Jews who don't keep their wealth hidden. And even in times and places where many or most Jews were very poor, their gentile neighbors frequently assumed that they were, in fact, stereotypically, loaded. And hated them for it.

Tznius is a key concept in Jewish life and Jewish philosophy. And that does not just refer to hemlines. It's ironic that showiness is common enough among some

Jews that it is often taken to be, in fact, a Jewish trait. But that's confusing a trait seen among some Jews with the Jewishness, or un-Jewishness, of that trait.

We know that the *neviim* preached it: "*Higgid lecha adam mah tov, u'mah Hashem doresh mimcha, ki im asos mishpat v'ahavas chesed, v'hatzne'a leches im Elokecha*" (Michah 6:8).

A primary source for this lesson, aside from the common sense and the Torah-based *hashkafah* of it, is found in Parashas Miketz.

Crop failure and famine prevailed in the world. Only in Egypt was there food to be had, in the storehouses Yosef had established. When everyone else was out of food, Yaakov's household still had. But he was careful, and he was concerned. He did not want his neighbors "looking at him," in the way that the envious look at the objects of their envy, in the way that gentiles sometimes look at Jews.

"*Lama tisra'u?*" he says to his sons. Why should you stick out, why should our neighbors look at you? Everybody is going down to Egypt to buy food. You go too.

And when you go, my beautiful boys, avoid an *ayin hara*: don't walk in all together, and don't let people see the money in your wallets. They're looking at you anyway.

Don't stick their eyes out. It's unhealthy.

That's really good advice. There is a Yiddish expression, when one ostentatiously exhibits something that makes someone else angry and resentful, "*Er hot im oisgeshtochen di oygen*" (He stuck him in the eyes); he figuratively poked his eyes out.

In the *Elokai netzor* prayer we append to Shemoneh Esrei, in the Nusach Sefard version, there is a prayer *she'lo saaleh kinas adam alai v'lo kinasi al acherim*.

We pray that others not envy us, and that we not envy others. This is so important that we say this prayer three times a day. And how many times a day do we say *bli ayin hara*?

The Gemara (*Sanhedrin* 29b) says, "*adam asui she'lo l'hasbia es atzmo...(v')es banav*," not to appear loaded with money, to avoid jealousy or *ayin hara*. Perhaps he doesn't need to be, as the Gemara puts it, like an *achbar* (a weasel), who sits on gold coins and has no benefit from them. A person whom God has blessed economically may, indeed, benefit from that blessing. But he is far better off not being too showy about it. It's just not healthy, it's not wise, and it's not fine.

This is a lesson derived from our forefather Yaakov, who sent his sons out into the gentile world with very sound advice. We should all take it to heart, individually and as a nation.

Parashas Miketz 5772

Truth and Beauty

> Thou still unravish'd bride of quietness,
> Thou foster-child of silence and slow time,
> Sylvan historian, who canst thus express
> A flowery tale more sweetly than our rhyme:
>
> . . . .
>
> Heard melodies are sweet, but those unheard
> Are sweeter: therefore, ye soft pipes, play on;
> Not to the sensual ear, but, more endear'd,
> Pipe to the spirit ditties of no tone:
> Fair youth, beneath the trees, thou canst not leave
> Thy song, nor ever can those trees be bare;
>
> . . . .
>
> When old age shall this generation waste,
> Thou shalt remain, in midst of other woe
> Than ours, a friend to man, to whom thou say'st,
> "Beauty is truth, truth beauty," – that is all
> Ye know on earth, and all ye need to know.

John Keats, the early nineteenth-century Romantic poet, in his famous "Ode on a Grecian Urn," contemplated the figures on an old Greek vase and envied, in a way, their lifeless lives. They can't accomplish anything, they cannot ever complete the acts they are in the midst of doing, but they also will never grow old or fade away as mortal human beings do. They will always be exactly as they are. To Keats, and to those whose mindset was shaped by the ethos of the culture that gave rise to them, the highest attainment of civilization is beauty:

> "Beauty is truth, truth beauty," – that is all
> Ye know on earth, and all ye need to know.

Did you ever look at a Ming vase? The Empire of the Great Ming ruled in China from 1368 to 1644. In that period and culture, this form of porcelain art was brought to perfection. As works of art, they are as breathtakingly beautiful as they are sought after and priceless. The society that produced this art also had a million men under arms and, with force and violence, widely expanded its empire.

I am no expert on Chinese culture. I have done some reading on twentieth-century China. There is much that is remarkable about it. What I did not come across (it may be there, but I did not discern it) was any emphasis on what we call *chesed*. Nor does one get much sense of it from other societies either, whether they find virtue and truth in factory production, widgets, or in "beauty," rather than in the kind of goodness we, in our culture, immediately recognize as a basic fundament of our own civilization, *chesed*.

Back in the dawn of civilization, when the world and its various aspects was divided among the families of man, Noach pronounced the blessing *"Yaft Elokim l'Yefes"* (Bereishis 9:27), apportioning special powers related to art and beauty to the cultures derived from his son Yefes. The beauties of Persian and Greek art are the result. Rome later appropriated that art. Indeed, the finest artists in the ancient Roman world were, in fact, Greek, carrying on their own more ancient traditions.

It was this emphasis on beauty and physical perfection that drove Greek culture. Indeed, the Greek pantheon of gods were representations of perfect human physical specimens (with a load of moral imperfections), imbued with superhuman powers.

They did anything they wanted with anyone and to anyone. Later incorporating Persian elements, Hellenism became the civilizational norm of the ancient word – except for those pesky Jews.

The Jews could not abide a civilization that rested solely on the physical and the man-driven rational. The Greeks could not tolerate a culture that insisted on the preeminence of God-driven morality. The result was the Chanukah story.

The struggle was not essentially political. The Jews did not revolt because of Greek military or political hegemony. They were resigned to that. They revolted because the Greeks would not let them be Jews. The Greeks would even not let them be *Greek* Jews. The Greeks would not let them cling to the God of their fathers, a God Who mandated a moral, legal, and spiritual approach to life that was inimical to Greek culture. They revolted because they could not subsist on just art and physical beauty and call that life. They revolted because they could not live in a world that extolled art and beauty, but in which cruelty was a way of life. They revolted because of what it meant to be the children of the Avos, and they could not give that up.

They revolted because they could not live in a world without God and without goodness.

They revolted because they could not live in a world without *chesed*.

They revolted because Yosef Hatzaddik cried, and because his brothers were overcome with shame and remorse.

Yosef's brothers were mistaken in their judgment of him, but even while they continued to believe him guilty, during all those years of separation, they also understood that they had acted with what amounted to cruelty to their father, and also came to realize that however guilty they thought him to be, in the end, they were cruel to Yosef as well.

When sent to Egypt to buy food, they had, in fact, fanned out all over, determined to find their lost brother and return him to their father. And now, confronted by the apparent cruelty of the viceroy, searching for what they might have done wrong in life to deserve this, so many years later, the conclusion was obvious to them. Clearly, over all those years, it had never left their minds and their consciences.

In what is, to me, one of the most moving passages in all the Torah, the brothers confront their sin: "They said to each other, we are guilty! Our brother! We saw the desperate misery of his soul [*tzoras nafsho*], as he begged us for mercy, and we did not listen! That is why this misery has now befallen us!" (Bereishis 42: 21).

It was not that they undertook to punish him for his perceived transgressions that was their main sin, as they understood it. It was that their little brother, aged seventeen, begged them to spare him, not to sell him into slavery; he fell at their feet and wept. They should have forgiven him for his youth. They should have softened their hearts, no matter how they resented him. They were not Canaanites, nor Greek nor Persian nor Roman nor Chinese. They were the first Jews and knew their mission well. They were the sons of Yaakov Avinu, grandchildren of Yitzchak, with whom they also lived, and of Avraham. They came into the world having been carried in the pure vessels that were the wombs of the Imahos. They had no right to be cruel. It was, for them, utterly out of place and out of character.

Yosef overhears their contrition and is overcome. Time and again, he must rush off, weep, and wash his face to hide his tears before returning to face them. The viceroy of Egypt, who is capable of firmly steering that empire through a catastrophic famine, centralizing political power in the process, is, at his core, a man of love and *chesed*, of emotion.

He weeps as well because he comes to learn, as the drama plays out, that his brothers, whom he thought cruel, who had mistreated him cruelly, are overcome with contrition and are, in fact, themselves at their core *baalei chesed* who had gone astray in this matter, but who have recognized their sin and wholeheartedly repented.

And then he is able to forgive them and reveal his true identity to them with the unparalleled graciousness and love that earned him the title, for all time, Yosef Hatzaddik.

This world, to be sweet, needs beauty in it, and indeed God has imbued it with great beauty. It needs ambition and industriousness to thrive, and indeed God has implanted in mankind the drive to achieve. It needs grace and charm, and those exist. But those things are not enough. They do not carry the world, nor are they sufficient rationale for its existence. Law is needed, but law without morality is neutral at best, and usually steeped in cruelty. Law, as God has given us to understand law as it should be, and morality, goodness, *chesed*, sustain the world.

Over the millennia, the message has emanated, through us, from Sinai and before, to the rest of mankind. Some have actually absorbed that lesson, on their own level.

Others, who think that art and beauty, money, commerce and industry, power and hegemony are what life is about, actually have no idea what life is about.

It is up to us teach them, if they are willing. It is up to us to us to be exemplars of morality and honesty and rectitude and kindness, of *chesed*, of conscience and the capacity for contrition and repentance, of love and mercy, of charity of coin and of the spirit.

It is up to us, as we are reminded by Yosef Hatzaddik and his brothers, as we are especially reminded by the brave and dedicated Chashmonaim on this joyous holiday of Chanukah, to bring light into what others have made a dark, dreary, and amoral world.

Parashas Miketz, Chanukah 5777

Vayigash

Everything Counts

The more one thinks about it, the more apparent becomes the amazing interaction and interplay of words and themes in the Torah, particularly in Sefer Bereishis. We, as a nation, are established in these *parashiyos*, and patterns of behavior and vital lessons for all generations are laid down for us. The actions of our forebears, even if they sometimes make us somewhat uncomfortable, are plainly stated so that we may learn and benefit from them.

A five-minute *derashah* that I heard yesterday from my good friend Rav Avigdor Burshtein, rabbi of the famous Hatzvi Yisrael (Chovevei Tzion) shul in Yerushalayim, blew me away. Allow me to recapitulate his theme.

After much travail, Yaakov Avinu finally breaks away from Lavan and returns to Eretz Yisrael, hoping there to live in peace and to establish Klal Yisrael. It is not to be as Yaakov has hoped. He must deal with Esav, who had sworn to kill him. His daughter Dinah steps out and is abducted and violated. Her brothers violently avenge the rape, and Yaakov is further upset, fearful that the local nations will now make war on them. Tragically, his beloved wife Rachel dies young, and he buries her by the roadside.

His eldest son Reuven, protecting his mother Leah's honor, interferes with Yaakov's personal marital business. His sons bicker. The sons of Leah are abusive to the sons of Bilhah and Zilpah. And then there's Yosef.

Yaakov loves Yosef exceedingly, igniting jealousy in the other sons, who come to hate Yosef, who makes no apparent effort to ingratiate himself with them. Rather, he stands apart and tells of his dreams, in which he rules over them. They bicker constantly. They complain to Yaakov about him, and he complains to Yaakov about them, bearing tales of their misdeeds. Ultimately, they sell him into slavery and fool their father into believing him dead, torn apart by a wild animal, and presumably devoured by it. Yaakov is absolutely inconsolable and remains so for twenty-two years. Yehudah, deposed by his brothers from his position of leadership, leaves town and faces public embarrassment in the Tamar affair.

Yaakov has anything but peace and tranquility. The story of his life.

Now let's look more closely at Yehudah – until now the leader of the brothers, and destined to be progenitor of Malchus Beis David and ultimately Moshiach.

It was Yehudah's idea to sell Yosef. Even though in the brothers' judgment Yosef actually deserved the death penalty, Yehudah convinced them to sell him instead. Later they complained that if he had insisted that they return Yosef to his father, they would have listened to him, and he was therefore responsible for the mess they wound up in.

What they actually did was slaughter a goat, dip Yosef's coat in it, and show it to their father. "*Haker na*," they said to Yaakov. Recognize this blood-spattered coat. Is it not Yosef's? Is it not the special coat you favored him with?

Irony: Yaakov himself had, years before, slaughtered goats and used them to fool his own father, Yitzchak, into bestowing the *berachos* upon him, rather than Esav, whose world then came crashing down. Yaakov fled to Lavan and encountered his brother again about twenty-two years later. Now, a slaughtered goat is used to fool Yaakov into thinking that Yosef was mauled to death, bringing his own world crashing down for the next twenty-two years.

Irony: Yehudah loses his wife, and then his two older sons, leaving him a widower with one son, for whose life he fears. Is that not what he had done to Yaakov, who lost Yosef and had but one son remaining from his own favored wife, Rachel, for whose life he feared?

Yehudah, meanwhile, is showcased in an aside placed smack in the middle of the Yosef story. Not by accident. Yehudah's son marries Tamar and then dies. The next brother marries her as a *yibum*, and he also dies. Yehudah is afraid to allow his remaining son to marry her. Then Yehudah's own wife dies. Tamar takes matters into her own hands and, disguising herself, fools Yehudah into being with her, thinking she is a *kedeshah*. He promises her, in payment, *a goat* (!). But he must leave an *eravon* (security deposit).

She asks for his seal, his staff, and his coat.

Later, when he tries to send her the goat, no one knows who he is talking about, and the goat is returned to him. As he looked at that goat, with which he had tried to pay a woman he thought to be a *kedeshah*, could he have not thought of the goat he and his brothers had used to fool their father, and which made him so miserable?

When Tamar, still maritally bound to the Yehudah family but now pregnant, is accused of adultery and condemned to death, she faces death rather than publicly embarrass Yehudah, imparting a lesson for all generations: it is preferable to allow oneself to be thrown into a fiery furnace rather than to embarrass someone publicly.

Instead, awaiting execution, she sends Yehudah his *eravon*: his seal, his staff, and his coat. And what does she say? "The man whose things these are is the father of my child. *Haker na* – whose are they?" The ball is now in his court. Faced with intense public embarrassment, Yehudah could have just kept quiet. Tamar would be dead, and no one would know. His response: *Tzadka mimeni*. Tamar is right and righteous, and I am wrong. I behaved in a shameful way and I admit it publicly. *Va'yaker Yehudah*. He recognized where truth, honesty, dignity, and *tzidkus* lay.

Irony: the brothers, instigated by Yehudah, showed Yosef's bloody coat to Yaakov and said "*haker na*" if this is your son's coat, setting off twenty-two years of miserable mourning.

Yehudah's public embarrassment, which he accepted upon himself, also came about with Tamar's words "*haker na.*"

And was it perhaps at the very moment that Tamar confronted Yehudah with the words "*haker na*," forcing him to confront not only his shame in his encounter with her, but his profound shame, and that of his brothers, when they used those very words with their father, showing him Yosef's bloody coat, that Yosef, whom the brothers wrongly judged to be a villain, in his own righteousness left his coat in the hands of *eishes Potiphar* and escaped sin?

When Yosef, as viceroy, tells the brothers not to return to Egypt unless they bring Binyamin with them, Yaakov refuses to allow it. But they must return to buy food. Yehudah convinces Yaakov by undertaking to be an *arev* – a personal guarantor, *b'olam hazeh* and *b'olam haba*.

Later, when Yosef says he will imprison Binyamin for stealing the cup, Yehudah confronts him. *Ki avdecha arav es hanaar.* Through my experience, through the hardships of my life, through my loss and my public embarrassment – through my shame – I have learned the lesson of the seriousness of personal responsibility, of *eravon*.

Irony: Yehudah's appeal to Yosef, dependent upon his personal responsibility as a guarantor, depends as well on his own history of failing his father in this regard, and the lesson in personal responsibility he learned from his deeply embarrassing encounter with the noble Tamar.

The intertwining connections, the lessons to be learned, the *middah k'neged middah* with which this entire story is replete can make you dizzy. In these *parashiyos* that center on Yosef Hatzaddik, two other tzaddikim stand out as well. Tamar, who was prepared to die by fire rather than to publicly shame someone, and Yehudah, who had the greatness of spirit to allow himself to be publicly shamed for the sake of truth, in order to do the right thing, and who thus indeed merited his father's trust in safeguarding Binyamin.

And together, Yehudah and Tamar merited becoming the progenitors of Moshiach ben David, even as Yosef Hatzaddik became the progenitor of Moshiach ben Yosef.

Parashas Vayigash 5772

Gracious

"Rabbi! Rabbi! Is there a blessing for the czar?"

"A blessing for the czar? Of course! May the Lord bless and keep the czar…*far away from us!*"

The famous joke from *Fiddler on the Roof* derives from the fact that there are, in Judaism, blessings for nearly everything. Everything we eat and drink. Things that we smell. Things that we hear. Many things that we see. The occasions of life. Good news. Bad news. Nearly everything. There is usually a *berachah*.

More on that later.

So, if it happened to you, what would you do? If your bigger brothers hated you and constantly ganged up on you, if your father did not help you, if your brothers finally threw you into a pit with snakes and scorpions and no water, if they later sold you into slavery, and then, no thanks to them, you survived and found yourself not only with power over them, but *absolute* power over them, answerable to no one, *what would you do?*

How would you respond, when you had the power and the opportunity, to their hatred and their betrayal? If you had, as a seventeen-year-old, powerless boy, pleaded with your big brothers, begged them not to sell you as a slave to a bunch of traveling Ishmaelites, begged them for your life, your home, pleaded with them, as their little brother, not to treat you so cruelly, and they heartlessly rebuffed you and gruffly sent you off, chained, to misery and a probable early death, what would you do if you had years to brood about it, and now you had them in your power?

We know what Yosef did. If one wishes to find the epitome of graciousness, an unparalleled example of being far greater in one's goodness than can be expected of anyone, Yosef is that exemplar. Yosef Hatzaddik.

Time and again, he is overcome with loving emotion. He weeps with its intensity. He is famous for it. And he is not a wimpy character; he is the viceroy of Egypt, its de facto dictator. And he is no fool, either. He knows full well that his brothers, agents of God's plan though they were, also had free will, and *chose* to act as they did. And yet, he weeps with loving emotion. He could have seen the big picture and, accepting it, could have also kept the message to himself, comforted *himself* with it. He did not have to comfort *them* with it. He did not have to tell them that they should not fret, that it was God's plan and His will that this incredible chain of events transpire. But, in his graciousness, he comforted them in their shame. His soothing words, an altar of gracious loving-kindness, brought them into his embrace.

Now look what happens when Yaakov Avinu passes on, and after the funeral the brothers fear that Yosef will, in their father's absence, take revenge upon them. After seventeen years of his treating them lovingly and kindly, their eating daily at his table, his providing sustenance for their families, the complete absence of recriminations, they still suspect that he will now turn around and act like most people would have. But if they thought that it was Yaakov's presence that held him back all this time, did they forget that Yaakov was indeed *not* present when, with tears, emotion, and loving embrace, he first revealed himself to them?

What made them think this way? *They saw something*. The *pasuk* only says that they saw that their father was dead, and that as a result, perhaps Yosef would now harbor a hatred against them. What, in fact, in relation to Yaakov's death, did they *see*?

Midrash Rabbah (100:8) offers two views. The first, quoted by Rashi, is Rabbi Levi's teaching that they saw that now that Yaakov was gone, Yosef no longer fed them at his table. They thought it must be because he hated them.

The real reason, Rabbi Tanchuma adds, was that Yosef wanted to *honor* his brothers. When Yaakov was alive, he placed Yosef at the head of the table, above Yehudah ("the king" and progenitor of Moshiach) and above Reuven (the *bechor*). Yosef reluctantly acquiesced, in deference to his father's wishes. Now that Yaakov was gone, Yosef could not bring himself to place himself above his brothers, so he stopped seating them at his table. The brothers did not see it that way.

The second explanation offered by the Midrash, by Rabbi Yitzchak, is profound indeed, and particularly telling with regard to who Yosef really was.

What the brothers saw, he says, was a side trip Yosef made while he was in Canaan to bury his father. They traveled north and east from Egypt to Chevron, and there they buried Yaakov in Me'aras Hamachpelah. Yosef was under Pharaoh's orders to return to Egypt immediately afterward. But he did make a detour. He traveled *further north* before turning back south to Egypt. He went to Shechem. He visited the pit his brothers had thrown him into all those years before.

The brothers, in their guilt, seeing him peer into that pit, concluded that he was brooding about what they did to him and nurturing a hatred for them.

The reality, Rabbi Tanchuma adds, is that he stood there and recited a *berachah*.

In that place, in the waterless pit that was a den of snakes and scorpions that his brothers threw him into, and from which his brothers sold him into slavery,

Yosef recited the *berachah* one makes at the site where a miracle was wrought on his behalf (*Berachos* 54a): *Baruch she'asa li nes ba'makom hazeh*. Praised is God, Who performed a miracle for me in this place.

What miracle was performed for Yosef in that place? There he was brutalized and degraded and sold into slavery and exile. It was only many years later, in Egypt, when he was brought out from prison to interpret Pharaoh's dream and was suddenly elevated from prisoner to viceroy of Egypt, that the miracle occurred. Why, then, did he make a pilgrimage to the pit, there to recite a *berachah* of thanks for a miracle wrought in that place, where there was no miracle?

Because, I submit, Yosef Hatzaddik, that consummately gracious tzaddik, in the depths of his misery and at the height of his power, never lost sight of the big picture, never despaired of God's guiding Providence, recognized the hand of God in every stage of his incredible journey, and, in his graciousness, no more blamed his brothers for his troubles than he credited Pharaoh for his rise to power. The snake pit in Shechem, the caravan of his enslavement into Egypt, the twelve years in the dungeon there, the dreamers, the dreams and their interpretations, the ascent to power, the saving of much of mankind from starvation, reuniting with his father and his brothers, setting the stage for the creation of the Nation of Israel and for the Revelation at Sinai, were all part of the same divine plan.

In Yosef's faith-driven benevolence, the miracle of salvation, the miracle that would ultimately lead to Sinai and to Jerusalem, started to play itself out as he sat helplessly among the snakes and the scorpions in that pit where his brothers cast him. And that is how he looked upon his brothers.

There are many tzaddikim mentioned in Scripture, and many good and kind-hearted people.

But only one do we identify by name as Hatzaddik, and one, in particular, stands out for the graciousness that marks his *tzidkus*. We are told his story not just to know how we came to be, but that we may learn how a person *can* be, and what we may, in our flights of aspirational fancy, dream and strive ourselves to be.

Parashas Vayigash 5774

Holy Shame

What's the worst non-medical faux pas a doctor can be guilty of? I did it.

It was an unguarded moment, one which I have never repeated and never forgotten.

I made reference, in speaking to the man in the exam chair, to his mother, who was sitting in the side chair. The "mother" responded, through clenched teeth, "I'm his wife."

I looked for a hole in the floor to open up, so I could jump in.

Wow. That was bad. I was terribly embarrassed. I never did that again.

Then again, there's embarrassment and there's embarrassment. In the larger scheme of things, there's worse.

Imagine the situation of Yosef's brothers when they learned the truth about his identity. Their shame and chagrin were so great that, according to midrashic sources, they actually, *literally*, died of embarrassment, and were immediately miraculously revived. (Several generations later, their descendants stood at Mount Sinai and, hearing the very voice of God, they too dropped dead, overcome, and they too were miraculously resuscitated with "dewdrops" from *techiyas hameisim*.)

It's interesting that Yosef, who was so emotional, so kind, so good-natured, so pure-hearted, so empathetically prone to weeping that he alone in Tanach bears the title "Hatzaddik," also put his brothers through a rather trying reconciliation process. As kind and giving as he was after his revelation, he was tough on them before. He needed to know if they had changed, if they had truly repented. He needed to see what they would do, during maximal stress, for Binyamin. And because there needed to be an accounting.

Yosef had engineered that Binyamin be snared, about to be enslaved for ostensibly stealing Yosef's chalice. What would the brothers now do to prevent that? Yehudah stepped forward and made their argument. "I see you are the spokesman," Yosef replied. "Why you? Is not Levi your older brother? And is not Shimon Levi's older brother? And is not Reuven older still, the firstborn? Why you?"

Yehudah replied that he had gotten Yaakov to agree to allowing Binyamin to travel to Egypt upon his, Yehudah's, assuming full responsibility for the boy (who was not his own mother's son). Yehudah promised their father and would now lay down his life for the boy if need be. "You took responsibility for the boy?" Yosef challenged him. "You cannot allow your father to be hurt? You will not allow your father to be bereft?" *If so, why didn't you do the same for another younger brother, when instead you threw him into a pit, and then sold him to a band of Ishmaelites for twenty pieces of silver and caused such pain to your father, telling him that the boy was torn to pieces by a wild animal?*

Hearing this, Yehudah broke down completely and wept, exclaiming, "How can I ever face my father again?" *Ki eich e'eleh el avi?* (Bereishis 44:34).

But Yosef was not finished. How would he know about the sale of the brother?

"Didn't you tell me that this one's [Binyamin's] older brother is dead? I know otherwise! *I'm the one who bought him! He told me all about it!*" And then Yosef called out, "Yosef the son of Yaakov, come in here! Yosef the son of Yaakov, come in here!"

At this denouement, the brothers desperately looked all about. Of course, no one came in. The breaking point had been reached. Yosef could stand it no longer. Don't look all around for Yosef, he told them. You're looking at him. I am Yosef. And that is when, tzaddikim and *baalei teshuvah* all, *parchah nishmasam*, in their extreme shame and in their distress, their souls left their bodies, and God had to bring them back to life.

Yosef, ever the man in charge, had additional *cheshbonos* as he engineered this revelation.

Not only could he stand it no longer emotionally, but he also knew what his brothers were capable of. He knew that they could destroy Egypt to get Binyamin back, and that they would, and indeed they were on the verge of doing so.

And so, in sending everyone out of the room – his entire retinue and his imperial guard – he was exposing himself to great personal danger. But he did so rather than risk embarrassing his brothers in public. How interesting that the very same Yehudah had also been spared public embarrassment some time before when Tamar was prepared to allow herself to be killed rather than to cause him public humiliation. What lessons we are taught by our forebears!

When Rabbi Elazar came to these verses, he would weep and say: if the effect of human reproof was so profound (as it was on the brothers), how much more so that of God! (*Chagigah* 4b).

אבא כהן ברדלא אמר: אוי לנו מיום הדין, אוי לנו מיום התוכחה!
בלעם חכם של העובדי כוכבים לא היה יכול לעמוד בתוכחתה של אתונו ....
יוסף קטנן של שבטים היה ולא הי יכולים לעמוד בתוכחתו ....
לכשיבא הקב"ה ויוכיח כל אחד ואחד ... על אחת כמה וכמה!

Abba Cohen Bardela says, woe is us for the Day of Judgment!
Bilaam, the wisest of the gentiles, could not withstand the reproof of his donkey;
Yosef was the youngest of the brothers, and they could not withstand his reproof.
When Hakadosh Baruch Hu comes to judge us, how much more so!
(*Bereishis Rabbah* 93:10)

We are taught that for everything that we say, for everything that we do, we will one day be called to an accounting. What a frightening prospect. But it is the reality of human existence: an "eye" sees, an "ear" hears, the "book" is open, all is recorded, and we will have to answer.

A hallmark of the Jewish People, inherited from their forebears, is that they are *baishanim*, prone to embarrassment. One cannot be conscience stricken unless one has a conscience. Antisemites mock Jews for their conscience. Yosef's brothers, the *shevatim*, literally died of embarrassment, so great was their regret and their shame at what they had done (even though when they did it, they believed that they had ample justification). And Yosef's response? He was kind and merciful and gracious and generous. The other attributes that mark the Jewish People are that they are *rachmanim* and *gomlei chasadim* (gracious practitioners of loving-kindness). Indeed, when Yosef, as the viceroy, put the pressure on them, the brothers concluded that it was because, all those years earlier, they should have had greater *rachmanus* for Yosef when he pleaded with them – even if he was guilty.

The Torah is not a storybook. It tells us what it tells us because these are things we need to know and to internalize, so that we may live our lives as we should. Life and its relationships are not simple. Our forebears, the great men and women who preceded us, contrary to a simplistic sense of our history, like us, had issues to deal with. Indeed, we can relate to those issues, because that is life, that is the nature of the world that the Creator placed us in.

But he also gave us holy role models who teach us how to cope, how to navigate our way through this life, as we reach and strive for the very goals those forebears sought to attain and taught us to seek as well: knowing and doing the will of God in this world, so that we may merit being close to Him in the infinite world to come.

Parashas Vayigash, Zos Chanukah 5776, Yerushalayim Ir Hakodesh

In God We Trust

There is a well-known *vort* on "*ach tov va'chesed yirdefuni*," David Hamelech's declaration that goodness and *chesed* pursue him all the days of his life, addressing the obvious question: Who would flee from goodness and *chesed* that they should need to pursue him? The answer, of course, is that in life it is not always obvious to us what will, in the end, turn out to be good for us. We may, in fact, flee from it, thinking it will be bad, and only God's *chesed* makes it turn out for the best, even if we did not know it from the beginning.

Every person is faced, constantly, with the question in life, for matters large and small, what is the right choice to make, the wisest path to follow? How many of us are so smart that we always know the right answer? None of us. Of course, our moral and religious compass will tell us, hopefully, what is the "right thing to do," the difference between right and wrong, in making moral or faith-based choices, but life is filled with choices, often fundamentally life-changing, that are not accompanied by those more obvious signposts.

And so, while *mazal*, God's blessing, His divine plan for us and for the world, affect the *outcome* of the choices we make, the paths we choose, *how we look upon* the outcome or even the path itself is a function of the spirit, the faith within us.

Yosef and his brothers, in their youth, did not get along well. He rubbed them the wrong way, so to speak, and they were not well disposed toward him. They thought him spoiled, indulged, and grandiose. They thought his manner and his path were destructive, interfering with their God-mandated mission to build Klal Yisrael. And so the stage was set for tragedy.

When they had had their fill of him, when they could tolerate him no more, when he persisted in behavior that, in their minds, went beyond all limits of acceptability, they tried and judged him, finding him guilty of sedition and high crimes, resulting in his being cast down into slavery in Egypt.

It could not have been easy for them. The Torah reveals a little, but only a little, of the dissent between them regarding the choices they made. Ultimately, majority ruled, and they presented a united front. They believed their actions to have been just. But they knew, as well, that what they had done, however just, however within the law, was also harsh and cruel. They were, after all, *shivtei Kah*, the holy, righteous sons of Yaakov Avinu and the progenitors of Klal Yisrael. And so they carried within them the burden of what they did.

It was, of course, harder still for Yosef. Only seventeen years old, his own brothers had thrown him into a pit filled with snakes and scorpions, ignored his cries for mercy, and sold him into slavery and the terrible unknown. It could hardly have been worse.

We all know what ultimately happened, how it turned out to be an incredible God-directed plan for salvation and the creation of the Nation of Israel. These are things we know after the fact. A measure of the man – the measure of *these men*, the players in this great drama, is what was going on *within* them, within their spirits, *before* the final outcome became apparent.

Yosef figured it out early on. He could not have known where it would lead, exactly, but this tzaddik, this man of faith, this dreamer, after his initial shock, understood that his dreams were not for nought, and he understood that the hand of God was at work. He had every right to be angry – as angry and as potentially vindictive as any human being could be – but he was, in his revelation to his brothers, as loving and as gracious as any human being could be. Not for nought, indeed, did he earn the title Yosef Hatzaddik, for his goodness as well as his faith.

The brothers could not know what would be the end result of their actions. But they did know, and carried with them the painful moral burden, that they had acted cruelly, even if within the law. For all those years, while life otherwise went on, that pain was with them.

(One of the "crimes" against the world that the Nazis accused the Jews of is introducing the concept of a guilty conscience.)

At the *denouement*, when Yosef finally confronts his brothers as Yosef, his natural, human reaction could well have been intense anger directed at them, typically described in the Torah as *charon af*. That, of course, is not what he does. Instead, not only does he graciously and lovingly explain away all their misdeeds against him as part of God's plan to save them all, but he also urges them, "*al te'atzvu v'al yichar b'eineichem*," do not be anguished or angry with yourselves over what you have done.

The Daas Sofrim here describes the difference between these two types of anger. *Charon af* denotes anger aimed at another person, a kind of *transitive* anger, with consequences for the object of that anger. *Charon einayim* denotes deep, internal anguish within a person.

Yosef Hatzaddik not only assures his overwhelmed brothers that he is not angry with them, for it was all the hand of God that brought them to this point for the common good, but he also urges them, for that very same reason, not to be internally anguished over their actions, not to be angry with themselves. Loving tears fell from his eyes as words of solace and encouragement flowed from his lips. It is the very height of graciousness and faith, the epitome of *tzidkus*.

It is especially striking that when, in the beginning, they judged him, they did so strictly, and did not give him the benefit of the doubt. Now, when he was in a position to judge them, he did so only to their benefit, waving away even the suggestion of guilt on their part.

We never know, when we embark upon a path, where the road of life will take us or what lay at the end of the road not taken. That is the nature of life in this world as it has been presented to us. We do have free choice, and we do have some measure of control, as God has granted us: we can decide on our own actions. But we do not control outcomes and we do not control the big picture. That is in God's hands, and people of faith take comfort in that.

But that faith and that comfort do not mean that things will go as we think we want.

We pray for a good *shidduch*, but it would be foolish to pray for a *particular* *shidduch*.

The enemy is coming for us – should we run this way or run that way? Who can really know? We pray for success in every endeavor in life. We do what we think is the wisest – but who knows, really? Who can know what's ultimately right and what's best for us?

What we do know, in the many choices we make, is that there is also a moral dimension to many of those choices. The outcome is up to God, but how we behave is up to us. And God, and our Sages, have taught us much about what our behavior should be. As painful as some outcomes may be – and, *lo aleinu*, many such outcomes have been, for our people, as painful as any human experience can possibly be – people of faith, we, the children of the Avos, can still find enough solace in placing our trust in God, no matter how things appear, to make life and hope still possible.

We do what we must, in God we place our trust, we pray for the best, and to God we leave the rest. Yosef Hatzaddik, orphaned from his mother as a child, torn away from his father as a youth, in the short time he lived with his family, absorbed this lesson well, and it sustained him through such difficult and trying times. In so doing he taught us, and set for us the example, of the meaning of faith, goodness, kindness, charity of thought and judgment, graciousness and *chesed*.

Yosef Hatzaddik is called Yosef Hatzaddik, I believe, because his life sets for us the example of what it takes for a person, by thought, word and deed, to be, in this challenging and often bewildering life, the kind of person God wants us to be, what it really means to be a tzaddik.

Parashas Vayigash 5777

Yaakov Revivified: Yosef in the Lion's Den

The Baal Hatanya teaches that a person who sins, in transgressing the supreme will, undoes his own specialness as a human being, and distances himself from his Creator. A lowly gnat, a *sheretz*, all creatures large and small live out their animal lives doing the will of the Creator. Only man, when he sins, acts against God's will, and thereby sets himself lower than the lowest creature. As the Gemara (*Sanhedrin* 38b) states, in such a circumstance, *yetush kidamcha* – even a mosquito takes precedence over a person who sins.

Upon emerging from the Ark, mankind was blessed with a special power: *Moraachem v'chitchem yihyeh al kol chayas ha'aretz*. The face of a human being will instill instinctive fear in all animals and birds. But that fear will only be manifest if the animal recognizes that face as that of a human being, reflecting the *tzelem Elokim*, the Image of God.

The Gemara continues: *Ein chayah raah sholetes b'adam ela im ken nidmeh lo k'behemah.* A wild animal cannot have power over a human being unless it does not recognize him as a human being, but perceives him to be just another animal: *k'behemos nidmu.* The Baal Hatanya explains that this distinction is a function of the *tzelem Elokim* that is manifest in the human being's visage. In a sinner, that *tzelem Elokim* is not apparent – he has distanced himself from God, and the animal has no fear. In a tzaddik, the *tzelem Elokim* is always on his face, instinctually apparent to all animals, and filling them with fear and dread of this human.

Daniel's survival in the lion's den was exactly the result of this phenomenon. The lions looked at Daniel and saw the *tzelem Elokim* on his face. In fear, they left him alone. One might even therefore argue that Daniel's survival, being consistent with this aspect of the divine plan of creation, was not actually a true miracle. Rather, it may be argued, it is this aspect of nature that can be said to be miraculous.

The principles stated above, I suggest, provide a deeper understanding of one of the most dramatic narratives in the Torah.

Yosef, whom we, in retrospect, refer to as Yosef Hatzaddik, was not always understood to be a tzaddik. His brothers, great men all, thought he was deeply flawed and accused him of various serious transgressions, even capital ones. They bickered with him and complained to their father. Yaakov, who loved Yosef and judged him to be pure and good, was vexed by their accusations. Were they jealous? Or were they God forbid right? Yaakov anticipated Yosef's vindication: *v'aviv shamar es hadavar.*

When Yosef's bloody garments are brought to him, Yaakov is devastated. Yosef has been, to all appearances, torn to pieces and eaten by a wild animal. Yaakov is beyond consolation.

Yaakov's devastation goes beyond the loss of his beloved son, tragic and unbearably painful as that would be. It is the *manner* of Yosef's presumed death that is particularly terrible.

All along, Yaakov believed in Yosef; he adored him, he favored him, he esteemed him, he trusted him in the face of his brothers' accusations. And now he appears to have been killed by a wild animal that did not perceive the *tzelem Elokim* on his face, exposing him as a *rasha* after all. In Yaakov's grief and despair, even the *ruach hakodesh* that has been his constant companion for so long deserts him.

Later, when he learns that Yosef is not only alive, but has proven himself over and over to be Yosef Hatzaddik, completely righteous, Yaakov's spirit comes alive again. He is revivified. The *ruach hakodesh* returns to him: *Va'techi ruach Yaakov avihem*. He goes on to spend the best years of his life in Yosef's realm, *mitaso shleimah*, his family complete, basking in the *tzelem Elokim* on *all* his children's faces.

Parashas Vayigash 5771

Vayechi

Asher Lo Hesir Tefillasi v'Chasdo Me'iti

He stood before the congregation, this remarkable, slightly built elderly man, and held their rapt attention as he recounted episodes of his extraordinary survival. Naftali was one of the very few Polish Jews who remained alive while under German control for most of the Holocaust period.

Afterward, one woman asked him how, after all he endured, he was able to remain religious. He smiled graciously and moved on to the next question. He was too much of a gentleman, and too respectful, to state publicly in a shul that he was no longer religious. Like many other survivors, his religion was a casualty of the Holocaust.

Not that he was overtly anti-religious. In fact, he belonged to a temple in his suburban community. His was not a "religious" way of life in the way Torah Jews think of "religious," but this Kohen, son of a distinguished Chassidic Galitzian family, retained a reverential nostalgia for the ways of his early life and that of his forebears.

Naftali was a *landsman* of my mother's. He published several books with tales of his eventful life and miraculous survival. And he told me many stories.

An incredibly resourceful person, Naftali (pronounce that Chassidic style, "*Naftuleh*") survived, in human terms, by his wits. When he finally managed to escape the Germans, late in the war, he fled eastward and, posing as a gentile Pole, "Jan Zaleski," a made-up name, ultimately became a high-ranking intelligence officer in the Polish forces, attached to the Soviet army.

At one point he was "in charge" of a prison, the real bosses being the Soviets (read KGB). Two Jewish boys, brothers, were kept in the dungeon, for reasons undisclosed.

Every day they were beaten to within an inch of their lives. It was clear to him that they could not survive much longer. Risking his own life, one night he went down to the dungeon and freed the brothers, telling them to run for their lives. They had no idea why Polish Captain Zaleski, a "*goy*," would risk his life to save them, but they ran. He did not hear of them again, and had no idea if they survived.

Some time in the early 1960s, Naftali's temple membership in New Jersey went on a field trip. Chartering a bus, they traveled on Simchas Torah night (yes, on *yom tov*) to visit the Chassidic *hakafos* in Brooklyn. At that time, the two most exciting *hakafos* to witness were in Crown Heights: Lubavitch and Bobov (before their move to Boro Park).

Standing in the crowded Bobover *sukkah*, they watched the joyous proceedings and the spirited dancing with the Torah. The Rebbe's *gabbai* got up to call those honored with the next *hakafah*. Standing with his group that arrived by bus, Naftali heard the *gabbai* announce, "*Pan* [Polish for Mr.] *Zaleski iz mechubad mit di nexte hakafah!*" Certain that he heard wrong, Naftali looked up at the *gabbai*, and found him looking right at him.

The *gabbai* was one of the brothers, both of whom had survived and now were Bobover Chassidim.

As the Red Army, with its Polish contingent, swept the Germans out of Poland, they entered a town moments after the Germans left. An intelligence officer, Naftali (in his guise as Polish Catholic Captain Jan Zaleski) entered the Gestapo headquarters and found only one person remaining there, the secretary, who had not fled with the Germans.

This young woman was a Volksdeutsch Pole. The Volksdeutsch were ethnic Germans who had been in Poland and other eastern European areas for many generations, becoming part of the new nation states, but retaining their German ethnic and cultural identity and their German language. When in 1939 the conquering German armies marched in, they were welcomed everywhere as liberating heroes by the joyous Volksdeutsch, who collaborated most willingly with the invaders. This treachery made them especially hated by the local Polish or other indigenous peoples.

Captain Zaleski drew his gun to shoot the traitor. Sitting at her desk, where she had served as a translator for the Germans, this ethnic German blonde young Polish woman who chose to betray her country and work for the Nazis, even though just as a translator and secretary, deserved to die. They all did, in his impassioned opinion.

Staring at her, he aimed and cocked his pistol. Seeing that she was about to die, she covered her eyes with her right hand and proclaimed, "*Shema Yisrael, Hashem Elokeinu, Hashem Echad!*"

Like him, she had miraculously survived by her wits and her knowledge of German, which allowed her to pose as a Volksdeutsch. Like him, she was a Jew who had posed as a gentile to survive. He did not kill her. Instead, he married her.

Many years later, a yeshiva, what we would call a right-wing, heavy duty, "black hat" *yeshivishe* yeshiva, undertook to establish itself in Naftali's suburban community. He no longer used the name Naftali, but was now known as "Norman" (there was a lot of water under that bridge). His neighbors were up in arms, determined to prevent this invasion by the undesirables. An emergency meeting was held in the temple. Speaker after speaker ranted about how their lives and property values would be ruined if the yeshiva came in.

Norman got up to speak. A respected member of the community, he had their attention.

"I want to talk to you about those people," Norman said. "*Those people.*" Like his fellow Temple members, he enjoyed a lifestyle that appeared to be essentially as secular as his neighbors', a light Jewish veneer on a decidedly American suburban existence. The *frumer* were an embarrassment and made them cringe.

"I want to tell you about those people. Those people are *me*. That is where I come from. That is where *all* of *you* come from. If you oppose them, you are opposing me. Are you sure you want to oppose *me*?"

The opposition withered, and the yeshiva succeeded.

Naftali had become Norman; the *chassidishe* young man became something very different. The events of a remarkably difficult period in life had overtaken him and changed his outlook and his way of life. And yet, on some level, on a visceral level, his core identity, something in his deepest sense of self, remained attached to who he once was.

Many Jews who suffered and struggled and experienced unspeakable loss and pain and travail did not budge at all from their steadfastness in Yiddishkeit.

Others were estranged, to a greater or lesser degree, from the faith of their fathers.

We who were not there and were not tested should leave judgment about those who were up to the One Above, the "*bochen kelayos*," Who knows what lies in the deepest recesses of every human heart.

It is clear, however, that some people come through difficult periods, even impossible periods, with their attachment to God undamaged or even strengthened.

Yosef Hatzaddik, unique in Tanach with the title "Hatzaddik" appended to his name, had more than his share of suffering and hardship. Motherless, resented by his brothers, ultimately cruelly betrayed by them (in the guise of a *beis din*), sold into slavery, falsely accused, imprisoned in a miserable pit for long years, Yosef was able to see beyond his suffering and disappointment and perceive the hand of God guiding him and directing history. His faith and his service to God remained intact. And so he ultimately became the instrument of *michyah*, life-giving sustenance for the nascent Jewish nation.

It's interesting that Yosef's father Yaakov also had many difficult and unhappy years, and he only grew in stature and holiness as a result. In the end, he was the perfect tzaddik, the perfect *oved Hashem*.

And David Hamelech too had a very difficult life, with much pain, sorrow, and disappointment. He too clung to God with all his might and became *ne'im zemiros Yisrael*.

Pain, suffering, and loss, for some people, result in a disconnection, to a greater or lesser degree, from God and His Torah. It is no surprise when people who suffer feel that God is not with them, that He is not there for them, that He does not hear their prayers, if they still pray at all. In fact, they lose their ability to pray.

That disconnection itself is part of the loss they suffer. It's a terrible loss, *lo aleinu*.

It leaves one essentially feeling alone and utterly vulnerable in the universe.

Others, like Naftali, become estranged, but not altogether. On some level, an important but certainly incomplete level, they remain connected.

And others, like Yosef Hatzaddik, like Yaakov Avinu, like David Hamelech, like countless others over the generations – *may we not be tested, Ribbono shel Olam!* – only grow from it, however painful it is.

David Hamelech famously wrote: "*Baruch Elokim asher lo hesir tefillasi v'chasdo me'iti*" (Tehillim 66:20). Blessed be God, *thank You, God*, Who has not removed from me the ability to pray or the perception that His saving grace, his *chesed*, is still with me.

Some of us appear to live charmed lives. Some seem to have a disproportionate share of hard luck, *lo aleinu*. These things are in God's hands, *cheshbonei Shamayim*, and in truth, we never know what's really going on in *yenem's* life. And we don't always know what's really a *berachah* and what is not. We certainly hope, and we pray, that God's blessing should be obvious blessing, and not require an act of faith to believe that it's really for the good. For aside from the suffering involved, that is a test that not everyone seems to be able to stand up to. We pray not to be tested.

Many of us, in the recent catastrophe (Hurricane Sandy, the flood, the destruction), have been tested, and continue to be. For most of us, that test is so much easier than what the last generation, and what many earlier generations, had to undergo. But tested we have been.

And so, as we see a sorely tested Yosef Hatzaddik rise above all his hardships to perfect *tzidkus* in Egypt, as we see Yaakov Avinu finally finding easement from his many travails in his final years in Egypt, as we are grateful that we have not had to deal with the unspeakable horrors that Naftali had to, we continue to be inspired by the words and the concepts immortalized by the Sweet Singer of Israel,

David Hamelech, who wrote, in gratitude for finding himself *able* to hold on, *able* to continue to pray, *able* to still feel the loving hand of God alongside him, *Baruch Elokim asher lo hesir tefillasi v'chasdo me'iti.*

Thank You, Ribbono shel Olam, for helping me still feel connected to You, that You are right here, still with me.

Please, dear Father in Heaven, stay with me. And keep me close to You.

Parashas Vayechi 5773

Remembrance of Things Past and Future

They don't really have an answer for it.

The Torah is our divine and eternal deed to this Holy Land. Remember the first Rashi in Bereishis. If the Torah is true, if everything in it is true, then our deed is a true deed. But then our obligations as laid down in the Torah are also true, and binding.

And if one sees the Torah as a thing less than the eternal word of the Living God of Israel, if one sees the mitzvos as historical, quaint reminders of ancient traditions, but not divine and certainly not binding, then we also have no valid deed. The eternal truth of one element validates the other.

And so the large number of Israelis who are fine people and in their hearts good and loyal Jews, who fully identify with Klal Yisrael, but who are uneducated as Jews and do not observe the mitzvos, cannot really delve too deeply into this question, because they have no good answer to this dilemma: either the Torah is literally true (which would obligate them to be *frum*) and they have every right to be here, or it is, *chalilah*, not, and they are, as the Arabs say, usurpers.

Enter the post-Zionists, the liberal left elites who have outgrown and left the Zionism of their parents behind (not to mention the Judaism of their grandparents), well represented in the media and in the universities, who do take it to the next step. They see no valid reason why the Jews should be here; they see only repression of the noble Arabs by the right-wing Jewish fanatic fascists and wish they themselves were in San Francisco. This is a point of view they do their best to propagate wherever they can. And given their prominent position in society, their voices are very loud.

Last year I visited the Palmach Museum in Tel Aviv. It is a beautiful presentation, honoring the dedicated and selfless young people who bravely put their lives on the line – and too often gave their lives – for the sake of the Yishuv of Eretz Yisrael.

As I emerged from the museum, it struck me as sadly ironic that it is situated in the shadow of Tel Aviv University, where the post-Zionist professors and their acolytes hold sway, and from where the utter rejection of what Israel means to the rest of us is the new, "politically correct" faith.

And the saddest part of that irony is that those professors are, literally and figuratively, the children of the very heroes of the Palmach that are honored in the museum.

This became possible because while the Palmachniks of old still had, as a driving force, the Judaism of their parents and grandparents behind them, their own children were even more cut off from their Torah roots, and in the end, could find no "moral" reason for them to be here, other than the lame excuse of "facts on the ground" and some vague reference to "history" or "historic rights." And so, enter the post-Zionists.

We see these people writing op-ed pieces in the *New York Times* (always a welcome home to Israel bashers and Jew haters) that routinely denounce the actions of their fellow Israelis and Jews, sanctimoniously and self-righteously taking the moral high ground as they do so.

I'm sure there are some very fine people at Tel Aviv University and other places like it – good, loyal Jews. But theirs are not the voices we usually hear. In fact, those "liberals" will often do their best to suppress any dissenting voice, painting alternate opinions as "antidemocratic" and unworthy of a hearing.

Now let's take a peek at the Department of Archeology at Tel Aviv University.

Traditionally, archeologists in Israel, even if not personally religious, reveled in uncovering archeological evidence of ancient Jewish habitation in this land. They walked around with copies of the Tanach in their hands, and they knew, from it, what they could expect to find.

Not these guys (or at least some of these guys). They have made it a point to deny any historical validity to the Torah. Avraham? Yitzchak, Yaakov, Moshe Rabbenu, Yetzias Mitzrayim, Matan Torah? David Hamelech? Never lived! Never existed! Fables, they insist, made up much later by people who wanted to fabricate a past to suit their sociological or political or religious needs.

I was at a site a few days ago that has been recently excavated. It is a fortification that sits exactly on the confrontation line with the Plishtim in Shaul and David's time, just as described in Tanach. It shows clear archaeological evidence of being Jewish (Torah words are etched in its stones) and an outpost of a central government (Yerushalayim!), and it has been radiocarbon dated to David Hamelech's reign. All things that are entirely inconsistent with the views of these committed Torah deniers and show their anti-religious and anti-Tanach biases to be just that: biased and untrue.

What's the response of the deniers? Uh, uh, uh, er, uh, *maybe it means something else! It must mean something else!*

They can't let go. *Nebech.* David Hamelech is laughing at them.

I believe it's about Chanukah, and about Parashas Vayechi.

The Chashmonaim and their followers of loyal Jews, we all know, fought the Seleucid Greeks, foreign invaders who tried to impose Greek culture upon the Jews. Greek culture and learning were seen by the world as the ultimate expression of human development, an enlightened "liberal" civilization and lifestyle. It had no tolerance for Yiddishkeit.

The external enemy were the Yevanim (Greeks). The war with the Yevanim, however, was really also a *civil war* with the Misyavnim, Jews who were so enamored of the non-Jewish culture that they abandoned their Jewishness to adopt the mode of the gentiles, and in the culture war, they sided with the Greeks.

The Misyavnim of that period are the "liberal left elites" – or some variation on that theme – of today. *The civil war with the Misyavnim has never ended.* May it never be an armed struggle, *chalilah.* But a struggle it is.

In every generation that there arise Misyavnim among our people, the result is always the same. Those who trade in their Judaism for some other *ism* have children or grandchildren who either disappear altogether from Klal Yisrael, or, if they're lucky, who become *baalei teshuvah.*

Parashas Vayechi marks the end of the saga of the Avos, culminating with the passing of Yaakov Avinu, who bequeathed to us our name, Yisrael, and our national character.

Albeit into Mitzrayim, a terrible but necessary station, our nation was launched.

Vayechi discusses the final days of Yaakov. The *haftarah* discusses the final days of David.

It's interesting to note the parallels between the final days of Yaakov Avinu, who represents our founding past, and those of David Hamelech, who represents not just the past, but the future as well, in the person and concept of Moshiach Tzidkenu.

Va'yikrevu yemei Yisrael lamus. Va'yikrevu yemei David lamus.

Yaakov Avinu lo meis (Taanis 5b). David Melech Yisrael chai v'kayam.

The *meforshim* teach us a truth about ourselves. We possess, as a nation, the power to transform death into life. Indeed, our tzaddikim can be even greater, more powerful and effective after their deaths than they were in life (*gedolim tzaddikim b'misosam mi'b'chayeihem*). How? When the lessons and the traditions of the fathers are passed on to the children, who thereby perpetuate those parents.

Our parents are alive, our holy forebears are alive, Abaye and Rava are alive, Rashi is alive when we *give* them life, by learning their Torah, following their example, by living the very life-giving lives they laid out for us.

While he was alive, the image of Yaakov's face saved Yosef from mortal sin with *eishes Potiphar*, and our nation came into being. And after his mortal life, the image of Yaakov's face, enshrined in the Kisei Hakavod, continues to save us.

Yaakov Avinu is "alive." David Hamelech, *ne'im zemiros Yisrael*, is "alive." They had the *koach* to impart to us and to all future generations the *koach* to perpetuate Am Yisrael as Am Hashem forever.

The Misyavnim? In the end, no one will remember them. In fact, it will be hard to believe that they ever existed.

Parashas Vayechi 5772, Yerushalayim Ir Hakodesh

Land O' Goshen!

Land O' Goshen!

This old-time exclamation refers to arriving in the land of plenty.

Goshen, of course, is the rich land, the best in Egypt, where Yosef, with Pharaoh's encouragement, settled his arriving father and brothers, where they would eat of the fat of the land. And that indeed is where they settled and grew and prospered tremendously.

We know, of course, that it also became, eventually, the land of their enslavement. And, in human terms, their engagement with it may well have been contributory to their enslavement.

Any surprise? As the Jews prosper, the others see them more and more as interlopers who have come to take what is rightfully theirs. This is the frequent fate of immigrant groups in general, and of Jews in particular. Jews, of course, are seen as outsiders even after a thousand years in a country. And their hard work and enterprise is not credited at all.

And so Pharaoh presumably had no trouble convincing his people that the Jews were a dangerous, ravenous race bent on taking over Egypt and usurping its wealth.

The Jews settled in Goshen, and they prospered. A new generation arose that knew only Goshen. Normal behavior – that backfired on them. Because the Jews are not a normal nation.

There is a hint, I believe, to the underlying nature of this process at the end of Vayigash. The last *pasuk*: *Va'yeshev Yisrael b'eretz Mitzrayim b'eretz Goshen va'ye'achazu bah va'yifru va'yirbu me'od*. Israel settled in Egypt, in Goshen, they possessed it, and they were fruitful and multiplied exceedingly.

Va'ye'achazu bah is typically rendered "they took possession of it." But look at the *dikduk*. It actually says "they were *possessed*." Their successful settlement of the land of plenty possessed *them*. They were entrenched in Goshen, and it possessed them.

What is normal for other nations is not normal for Israel. True, God has His plan. But we have ours. We find ourselves in foreign lands. Sometimes they are the land of plenty. Sometimes they are dire places. But they are not our place.

We may, indeed, have every political and moral right to be there and to prosper there, just like any other people. But that is from the perspective of the others. From our own perspective, while we find ourselves there, and while we may appropriately assert our rights there, we must not lose sight of who we are, and what our real place is – physically *and* spiritually.

The Jews settled in the land O' Goshen. They possessed it and they were possessed by it. How long was it before that illusion was broken, and how bitterly was it broken?

As the Jews came into Egypt, Yosef encouraged them to settle the land successfully. But he also reminded them that it was not their true place and that God would redeem them and return them to the Land of Israel. Much later, when the Jews faced exile in Bavel, the prophets told them to build lives there, to settle in. But they also told them that they would ultimately be redeemed, and yet again tend their vineyards in the Land of Israel, their true place.

It's good to have possessions. May we be blessed with them. But we should not be possessed by them.

It's good to be free and successful in the Land O' Goshen. Hopefully, without the enmity of our non-Jewish neighbors, we should possess it. But we should not be possessed by it.

We are, in fact, not a normal people. Who we are, what our mission in this world is, what God has given us, is what we truly possess. And that is the reality that should possess us.

Parashas Vayechi 5772

While You Are Still Visible

My big brother is a very smart and observant man. A psychiatrist, he is also well attuned to the nature of the human mind and spirit. He shared with me an observation about himself – or, more precisely, about how others appear to relate to him.

He is a family man. He is a doctor. He is a scholar and thinker. He is a well-respected writer and professor. He has been a man of considerable importance. He is a man of dignity and distinction. Except for those who relate to him as one of the above, he has noticed that others, especially young others, as he has aged, don't really see him, even if he walks right by them. He is as if invisible, someone not necessary to notice, unless there is some reason to.

Alas, that is part of what aging is about. It is as if we contract, as we become old, as if we occupy less visible space in the universe. We continue to be an important part of the lives of those near to us, those who need us, but for others, especially the young, we are only noticed when necessary. It is as if our power of making others aware of us – and that is a very considerable human power, the power of presence – wanes and tapers off once one reaches older age.

In a practical sense, our visibility to others, especially young others, it seems, is in proportion to how useful (or bothersome) or how interesting we may be to them, in reality or in fancy. I believe, however, that this is also a function of the very nature of the life force itself.

As Yaakov Avinu's life approached its end, he appealed to Yosef not to bury him in Egypt, but to bring his remains for burial to the land of his fathers, in Me'aras Hamachpelah in Chevron.

The language of that request is telling: *"Im na matzasi chen b'einecha…v'asisa imadi chesed v'emes"* (Please, if I have found favor in your eyes…do for me this kindness; Bereishis 47:29). A plea spoken as if to a superior. A lesser or weaker petitioner making a request of someone greater, more powerful. It is not the command of a father to his son.

The Midrash takes note of this weakening and, citing Koheles 8:8, which describes how a man, as the end approaches, becomes powerless, compares I Melachim 1:1 with 2:1.

The opening line of the first chapter describes King David as he grows older. He is more vulnerable than he was, he feels cold, but he is still in his power. He is referred to as Hamelech David (David the King). The next chapter describes him as he feels death is approaching. He calls his son Shlomo to instruct him in what he must do as he assumes the kingship.

The opening line of this chapter simply refers to him as "David," not "David the King."

He was still there, but at the same time, as if not fully there. Becoming invisible.

The great King David, loyal and dedicated servant of God, "Sweet Singer of Israel," while ascendant and triumphant, had a very difficult and challenging life. Deeply spiritual, beset by problems, he produced the great body of Psalms, which became the staple of comfort, hope, prayer, and spiritual inspiration for all time, not just for Jews but for all the world.

At the height of his power, he is well aware of the limits of life and of power. They fade. The have their time and then they are over. Gone. Powerless. Invisible. That which we must accomplish in this life is for us to strive to accomplish while we still can. For afterward we cannot.

In Tehillim 39:14 he states this starkly and dramatically. He appeals to God, "*Hasha mi'meni v'avligah – b'terem elech v'eineni.*" Ribbono shel Olam, please relieve me of my burdensome afflictions, that I may be strengthened (to serve You, to occupy myself with the Torah, to accomplish my goals and my duties to my people) *before I must go – and be no more.*

B'terem elech v'eineni.

Most of us have goals that we wish to achieve in life, accomplishments we envision for ourselves, both temporal and spiritual. Most of us also have a tendency to defer for tomorrow what we might have to strain to accomplish today. But in normal life, we can hope, we can expect, but we cannot know how many tomorrows we have.

In medical school I saw a remarkable and deeply memorable short film made by a young man who was dying. Most of us, when we are in our strength, cannot conceive of the world going on without us. This young man knew that he would, before long, be gone. But he could not quite grasp the idea that the world, the world he knew, the world that he affected by his presence, would just go on without him. He asks, repeatedly, "Can the sun still shine without me?"

Of course he knew the answer, but he could not fathom it. He had so much more to do, so many more miles to travel, so much to accomplish. But he would not. The sun would continue to rise and to shine, somehow, even without him.

The Midrash above speaks of some of the greatest men in our nation's history and formation, Yaakov, Moshe, David, and Shlomo, in the context of this reality. Koheles 8:8:

אין אדם שליט ברוח לכלוא את הרוח ואין שלטון ביום המות.

> There is no man that has power over the wind to retain the wind, nor power over the day of death.

No one escapes this reality. The obvious lesson, of course, is to impact the world the way you need to, the way God wants you to impact it, while you still can. Accomplish what you ought to accomplish while you are still able to accomplish. Time, life, and opportunity are too precious to waste. The wisdom of our Sages teaches us this; indeed, the wisdom of the world teaches us this. The wisdom of our parents, the wisdom of life teaches us this. Yaakov Avinu, whose face is etched into the very Throne of God, as his life force waned, taught us this. Do it now. Do it every day. *Do it while you are still visible.*

Do it *b'terem elech v'eineni.*

Parashas Vayechi 5777

ספר שמות

Shemos

A Rose by Any Other Name

"Albert, what's your real name?"

The young boy, eight or nine years old, a third- or fourth-grader at a local yeshiva day school, looked at me uncomprehendingly. "Albert," he answered.

"Albert, what's your *real* name?"

"Albert." He's bewildered.

"What name were you given at your *brit milah*?"

"Albert!" He has no clue what I'm talking about. His name, his self-identity, is Albert. Period.

His mother, looking a little uncomfortable at Albert's total cluelessness in this regard, says to him, "He wants to know your Hebrew name."

"Avraham."

"Avraham! Wow, what a wonderful name! Like Avraham Avinu! Wow! *With a wonderful name like Avraham, what do you need 'Albert' for?*"

Blank look.

Poor Albert, a nice boy, has no idea what I'm doing. His mother does. She also realizes that I'm talking to her as much as to Albert. I am well aware that I cannot, and will not, and am not mandated to change the sociological dynamics of Albert's particular sector of Jewish society. But let him also have some awareness of the issue. And it is not an unimportant one.

Everyone knows that one of the merits the Jewish slaves earned in Egypt, by virtue of which they were ultimately redeemed, is that they clung to their Hebrew names despite, for many of them, near total acculturation into corrupt Egyptian society, with the depravity that entailed.

The book of Shemos, known to the world as Exodus – referring to the central event of our becoming a nation – for us, refers to names: *Shemos Bnei Yisrael*. It opens with the listing of the names of Yaakov's twelve sons. Every one of those names is still in use among their descendants today. We carry, in the legacy of those names and the other classic biblical Hebrew names, the names of the founders of our nation and our faith, those righteous tzaddikim and *tzidkanios* whose character and whose actions provide the foundation for who we are.

A word, please, about the brothers – Yosef's brothers, who threw him in the pit, who sold him into slavery, who treated him wrong, and whose names are now presented as the paragons of virtue and of rectitude.

They were. Indeed they were. Yaakov's children were all righteous, all great tzaddikim, *shivtei Kah*, God's chosen tribes. In my own recent essays, I refer to their treatment of their younger brother as brutal and cruel. Please understand that that was the case from *Yosef's* perspective.

They were anything but intentionally cruel. Their perception and judgment of him was mistaken, but they did believe he was actually bad, a spoiler of the legacy of Avraham, Yitzchak, and Yaakov, a bad influence, a rotten apple. It was their understanding that he had to be removed from their midst, and that he brought it upon himself. They held an inquest. And he was, we are told, actually tried and convicted. They did what they were convinced they had to do, however distasteful.

Even so, what they did to him (and thereby also to their father) obviously plagued them. Twenty-two years later, when they went down to Egypt to buy food, it was also their agenda to search for Yosef and to redeem him. And in what is to me one of the most moving passages in the Torah, when it appears to them that the world has come crashing down upon them as their youngest brother Binyamin has been seized by the Egyptian viceroy, they immediately recognize the reason: "This catastrophe has befallen us because when our brother Yosef pleaded with us, begged us for mercy, *we did not listen*." They understood that they could have and should have let their natural compassion for their brother overcome their strict judgment. They had been wrong, and they were ashamed. And when Yosef revealed himself to them, they were speechless with shame, and with remorse.

They were *baalei teshuvah*.

Having just enumerated the brothers who moved from Canaan to Egypt at the end of Bereishis, Shemos begins with enumerating them yet again. Rashi offers the midrashic explanation that they were so precious and beloved to God that, having named them and counted them just before, while they were still alive, He does so again now that they have died. They were His precious stars.

And, the Kabbalists teach, they had a particular cosmic purpose for their descent into Egypt.

Many holy sparks were distributed in the world upon its creation, and one mandate of Israel is to collect them wherever they are and to incorporate them, liberating them, as it were, for the service of God. The power and the ability, the key to unlocking and gathering those holy sparks, the *nitzotzos hakodesh*, that were in Egypt, required the power that comes from *teshuvah*.

When, in the course of their bondage, their condition ever worsening, ever more bitter, the Jews cried out in their anguish, and God heard them: *va'yizaku va'taal shavasam el ha'Elokim min ha'avodah. Va'yishma Elokim es naakasam. Va'yar Elokim es Bnei Yisrael va'yeda Elokim.* God saw Bnei Yisrael and He knew. What did God see and what did He know? *She'asu teshuvah* (*Midrash Rabbah* 1:36). That they did *teshuvah*. The *beinonim*, neither tzaddikim nor *resha'im*, did *teshuvah* and became like tzaddikim. And even the *resha'im* had at least had *thoughts* of *teshuvah*. This is what God saw, and this is what He knew. And what followed was Moshe and their redemption.

The example that they were able to draw upon, the lesson in spiritual life from which they could learn how to do this, was provided by their grandparents, Yosef's brothers, who themselves repented wholeheartedly, in all humility and in all sincerity. Thus, through their own *teshuvah*, they made possible the subsequent mass *teshuvah*, which in turn gave their descendants the spiritual strength not just to merit redemption, but, in their glorious exodus, to carry all the holy *nitzotzos* in Mitzrayim with them on their way to Sinai and to the Promised Land.

We read the *parashiyos* known as Shovavim – an acronym for Shemos, Va'era, Bo, Beshalach, Yisro, Mishpatim – as the winter sets in, four months after Rosh Hashanah. Perhaps the spirit of *teshuvah* and commitment that imbued us during the Yamim Noraim has worn off somewhat by this time. Life's demands take up our attention and energies. The stresses we all face distract us from that spiritual commitment we made four months ago. And just as it worsens, as the cold and the damp set in, the inspirational and powerful *parashiyos* of Shovavim, with their theme of redemption and rebirth, come to rekindle that awareness and that commitment. The *teshuvah* that made those *parashiyos* possible, that made the Exodus possible, that made the recapturing of the *nitzotzos* possible, inspires us to keep gathering those holy sparks, especially at this propitious time of the year, which is *mesugal* for it.

These are the names of the children of Israel "haba'im Mitzraimah," literally *"who are coming"* to Egypt, in a sense, even to this day, for the purpose of learning to do *teshuvah*, to gather the holy sparks, to be redeemed and formed into the nation that stood at Sinai. The Imrei Noam notes that the *sofei teivos*, the final letters of *Mitzraimah es Yaakov ish u'veiso* (מצרימה את יעקב איש וביתו) spell out *teshuvah* (תשובה).

What's in a name? Would not a rose by any other name smell as sweet?

Many of us, if not most of us, do carry "outside" names in addition to our Hebrew ones.

My own parents, recently off the boat as refugees, were told, when I was born, that everyone in America must have such an "outside" name, and thus I received mine. It has been a central part of my identity, I use it professionally and in civil matters, and that is, I believe, fine. But if you wake me up in the middle of the night and ask me my name, my *real name*, my groggy answer will not likely be "Raymond."

We understand that what a person's name is informs, to some degree, who he is and what he is. To whatever extent that is true for the world at large, it is especially true for Jews. It is part of the metaphysical bond that ties us to God, it is part of the glue that binds us to each other, it is part of the fixative that places us in the continuum of Jewish history and civilization. It affects our character and our strengths. It is a key part of our definition.

And so a Jew who is so poor in his Jewish connection and so unlucky that he does not have or is not aware of his Jewish name is poor indeed, and cut off. And a Jew who is lucky enough to be blessed with a holy name that binds him to his holy forebears, that allows him to inherit their strengths and their connection with the Eternal, but who is so clueless, so uninformed, so uninspired, so uneducated, so disconnected that his awareness of it is relegated to a foggy, distant memory bank and that it is not, in his mind and in his spirit, part of his self-awareness, but rather an unimportant detail, is perhaps poorer still. For that tragic loss is self-inflicted, unnecessary, such a waste, and so, so sad.

Parashas Shemos 5774

Dan v'Naftali

Sefer Shemos opens with the names of the sons of Yaakov who migrated to Egypt.

A set of *pesukim* lists the names, several to a *pasuk*. The last name in each *pasuk* is preceded by a *vav*, meaning "and," in expected and proper grammatical form. Reuven, Shimon, Levi v'Yehudah. Yissachar, Zevulun u'Vinyamin. But the last breaks with the pattern, even as it fulfills it. It lists Dan, Naftali, Gad v'Asher. But it doesn't say Naftali; it says Dan v'Naftali, Gad v'Asher.

Why the extra *vav* before Naftali?

You might think that it's because Dan and Naftali were a pair, from one mother, as were Gad and Asher, so the pasuk lists them as pairs and adds the *vav*.

But the absence of a *vav* from Zevulun, which completes the listing of Leah's children, suggests that that is not the form mandated by the *pesukim*.

So why the extra *vav* before Naftali?

Perhaps it has to do with the nature and the origins of the names themselves.

Rachel gave her maidservant Bilhah to Yaakov as a wife in the hope that she, Rachel, would merit having a child herself. She named the first son of Bilhah Dan, referring to judgment: God has judged me and found favorably for me.

But we know that one who invites judgment into the world is often singed by that very judgment. Sarah said to Avraham, also in relation to having children, "*Yishpot Hashem beini u'veinecha.*"

Says the *Midrash Rabbah*, whoever pursues *din* will not likely come away unscathed himself. Sarah should have lived as long as Avraham, but her calling for *din* caused her to be judged for the *ayin hara* with which she regarded Hagar's initial pregnancy, which she lost (and subsequently conceived Yishmael). See also *Bava Kama* 93a on this.

And so the concept of *din* is so powerful and potentially dangerous that in listing Dan, he is "insulated" or protected from *din* by appending his name, and his concept (all the *shevatim* had concept names) to that of Naftali, which evokes positively answered prayer.

Hence, the one exception: Dan v'Naftali.

Parashas Shemos 5772

Heart on Fire

Why Moshe?

The young Moshe was a prince in Egypt. He had power and privilege.

Within the system, he had everything to gain from the status quo.

In rebellion, he had everything to lose.

Va'yigdal Moshe, va'yetzei el echav, va'yar b'sivlosam (Moshe grew up and went out among his brethren, seeing their burdensome suffering; Shemos 2:11).

Moshe, prince of Egypt, understands who his brethren are, steps out from his royal sphere of privilege, and goes out to mix with those brethren, to see their condition in their plight. Unable to tolerate their misery, he slays the Egyptian and sacrifices all for their sake.

Later, exiled to Midian and tending Yisro's sheep, he follows a stray sheep and tends to it tenderly and lovingly, demonstrating his fitness to be the shepherd of Klal Yisrael.

God sees Moshe's heart, sees what Moshe has made of his heart, sees the depth of feeling he has for his brethren, and identifies him as the redeemer who will lead Klal Yisrael out of Egypt, out of bondage, and into the nationhood of Israel.

And so Hakadosh Baruch Hu reveals Himself to Moshe in the Burning Bush.

The very language describing this encounter is itself, I believe, most telling.

Va'yera malach Hashem elav, b'labas esh mi'toch hasneh, v'hineh hasneh bo'er ba'esh v'hasneh einenu ukal (And the angel of the Lord appeared to him in a flame of fire out of the midst of a bush; and he looked, and, behold, the bush burned with fire, and the bush was not consumed; Shemos 3:2).

Rashi explains regarding the choice of a *sneh* as the vehicle for His Presence for this particular revelation. Why a lowly thorn bush rather than a majestic tree? *V'lo ilan acher mi'shum imo Anochi b'tzarah* (And not a different tree because of [the *pasuk*] "I am with them in their troubles" [Tehillim 91:15]).

Other trees would be too grand. If the Jews were in misery, a lowly thorn bush would do as the vehicle for God's presence. Rashi also elucidates the meaning of "*b'labas esh*": *shalheves esh, libo shel esh,* the heart of fire, and he cites similar language in Scripture. The key words here, I believe, are *libo shel esh* (לבו של אש), the heart of fire.

Why Moshe? By what merit? *B'labas esh* (בלבת-אש), the heart of fire.

Because Moshe's heart was afire with love and compassion for his brethren.

Moshe's heart was that of a true leader, a loving shepherd, fiercely loyal, ready to sacrifice everything for them. His heart burned with love for his fellow Jews.

And so when Hakadosh Baruch Hu manifested Himself as a fire in the lowly thorn bush, when He "lowered" himself, *k'v'yachol,* as an expression of *imo Anochi b'tzarah* (I am with them in their troubles), He chose to do so to someone who, in human terms, had a heart to match. A heart on fire. And yet, like the *sneh,* the lowly thorn bush, and like the modest mountain itself, a heart of utter humility.

And as God manifested Himself, *k'v'yachol,* as a fire in the humble thorn bush, so too the holy flame of human Godliness manifested itself in Moshe, who was the most humble man on earth.

Why Moshe?

Because he possessed the key element for this mission.

Because he had perfected his heart.

Because he lived his life *b'labas esh.*

In undertaking to bring about the seminal event in Jewish history, which would set the course of all human history – the Exodus from Egypt – God chose as His human "partner" someone who demonstrated time and time again, like Hashem, a seemingly limitless capacity for *imo anochi b'tzarah, I am with them in their troubles.*

In that desert, on that mountain, Hashem identified and designated Yisro's shepherd as the Raya Mehemna, the loyal and devoted shepherd for His Chosen People.

Parashas Shemos 5768

Ten Years a Slave

An insistent bang on the door in the middle of the night. Everyone lived in dread of that signature arrival of the NKVD to drag them away. That night, in 1938, at the height of Stalin's campaign of terror, it arrived at the Bogatin household in Moscow. Noach and his father, Rabbi Bogatin, were taken by the dreaded secret police. The incriminating evidence was right there: Jewish holy books. *Guilty!*

Guilty of what, exactly? Freedom of religion was guaranteed under the Soviet Constitution. The obvious answer, known to all, was that the law, and the Constitution, and decency itself, were all irrelevant in the hell on earth known as the Union of Soviet Socialist Republics.

Noach was sentenced to ten years of slave labor in the frozen taiga. The camp was so remote and in such a hostile, harsh location that there was no possibility of escape. The possibility of survival outside the camp was virtually nil, so that fences were not even necessary. No one could get away.

The likelihood of survival within the camp was quite small as well. Starvation, disease, exposure, and violent attack by other prisoners lurked constantly. The biggest killer, though, was the work itself. The backbreaking labor of felling huge trees in the frozen wastes was bad enough. Quite often prisoners died as the trees they or their fellow prisoners chopped down fell upon them and crushed the life out of them.

Noach's work partner was a Korean fellow (his "crime" who can know – he himself probably did not know) who toiled alongside him for eight years. They looked out for each other, to the degree that was possible. They worked out a system, in bringing down the trees, that helped them avoid being crushed. Until one day a tree did fall upon him as he stood right next to Noach, and that was his end.

Upon the completion of Noach's sentence, he was duly released. After all, the law is the law. And so, in 1948, he made his way back from the slave labor camp and discovered, only then, *that there had been a war while he was there.* Incredibly, they were so remote, and so cut off, that none of the prisoners had even heard about World War II.

There was no word about the fate of his father, the rabbi. All inquiries were met with stony silence. Where was he? When would he be released?

After 1953, when Stalin finally *peigered* (a wonderful Yiddish term used for an evil person who drops dead, derived from the Hebrew *peger* [פגר], "carcass," referring to the corpse of someone too evil to refer to in a more respectful way; it is the opposite of the respectful *niftar*, or "passed away"), some information finally became available. Rabbi Bogatin had been shot in the back of the head in the basement of the NKVD prison within a day or two of his arrest, and his body disposed of somewhere.

I know these things because they were told to me by my dear friend and shul mate, Reb Noach himself. And, he told me, what I do know is but a small fraction of the story.

This history, true in every respect, was typical of millions of such stories in that time and place. A variation on that story was the fate that befell the hundreds of thousands of Polish citizens, most of them Jews, who fled the Germans to find refuge in the Russian-conquered areas of Poland.

As the Russians consolidated their hold on eastern Poland, territory was not enough. The millions of inhabitants, native as well as refugees, now had to become citizens of the Soviet Union. Most understood that if they indeed became "Russian," they would *never* escape that cruel fate, even when peace would come. In the hundreds of thousands, they refused. And so, in the hundreds of thousands, they were declared enemy aliens and were deported to slave labor camps in the East, typically Siberia.

They were packed into cattle cars and shipped for days and weeks ever eastward.

They could not know, at the time, that for those who would survive this ordeal (and so many did not), it saved their lives, as they were no longer present when the Germans attacked and murdered every Jew in the very areas they were deported from.

Onward they traveled, locked up in the cattle cars. Three days alone were spent traveling along the shores of Lake Baikal, as they continued ever eastward, and northward, into the heart of the Siberian forests. Slaves were needed to chop down those forests, and to build, and to lay down the tracks of the Trans-Siberian Railroad.

Perhaps not all wound up in places as harsh as Noach's, but very many did.

Shimon and Chana, in their thirties, were in fact enslaved in a manner quite similar to that of Reb Noach. Shimon, in his slavery, toiled incredibly hard, and dangerously, in the frozen wasteland. He too chopped down giant trees, laid railroad tracks, and fended off the unexplained hostility of his overseer. Chana was overtaken with a severe intestinal malady that made even standing, let alone working, impossible. For this she was convicted of "parasitism" and sent to prison.

The miracle of her survival of that ordeal is recorded elsewhere in these essays.

After some time of this, the Soviet government reached an agreement with the Polish government-in-exile, operating in Britain, to free the Polish slaves. Perhaps this was connected to the massive arms help the American and British Allies provided to the Soviets, which helped them survive and carry on the fight.

Shimon did not know where Chana was. There were many prisons in the Soviet hell.

He ran from prison to prison, standing outside, running along the perimeter, calling out her name. In this he was helped by his brother-in-law, Binyamin (Yumek) Pfeffer, who was married to Shimon's sister and had been his business partner. They could not know, at the time, that Yumek's wife and little children, too tender to flee the Germans, thought to be reasonably safe at home in Reishe, were, by now, ashes in the pits of Belzec. As were Shimon's other sister and her children. Shimon's elderly mother never made it to the death camp. The Germans dealt her that blow in Reishe, when, ordered to run to the train that was to carry her to her death, "*Schnell! Schnell!*" but unable to run fast enough, she was shot down in the street like a dog, the body of that elegant, aristocratic princess of Galitzianer Jewry discarded like so much rubbish. A Polish gentile witness, who was an acquaintance of Shimon, my father, years later described the scene to him.

He found Chana. He had been to many prisons already, but refused to give up. She heard him calling her name and made her way to him. She weighed next to nothing in his arms as he carried her off.

The actual slavery part of their ordeal was over, but their bitter travails were still far from over. That story will follow in another essay. These tales here relate to the historical prototype of our enslavement, our bitter bondage in Egypt, as related in Parashas Shemos.

V'eleh Shemos Bnei Yisrael haba'im Mitzraimah – These are the names of the children of Israel who *are arriving* in Egypt. It does not say, who *arrived* in Egypt, past tense, but strangely, who *are arriving*, using the present tense. The Chiddushei Harim famously says that the present tense is used because we, the Children of Israel, seemingly are *constantly* arriving in one exile or another, driven from pillar to post, and have spent most of our existence doing so. But wherever we wander, we bring with us the names, and thus the memory, the spirit, and the strengths of those very forefathers who preceded us into exile, that very first and formative exile into Egypt, and thus showed us the way to survive and, in the end, to triumph. Their merit continues to stand for us, their example continues to inspire us, their very names persist among us, and thus fortified, we manage to persevere.

And so, our forefathers – we – were enslaved, in a pattern that would be repeated time and again, with variations dictated by history. *Va'yakam melech chadash al Mitzrayim asher lo yada es Yosef.* A "new" king arose in Egypt – literally or figuratively – whose policy was to deny the previous benevolence toward the Jews. Never mind that Yosef saved Egypt from starvation and massively increased Pharaoh's wealth and power. Never mind that the presence of the Jews in Egypt was a great blessing, starting with the cessation of the famine upon Yaakov Avinu's arrival there. Never mind that they excelled there – as the Haggadah says, "*she'hayu Yisrael metzuyanim sham.*" The pattern for future relations with the other nations of the world was set: recognize the Jews' unique and outstanding qualities and *hate* them for it. *Hava nischakmah lo* (1:10), we need to outsmart those *foreigners*, those usurping Jews, who think they're so smart! *Va'yakutzu* (1:12) – they couldn't stand the sight of them.

And so they enslaved the Jews, to use them up in the process of making them disappear.

As the decades of oppression and slavery passed, as the terrible became the unbearable, as time seemingly stood still for them, with no sign of an end to it, with no relief at all, *va'yehi ba'yamim harabbim hahem* (2:23), *in those unending terrible days*, something happened.

Pharaoh, the chief oppressor, died.

Yet nothing changed. It would have been reasonable, as was the custom of the time, to expect some lightening of the burden. But there was none. The collective groan of misery from the Children of Israel – *va'ye'anchu Bnei Yisrael min ha'avodah* – pierced the Heavens, and God "heard" them, He "remembered" His covenant with Avraham, Yitzchak, and Yaakov, He "saw" the Children of Israel, and He "knew" the time of their salvation had arrived.

Despite the depths to which they had fallen in their misery, to the extent that they could, the Jews had held on. They still remembered who they were. They did not change their Hebrew dress, their Hebrew names, or their Hebrew language. Much of Egypt's depravity, after all those years, had seriously tainted them in various ways. But in their core, they knew who they were, and they held fast. And for that, as difficult as it was for the Jews to hold fast, they were redeemed.

A great tragedy in the enslavement and violent transshipment of millions of Africans to America was, in addition to the enslavement itself, the cruel dehumanization that was integral to the enslavement process. Those poor, wretched people were not just stolen from their homes and their homelands. Their homes and their homelands were stolen from them. Their names, their languages, their customs, their identities, their origins, were so ruthlessly ripped away that whatever and whoever they had been was soon lost. And the price of that tragedy has reverberated through the generations, all over America, long after legal emancipation.

The Children of Israel have suffered many terrible tragedies over the millennia. At times it was clear that we brought it upon ourselves. Other times, the reason is not so obvious at all. But, as *maaminim bnei maaminim*, we know that it is God's judgment. As in Egypt, many were lost along the way. And as in Egypt, the core held on, in whatever way they could. And one way that was possible, after all that, was that God not only remembered our Avos – Avraham, Yitzchak, and Yaakov – and His relationship with them, He made sure that we too, despite all the troubles in our history, in the depths of unspeakable national and personal tragedy, *we* remembered as well. And that made holding on possible.

He did not let us forget, and here we are.

Noach Bogatin was raised in an oppressive, Godless society, he was ten years a slave in a frozen gulag where privation and death were the daily menu, but in the end, he was our cherished *shaliach tzibbur* on Rosh Hashanah and Yom Kippur. Who better to represent us at such an awesome time? His father sacrificed that he might remember, he sacrificed to remember, and by God's grace, he remembered, he persevered, and he overcame.

Shimon and Chana, and so many like them, were blessed with upbringings that made it possible for them to hold on, as best they could. What more can one ask of a human being? And the same God, the God of their fathers, the God Who brought their forefathers into Egypt and caused them to be enslaved in its cruel *kur habarzel*, the roiling smelting furnace that was Egypt, and then "remembered" them and made them into the nation that stood at Sinai, also blessed my parents not just with survival, but with the memory that made that survival so much more meaningful than just physical survival itself.

As difficult as things become, He has not forgotten us, we have not forgotten Him, and we are here. It is a bond that shall never be broken.

To Gehinnom with our oppressors. They will disappear. We are here.

והיה כאשר הייתם קללה בגוים בית יהודה ובית ישראל

כן אושיע אתכם והייתם ברכה

אל תיראו תחזקנה ידיכם

כה אמר ה' צבאות

צום הרביעי וצום החמישי וצום השביעי וצום העשירי

יהיה לבית יהודה לששון ולשמחה ולמעדים טובים
האמת והשלום אהבו
(זכריה ח')

Parashas Shemos 5775, Yerushalayim Ir Hakodesh

The Evil Professor Pharaoh

Pharaoh ordered the Jewish midwives to kill the male Jewish children immediately upon their birth, while letting the females live. The Gemara (*Sotah* 11b) tells us that he gave them important medical signs to help them in this nasty work. Rabbi Chanan says, *siman gadol masar lahen*, he gave them an important sign, that *when they crouch to give birth, their thighs turn cold as stone*. Rabbi Chaninah says, *siman gadol masar lahen*, he gave them an important sign, *a male child faces down (upon emerging), while a female faces up.*

1. What is the *siman gadol*, the great significance, or even the relevance of these two signs?
2. The facts of nature are different from the common explanations of these two "signs."

Is it really necessary to postulate that "nature has changed" in order to understand this Gemara?

Some posit that Pharaoh wanted the Jewish mothers to think that the babies were stillborn (rather than killed – or, if you will, *late-term aborted*) in order to keep them quiet, and to keep them from ceasing to have children altogether. He wanted the female children to be born alive. He therefore needed a way for the midwives to recognize a boy *before* the birth was complete, at a time when the mother would not be able to concentrate and not realize what was happening.

(The Midrash famously describes how the Jews, upon learning of the decree, indeed all separated from their wives, but Miriam convinced her parents, and thereby all of Israel, to push on with making life, lest the nation disappear altogether.)

And so Professor Pharaoh gave the Jewish midwives *simanim gedolim*, great natural signs, by which they would know if the child that had not yet fully emerged was a boy or a girl.

But women's legs do not, in fact, turn "cold as stone" when the baby is about to emerge.

And while there are exceptions (and these cases can be problematic), children are normally born occiput anterior, facing the rear, regardless of gender. The common understanding of the Gemara is that the boys were born facing rear, while the girls were born facing forward (occiput posterior), contrary to nature.

Let me offer an explanation.

The Gemara says that when they were about to give birth, the women's legs became *mitztanenos k'avanim*, cold as stone. But stones are not inherently cold or warm. They are as cold or as warm as the environment makes them. The word *avanim*, stones, here may refer to something *sensory*.

The Jewish women were giving birth to six babies at a time. As this mass of babies descended into the pelvis, the nerves in the region were impinged upon, making the legs numb during the birth process: *mitztanenos k'avanim*. Their legs would feel like a stone – *numb* – not to the midwife, but to the mother. And this was a sign to the midwife that birth was imminent and she should prepare to fulfill Pharaoh's orders.

The common understanding of *ben panav l'matah, bas paneha l'maalah*, a boy faces rearward, and a girl faces frontward, may be fallacious based upon our modern-day experience of women giving birth while lying on their backs, in bed. Historically, however, women would squat to give birth. The baby's head would emerge, typically, as is natural in childbirth, occiput anterior, the back of the head emerging in line with the mother's front.

Now, with the head out, dangling, but with the rest of the body still obscured inside the mother, Pharaoh's plan required the midwife to know at this point if it was a boy, so she could wring its neck, or a girl, so she could let it live.

I suggest that Pharaoh's sign referred to where the baby was facing once its head was out and dangling: the boys faced down to the ground (*l'matah*), and the girls faced up (*l'maalah*), back toward the mother.

The *siman gadol* is the remarkable insight this implies: the male faces toward the earth, whence he was derived (Adam); the female faces toward the human body, whence she was derived (see *Niddah* 31b). The male faces toward the earth, from which he must somehow scratch a living his entire life; the female faces toward the womb: family, child-rearing, the things that occupy a woman's life. The male faces toward the earth and stone, reflecting his harder nature; the female faces back toward her mother, reflecting her softer nature. The male faces down, reflecting his propensity to the mundane; the female faces up, reflecting propensity for sensitivity, for the spiritual. To face the ground, the male must stick out his chin, jut his jaw, a typically male assertive, even defiant stance; the female turns her face up, hiding it, reflecting her shy, even retiring nature. The male faces down, direct and abrupt; the female faces away, subtle and mysterious. The male faces down, bold and adventurous; the female faces up, back to her mother, meeker and home-oriented.

The macho male faces down to the earth, fixed on *l'an ata holech*, where are you headed; the female faces her mother's womb, *me'ayin basa*, where do you come from.

Now, I don't know if those boy babies actually arched their necks and faced down to the ground as they emerged from their mommies, and the girls arched their necks the other way and faced back up toward their mommies, but maybe they did. Those were remarkable times. A nation was being miraculously created. Even in the midst of bondage, indeed perhaps *because* of the bondage, Israel increased at an astounding, unnatural rate, which strengthened the Jews and alarmed the Egyptians. Perhaps accelerated this way, maleness and femaleness were already being expressed even as the children emerged from the womb. Egypt was a place of great learning and science. Something so remarkable would not have escaped the notice of the Egyptians, and Pharaoh tried to use this information in fighting Jewish increase.

The Jewish midwives, Shifrah and Puah, of course, feared God and did not do as Pharaoh demanded. And so Pharaoh resorted to other evil means.

How strange that Pharaoh should have access to such knowledge, such insight, such *simanim gedolim*, and yet be so blind to the obvious truth. Soulless science also powered the evil Nazi and Soviet empires. Such is the power of evil.

Parashas Shemos 5767

Those Jews...

Many of the *parashiyos* of Bereishis and Shemos set the patterns for the future with regard to Israel and the other nations – Yaakov and Esav, Yosef and Mitzrayim (Yosef and his brothers), Yitzchak and Yishmael, and so on.

Lo yada es Yosef: here, the king of Egypt "knew not Yosef." Yosef had, on behalf of Pharaoh, centralized virtually all the wealth and power of Egypt in the hands of the king. Now there is no acknowledgment or appreciation. *What have you done for me lately? Besides, whatever you did, you did for yourself.*

Am Bnei Yisrael rav v'atzum mimenu. The Jews are so many and so powerful! There are so many of them! They multiply like vermin! Disgusting! *Va'yishretzu.* Much like the Nazi propaganda films depicting the Jews as propagating rats and vermin.

Va'yakutzu mi'pnei Bnei Yisrael. They were disgusted by the Jews.

Hava nischakmah lo – they are so clever: watch out! Let's be more clever! Let's outsmart them.

Rav v'atzum mimenu – emphasis on *mimenu* (from us). They got rich off of us. What they have we should really have. It's *ours*. Like that charlatan and rabble-rouser Sharpton about Jewish (or Korean) merchants.

V'nosaf gam hu al soneinu. They will join forces with our enemies – they're a fifth column! They are not loyal. They're not really us! They are *other*. Hence, the Midrash explains the use of the present tense in *haba'im Mitzraimah* – they just got here. No matter how much they have become vested in society, they are still viewed as newcomers, outsiders.

But who knows? Maybe the Egyptian people were not particularly antisemitic. Maybe they lived well with their Jewish neighbors. And like many demagogues over the years, this was an attempt to deflect anger or frustration onto the stranger. The state had taken all the land, all the cattle, all the wealth, and even had claim to the very persons of the Egyptians, as documented in Parashas Vayigash. Who's responsible? The Jews! Yosef! Those capitalists! Those communists! Blame them! *The reason you don't have is because those Jews do have!* (Sound familiar?)

Va'yomer el amo: Pharaoh did not just order measures taken against the Jews, he appealed to the people to hate them, to fear them, to despise them. To be disgusted by them.

Amo: "My people." That's you, my fellow Egyptians – not them, not those Jews. We're in this together – against *them*. Help me in this noble and patriotic struggle against the money-grubbing, avaricious alien outsider!

The Torah is telling us that we will always be seen as alien to the other nations, that we cannot pin our hopes on them, that salvation does not come from London, or from Basel, or even from Washington. We can rely only upon our Father in Heaven, and we must turn to Him to help us. And if we do, as a nation, turn only to Him, we will, in fact, be redeemed.

Parashas Shemos 5770

Why Moshe? Why Me?

The four-month-old grave was not hard to spot. The neat rows of stone slabs, horizontal on the ground as well as vertical at the head, as is the custom in Israel, were interrupted by the grave we sought, which as yet has no *matzeivah*, no monument. A little mound of earth and a small name tag.

Ninety-nine years in this world. A life. And now, a little mound of earth. With a random wild weed trying to sprout.

It does lead one to reflect. In the ninety-nine years between my mother-in-law's birth and that little mound of earth, what was accomplished by her being on this earth?

The question is, really, for each of us, why are we here, and what are we doing with our lives to justify our having been here? We Jews believe that life has a purpose, that this world has a purpose, and that each person is here as part of that purpose.

Our challenge is to fulfill that purpose. But God doesn't normally whisper in our ears what great projects to undertake to fulfill that purpose. He has given us guidelines on how to live our lives. It is then our duty to live our lives, and to think of His will as a guide for all our actions.

That's a tall order. But what else is there? The Ribbono shel Olam's *hashgachah* runs the world according to His wisdom and His plan, to which we are not privy.

And so, each day, in each encounter with God and in each encounter with our fellow human beings, we never know what universe-changing result may ensue.

What was the result when the daughter of Pharaoh heard a child's cry, saw the little basket floating in the Nile, and decided not to ignore it?

Ida Hilsenrad was not Pharaoh's daughter. Born in Poland, a child immigrant, she had an upbringing and an education quite typical for a girl of her time in Williamsburg, Brooklyn. She did not have what the world today would consider a distinguished career.

She was not a professional, she did not write books, she did not hold public office.

And yet, in the ninety-nine years she spent on this earth, she enabled, with her husband through their Keren Hachesed, many hundreds of families of desperately poor people to live and to sustain themselves as perpetuators of Torah life in Eretz Yisrael. Who but God can say who and what will, over the long term, emerge from that effort?

She raised a fine family *al taharas hakodesh*. Who but God can say who or what will emerge from her generations?

She interacted kindly, always, with those with whom she dealt in all spheres of life. Who can say what will, in some way known only to God, result from that?

She was not unique, except in the way each of us is unique. But that itself is the very lesson. God's world is built primarily not on Great Men, but on regular people who, striving to live as God wants them to, bring the greatness of God's plan into the world and make Him manifest.

Certainly, the great men and women in our history, the Avos, the Imahos, Moshe Rabbenu, were the necessary giants around whom the great events that shaped our history and our civilization happened. But the greats of each generation, who sustain that civilization, are, in turn, enabled and supported by the actions of the rest of us. It is up to us, as well, to sustain that civilization. And who but God can say which of us – and by which particular choices we make in life – will affect the whole world in the most profound way?

Harbeh shluchim la'Makom. God has many messengers. Moshe Rabbenu was the great messenger sent to take us out of Egyptian bondage and form us into the Torah nation, the Raya Mehemna, the strong and loving shepherd. But every one of us, every living person, has a role to play in sustaining the world.

And so I will share with you a story I heard this week in Yerushalayim, from my cousin who is a descendant of the great Rebbes of Dzhikov and Ropshitz. It is a story he was told by one of its chief protagonists. And the story is absolutely true.

When my cousin was visiting a certain city, he met with an elderly man.

In his youth, the man had been *hausbachur*, a live-in assistant to the Rebbe Reb Alter of Dzhikov, H"yd. Although quite elderly, and no longer the least bit observant of the Torah and mitzvos, he remembered much Torah taught by the Rebbe, he remembered *minhagim*, and he remembered many unique *niggunim*.

He and his brothers survived the war, although the rest of their families did not.

He showed my cousin a picture of his father. He had been a beautiful Jew, a Chassid and a *talmid chacham*, a *hadras panim*. Not one of the surviving sons, as they emerged from the Holocaust, retained his religion.

This particular man had a daughter who, raised without Yiddishkeit, married a non-Jew.

I don't know if it bothered him; I will assume it did. Nevertheless, the son-in-law was a very fine fellow. In fact, he was so fine that he took a great interest in the people he married into. And, you guessed it, his interest grew until one day he told his wife that not only did he wish to become a Jew, he intended to become a *real* Jew. The whole deal.

She had never lived a religious Jewish life, and did not want to. But she did want to stay married to her husband, who was determined to proceed, even if it were to cost him his marriage. She had to choose. And so they did it and raised a family.

The old man told the visiting rabbi that his grandchildren were not what he had expected. You see, they were not only religious, they were also heavily Chassidic.

The children attended Chassidic yeshivos. Their mother too was now fully with the program.

My cousin met this family. The sons had long *peyos* and learned day and night.

The father had a big beard and *peyos*, dressed Chassidic, and was fully integrated into Jewish life. His Shemoneh Esrei, my cousin reported, was an inspiration.

He was the real thing. A smart man, he became quite learned, and even taught *shiurim*.

My cousin looked at the picture of the old man's martyred father. How many generations of great, loyal Jews had come to an end, just in his line, when he was murdered by the Germans and his surviving sons turned away from the faith of his fathers? And yet, here they were again, the chain picked up and ongoing. What great things will come out of them?

Only God knows. But that beautiful grandfather, that *hadras panim* of a Jew, *hut zich fardint*. He and his holy forebears somehow earned the merit that life be reinfused into their generations.

My cousin was in town again some years later. He saw the sons in shul, young men, beautiful Jews, davening and learning. "Where's the father?" he asked. "Strange thing," he was told. "He became a non-Jew again." He left. The mother runs their Torah household.

Harbeh shluchim la'Makom. God has many messengers.

Each one of us is God's messenger. With some people, such as Moshe Rabbenu, and the great leaders and teachers of our people in every generation, that role is more apparent and more fundamental. But that role, in some manner, is, in fact, part of the mandate each one of us has in this life. In our actions and our interactions every day and in every sphere of life, we can never know – only the Creator can know – what the longterm effects and ramifications of our deeds will be.

God does have a divine plan. Some are *zocheh* and earn the privilege to be a Moshe Rabbenu or a Rav Moshe. Some might be a *bas Pharaoh*. Others are an Ida Hilsenrad. Most of us never know, and never see, in this life, the big picture of what we have brought about, or what we *could have* brought about, had we made the right choices.

For God has many messengers, and His will be done. In whatever number of years we do have, we must choose always to be God's messengers for good, so that when it is over, what's left is considerably more, and considerably greater, and considerably more lasting, than a little mound of earth.

Parashas Shemos 5772, Yerushalayim Ir Hakodesh

Va'era

Raya Mehemna

The surgeon, working meticulously, suddenly encountered a situation that required rapid and urgent intervention. He asked the circulating nurse, whose duty it is to fetch and deliver to the sterile field such items as may be needed during the operation, to bring him what he needed.

The woman looked at him for a moment. After another moment she slowly rose from her seat, and slowly, leisurely, ambled over to the supply closet, rummaged a bit, found the item, and then strolled over to the scrub table and delivered it.

From the perspective of the circulator, it was normal – perfectly fine and timely. From the perspective of the surgeon, and the urgent situation at hand, it took an eternity.

The scrub nurse assisting the doctor with the surgery, a *geshikte* woman who went about her business always with energy and diligence, with little tolerance for laziness, shook her head and muttered, in an undertone, "Sittin' on the dock o' the bay!"

She was referencing a slow-moving popular song from the sixties in which the protagonist just sits there, on the dock of the bay, watching the tide roll in and hours later roll out again, not doing much else, "wastin' time." No hurry. The protagonist, of course, accomplishes nothing, and he knows it. He is sad about it.

For many people, it is a way of life, and they are not at all sad about it. They do go about life, but wrap everything they do in listless lethargy – not because they are ill, but because that's how they do life. The idea of diligence or alacrity is alien to them. Don't expect too much accomplishment from them. And many of them completely fail to make the connection between their limited accomplishments in life and their utter lack of diligence.

The Torah sends us a message on this. Moshe is instructed, *"hashkem,"* get up *early* in the morning, and stand before Pharaoh. The Midrash (*Pesikta Rabbasi*) points to the wisdom of God as presented by Shlomo Hamelech in Mishlei (22:29) on this subject: *"Chazisa ish mahir bi'mlachto lifnei melachim yisyatzav."* The man who is quick in his work, who works with alacrity, will succeed; he will stand before kings. This is Moshe, says Rabbi Tanchuma bar Abba. Moshe was a *zariz*, who was diligent in his life before this, and whose alacrity in all things, in addition to his other superior qualities, brought him to his present station.

Rabbenu Yonah expands on this formula for success and accomplishment. When you have a task to accomplish, do not relax until you have completed it. Doing it with alacrity also means not putting off getting started or preparing for it, and not dillydallying while doing it. *Lifnei melachim yisyatzav:* such a man is sought after by kings; he is in demand, and he will likely succeed in life.

Rabbenu Yonah brings it to the next step. Such a person is a *zariz*, diligent in religion too, careful and punctilious in carrying out his religious requirements. He ties it to the preceding *pasuk, al taseg gevul olam, asher asu avosecha.* Do not move back the longstanding boundary markers established by your forefathers. Homiletically, this refers to *syagim*, enactments placed around a Torah law in order to protect people from serious violations. The Torah itself tells us to do this: *u'shmartem es mishmarti,* regarding holiness (Vayikra 18:30), which tells us to be zealous and to set up safeguards around the mitzvos (see *Moed Katan* 5a).

The Midrash associates this quality of Moshe's with his behavior while working as a shepherd for his father-in-law, Yisro. We are told, elsewhere, that Moshe's great compassion and humanity in how he tended the sheep, going so far as to search for and find a lost sheep and, finding it tired and frightened, carrying it home on his shoulders, demonstrated his worthiness to be the Raya Mehemna, the faithful shepherd of Israel.

And so here we come to what appears superficially to be a bit of a contradiction, but which I believe is not.

For eight days at the Burning Bush, the very modest and self-effacing Moshe fended off God's demand that he go to Egypt to be the leader and spearhead of the Exodus. He pleaded: *Send someone else!* God insisted: *Only you, Moshe!* In the end, Moshe went. Over the ensuing forty years, Moshe was more than exasperated with this stiff-necked and difficult people. And time after time, he stretched himself to the limit to defend them before God, begging Him to forgive their many serious trespasses. Only Moshe could have done that. And, after all that, only Moshe could have still remained in the good graces of both God and the people.

But it was his very loyalty and dedication to his brethren that earned him a stern reprimand from God right at the outset, even before the first of the *makkos* (plagues).

As the process played out, Moshe first presented himself to Pharaoh, stating God's demand that Egypt "let my people go." He showed the king of Egypt the wondrous signs. Pharaoh was unimpressed and punished the Jews by making their work much harder. They were now much worse off than before Moshe came.

Moshe confronts God: "*Lama hare'osa la'am hazeh?*" (Why have You harmed this nation?) "*Lama zeh shelachtani?*" (Why did You send me?) "*Hatzel lo hitzalta!*" (You have not rescued them!) *Since I arrived on Your mission, it's only gotten worse!*

Moshe presses the point further (see *Shemos Rabbah* 5:26), with language that is shockingly suggestive of anger. I know history, he argues before God. I know what the generation of the Flood did, I know their evil deeds and how they were judged and punished. I know what the generation of the Dispersion did, I know what the people of Sedom did, I know their evil deeds and how they were judged and punished. *What did the Jews do that You should punish them so?* And if it is because Avraham asked You, by what can I know that I will indeed inherit this land, and You told him that his descendants would be strangers and slaves, well, Esav and Yishmael are also Avraham's descendants! Why not enslave *them*?! Why not the generation of Yitzchak, or of Yaakov, rather than my own contemporary Jews? If this is what You do, I protest that You sent me! Save them through somebody else!

God responds somewhat "testily," *k'v'yachol*, criticizing Moshe for his argument, indeed his *apparent* weakness of faith. *Chaval al d'ovdin v'lo mishtakchin!* Woe for the loss of those who are gone but not forgotten, God chides Moshe. The Avos received only promises but no fulfillment, yet they did not question Me. *You, who have been chosen to be the redeemer, to actually see the fulfillment of those promises, you challenge Me!*

Oy!

So, did Moshe actually do wrong here? Does that make sense? He was the greatest of all the prophets ever. He merited to speak with God "face to face," which no other prophet could. He was the perfect tzaddik.

I submit that this was, in fact, part of God's calculation in choosing Moshe. What Moshe faced was forty years of challenges no other man could meet. He had to be a unique individual who had it in him to stand up to God, *as it were*, as well as to a tough people, not to mention Pharaoh and his mighty empire. And he had to be the gentle, loving shepherd of his flock.

At the Burning Bush, Moshe, understanding who he was, knew that he might well say things in defense of his brethren that might provoke God's criticism, which he in fact ended up doing, and he therefore, along with his other reasons, demurred.

At the Burning Bush, indeed long before the Burning Bush, God knew very well that it was Moshe whom He wanted for this special role, just for those qualities of his.

For his loving compassion. For his strength and his utter dedication. For his piety and his humility coupled with his determined loyalty to his people and his willingness, time and again, to put himself on the line to defend them and promote their cause. For his *zerizus*, his zeal, his alacrity, and his diligence in all things.

God knew that Moshe would argue, *why have You harmed this nation?! Why did You send me?* When, later on, upon encountering the Golden Calf, Moshe took the very *luchos* that God had fashioned with His own hand and shattered them, we are told that Hashem told him, *Yasher kochachem!* What he did had a purpose and served a higher end.

Here too, I think, Moshe's argument had a purpose and a higher end, one which God undoubtedly anticipated and might even have welcomed, even with the declaration, indeed the complaint, of *Chaval al d'ovdin*, because that was the kind of dedicated leader that was needed, that was the person who could, and would, for all time be known as our people's faithful shepherd, our Raya Mehemna.

Indeed, indeed, Chaval al d'ovdin.

Parashas Va'era 5777

The Language of Redemption

Parashas Va'era opens with some of the most soaring, redemptive language anywhere in Scripture.

Here are enshrined the four immortal *leshonos* of *geulah*: *v'hotzeisi, v'hitzalti, v'gaalti, v'lakachti*. Chazal established the four *kosos* of wine at the Seder corresponding to these four *leshonos*. Wine is one way that we separate ourselves from the *nochrim*. We do not drink gentile wine. It was this very halachah that Haman, in his quest to destroy the entire Jewish race, used to turn Achashveirosh against the Jews: "If a disgusting fly falls into their wine, they will remove the fly and drink the rest. If you, the king, even touch their wine, they will pour it out and not drink it. They consider you, and all gentiles, more disgusting than an insect." Of course, Haman got his comeuppance at a wine party. And thus, at the Seder, we raise the cup of wine when we sing V'hi She'amda, signifying the role, in our miraculous continuity, of our keeping ourselves apart.

And yet, how well do we keep ourselves apart? We know very well that those who survive as Jews also are those who have, on a fundamental level, maintained themselves as a group apart. Throughout the generations, however, there have always been Jews who, for one reason or another, have fallen away, disappearing into the multitude of nations.

I once read – and I do not know if this is so – that at one point in history, the number of Jews and the number of Chinese was about the same. Imagine that.

That this can be so is supported by the Gemara (*Sanhedrin* 111a) and *Midrash Rabbah* (Shemos 5). Chazal tell us that only a small fraction of the Jews actually left Egypt, the rest too far gone to be redeemable. Terrible forces, usually imposed by the outside world, but sometimes, *nebech*, from within, have torn away large chunks of our people over the ages.

It's interesting that when Hashem ordered Moshe and Aharon to tell Pharaoh to let the Jews leave Egypt, a simultaneous mandate was given to them to tell the Jews *themselves* that they must, in fact, leave Egypt. It was not optional or voluntary. Leave Egypt. Leave as Jews or disappear. *Va'yetzavem el Bnei Yisrael v'el Paroh melech Mitzrayim l'hotzi es Bnei Yisrael me'eretz Mitzrayim* (6:13).

And yet the Jews, even the "good ones," who merited redemption, had a hard time with it. Moshe announces the impending redemption in the soaring language of the four *leshonos* of *geulah*, but they don't listen to him. *V'lo shamu el Moshe mi'kotzer ruach u'me'avodah kashah* (6:9).

An amazing concept, I believe, is couched in these words, and in the Torah's stating them. There have been countless times when Jews, as a people and individually, don't do the right thing. With this *pasuk* the Torah is establishing a defense of the Jewish People for all generations. The world has been very hard on us. For most of our history, we have been under foreign domination, oppressed, persecuted, and poor. We have suffered from *kotzer ruach* and *avodah kashah* to an incredible degree. With this *pasuk*, one can argue, God is cutting us some slack. "Here's a reasonable excuse. Go ahead and use it in your defense when you have to." It is a loving God that we have.

Now remember what distinguished those Jews who did make it out of Egypt.

They kept their Jewish names, their Jewish clothing, and their Jewish (Hebrew) language.

It's easy to see how that attachment to their roots helped them hang on and created for them a Jewish future.

And so I will relate an observation that I have made in Israel. It's hard to be an immigrant. New language, new social mores, new culture, new way of life.

The task of integrating, holding down a job, and caring for a family must be very daunting. It's hard to be a stranger. And if one can learn the new language, it is usually lacking in fluency and spoken with a readily identifiable foreign accent.

Immigrants, speaking among themselves, will typically do so in their native language. That's only natural. It's so much easier, and it's instinctive. I would do it. And if I were working hard to speak that new language, and someone, recognizing my American accent, switched to English, I would happily revert to English as well.

So here is something I have noticed. In our area of Brooklyn, many people from Russia do speak English, with varying degrees of facility. Address them in Russian, however, and they will very likely switch to that language. It's only natural, and this has been my experience with speakers of other languages as well.

In Israel, Americans I know who have been living there a long time still typically speak English with each other. If they are speaking Hebrew, address them in English and they will switch to English. Too many times to be a coincidence, however, my experience with Russian immigrants in Israel has been somewhat different. If they speak to me in Hebrew, and, hearing their heavy Russian accent, I switch to Russian (yes, I can do that a little), they will typically continue to determinedly talk to me in Hebrew. And to my delight and embarrassment, they are sometimes visibly somewhat offended, or at least annoyed, by my innocent attempt to derail their use of Hebrew.

I just love that. The message that I get is that this language, Hebrew, although new to them, is also the old, original language of their souls, and that this land, new to them, is the birthplace of their souls. Deprived for so long of this connection and source of oneness with their people and their essential identity, they now cling to it with a fierce determination. It's a statement that now, this new language may "break their teeth" a bit, but it is *theirs*, and not the language of their oppressors. It is a real advantage that Jews in Israel have over us Americans.

We Americans, blessedly free, do not need that particular declaration of freedom; we can easily express our Jewishness in multiple ways. There may still be a lot that's missing from a full Jewish life for many of those immigrants in Israel from the former Soviet Union, but, like their forebears in Egypt, the ancestral, holy language of the Jews is something fundamental to hold on to while the rest develops.

In the Torah (Devarim 30:4), God promises that He will bring home the exiles from the far corners of the earth. But it does not exactly say that. The actual words are *im yihyeh nidachacha bi'ktzeh hashamayim mi'sham yekabetzcha*. If your exiles are in the outer reaches of Heaven, from there I will gather you. "Heaven"? It should say "earth."

The Lubavitcher Rebbe suggests that "the outer reaches of Heaven" here is not simply a poetic way of saying "far away." Rather, it refers to where those Jews are in relation to heavenly matters. That is, they are very far away from Torah. But if still connected, they can be drawn in, and they will be.

People sometimes mock those Lubavitcher fellows who chase people in the street with a lulav or get them to put on tefillin once in their lives. What difference does it make, the scoffers ask. They'll never do it again.

Sadly, that may be true. But, the Rebbe teaches, when a Jew does anything that connects him to Judaism, to Torah, to mitzvos, to other Jews, when he shakes a lulav even once, or recites Shema even once, there attaches to him a kind of spiritual string. And with that string, God, in His wisdom, His kindness, and His love, may some day pull those Jews in. They may be at the outer edges of Heaven, but they are not inevitably or irretrievably lost.

The Jews in Egypt who merited redemption were those who remained attached by the "strings" of their particular time. They were down to the forty-ninth level of *tumah*. But that Jewish garment, that Jewish name, that stubborn continued use of Hebrew were the strings that God used to draw them from the edge of the fiftieth level of *tumah* to the foot of Har Sinai and the very heights of *kedushah*.

And so, *bravo!* to our brethren who have been robbed of their background, robbed of their inheritance, and robbed of the necessary tools, except for their determination to hang on in some way. And as one family, may Hashem soon pull upon all our connecting strings and draw us to Him and to each other, and redeem us, and again establish us as the nation of Torah, safely in our Holy Land, even as He did for our ancestors in Egypt.

Parashas Va'era 5772

The Lightness and Heaviness of the Spirit

Parashas Va'era depicts events quite early in Moshe's career; in it a startling pattern is set, which Moshe perhaps gets used to but does not seem to get over. And who can blame him?

God sends him to Bnei Yisrael with a message, a promise of redemption couched in the most sweeping, glorious, and exalted terms. But do they listen? No. "*V'lo shamu el Moshe*" (Shemos 6:9).

There is no comment on what his reaction was. We know from his dialogue with God at the Burning Bush that he doubted their worthiness for miracles to be performed on their behalf (see Rashi on "V'chi otzi es Bnei Yisrael mi'Mitzrayim" [Shemos 3:11]). However disappointed he must have been, one suspects that it was fairly benign, because later on, in the *midbar*, he does react forcefully, presumably because of higher expectations, and we *do* know about it.

But when he reacts forcefully, while he might in fact be angry with them, his forceful action is typically to pray for them, begging God, *insisting of God*, for their forgiveness, to save their apparently ungrateful selves. Is that what happened here? Was this the opening act in a play that was to become a repertory? And why was Moshe so understanding?

Once before, upon his initial presentation to the Jews when he arrives from Midian, the Torah tells us that they believed him: "The people believed; they heard that God remembered and designated Israel for redemption, that He saw their oppression, and they bowed and prostrated themselves [before God]" (Shemos 4:31).

This is now the second time Moshe comes to announce to the Jews their impending deliverance. Their reaction is different this time. What changed now? Further, asks the *Mechilta*, is there a person who hears very good news, especially news of his impending freedom from slavery, and is *not* happy? You won the jillion-dollar lottery and you're *miserable* to learn of it? Not likely. Why were they happy the first time, and not now, especially with all the lofty promises of divine blessing?

So let's compare the two messages. In the first, Moshe told them that the time for redemption had arrived. He spoke the "code words" that first Yaakov, then Yosef told them the redeemer would use to signal the redemption: "*pakod yifkod,*" which the most senior elders knew of and awaited. So they knew that Moshe was the true redeemer, and that they were, at long last, to be freed from their bondage. They were told nothing of any expectations *of them*. And so they were happy.

Now comes Moshe with a beautiful message from God, that He has heard their groans, He has seen their bitter labor, that He remembers His covenant with their forefathers, that He will take them out (והוצאתי) from their state of suffering, that He will save them (והצלתי) from their backbreaking labor, that He will redeem them (וגאלתי) with an outstretched arm and with great signs, that He will take them (ולקחתי) to be His, *that He will be their exclusive God, and they will know that He, the Ribbono shel Olam, is their Redeemer* from Egypt. And He will bring them to the land that He has given them as their eternal inheritance, the Land of Israel.

Sounds wonderful! Except remember where they have been for over two hundred years, what life was like for them, and how much of Egypt had already rubbed off on them. Yes, they retained their Jewish identity (clothing, language, names), but some behavior patterns learned from the Egyptians that they enjoyed they would now have to give up, *and they weren't ready for that.*

God wanted an *exclusive* relationship (no *avodah zarah!*), but they were reluctant. God also demanded chastity, but they were reluctant. Of course they wanted to be free, and of course they wanted to be good Jews...*but not quite yet.*

They did not listen to Moshe, the Torah says, *mi'kotzer ruach u'me'avodah kashah.* Usually understood to mean, essentially, from shortness of breath, of *spirit*, due to their terribly hard labor. The Midrash (*Shemos Rabbah* 5) offers a twist: It was *kasheh*, hard for them to undertake God's mandate that Moshe brought them, *mi'kotzer ruach*, for lack of the proper spirit. They were still too tied in with the *avodah zarah* and the fleshpots of Egypt. They weren't quite ready to give that up.

They were contaminated. And God, in His mercy, seeing that it would only get worse, brought them out before they were altogether gone.

People do resolve to do good, to be good, to reform, to quit their bad habits... tomorrow. (*Like that diet and exercise program we're going to start, any day now.*)

Moshe, it would appear, understood this, even as he was undoubtedly repelled by it. Ever their loyal defender, he forged ahead, under God's direction, with the process of Redemption, hoping and expecting that they would wake up and fall into line. And he was correct in that assessment. They certainly did.

Yet, for the next forty years, and thereafter, some of that pattern would reemerge. Human nature. Even for the generation that proclaimed at Sinai, "*naaseh v'nishma.*"

L'havdil, one of the great formative thinkers of another religion, in describing his progress from pagan to saint, famously describes his early prayers, which reflected his mindset and readiness for reform at that early stage: "Grant me chastity and continence," he prayed, "*but not yet.*" He was too busy enjoying certain aspects of his old life. That is human nature.

There were many prophets in ancient Israel, probably in the thousands, but we know of only a few. We know nothing of all those other prophecies. There were many occurrences in the lives of the Avos, but we know of only those few recounted in the Torah. What is preserved for us and transmitted to us is that which is necessary *l'doros*, what all generations of Jews until the end of time need to know in order to fulfill our role and our mission in the world.

Sometimes there is information about great people that is less than complimentary, but the Torah and the Navi spell it out because we need to know, that we may understand. Sometimes there is such information that is not spelled out, but quietly known to masters of the *mesorah*. And when one of them does spell it out, makes it public, as it were, he may well be chastised by his colleagues for needlessly publicizing that which the Torah clearly "chose" to keep hidden.

Why do we need to know that Bnei Yisrael in Egypt were contaminated by *avodah zarah*, to the point that even when told by the one whom they already acknowledged had been sent by the God of their fathers to redeem them, they *still* held back, reluctant to give up what they *knew* was *avodah zarah*?

Because, I submit, in this we recognize a key element in human nature that we also recognize within ourselves. It is the inner demon we each struggle with, at whatever level we are, in the ongoing battle to bring ourselves from where we are to where we need to be. And importantly, perhaps most importantly, it sensitizes us to that very struggle within those around us, a struggle that may be more difficult, more demanding, more of a test than our own.

It is a struggle that, we are taught, Moshe Rabbenu himself went through before he perfected himself to the point that he indeed became Moshe Rabbenu. It is no surprise at all that he must have understood and even tolerated, at that point, the process, the struggle of purification that Bnei Yisrael had to go through.

It is a struggle about which God and our *chachamim* want us to know that it is inherent to the human condition, and that the same Creator who made us that way also created within us the power and the ability to win that struggle. The *will* to do so is up to us.

We sometimes read biographies of great men who seem to have lived, as the book reads, in a phantasy world of improbable perfection, seemingly from the moment of conception, divorced from the reality of human nature. It makes the rest of us feel that this kind of achievement is utterly beyond the reach of us mere mortals, who live in the real world, and there's no point in even trying. Some years ago, a biography appeared about one of the great *chachamim* of nineteenth-century Europe that depicted him, especially early in life, as a real person, with real struggles, who overcame and who excelled. There were those who lambasted the book for that reason. I believe they did no one a service in doing so.

Ironically, even paradoxically, the very fact of the Jews' *kotzer ruach*, their spiritual decline, served to hasten their departure from Egypt. God would not allow them to fall any lower. He had to get them out of there before they were beyond redemption. And the severity of their servitude, four hundred years' worth of slave labor crammed into 210, but actually eighty-six brutal years, fulfilled their "sentence," their quota of misery, ahead of schedule.

It was by God's mercy, His loving-kindness coupled with His commitment to the Avos, that our forefathers were snatched out of Egypt before it was too late. And even so, even though we needed to be snatched out in a hurry because of our state of *kotzer ruach*, God also knew whom and what He was dealing with, the children and the heirs of Avraham, Yitzchak, and Yaakov, Sarah, Rivkah, Rachel, and Leah. By the time the Redemption came, they were the Dor De'ah that merited witnessing and benefitting from all those miracles in Egypt, at the Yam Suf, at Sinai, and in the wilderness. The soaring, sweeping language of redemption promised in the opening lines of Parashas Va'era, in the end, reflected their true legacy.

And Moshe Rabbenu, the Raya Mehemna, the patient, loving shepherd, as unique and giving a leader as there ever was, helped bring them from *kotzer ruach* in Egypt to *naaseh v'nishma* at Sinai.

Parashas Va'era 5775, Yerushalayim Ir Hakodesh, on a blustery, rainy, dreamy day

U'shmi Hashem Lo Nodati Lahem

Can man bless God?

Three juxtaposed words pronounced by Jews many times each day are "*Baruch Atah Hashem.*"

And the expression "*Baruch Hashem*" is ubiquitous.

And yet, the very source of blessing is the Ribbono shel Olam, the Creator, Whose will informs the universe. How can He be blessed? Who is there to confer blessing upon Him, to change something on His behalf, as a result of that blessing?

What, then, is meant by *Baruch Atah Hashem*?

This question has been addressed in several ways, broadening the scope of our understanding of our prayers. There is a fair amount written on this subject in the literature.

The various explanations offered are beyond the scope of this essay. It is the question itself, rather, that helps elucidate the question at hand: How does one explain the seemingly difficult grammatical construction of the words *u'shmi Hashem lo nodati lahem*? One would think that it would say *u'shmi Hashem lo hodati lahem* or *b'shmi Hashem lo nodati lahem*. That is what *dikduk* would dictate.

Rashi offers the classic and standard understanding of the intent of the *pasuk*: until this time, to the Avos, God revealed Himself with only certain of His attributes, and thus, with only certain of His names, which reflect those attributes. They experienced God's promises, but not His fulfillment of those promises. The names and attributes associated with this fulfillment were as yet unrevealed.

Specifically, the Avos knew the God of promise, but not the God of fulfillment of those promises, the names and associated attributes of E-l Sha-dai, He Who is all powerful and can make things happen according to His will, but Who has not yet fulfilled His promises. The attribute associated with Elokim is *middas hadin*.

Now the Ribbono shel Olam reveals to Moshe another side of Himself. He is also the God of fulfillment, the God of *middas harachamim*, Whose name is also Y—H.

Let us now revisit our pasuk: *Va'yedaber Elokim el Moshe va'yomer elav Ani Hashem*.

Elokim – the God that Moshe was familiar with, the God he knew from his *avos* – addresses Moshe and now identifies Himself as Hashem (Y—H).

He then explains: "*Va'era el Avraham, el Yitzchak, v'el Yaakov b'Kel Shakkai*" (6:3). I "appeared," I was known, to the Avos as One Who judges and also promises. I.e., My name that signifies *middas hadin*.

BUT: "*U'shemi Hashem* [Y—H]!" I.e., My name that signifies *middas harachamim*. My name is not just *also* Hashem (Y—H), but that is My preferred name!

That is the name by which I wish you – Moshe and Klal Yisrael – to experience Me.

That is the name and the attribute (fulfillment, mercy) I prefer you know Me by.

That is the name and the attribute that I now reveal to you – and to Klal Yisrael. *Shemi Hashem*.

The Avos did not fully see this side of Me. They did not fully experience or understand this side of Me. They did not quite get the whole picture, which I now reveal to you: "*Lo nodati lahem!*"

"I was not known to them" in the way that I am now known to you, in the way that I will soon make Myself known to all of Israel, and to all the world, as I perform miracle upon miracle on behalf of My people.

Thus, the concept and the *dikduk* coincide nicely.

And the configuration of the *trop* supports the notion that "*U'shemi Hashem*" and "*Lo nodati lahem*" are, in fact, separate phrases: "*U'shemi Hashem*. [Stop.] *Lo nodati lahem*." My Name is Hashem (Y—H). I was not (fully) known to them.

In this light, we can perhaps understand somewhat better the classic Gemara in *Berachos* 7a. Rabbi Yishmael ben Elisha, the Kohen Gadol, enters the Kodesh Hakodashim and experiences God. Hashem says to him, "Yishmael, My son, bless Me!"

How is such a thing possible?

Rabbi Yishmael the Kohen Gadol knew just what to answer: יהי רצון מלפניך שיכבשו רחמיך את כעסך ויגולו רחמיך על מדותיך ותתנהג במדת הרחמים אם בניך ותכנס להם לפנים משורת הדין.

Please, Ribbono shel Olam, let Your attribute of Mercy overcome Your attribute of Judgment. Put aside *din* and show them *rachamim*!

And the Ribbono shel Olam, our loving Father in Heaven, was pleased with this "blessing."

"*Na'na li b'rosho*," Rabbi Yishmael reported. God accepted it, He appreciated it, and *k'v'yachol*, He nodded His head, as if to say *amen*.

Just as in our *parashah*, Hashem is making a statement.

The system that He created for the world allows for Him to manifest Himself through *middas harachamim*, or through *middas hadin*, as the situation demands, and as He judges fit.

For His beloved Children, Yisrael, He prefers *middas harachamim* – *Shemi Hashem!* – as He "allows" Himself, so to speak, to operate within the "confines" of the system He ordained for the governance of the world.

This is what He revealed to Moshe in our *pasuk*. And this is the *berachah* He was so pleased to receive from Rabbi Yishmael: that He may indeed preferentially manifest Himself as Y—H and show His attributes of mercy and fulfillment to His beloved children.

And so may it be His will.

Parashas Va'era 5767

The World Is a More Dangerous Place Than You Thought

In the unlikely event that you're not familiar with Ralph Kramden, just as well. Suffice it to say that he is a perennial loser whose view of life is based on his life history–driven assumption that for every "up" in life, there's going to be a "down" that more than undoes the "up." As they say, "Be kind to the little people you pass on your way up the ladder of success – you'll meet them again on your way down." May God protect us, that does seem to be the reality for some people.

For most of us, even when it's going well, we are aware, or should be aware, that lurking out there somewhere is the possibility that, for no reason apparent to us, from out of left field, something can come along to spoil things.

We pray for God's blessing in life. Everything is from Him. But we don't really have a full grasp on how it all works, and why. We just have to do the best that we can to earn God's blessing, and hope and pray that what we are dealt in life is, in fact, also experienced by us as blessing, without having to resort to tests of faith to believe that it is so.

And we must bless each other. This is part of our mandate in life in how we relate to each other. God wants us to bless each other, and He is listening for those blessings.

We've all heard people, when conferring a *berachah* on someone in a public address, identify that *berachah*, humbly (with real – or, well, perhaps less than fully genuine – humility), as a *birkas hediot*, the blessing of a plain person.

We are taught that the blessing of even a plain person has power: *al tehei birkas hediot kalah b'einecha*, do not discount the importance, or the power, of the blessing of a plain person. Based on a *gemara* (*Megillah* 15a), this is a nearly universally known and recognized saying in Jewish circles.

We all recognize that *berachos* are important, and that they must have some efficacy. After all, we resort to them all the time. We wish each other mazal tov on happy occasions, we wish each other health and life and all manner of good things, and the recipient of those blessings always says *amen*.

And so it's a bit odd that while we take *birkas hediot* seriously, and we certainly take the *berachah* of a tzaddik seriously, there seems to be something of a sociological divide on what kind of tzaddik's *berachah* has value.

Some Jews prize the *berachah* of all tzaddikim, and some, of their particular Rebbe especially. Others seem to prize the *berachah* of the great *rosh yeshiva*, as much as any Chassid prizes the blessing of his Rebbe, but turn their noses up skeptically at the power of the *berachah* of a tzaddik of a different style. Well, that's human nature.

Be that as it may, everybody does seem to agree that *birkas hediot*, at least, has power, or may have power. Chazal have told us so. Perhaps it is because the action of that *hediot* evokes a judgment for the good on behalf of the recipient, and he thus serves as a kind of conduit for that *berachah* to reach the one who is blessed.

Unfortunately, while we often think about *birkas hediot*, there is another potential reality in the world, the power, *lo aleinu*, of *kelilas hediot*, the curse of a plain person. The Gemara documents that as well on the same page in *Megillah*: "*Al tehei kelilas hediot kalah b'einecha.*" Do not discount the importance, or the power, of the *curse* of a plain person.

After the plague of darkness, Pharaoh says the Jews can leave – but he attaches unacceptable conditions, and then he promptly reneges altogether. Moshe and Pharaoh have a sharp exchange. Pharaoh tells Moshe, "Get away from me, and watch out: *al tosef re'os panai* (you will no longer see my face), for on the day that you see my face, you will die!"

The Baal Haturim reminds us of the other place in the Torah where this phrase is used, in Devarim 3:26. It is, indeed, on the day of Moshe's death, when, in response to Moshe's pleading to be allowed to enter the Land of Israel, God tells him, sharply, "*Rav lach!*" (Enough!) "*Al tosef daber Elai od ba'davar hazeh!*" (Do not speak to Me any more regarding this!) Moshe is told that his fondest wish is to be denied, and that he will now die.

The very language, the phraseology, Pharaoh used to curse Moshe regarding his death was used in Moshe's actual "death sentence" forty years later. Somehow, Pharaoh's *al tosef re'os panai* connects to *al tosef daber Elai ba'davar hazeh*.

But why should that be? Pharaoh was the bad guy, evil, cruel, arrogant, without merit. And yet his curse was not altogether without efficacy. The Gemara offers the example of Avimelech complaining to Sarah, that she had fooled him, "covered his eyes" from the truth that she was Avraham's wife, and in so doing, he slipped in a curse that Sarah's offspring should suffer from blindness – have their eyes "covered" – as indeed happened with Yitzchak, and later with Yaakov.

Of course, the world that God runs is not random. There is a reason and a *cheshbon* for everything. The Imrei Noam points here to the teaching that the words *rav lach* refer to an area of responsibility, indeed culpability that Moshe brought upon himself, which ties into his encounter with Pharaoh and to much of the trouble that befell the Jewish People in the *midbar*.

And that is those pesky troublemakers, the Erev Rav, the "mixed multitude" of non-Jews that Moshe allowed to join Israel in the Exodus. They not only were a terrible, instigating thorn in their side during the forty years of their wandering, inducing them to terrible sins, but they also apparently have never left us, and to this day are discernible as the bad Jews among us – and there are, unfortunately, some very bad Jews indeed among us – who are disloyal, and instigate, and lead the people astray in every which way.

Rav lach: those bums the Erev Rav are *yours*, Moshe. They are on your head. They are your responsibility. It was your decision to let them join Israel in the Exodus, and all the bad that they did, all the harm that they caused, played a role in God's ultimate judgment to deny Moshe his wish to enter the land.

One can argue that Moshe, a very kind man, was being kind to those people who also wanted out. Apparently it seemed like the right thing, if you will, the liberal-minded thing to do. But Moshe's kindness to that rabble was, in fact, catastrophic for his own people.

God has a *cheshbon*, by which the world is run. All things are weighed and infinite factors play a role in that *cheshbon*. Sometimes things may hang in the balance, waiting for another factor to kick in before a judgment is made. And every person in this world is a conduit of some kind. God hears a *berachah*, and God hears, *lo aleinu*, a *klalah*.

The *berachah* of a tzaddik carries the power of the *tzidkus* of that tzaddik. The *berachah* of a *hediot*, in the system God put into this world, has its own efficacy. Do not discount its power. And, unfortunately, every dog has its day. The *klalah* of a *hediot*, even a *rasha*, *lo aleinu*, cannot be discounted. God may not listen to it, but then, He may have a reason to. May God protect us.

The world is, indeed, a more dangerous place than you might think. What we do and how we act in every sphere of life has consequences. How we interact with others has consequences. Why are the Ralph Kramdens, the *lo yitzlachs* of the world, the losers of the world, *lo yitzlachs*? Who can know? *Cheshbonei Shamayim*, a matter of heavenly judgment beyond our ken. We can make no assumptions and must always strive to do the best. And yes, be kind to the little people we pass on our way up the ladder of success, even as we hope, and pray, not to have to meet them, God forbid, on the way down.

The lesson, I think, is to take every person entirely seriously. The tzaddik of course, but the plain person too. We do not know who is imbued with what power to affect us at any given moment. But if we act kindly toward everyone, if we are honest and pleasant in our dealings with people, if we are careful not to give offense, if, to the extent possible in life, we avoid conflict and strife, which are cloaked in *klalah*, if the face we show others bears a smile rather than a sneer or indifference, if we are polite to the stranger as well as to those who are close to us, if, by the way we conduct ourselves with others we evoke in them only positive feelings, then we will have gone a long way in evoking *berachah* in life, for ourselves and for our loved ones.

At the same time, the trick – the art, really – is to do so wisely. My father, who was well schooled in the wisdom of life, and who was a very fine person, taught that "too much" of anything is no good; even "too good" can be no good. Witness Moshe Rabbenu and the Erev Rav.

And when it's over, when the story of our lives on this earth is done, having lived that exemplary life of goodness and *chesed*, having touched the world with kindness and piety, decency, friendliness, and respect, those we have left behind, those who knew us, will say of us, "*zichrono li'vrachah.*"

Parashas Bo 5777

Blood Libel

Mendel was, at heart, a cheat. So when he saw an opportunity, he grossly overcharged Janush the peasant and sold him defective goods. Bad move. Janush figured it out. Mrs. Janush went ballistic. Together, they raised a terrible ruckus.

Some years before, there had been a pogrom in town. No particular reason other than the hatred and the superstition bred by generations of religious and ethnic bigotry, potentiated by the church and fueled by envy and greed. They came from all around the district to pay the Jews a well-deserved lesson.

Now Janush cried, "Thief! They're *all* thieves! Zhids! They rob you blind. It's not enough for them that they killed our god, they still want to kill us! They kill our children to use their blood for their matzos! It must be true – everybody says so! They want to take over the world. Let's get them! Get them! Get the Zhid! Zhid! Zhid! Zhid!"

It was terrible. Mendel was a knave. For those who hate us, his foolish behavior was an opportunity. Remember Haman? Why bother with just Mordechai, when we can get them all?

For the past weeks, media outlets in Israel have been on a rampage, indicting all the *frumer*, the so-called *charedim*, painting them as Neanderthal primitives who hate and degrade all women, hate freedom, hate anybody who is not like them, and who are planning to take over all of Israel and force their despicable and fanatical ways upon everybody else. It must be true. Everybody says so. They want to take over the world.

And so, it seems, they've decided: let's get them.

A moron in Beit Shemesh reportedly spat on or at a little girl whose dress, he judged, was not long enough. Some of her eight-year-old calf was showing. That opened the floodgates. His idiocy brought the haters out of the woodwork and gave them license.

Buses in Israel can be very crowded. Many *frum* people, men and women, are not comfortable being jostled up against people of the opposite sex. They would like to open their own private bus lines, where that kind of *tznius* consideration can be addressed by separate buses, or separate sections within buses. But Egged has a government-granted monopoly, and a license for a private company for a regularly scheduled public service run (which we in America would think is their right and an obvious solution) is refused them. The solution offered by Egged is for "*mehadrin*" buses within the Egged system. They run parallel to the regular buses and are available to those who desire such arrangement.

That the basic halachah permits men to travel with women on crowded public buses does not mean that the men and women who are squeezed together do not have the right to seek transportation that does not force them to do so. They do not seek to impose that on the general public, who can travel any way they want to. Why is their right to privately avoid unwanted touching inferior to anybody else's right?

And so there are separate arrangements for those who want it. No one is forced to use those buses, and no one is inconvenienced by them.

Great. Except the haters have decided to create provocations, in which women intentionally board *mehadrin* buses and self-righteously refuse to abide by the rules.

They have been creating photo-ops and sensational headlines, which is what they set out to do. It's staged. "The *charedim* hate women! They want to keep them locked up and repressed! They want to impose their medieval superstitions and

Taliban ways upon all of Israeli society, and we won't have it! Taliban! Jewish Taliban!" ("Zhid!")

Charedi behavior is universally loathsome, they say, and must be outlawed in a free and democratic society. Those fanatics have no right to impose their lifestyle upon the rest of society!

That these secularists and militant feminists wish to impose their own lifestyle upon the *frumer* is, for them, not a problem. After all, they're right, and so they have that right. The first provocateur in this wave was hailed as Israel's Rosa Parks, the woman who bravely defied forced racial segregation on buses in America's South fifty years ago.

While there have been some op-ed pieces and letters to the editor in the Israeli press that decry this "blood libel" against the *charedim*, journalists publish and air what they want, and it has been open season on the *frumer*. And it's not just from the far left. Even Modern Orthodox voices have been heard on the attack. It seems that if you're on my left, your attacks on me are a blood libel. If you're on my right, I don't like you, you fanatic, and you deserve some blood-libeling. And because I don't like you regarding some other matter, I don't mind if you get it in the neck over this, even if you don't actually deserve it.

I have heard a feminist activist on Israel radio, who described herself as Orthodox, declare that the *charedim* hate women and want to keep her chained up. *Huh*?

A fellow I know, seriously religious but not in the so-called *charedi* camp, told me that he has a brother who is *charedi*. An able accountant, the brother represented his firm in a complex audit at a company headquarters in Tel Aviv. When he finished, at the close of the meeting, the Tel Aviv CEO sneeringly asked him if he keeps his daughter locked up. It's what he reads in the newspapers, sees on TV, and hears from his friends.

Too often, it's what they want to hear and what they want to believe. It gives them license to sneer and validates their distaste for the *frumer*.

Last year there was a brouhaha over alleged "racism" by Ashkenazi *charedim* who were accused of excluding Sephardic girls from their school system supposedly because they are darker skinned. It was a total crock. It was all about standards of *tznius* and observance in the homes, so that classes would be comfortably homogeneous in that regard. The fact that many of the girls within the school were, in fact, Sephardic, from very frum homes, with similar values and standards, made no difference to the accusers. It seemed then that every other word in the press was "racism!" angrily and gleefully flung at those barbaric Neanderthals with dark clothing and black hats.

There is a popular columnist in the *Jerusalem Post* who one day complained bitterly about the "blood libel" of false accusations by the Europeans about Israel, which are reflexively accepted as truth by the European masses and fed by their media, and the next day this same columnist accepted, without question, the libelous assertion that the *frumer* are "racists" with regard to Sephardim. It was obvious that she just wanted to.

It's OK, it seems, to blood-libel the *chnyoks*, the "fanatics," without any serious regard for the truth, because she doesn't like them.

It's not such a simple question. There are many normal people with serious and arguably justifiable gripes about certain aspects of the *charedi* world in Israel as it has developed, and how it impacts on the rest of Israeli society.

The basic complaint is that they by and large don't go to the army, and many learn and don't work, but collect social welfare, both seemingly at everybody else's expense. There is really a lot of resentment about this, and it's hard to dispute this with people who carry a heavy burden of taxes and long years of army service and reserve duty.

A man can't really work in Israel unless he's been to the army. And for the *charedim*, there are truly very serious problems with going to the army. Putting aside any ideological problems with acceptance of the state, which in practical terms really applies only to a small minority, drafting young *charedi* boys would destroy those communities. And, in truth, the Jewish People and the Jewish state need those communities to exist and to thrive, even if not all Israelis see that.

A relative of a relative lives on a religious kibbutz. He has told me that most of the boys return from the army religiously damaged. They are young when they go, like all other Israelis, and are subjected to…well, very low moral influences in the army camps.

Many of those boys eventually straighten out, but it is a serious problem.

There is a movement that speaks of forming strictly *charedi* army units, so that they can serve and then get on with life, have jobs and careers, and support their families. This has not yet been firmly established or accepted in most sectors of the *charedi* community, partly on ideological grounds, and partly because an acceptable model has yet to be achieved. And the common yeshiva ethic that men stay in *kollel* learning forever and never enter the workforce is strongly held by many. From the standpoint of the average Israeli, who cannot understand that lifestyle choice, or the benefit to all of Israel that derives from their Torah study, that ethic is seriously problematic, as those same men who do not work, in the usual sense, also collect stipends or welfare, provided by the taxes of those who do go out and work.

And so, there is friction and there are hard feelings. But beyond that, much of the attack is driven not by facts, but by anti-*frum* ideology. Sadly, there are committed secularists who are at war with Yiddishkeit.

There is an intensity to *frumkeit* in Eretz Yisrael that, generally speaking, surpasses that of the rest of the world. Literally, it goes with the territory. In a historical sense, many of the fervently Orthodox in Israel see themselves as continuing the struggle for the *kedushah* of Eretz Yisrael that started when the secular, non-religious or anti-religious Zionists appeared in the Holy Land and introduced public *chillul Shabbos* and other violations of the land's *kedushah*.

The mindless fools who thoughtlessly provoke the rest of society with rash actions, however, such as the spitter, or the man who publicly screamed "*Zonah! Zonah!*" at the female soldier – who puts her life on the line to keep him and his family safe – when she sat down in the front of a *mehadrin* bus, needlessly inflame the situation and offer the haters a golden opportunity.

And it's not just the *charedim* who are under attack. The other group that the haters love to hate is the so-called "settlers," practically the last pioneering, *moser nefesh* Zionists left. That same North Tel Aviv cafe crowd hates them with a passion. "Why are they ruining everything with their fanatic aggressive Zionistic behavior? Why can't they be normal and live in the Tel Aviv area, where they belong? Then everything will be fine and everyone will love us. We're so Western, so hip. Of course they'll love us. Things will be quiet, and we will be free to pursue our materialistic lives. These guys make the rest of the world hate us."

The culture war that we fought in the days of the Chashmonaim is not over. The divisions and the intolerances that have plagued our people throughout history continue to plague us today. And, it seems, the lure of the foreign, the anything-but-Jewish, continues to be a powerful one for some Jews.

Every born Jew who is alive today is the descendant of generations of loyal Jews who stuck it out and held on to their Yiddishkeit with uncommon determination.

It's such an interesting and disturbing fact of Jewish history that these negative forces continue to worm their way into the mindset of segments of our people.

Many have been led astray by alien philosophies. But they are, in the end, the children of holy *zeides* and *bubbes*. They *can* be reached. I believe, and I hope not naively, that a loving and patient approach would go a long way. And we must pray that those who act so hatefully toward those Jews who represent the very Judaism that they think they have outgrown will again find the love in their hearts for their fellow Jews and for Judaism that must surely still be there.

Life is not easy in Israel. There is much stress in everyday life. Presumably this factor plays a role in all this discord as well. Let's be *melamed zechus*. In these *parashiyos* we read about God's redemption of the Jewish People and their delivery from bondage. What we are witnessing now is also a form of bondage, one of the spirit.

The descendants of Yaakov were not unified or of one heart in Egypt, and many disappeared there. We have seen what the midrashic and Talmudic sources say happened during *makas choshech*. God brought our ancestors out of Egypt and led them to Har Sinai. There they finally truly came together. *Va'yichan sham Yisrael neged hahar*. The Midrash famously explains the use of the singular, *va'yichan*: *k'ish echad, b'lev echad*.

When our ancestors were of one heart and of one mind, when they were bound together as of one body, one *corpus*, one whole, at peace with each other, they were ready for their encounter with God at Mount Sinai, and the Revelation that would put God's stamp on each and every one of us, individually and together, forever.

That unity, that love, that brotherhood, is something we should pray for, and something we should strive for. It will awaken the many Jews who are spiritually asleep. It will straighten the crooked. It will open our hearts and bring us light. And in the end, it will redeem us and bring us peace.

Parashas Bo 5772

That You May Know God

Can man know God?

The first verses of Parashas Bo mirror some of the first verses of Parashas Va'era.

Here Hashem instructs Moshe to present himself to Pharaoh, who will stubbornly continue to deny God's command to let the Jews go. This will result in great manifestations of God's power on behalf of His people, making so great an impression that the Jews will continue to tell their children, and their children's children, of these great miracles, until the end of time: *"vi'datem ki Ani Hashem"* (Shemos 10:2).

In Va'era, amid some of the most gloriously soaring redemptive language in the Torah, Hashem also speaks of the imminent *geulah*, including the famous four terms of *geulah*: *v'hotzeisi, v'hitzalti, v'gaalti, v'lakachti*. This great buildup leads to the ultimate divine promise: *vi'datem ki Ani Hashem Elokeichem hamotzi eschem mi'tachas sivlos Mitzrayim* (6:7).

In the midst of the most dramatic story in history, the most dramatic and fantastic rescue of any people, the emphasis is placed on the Jews *knowing* just Who saved them.

On one level, this initial knowledge of God may be said to serve as a necessary prelude to make possible their exposure to the divine Revelation at Har Sinai and their ability to receive the Torah.

Beyond that, the Kedushas Levi explains, it is impossible, of course, for a human being to understand God: *leis machshavah tefisa Bei klal* (no mind can grasp Him at all). But we also know that *Kudsha Brich Hu v'Oraysa chad hu*…the Torah is a continuous manifestation of Hashem. And by studying the Torah, by absorbing it, a Jew may, to some finite degree, gain some understanding of Him. And so *V'lakachti eschem Li l'am* (I will take you, God says, by virtue of giving you the Torah, to be My nation) makes possible, in some some small measure, *vi'datem ki Ani Hashem* (you will know that I am Hashem).

L'aniyus daati, I would suggest an alternate understanding. It's about love, and the power of love to affect people, to affect memory, to affect history.

As a resource for this theorem, let's learn a Mishnah – by a quirk of my personality, my favorite Mishnah. Quoting Rabbi Akiva (*Avos* 3:18):

"*Chaviv adam shenivra b'tzelem; chibah yeserah, nodaas lo she'nivra b'tzelem*" (Beloved [to God] is man, who was created in His image; an indication of *surpassing* love is that Hashem *let man know* that he was created in God's image). That knowledge itself is an extra and a special gift.

"*Chavivin Yisrael shenikre'u banim la'Makom; chibah yeserah, nodaas lahem shenikre'u banim la'Makom*" (Beloved [to God] is Israel, who are called God's [special] children; an indication of *surpassing* love is that Hashem *let them know* that they are God's special children). That knowledge itself is an extra and a special gift, which sustains them.

"*Chavivin Yisrael she'nitan lahem kli chemdah; chibah yeserah, nodaas lahem she'nitan lahem kli chemdah*" (Beloved [to God] is Israel, who were given the Torah [the most precious commodity possible, which makes life as a Jew possible, which makes it possible for them to have knowledge of God]; an indication of *surpassing* love is that He *let them know*…). He made them aware that this precious commodity, the Torah, is the key to life and worth clinging to at any cost. And that in His love, it is His exclusive gift to us. That knowledge itself is an extra and a special gift, and it sustains us.

Any person who loves another deeply understands the power of this concept. Nothing so engenders love as the perception that one is loved. Nothing so engenders abiding love – and all the strength that brings to bear – as abiding love itself.

In bringing us out of slavery in Egypt and forging us into His special nation with whom He is eternally bonded, He cemented that bond by making it clear to us that *it was Hashem Yisborach* Who did this for us – not a mighty army, or a clever leader, or skillful diplomacy, or an accident of history, but our Father in Heaven, Who loves us, Who watches over us, Who guides us, Who is lovingly with us always (even when it is not obvious). And not only did *we* know it, but Pharaoh and all Egypt, and indeed all nations knew it, and we *knew* that they knew it. That too was part of the gift – that extra and special gift in itself that, in our national heart, made us His.

L'maan tesaper b'oznei bincha u'ven bincha – that we as Jews will have the strength to perpetuate our relationship with Hakadosh Baruch Hu for all generations, for all time, in all places, forever, is borne of this priceless gift: *vi'datem ki Ani Hashem Elokeichem hamotzi eschem mi'tachas sivlos Mitzrayim.*

Parashas Bo 5771

The Way to Go; the Way to Stay

I have it on good authority: the first *chassidishe* Rebbe was Moishe Rabbeini.

I'm not kidding.

If you have ever visited a Rebbe's shul and watched as the Rebbe davens, you have probably also seen how children of various ages hover as close to him as possible, watching his every move, listening to his davening, absorbing everything.

The truth is, more or less the same holds true in the non-Chassidic settings of the fervently Orthodox. The *rosh yeshiva* is closely watched and emulated by the young. It is an amazing departure from the world around us. The youth "out there" worship the young, the hip, the ignorant. They are focused on collecting baseball cards (which I am not criticizing), while our youth collect *gedolim* cards. They respect youth and immaturity, whose loudest voices set the agenda and whose outrageous escapades they try to emulate. Our youth look to graybeards to learn how to live. How odd. How different. How telling.

We are still here today, still going strong, because thirty-five hundred years ago, when Pharaoh demanded to know who would be involved in the new Israelite movement, Moshe told him plainly and emphatically: "*b'ne'areinu u'vi'zkeneinu nelech*" (Shemos 10:9). In this endeavor, in this nation of God we are building, we are all in it together. The youth are as involved as their elders. We are one, with one agenda. Because, like the Chassidim, but really like every fervent Jew, *chag Hashem lanu*.

Literally, "it is a holiday unto God for us." But I submit that there is another sense to this declaration. The worship of our God is, for us, itself a joyous event, a holiday. God *is* our holiday. And so it is for all of us, old and young, men and women. The God of Israel is our joy. How that joy is expressed may differ somewhat from community to community. Among the Chassidim it is obvious in certain ways. Other groups have their own means of living that joy.

Moshe Rabbenu (however you choose to pronounce that) set the tone for our people, while we were still in Egypt, that would ensure our eternal existence, our national persistence in the face of all odds. The children are as fervent and as enthusiastic as the adults, and as involved, an attitude nurtured from earliest childhood. And they are taught, as well, *that it's good to be a Jew*.

Our "holiday," our joy, our celebration, is God Himself, and the intimate relationship we have with Him, each and every one of us. And we celebrate, as well, the fact that we are all in it together.

Where this has held true, we have succeeded and persevered. Where it is forgotten, the children are at great risk of being lost. It is inherent in human nature, and it is especially inherent in the nature, the makeup, and the history of the Jewish People.

Chag Hashem – lanu. It is ours, and it is what makes us.

Parashas Bo 5776

Beshalach

Jewish Malaise: The Peculiar Disease

It is well known that different ethnic groups have different incidences of various diseases, a function of their genetic makeup. We, as Jews, are not exempt. Hence, there are various illnesses, *lo aleinu*, that are more common among Jews. As the inheritors of the greatest spiritual infusion the world has ever known, Yetzias Mitzrayim, Krias Yam Suf, Matan Torah, and unceasing miracles in the *midbar*, our spirits have been elevated and refined to a point that they have become, paradoxically, exceptionally vulnerable.

And so Jews are vulnerable as well to disorders of the spirit in a way that others, as a group, are not. It's easier to slip off a peak than a trough.

In the past 150 years, or so, our people appear to have been especially susceptible, especially the young, and especially to disorders whose names end in ism. It's true that this kind of thing has been going on since time immemorial (think of the Chanukah war against the Greeks, which was, in part, a civil war with Jews who had slavishly adopted Hellenism), but the various isms have been particularly virulent in modern times. Napoleon's armies carried all sorts of notions eastward across Germany, Poland, and Russia, which can be described as political liberalism, a product of the Enlightenment.

Many of these ideas did have merit. And so socialism (a really big ism among Jews), liberalism, communism, secularism, Bundism, Yiddishism, political Zionism, etc., etc., etc., swept through the ranks of young Jews, who, in their idealistic spiritual and intellectual zeal, adopted these alien ideologies with great fervor – gevalt: ironically, with *messianic* fervor! – to replace their real, one true ism, Judaism, as the purported new hope for mankind and for the Jewish People.

A sad, typical case in point: the late Golda Meir, who certainly dedicated her life and her considerable energies to – and clearly identified very strongly with – the Jewish People, was not at all shy about proclaiming herself totally alienated from what we consider Judaism. She openly proclaimed this in her autobiography (in shockingly dismissive language), and, when asked by journalist Oriana Fallaci whether she was religious, she replied, emphatically, "Never!"...and then went on to speak in eloquent *religious* tones about her two real religions, socialism (her number 1) and Labor Zionism.

What happened to the thousands upon thousands of Jewish youth who were similarly carried off from the faith of their forefathers, turning to foreign and strange ideologies, often even redefining Judaism to conform to their new beliefs? Sadly, Jews appear to have a particular propensity for this kind of behavior.

I have always felt that it is exactly the heightened spiritual awareness of the Jew, developed by the Avos and the Imahos and then reinforced and driven home during Yetzias Mitzrayim, Krias Yam Suf, Matan Torah, and the miracles in the *midbar* to become an essential and inalienable part of the Jewish character, that predisposes the Jew to susceptibility to err this way, *lo aleinu*, when something goes awry with the system of Jewish life. That spirituality, that striving for truth and justice, that essential goodness becomes perverted when it is redirected away from the Judaism of our forebears. For the Jew, the search for social justice outside of Torah Judaism becomes a snakepath to evil and to oblivion.

Last week's *haftarah* and this week's *parashah* provide a redeeming promise, and a remedy.

Yirmiyahu Hanavi (46:27) comforts us: "*Al tira avdi Yaakov, v'al techas Yisrael, ki hineni moshiacha me'rachok v'es zaracha me'eretz shivyam v'shav Yaakov*"...the children who have been captured, "carried off" into the captivity of "*rachok*," alien philosophies, will be returned to the fold.

That return is a gift from Hashem, and will take place, deserved or not (*b'itah achishenah*, Yeshayahu 60:22), as a result of His promises. But our *parashah* contains within it a medicinal formula for the prevention of this peculiar disease altogether.

Fresh from Krias Yam Suf, when they run out of drinking water, the Jews do not just ask for water, they angrily and complainingly demand it. *Attitude!* This was a pattern repeated multiple times in the *midbar*. Tough, uptight people (sound familiar?). God sweetens the bitter water at Mara and offers them an even sweeter lesson that, if followed, is a promise to sweeten their lives: "*Im shamoa tishma l'kol Hashem Elokecha...v'haazanta l'mitzvosav, v'shamarta kol chukav, kol hamachalah asher samti b'Mitzrayim lo asim alecha, ki Ani Hashem Rofecha*" (Shemos 15:26).

Egypt was the world's most advanced and powerful society, with knowledge, with science and medicine, with wealth and power, a mighty empire. And morally, totally corrupt. Spiritually debased. Worldly achievement, no matter how great, without God, will be morally empty and ultimately depraved. And if that is true of the Mitzrim, who were *shtufei zimah* and *avodah zarah*, what of the Jews, God's holy nation, who were witness to His Revelation at Yam Suf and at Har Sinai, when even the most humble person saw more than the prophets, and who heard the very voice of God?

From that awesome peak, beware the slippery slope on all sides. It's very easy to slip and fall, to lose one's perch, to get dizzy, to get hurt, to get sick. Hashem, in our *parashah*, sees where the people are headed, and, like a good doctor, He offers them the best cure of all, prevention. *Ani Hashem Rofecha*: Hashem knows His people and their susceptibilities.

Follow this formula carefully, says Hashem, follow it in all ways, and you and your children will always remain spiritually healthy. Let your children see you doing good always, let them see you learning Torah, let them see you living Torah, let them see you praying with devotion, let them see you being kind and charitable and truthful, let them see you dealing honestly at all times, let them see you being punctilious in observance of the mitzvos, let them see you being enthusiastic and happy in your Yiddishkeit, let them see you following the path of peace and pleasantness, let them see you being a loving person, let them see you utterly and entirely and sincerely and lovingly dedicated to being Hashem's servant, and Hashem, the Divine Healer, will keep them healthy and free of that peculiar Jewish malaise. It is an offer and a promise that we, as God's nation, cannot afford to ignore.

Parashas Beshalach 5771

Tu b'Shevat on Shabbos Shirah

This year Shabbos Shirah and Tu b'Shevat coincide.

It is most interesting that they do, as I submit that their underlying themes coincide as well. Krias Yam Suf, celebrated in the *shirah*, marks the act of redemption that finally freed us of our Egyptian slavemasters. Tu b'Shevat, simply understood in agricultural terms, is actually central not just to our cycle of the year, but to our hopes for the coming Redemption.

On Tu b'Shevat, a process begins. It's subtle, but it's quite real. The sap begins to rise in the trees of Eretz Yisrael, we observe Rosh Hashanah la'Ilanos, we eat the fruits of the Holy Land, and a slow but clearly discernible process begins.

While yet in the grip of winter, our thoughts and our spirits start to look toward a rebirth.

Within two weeks of Tu b'Shevat is Rosh Chodesh Adar, and *marbim b'simchah*.

Purim arrives, and with it, the preparations for Pesach. *Sho'alim v'dorshim b'hilchos Pesach shloshim yom lifnei haPesach.*

With Rosh Chodesh Nisan, we dispense with saying Tachanun, and we are geared up to celebrate our national *geulah*. Pesach is Chag Ha'aviv, the Festival of Springtime; the days are longer and the world is getting brighter every day.

And on Pesach we already begin to count the days and prepare ourselves spiritually for *kabbalas haTorah*. Day by day, week by week, attribute by attribute, from *chesed she'b'chesed* to *malchus she'b'malchus*, we prepare for the ultimate realization of the process that began, in a real sense, months before on Tu b'Shevat: the rebirth, the culmination of the awesome and uplifting process that brings us to our own spiritual recreation of *maamad Har Sinai* and our national and personal encounter with Hakadosh Baruch Hu.

It should be, and it is, a time of great joy. The Ribbono shel Olam chose us, revealed Himself to us, entered into an everlasting covenant with us, and gave us His blueprint for Life. *Ashreinu, mah tov chelkeinu.* And yet…

For me, as I'm sure for many others, this passage from Pesach to Shavuos is not quite as smooth as it would appear.

I'm not referring here to the partial mourning period, the *ketzas aveilus* of the Sefirah period, although that is, in fact, an outgrowth of the primary problem.

I do not remember a single Pesach in my adult life that did not bring with it, upon its conclusion, a profound sense of disappointment.

Even as we count the days and prepare ourselves for a renewal of *kabbalas haTorah*, something is missing; something is depressingly wrong.

The Gemara (*Rosh Hashanah 11a*) says, "*B'Nisan nigalu, b'Nisan assidin ligael.*" The Jews were redeemed in Nisan, and in Nisan they will, in the future, be redeemed.

True, there are other points of view on this question, but this is the classic view. And each time Nisan comes and goes without the Geulah, without the final Redemption, I cannot help but feel the pall it casts on all the rest, on all the festivities of *yom tov* and its aftermath. How can it be so long, so hard, so terrible, so painful? Will our bitter suffering never end? Do we remain, after so much, still so terribly guilty? Has all our suffering as a nation not expiated our guilt? Ribbono shel Olam, how long? How long!

How do we cope with this?

Yes, it is true, and our history has proven, that we *can* exist and even thrive spiritually in *galus*, our seemingly never-ending exile. And it is perhaps for this reason that the Torah was given outside of Eretz Yisrael, rather than within it, to teach us that the life of Torah is possible even outside the land for which our national life of Torah was designed. But it remains a Torah only partially fulfilled. At its best, such a life is glorious but incomplete.

The long, dark night of our exile, with all its horrors, points out only too clearly how far we are from where we want and need to be, how far we are from being complete, how far we are from the true, ultimate fulfillment of the Torah life.

And so, as Nisan, with its hopes and prayers unfulfilled, gives way to Iyar, Sivan, and Shavuos, we need, I believe, to deal with this issue: celebrating the glorious ascent from bondage to physical freedom – from that bondage on Pesach to the spiritual freedom and the encounter with God on Sinai on Shavuos – while keenly aware that we remain, yet again, yet another year, in a state of bondage and in *galus* after all, with the *ol hagoyim al tzavareinu*, their heavy heels on our necks.

I believe that what we in fact do, what Jews do everywhere and every day, in their homes and in *batei knessios* and in *batei medrashos*, and what we conspicuously gather together on Shavuos to do, is our individual and our national method of coping: we cling to our Father in Heaven and to His Torah.

With all our troubles, we remain so blessed and so exalted by our chosenness, so ennobled by the Torah, that we declare, with great fervor each morning: *Lefichach, therefore, we are obliged to thank You, praise You, glorify You, bless, sanctify, and offer praise and thanks to Your Name. Ashreinu, we are fortunate, how good is our portion, and how beautiful is our heritage! We are fortunate when we come in the early morning, and we are there late at night, in the synagogues and the study halls, and unify and sanctify Your Name each day, continually, and lovingly proclaim twice each day, Shema Yisrael Hashem Elokeinu Hashem Echad!*

Even as a child who has been spanked turns, for solace and comfort, to the very father who administered the spanking – for the child knows, instinctively, and even intellectually, that the spanking was, in essence, an act of love, an unpleasant but necessary act – so too we turn to the Ribbono shel Olam for solace and comfort from the pain He has, in His wisdom, judged it necessary to administer to us.

In our love, we cling to God.

In our pain, in our disappointment, in the long night of seeming endless *galus*, we cling to God. In our hope for a brighter future, in our belief in and expectation of a brighter future, we cling to God.

The daily language of that clinging to God is prayer and the study of Torah, and the physical manifestation of that clinging to God is living the life of Torah.

And in so doing, we regain the warm embrace of our loving Father in Heaven.

"*Zos nechamasi b'onyi ki imrascha chiyasni*" (This is the consolation for my suffering: Your words have restored my life; Tehillim 119:50).

And so, as we exult in Shabbos Shirah, with the glory, the promise, and the hope contained therein, we also mark, with Tu b'Shevat, the beginning of a new cycle of hope and redemption, a new opportunity to rededicate ourselves, as we begin our annual march toward *kabbalas haTorah*. And it is the unique gift of the Torah, and our own immersion in it, that, even in our ongoing bondage, sets us free.

Parashas Beshalach, Tu b'Shevat 5770

Vus Vilst Du fun Mir Hub'n?

It seems strange, doesn't it, that God seems to chide Moshe for praying to Him: *"Mah titzak Elai?"* (Why are you shouting [i.e., praying intensely and urgently] at Me? Shemos 14:15).

Tell the Children of Israel to get moving!

Some *meforshim* explain that it was because God had just told him that Pharaoh was coming for them, but that He (Hakadosh Baruch Hu) was going to destroy Pharaoh and his army and save the Jews. So it seems to become a case of "What do you want from Me? *Vus vilst du fun Mir hub'n?* I told you already!"

But that does indeed seem strange, and "out of character," *k'v'yachol*. We know that God not only welcomes prayer, He very much *desires* it, especially from those close to Him. Thus, Sarah Imenu was barren for so many years, and Rivkah Imenu was barren for so many years, and Rachel Imenu was barren for years, at least in part because God so desired their prayers. Regarding Yitzchak Avinu's intense prayers that Rivkah conceive, *va'ye'etar Yitzchak*, the Gemara (*Yevamos 64a*) says that Hakadosh Baruch Hu *misaveh*, intensely desires, the prayers of His tzaddikim.

Of course God is not mean or a tease, *chalilah*. That's not the whole story of the wait for children. But Chazal tell us that that is part of the story.

And so what's the problem with Moshe praying now, as the Jews are in trouble?

Pharaoh and his army are bearing down on them, and they are pinned against the sea.

If ever there was a time to pray, this is it! That's what Jews do!

Well, maybe not. You have to pray. But sometimes you have to put the *siddur* down, or perhaps even the Gemara (!), and *act. March* – into the sea, in this case, where God says He will do it all for them, or *pick up the sword, or the gun*, where they must defend themselves in a natural way, or *do whatever has to be done*, in life, according to the circumstances.

As the Baal Haturim puts it, there is a time to daven long and there is a time to daven short (to be brief). But this (the encounter with Pharaoh's army at the Yam Suf) is not the time to daven at all, but to act.

Rashi explains that as Pharaoh's army approached, Moshe stood engaged in prayer. God says to him: *This is not the time for drawn-out prayers! Israel is in trouble! Act!*

And clearly, here, "act" means something other than to pray.

Which raises an interesting question. There is a declaration in the Gemara (*Bava Basra* 7b) that tzaddikim (i.e., *talmidei chachamim, rabbanan*) do not require extra or extraneous protection. The discussion there is about whether they ought to be exempt from the costs of building protective walls around an endangered community that they live in.

One may wonder, if that means that they are somehow personally safe even when everyone else is at risk, aren't they obligated in any event to help protect the entire community? Don't they have a stake in the community as a whole? Don't they benefit from the community as a whole? Is the well-being of the community as a whole not their affair? Are they not obligated in that sense?

Clearly, they would be. So if the view is held that they are indeed exempt from any financial burden in defense costs, such as the cost of building a wall, that must mean that they have *already* done their part, they have *already* contributed, *just by being who they are*. Not every *talmid chacham* is moneyless, but a whole lot of them are. If you spend your time and energy and creativity being a *talmid chacham*, if your focus is on development in *tzidkus*, chances are your focus is not on development in real estate. For the most part, the lifestyle necessitated by pursuing *tzidkus* involves the sacrifice of financial benefits others are freer to pursue.

So, how does it make sense to say that *talmidei chachamim* do not *require shmirah* (protection), which is what the Gemara actually says? That they are already protected, by their merits? The reality of the world, and all of history, clearly demonstrates otherwise. They are just as vulnerable to the sword or to the bullet, or to hunger or to freezing or to Zyklon B gas as anybody else.

My own sense of it is that *shmirah*, here, must refer to a state of protection that is not what we usually understand "protection" to mean. Protection from what? From physical harm? That's not the reality. I believe it must refer to a state of protection that is more fundamental to our presence and position in the *universe of existence* than to the physical reality of the moment. A bullet may do its nasty work, but it can never erase the imprint on *all* the worlds of existence, on the infinite as well as the finite, of the life of a tzaddik.

The tzaddik is safe, in a spiritually existential way, because of the lasting impact of his life and his good works on this world and on the world Above. His eternity, his supernal merit, is already assured, earned by his efforts, and cannot be undone, whatever physically happens to him. The rest of us still have our work cut out for us. We are not yet safe, in that sense, and so our physical existence needs extra protection now, so that we may still have a chance to earn the merit we need to achieve our place in the greater infinity of *eternal* existence. The tzaddik is already safely there, no matter what else happens to him here.

So, what about prayer? *Hakadosh Baruch Hu misaveh l'tefilasan shel tzaddikim.*

God intensely desires the prayers of His tzaddikim. And that's why the tzaddikim have their own special stories, such as Yitzchak and Rivkah. But of course it's not just tzaddikim whose prayer He desires. Prayer is for all of us, and He desires that too, even as He expects and demands it of us. It is good for us, and *we* need it. In times good and bad. It elevates our *neshamos* and brings them closer to Him. It unites us with Him – along with the other pillars of Jewish existence – which defines who we are in this world and in the world Above. Torah, *avodah*, *gemilus chasadim*. *Teshuvah*, *tefillah*, tzedakah.

These are what make us who we are, whatever category of Jew we fall into, whether we have as yet assured our position in eternity or not. That is who we all are.

Rabbi Yehudah Nesiah, son of Rabban Gamliel III and grandson of Rabbi Yehudah Hanasi ("Rebbe"), ruled, in those turbulent times in Israel (third century CE), when a protective wall needed to be built, that everybody had to participate in its expense, including the *talmidei chachamim*. His contemporaries, Reish Lakish and Rabbi Yochanan, objected, citing teachings that indicate that *talmidei chachamim* do not require *shmirah* (see *Bava Basra* 7b–8a).

Clearly, there are more ways than one to look at this question. We understand that tzaddikim are protected, in whatever way one understands that, and we also know that God wants us, and especially the tzaddikim, to pray for His help and His protection, and beyond that, to put prayer aside when it's time to act, and *to act*. Like everything else in life, it appears, there must be some combination, some middle path, some *way of the just* that fits both notions.

Perhaps Rabbi Yehudah Nesiah and his colleagues had different opinions about what was practically appropriate when, and what to emphasize when. It's certainly interesting, and perhaps telling, that Rabbi Yehudah Nesiah, who advocated *action* on the part of *everyone* at that time, including the *talmidei chachamim*, is, today, buried, together with his *beis din*, in the town of Ovnit, literally beneath a camp of the Israel Defense Forces.

But no one disagrees that, as much as there is a time for prayer, and a need for prayer, there is also a time for action. *Mah titzak Elai?* God chides Moshe: *Vus vilst du fun Mir hub'n?* What do you want from Me? The Egyptians are upon you! Tell the Children of Israel to get moving! Act! Now!

Life is a tricky place, and we don't always know what to do. We pray for God's help and for His protection. We pray that we should know how to pray. We pray that we should know how to act. And we pray that we should have the understanding to know when, as well as how.

And it is for us to strive to reach that level that, come what may in this physical world (and may God grant that it indeed be good and safe for us), we merit that state of Heavenly protection that transcends this physical world and assures us that safe place in the Eternal World in His infinite, loving, protective embrace.

Parashas Beshalach 5777

When a Good Heart Is Not Good Enough

They witnessed ten miraculous plagues visited upon their Egyptian tormentors, while they were spared. They saw a tightly locked country where barely a single slave had ever escaped, and they were part of a mass exodus of slaves, their former masters lavishing wealth upon them even as they hurried them out. And now they saw the full might of Egypt, thrown at them with a nightmarish fury just as they were hemmed in by the desert with their backs to the sea, washed up dead on the shores of the waterway that had parted for them and drowned their enemies, leaving a fortune in spoils for the taking.

Va'yaaminu b'Hashem u'v'Moshe avdo. They sang the immortal *shirah.*

How long did it take for them to start complaining?

At their very next stop they complained about water. God gave them sweet water.

Then they complained about the pots of meat they had back in Egypt and now didn't have. God gave them miracle food from the heavens. Then they complained again quite bitterly about water. God gave them a river of water from a rock. They demanded: Well, is God in our midst or not? *Hayesh Hashem b'kirbeinu im ayin?*

What kind of question is that? What kind of attitude is that? After all they saw and experienced and benefited?

They were in Refidim at the time. And that's where Amalek attacked them.

Tanchuma explains "Refidim": *she'rafu yedeihem min haTorah*; they became weak in Torah (even though they had only a few mitzvos at that time). *She'ein hasoneh ba ela al yedei rifyon yadayim min haTorah*: the enemy comes upon us as a result of the weakening of Torah in our hands.

Midrash Rabbah interprets their bizarre questions about God's presence among them: Does God know what we are thinking? Does He know what is in our hearts? Do we have to spell it out, or will He do what we want if we just think it? If yes, we will serve Him; if not, we will rebel.

Now, what does *that* mean?

The Kesav Sofer tells us. He cites a *pasuk* in Parashas Ki Savo: *Arur asher lo yakim es divrei haTorah hazos laasos osam*. Cursed will be the person who does not fulfill the requirements of the Torah, *laasos osam* (to do them).

We all recognize the syndrome, the many Jews, far removed from Torah, who argue that they are really good Jews because what God really wants is for them to have a good heart, and they do. They are Jewish in their hearts. The commandments are for people who do not have their great sensitivity of the heart, or their inherent goodness. And so we have witnessed Judaism redefined by these people as, essentially, a message: social justice, kindness, liberal Democrat politics, trade unionism, or whatever the PC of the hour might be. But certainly not actually *doing mitzvos*, which are a primitive throwback to the pre-enlightened times when they were necessary.

And so the noble Torah concept of *Rachmana liba ba'i*, that God wants our hearts, has been perverted by these people into the "good Jewish heart" as the total fulfillment of Judaism. Our old shul mate, Rav David Rubin, *a"h*, used to call them "cardiac Jews."

Hayesh Hashem b'kirbeinu im ayin? Isn't it enough to have God in your heart?

If yes, we will serve Him that way. If not, we will rebel; we will not accept Him on those terms, which are too primitive for our refined, cultured, and advanced intellect and sensibilities.

Refidim: *she'rafu yedeihem mi'divrei Torah*. They might have believed and were ready to serve God *conceptually*, defined according to their own will rather than God's.

And so along came Amalek to give them a slap.

The Midrash gives the classic parable for their question, is God really in our midst?

A man carries his child about on his shoulders, He gets him whatever he wants. Riding high, the child forgets that he is, in fact, being carried, and who it is that is carrying him. The brat wants something. So he asks someone, "Hey, have you seen my father?" Hearing this, the annoyed father casts him down. And along comes a dog and bites the boy.

So too, God says to Yisrael, I carry you about on My shoulders, I do everything for you, and now you wonder where I am? Okay, here's Amalek for you.

Yes, *Rachmana liba ba'i*. God wants our hearts. But if that's all there is, the pretense of a good heart, we are not serving God but our own inflated image of ourselves. The real blessing is the true service of God, to follow faithfully the blueprint for life that He has laid out for us, *laasos osam*. He Who created our hearts also knows what our hearts and our bodies need to achieve the fulfillment of the purpose of creation: Torah and mitzvos.

And in so doing, in fulfilling the mitzvos, we bear proud public testimony that the Creator of the universe is our Father in Heaven, Who has chosen us to be His.

Parashas Beshalach 5772

Will These Bones Live

Moishe ("Munke") Wein, *a"h*, was a great guy. He was a landsman of my mother's, a real Galitzianer from Kolbesov. He was several years younger than she was, and, as he never tired of telling me, a great admirer of hers as he was growing up. She was quite an accomplished young lady, and he, a maven.

Like my parents, Munke and his wife, a very fine lady, were Holocaust survivors. They managed to rebuild their lives and raise a family. Munke had a little hat store, where he sold mostly black fedoras. Brooklyn, you know. It was situated in a Jewish neighborhood, but close to an Italian one. Always ready with a smile and a joke, he once told me that he had two types of customers who favored those black fedoras: Jews and Mafiosi.

And so I particularly appreciated Munke's explanation of the well-known disparity between the number given in the Torah for the period of servitude our forefathers spent in Egypt, 430, and what we know to be the actual number, 210.

U'moshav Bnei Yisrael asher yashvu b'Mitzrayim shloshim shanah v'arba me'os shanah (Shemos 12:40). Literally, the period that the Children of Israel dwelt in Egypt was 430 years. But we know the numbers signify something else, as has been elucidated by Chazal. There are multiple layers of explanations, involving the various figures 210, 400, and 430 years, all timed from different events. One approach, however, states simply that the slavery and the oppression were so bad and so bitter that in 210 years our forefathers suffered 430 years' worth of pain, and thus were redeemed earlier than they might have been.

Now, for Munke's *perush*, you need to have a good sense of real, down-home Yiddish.

There is a Yiddish word for a mess (as in when things are not too clean and all strewn about) that is not heard too often these days among American-born speakers of Yiddish, whose vocabulary is often limited. "*Moyshif*" refers to such a terrible mess.

According to Munke, we know from that *pasuk* that in the 210 years the Jews were in Egypt, *moyshiv Bnei Yisrael asher yashvu b'Mitzrayim, hob'n zei ibergelozt aza moyshif vi fun 430 yuhr*; they left such a mess behind after those 210 years as if they had been there for 430 years.

OK, it's cute. But I cite it here for a reason. Munke is gone and his children, while very good, just don't talk like that, and are unlikely to perpetuate quite what Munke was, the flavor of that Yid, in their future generations. "Gone with the wind" – or, to put it bluntly, *up in smoke*: gone in the smokestacks of Auschwitz.

In shul the other day, I was contemplating the *pasuk* in Beshalach that makes a point, upon describing the triumphant departure of the Jews from Egypt, that Moshe occupied himself with taking along with them the bones of Yosef. While the other Jews were busy emptying the treasures of Egypt, Moshe was busy locating and retrieving Yosef's casket containing his bones, referred to twice in the same *pasuk* (13:19). At the same time that Yosef promised the growing and increasingly entrenched Jewish nation in Egypt that God would eventually redeem them from that place (*pakod yifkod Elokim eschem*), he also exacted from them the promise that when they would finally leave, they would not leave his bones behind. Their future was not in Egypt but in Eretz Yisrael. And while he yearned to be brought, ultimately, to rest in the land of his forefathers, which he himself had left ninety-three years earlier, I suspect that he also understood that the living Jews arriving in that Holy Land, so many years later, would *need* to have his bones with them in order to be successful in their settlement.

At this point in my *étude*, hearing a familiar little voice, I looked up and saw a familiar little figure. The little fellow before me bears a striking resemblance to me at his age, despite his hair being, inexplicably, not red. Contemplating this magical *einikel*, a deeper understanding of the inclusion of the reference to Yosef's bones in the Exodus narrative occurred to me. And I thought of Munke Wein as well.

Yechezkel Hanavi famously stands in a valley before a huge mass of dry bones. The Jewish nation is reeling from the recent destruction and exile into Babylon. They are in despair. And behold, the bones are *very* dry, and there are a great many of them. God asks him, "Can these bones live?" God then directs Yechezkel to prophesy regarding those dry bones: "Thus says the Lord God, behold, I will infuse you with the spirit of life, and you shall live. I will rebuild you; I will place upon you sinews and flesh and skin; I will emplace into you the very spirit of life, and you shall live, and you shall know that I am God."

Yechezkel (chapter 37) recounts that he prophesied as commanded. A noise arose from among the bones as matching bones joined together into whole skeletons, sinews, and flesh, and finally skin was added, but still they did not live. And God then commanded him to prophesy regarding the spirit, the spirit of life. From all four directions, let the wind blow the spirit of life into these bodies, the multitude of the slain, and let them live.

Yechezkel recounts further that he prophesied as commanded, and they lived, a great multitude.

God then says to Yechezkel: These bones are the House of Israel. They say, in our exile, in our state of destruction, we are but dry bones, devoid of life, all hope lost and gone. We are doomed. Therefore, Yechezkel, you now prophesy to the House of Israel. You tell them. *Tell them! I, God, will open your graves and will raise you from those graves, My people, and I will bring you to the Land of Israel. And you will know that it is I, God, Who has opened your graves, Who has raised you up again, Who has given you back life. I shall put My Spirit into you and you shall live! I shall set you upon your own soil, and you shall know that I, your God, have done this. I, God, have spoken, and it will be done.*

It will be done.

We read this chapter as the *haftarah* on Shabbos Chol Hamo'ed Pesach, the holiday that recounts the Exodus, when the broken remnant of the enslaved Children of Israel were brought up out of bitter bondage and were spiritually raised up, marching out of a defeated Egypt *b'yad ramah*, with a triumphant arm held high. In Yechezkel's time it was meant to keep alive the hope and the spirit of the broken remnant of Jews who survived to reach the Babylonian exile. In our time, the message is all the more important, and all the more powerful.

The very big deal that is the Exodus from Egypt, while a prelude to Matan Torah and our formation as the nation we are, marks the end of a bitter exile that lasted 210 years, and not all of those years were bitter. We are now in an exile that is *ten times as long, and if I may say, a million times more bitter*. How can we possibly still be here? How can we possibly still have hope? How is it possible that we have not withered away altogether?

The bones. The bones of Yosef Hatzaddik were preserved in Egypt, and were reverentially carried by our forefathers out of that exile and into the holy Land of Israel. Those bones, a remnant of the Avos, *a symbol of the continuity of the Avos*, helped anchor the people to who they were and who they needed to be. And in that renewed life of the nation, those bones lived again.

The bones. The bones of the slaughtered Jews strewn in the Valley of Dura miraculously came to life to give hope to the broken and defeated people that the nation would one day return to life. Whatever the actual origin of those bones (see *Sanhedrin* 92b), the message is the same. The bones of those who came before us will live through us. And as God has promised that they will live, so shall they, so shall we.

I looked upon my grandson עמו"ש in shul, just as I was learning the *pasuk* regarding Yosef's bones, and I thought about what had filled my mind as I looked upon my father's casket at his funeral, contemplating the passage of generations: "Will these bones live?" When God asked that question of Yechezkel, his response was, "Lord God, You know." God does, indeed know, and He has told us.

The number of years our people spent in Egypt was 210. And yet, the numbers 400 and 430, each signifying a different accounting, are also associated with the period of *galus* of Mitzrayim. Rabbenu Bachye, drawing upon Rabbenu Chananel, shows a remarkable parallel in Sefer Daniel to the different numbers given for the length of the exile. There too, in the inscrutable *cheshbonos* regarding the final Redemption, three different numbers, three different calculations, are discernible. Clearly, they are connected. They are meant to bring us comfort in this long and terrible final exile. Just as there were three different time periods associated with the redemption from Egypt, so too there are three different time periods alluded to in the prophecies that coincide with possible times for our ultimate redemption. And if we are disappointed that it is not earlier, we should take heart that it will also not be later than the final possibility. It *will* happen. Whatever the final calculation is in God's judgment, it will happen, and *it will not be delayed*.

The bones, the precious bones of our forebears, serve as a metaphor for us, an inspiration, the preciousness of the legacy of lives past that assure us of life in the future.

Our precious children may uncannily remind us, physically or characteristically, of ourselves or of our parents, but really, they are a vehicle for the continuation of what we are, hopefully, about, and what our parents and holy forebears were about. Through them, may Hashem bless them, those bones come alive. And without those bones, without *atzmos Yosef*, without the dry bones in the Valley of Dura, they would not know what to become.

Much of what my parents and their generation saw, no one should ever see again. And other things that they saw, the Jews of old, the Torah culture and the civilization that the Jews built over thousands of years and hundreds of genera-tions are an indescribably precious legacy, carried in the bones of our nation, that will continue until the end of time. God has promised.

The Old World flavor of Munke Wein's *peshat* on *moyshiv Bnei Yisrael* may well be disappearing. Sad, but that is the way of the world. The fundamentals, please God, never will. Because the Exodus was not just an escape. It was a triumphant march, divinely planned to be not even one minute later than originally decreed, and divinely ordained to be so formative of a national character that would last until the end of time that in the midst of the hurried Exodus, the "bones of Yosef," our national purpose, was not only not forgotten, it was a centerpiece of that march.

Will these bones live?

A nation that remembers and reveres the holy ways of its forebears ultimately merits to see those holy ways perpetuated in its children, and in their children, forever. We have our duty, and our obligation, to perform in this regard. But we also have God's promise. The generation that arose from the ashes, *my generation, my children and their children, and all of our nation, has God's promise: Tell them! I, God, will open your graves and raise you from those graves, My people, and I will bring you to the Land of Israel. And you will know that it is I, God, Who has opened your graves, Who has raised you up again, Who has given you back life. I shall put My Spirit into you, and you shall live! I shall set you upon your soil, and you shall know that I, God, have done this. I, God, have spoken, and it will be done.*

It will be done.

Parashas Beshalach 5774

Yisro

Gold – Only Gold

Her throat tight, mouth dry, she entered the office and faced the committee.

How would she do this? She and her husband were prepared to make any necessary sacrifice to accomplish what they must. But would that sacrifice, large as it would be for their means, satisfy this group of judges?

Sacrifice was nothing new to them. They had just emerged from years of privation and loss beyond description. Miraculously, they were among the few who had remained alive.

They had arrived a few years earlier with just the clothes on their backs and a little boy in their arms. They had no money. Her husband worked long, hard hours just to keep food on the table. They could barely manage with the new language. And now she had to convince these people, undoubtedly good Jews, but Americans all, who could not really relate, she thought, to who her family was, and to their determination not to compromise.

She faced the tuition committee of the yeshiva they were determined to send their little boys to, because they had been told that it was the best. But it also cost the most, significantly more than they could possibly pay, even with a generous scholarship.

"We're sorry," they said. "We appreciate your determination and understand your position, but we also have obligations. We have a payroll to meet, we have a mortgage to pay, and we have expenses. We suggest you seek another school for your children."

A woman not easily daunted, she appealed to them to understand who she was, who her husband was, where they came from, who their families were, and who her children could be, and had to be. Why they could not settle for second best when it came to a proper yeshiva education for those children. They would make any sacrifice they could. They would gladly pay more when it became possible.

A voice, previously silent, from the committee: "Reich? *Efsher fun Reishe?* Are these children Zalke Reich's *einiklech*? Reb Elya Reich's descendants?" Yes, they were.

Although he had been in America many years, Mr. Silver was, in fact, a *landsman*, who remembered their family well, and with respect. She had no idea who he was, other than God's messenger.

The president of the institution turned to his colleagues. "There is no way that we will allow these children to attend any other yeshiva. Even without any money at all, they will learn here. Period. If you knew where they come from, what they come from, you would agree with me. You will not regret it. This is on my responsibility."

Dizzy with relief, she thought, "Blessed is the God of our fathers Who put the solution in place decades before we arrived here."

And my brother and I did learn there. No payment at all was required, but my parents paid a few dollars per month for the two of us, at their own insistence. And within a few months, when they could, they voluntarily doubled their tuition payment. They were told that it was the first time in the history of the school that anyone had volunteered to raise their own tuition. And they continued to raise it as circumstances permitted.

The great Rav Meir Shapiro, who founded Yeshivas Chachmei Lublin in the interwar years, offers insight into this kind of determination from Parashas Yisro.

The Second Beis Hamikdash, destroyed by the Romans 420 years after it was first built by the Jews returning from the Babylonian exile, was not, at the end, the same structure that was originally built. The Temple the returnees built was poor and quite modest. It was the best they could do. Although the joy in the rebuilding and the resumption of the Temple service was very great, anyone left who had seen the original Temple built by King Shlomo knew that it was very poor indeed, and they wept at the comparison. Later it was upgraded. And in the end, the evil, murderous Hordos (Herod), megalomaniacal non-Jewish king of the Jews appointed by the Romans, in his quest for glory, rebuilt the Beis Hamikdash and its associated spaces in the grandest way imaginable, so that it was one of the most magnificent structures in the Roman world.

The Torah spells out what vessels and utensils to make for the Mikdash, and what materials to use. Many of these major vessels and utensils were to be made of pure gold.

But what if the Jews are poor, and have no gold? Under those circumstances, substitute materials are permissible.

Immediately after the Revelation at Mount Sinai, when the Torah was given to us, there is a strict admonition: *Lo saasun iti elohei kesef v'elohei zahav lo saasu lachem.* Literally, it refers to not making representations of heavenly bodies, lest they come to be worshiped, a common practice at the time. But Rashi concentrates on something else. He quotes a midrash that this *pasuk* is quite specific about the *keruvim*, winged structures with childlike faces that adorned the cover to the Ark, the Aron Hakodesh, in which were placed the two tablets, the *luchos*, bearing the Aseres Hadibros, the ultimate holy objects in the possession of the Jewish People.

Rashi states that this *pasuk* comes to instruct us strictly that while for all the utensils in the Mikdash, silver may be substituted for the mandated gold if there is no gold available, not so for the *keruvim*. In fact, in this one particular case, substituting silver for gold is tantamount to fashioning an idol, a false god.

Why? Rashi does not say. The *Mechilta* does not say. But Rav Meir Shapiro does say.

These strange structures, angel-like depictions rendered from pure gold, with stretched-out wings and the pure faces of children, served as a cover for the *luchos* and the Torah in the Kodesh Hakodashim, the Holy of Holies.

The lesson here, says Rav Shapiro, is that the Torah and our children are inextricably intertwined. Indeed, even as without them we have no future, the Torah too, as the repository of Godliness among humans, has, as it were, no future without those Jewish children. And so the Torah education and the Torah upbringing of Jewish children must be very pure. There can be no compromise, and no price is too high. It must be pure gold, and only gold. In this context, even silver is tantamount to idolatry.

And so we have seen generation upon generation of Jewish parents ready to make any sacrifice to inculcate their children with the best Torah education possible. For they have always understood that the Torah, our children, and our very survival as a nation are, in fact, inextricably intertwined. Of all things in life, *this* requires gold. Only gold.

Parashas Yisro 5772

Oy, Oy!

Yisro journeys to meet Moshe and the Jews after Krias Yam Suf, bringing Moshe's family: his wife Tziporah and their two sons. The Torah presents Moshe's sons:

Gershom, *ki amar ger hayisi b'eretz nochriyah*, and Eliezer, *ki Elokei avi b'ezri va'yatzileni me'cherev Paroh* (Shemos 18:4).

It is interesting to note that upon the birth of Gershom, as recorded in Parashas Shemos, the Torah presents the facts just the same way: *Va'teled ben va'yikra shemo Gershom ki amar ger hayisi b'eretz nochriyah* (2:22). The birth of Eliezer is deduced from the later text, but not specifically recorded.

Several questions come to mind.

1) Why, in each instance, does the Torah spell out that Gershom's name was chosen *ki amar*, because Moshe declared (*ger hayisi b'eretz nochriyah*), but with regard to Eliezer, it makes no reference to any declaration on Moshe's part, but simply states the rationale for the name (*ki Elokei avi b'ezri va'yatzileni me'cherev Paroh*)?

2) Historically, the order of events was that Moshe slew the Egyptian; Pharaoh, according to midrashic and Talmudic sources, ordered Moshe killed, but he was saved when his neck turned to stone in the face of the executioner's sword; and Moshe escaped and found his way to Midian, where he settled in with Yisro, whose daughter he married. He made his life there.

Now, one would think that Moshe's first son's name would commemorate the great miracle of Moshe's salvation from Pharaoh's sword. Instead, the first son's name reflects Moshe's distress at being in a foreign land (as if Egypt were not a foreign land!) and only the second son's name commemorates the initial miracle that made Moshe's life in Midian, with a home, a job, a wife, and children possible.

I would suggest that the language and the form that the Torah uses to tell us about the names also subtly (intentionally so) tells us something about human nature, and life, and what can be expected and accepted of people, great and small.

Ki amar: Moshe declared. It says this twice, in Shemos and in Yisro, that Moshe named his firstborn son Gershom, because he declared, in his distress over his separation from his family and from his people, *ki ger hayisi b'eretz nochriyah*. Moshe was saying, *Oy! It hurts*. Certainly Moshe was well aware and appreciative of the fact that God had saved him from Pharaoh's sword. But he couldn't help himself. *Ki amar: Es hut zich aroisgeshrigen fun ihm* – his pain, his angst, his helplessness upon separation from his suffering people burst forth from him. His mind and his spirit were on his people, not on himself.

When young Moshe, the prince of Egypt, Pharaoh's adopted grandson, first went out among his people and saw their enslaved misery, he was overcome. The Midrash describes Moshe's encounter: He went out and he wept upon witnessing their bitter bondage, and he said, "*Chaval li aleichem!*" (How intolerable your situation is to me!). "*Mi yiten musi aleichem!*" (Would that I would die for you!). He ran frantically from slave to slave, helping them shoulder their burdens.

And so he encounters the Mitzri taskmaster mercilessly beating and persecuting the Jew. In his rage and misery, he slays the murderous Mitzri, for which his own life becomes legally forfeit. He is saved by a miracle, his neck turning to stone and undamaged by the headsman's sword. He flees. He arrives in Midian and settles in with Yisro, marrying Tziporah and tending Yisro's sheep. But his soul remains in torment over his enslaved people. In his safe haven, Moshe laments that he is a sojourner in a strange land, when he longs to be back in Egypt, in the midst of all the misery, because that is where his heart and his spirit want to be, with his people.

Of course Moshe recognized the great miracle Hashem performed for him, saving his life. But Moshe had declared, "*Mi yiten musi aleichem*," would that I could die for you!

Moshe's life was less important to him than his people's welfare. And so his acknowledgement of that miracle saving him comes second, after his *ki amar*, his "primal scream" on behalf of his people. *Ki amar, ger hayisi b'eretz nochriyah.*

One can argue that Moshe's first obligation was to declare "Baruch Hashem for saving me" (Eliezer: *Elokei avi b'ezri, va'yatzileni me'cherev Paroh*) and only then express his personal feelings of pain and distress (Gershom: *ki ger hayisi b'eretz nochriyah*).

One lesson that can be drawn here, I believe, is that in life, it sometimes hurts. *Lo aleinu*, may we never be tested, it can hurt so badly as to be unbearable. We cry out.

And sometimes we cry out in a way that's self-centered, placing our own problems at the top of the world's heap of problems.

The Torah is telling us here, however subtly, that it's OK. It's understandable and it's acceptable. We should not judge others for doing so; we do not feel their pain. This is part of life. We can only hope that the pain will not be too bad, and that we are able to deal with it, to keep it in perspective. And that we will sympathize fully, when things are well with us, with others who are in pain.

Moshe's utter selflessness resulted in a paradoxical self-centered cry of pain. But that cry was for the pain of his people, which, in turn, pained him so deeply that he might have lost a bit of perspective in which declaration to make first. But he was so good, so selfless, so pure, so driven on behalf of his people, that in the end he makes only one declaration, *ki amar*, about his people, and not about himself.

And thus the Ribbono shel Olam, our loving Father in Heaven, chose this gentle, loving, caring shepherd, whose "Oy, Oy!" on behalf of his people – uttered perhaps indeed contrary to proper protocol – pierced the very Heavens, to be the very shepherd to lead them out of slavery and to the Promised Land, and to eternity.

Parashas Yisro 5771

Mishpatim

Eating Ham for Uncle Sam

Parashas Mishpatim is famous for introducing, immediately after the sublime and lofty scene of Matan Torah on Har Sinai, a veritable blizzard of seemingly mundane laws, rules, and regulations governing all manner of civil relations, and seemingly disconnected from the refined dicta of the Aseres Hadibros. The ox that gored follows hard on the heels of *Anochi Hashem Elokecha*. Rashi, quoting the Midrash, immediately makes clear: *mah harishonim mi'Sinai, af eilu mi'Sinai*. All these laws are from Hashem at Sinai.

We do not have a concept of secular, civil law apart from religious, sacral law.

Torts and ritual are not of two separate, parallel systems. They are one. Hashem teaches us – and commands us – how to relate to Him through Himself (*bein adam la'Makom*) and how to relate to Him through our fellow human beings (*bein adam l'chaveiro*), who are created in His image.

The prime imperative is that we be a holy nation, one that serves Hashem in all our actions and all our relationships. Systems of secular civil law, borne of logic, reason, pragmatism, and moral humanism, are also subject to rationalization, relativity, selectivity, erosion. The two Luchos Habris of Har Sinai, one apparently *bein adam la'Makom* and the other *bein adam l'chaveiro*, are not separate mandates at all; they are one. They are the same. The same voice of God enunciated them both. The same *etzba Elokim* engraved them both, on our national character as well as on the two tablets of stone.

Hashem set up an interesting and challenging system for us. The rationale, the legal and the moral basis for the latter commandments is the first commandment: *Anochi Hashem Elokecha*. The road to God leads directly through our fellow human beings, and there is no detour possible.

A perusal of the long list of mitzvos in Mishpatim reveals that virtually in the exact middle of them all are two specific ones that are treated differently from the rest, but which, by the nature of their mandate, define the others. And they are treated similarly to each other, with good reason.

They share an unusual grammatical form. Introducing them is a third mitzvah that shares the same grammatical form, and which thereby sheds light on our understanding of the other two. "*Al kol devar pesha*," with regard to every manner of wrongdoing, judgment will be made in courts with regard to "*asher yarshiun elohim*." The Gemara in Sanhedrin analyzes the extra *nun* in *yarshiun*, understanding that it denotes the plural. But *yarshiu* without the *nun* already denotes the plural. Clearly, the additional *nun* is an *emphasis* on the plural.

Two more of the many mitzvos in our *parashah* are marked by this seemingly superfluous *nun*. *Kol almanah v'yasom lo s'anun*. Do not oppress the widow or the orphan. Why the extra *nun*? Rashi paraphrases Rabbi Akiva: We may not oppress anyone. But the widow and the orphan are specifically mentioned because they are defenseless, they are powerless to fight back, and *diber hakasuv b'hoveh* (Scripture speaks of the usual case): it tends to happen to them. Such is human nature. People will often exert their petty tyrannies on those upon whom they think they can get away with it. They may not even realize they are doing it. They're just imposing their will where they can. To the powerless, however, sensitized by their lot in life, it is yet another blow to their own dignity, reinforcing their own helplessness and keeping them down.

God says that He will not let you get away with bullying the weak. It reveals who you really are. Several additional *pesukim* are given over to His response to such behavior. You were at Sinai. You saw and you heard. You heard *Anochi Hashem Elokecha*. You know My mandate to emulate God. This behavior is the opposite of Godliness and will not be tolerated. If you transgress in this, you will anger God. You may well die as a result, and your wives will become widows and your children will be orphans, helpless in the face of their own oppressors.

The extra plural *nun* means that society has an extra obligation to safeguard the interests of the helpless, such as through protective acts of *beis din* (Torah Temimah). The extra plural *nun* means that to a greater or lesser degree, this type of behavior is so ubiquitous, so common to human nature, and it can be so subtle that we are all at risk, in one form or another, of transgressing, at terrible cost, *lo aleinu*. The extra plural *nun* means this is not just about the obvious bully. It means me and you. It means most people, by their very nature, unless that nature is modulated by the imperative to Godliness in our day-to-day behavior.

Historically, the most prominent mitzvah that has defined a Jew, especially before the world, is *kashrus*. More so, I believe, than more *chamur* mitzvos. Perhaps even more than Shabbos, as central as that is to Yiddishkeit. It is, in a real sense, the face of practicing Judaism.

V'anshei kodesh tihyun li, u'vasar ba'sadeh treifah lo socheilu, l'kelev tashlichun oso.

Perhaps it is because we absorb and we become what we eat that it is so. And we are taught that eating *treif* has the terrible effect of *timtum halev*, creating a barrier between the Jew and God, so that as a result, the transgressor becomes more and more distanced.

The generations before mine, in America, who ate kosher but were *mechallel Shabbos*, raised children who dropped *kashrus* as well. It was actually quite common for people to work on Shabbos, unable to withstand that *nisayon* in this new land, but to still keep strictly kosher. Many, even if they wanted to, could not readily bring themselves to actually ingest – and absorb into themselves – what had been anathema to all their previous generations. They still understood the concept of and the connection between *anshei kodesh tihyun li* and *basar...treifah lo socheilu*. Their children, however, poorly or entirely uneducated in Judaism, did not have such a hard time making this break.

Interestingly, a major vehicle for this break with young Jews was World War II, when large numbers of young men left home for the army, and tough circumstances.

A very interesting history of that overall experience was published a few years ago under the title *GI Jew*. And one important chapter in that book, titled "Eating Ham for Uncle Sam," describes how Jewish boys who had never eaten *treif* before began doing so because they felt they had no choice, or because they were no longer under the restraints of home and their mother's kosher kitchen. And they never went back.

By the grace of God, the physical Holocaust in Europe never reached these shores. That same war, however, produced a terrible spiritual devastation here. Things changed – in many families, irreparably. What set the stage for it was *chillul Shabbos* and lack of education. The *timtum halev* that resulted from eating *treif*, however, was explosive in its consequences.

A generation ago, nearly every shul in New York had a large turnout of non-shul-goers for Yizkor. In our own shul, the basement was set up with benches and was filled to overflowing for Yizkor services by people who did not normally come to shul, who were not observant, but whose parents to some degree still had that connection.

How terribly sad that the children of these people, however, by and large do not observe Yizkor at all. In a Jewish sense, their souls have been forgotten. Many of their grandchildren are not Jewish, or are not at all connected to Judaism. It is, from a Jewish perspective, for many of them, as if they had never lived. *Timtum halev.*

There have been times and places when Jews have been forced to eat *treif, lo aleinu*.

In about 1912, before he was *niftar*, the great Dzhikover Rebbe, the Ateres Yeshuah, who foresaw much, looked upon his Chassidim at a large gathering and said to them, "I see you all in uniform. Some of you will be forced to eat *neveilos* and *treifos* to stay alive. But I beg you: when you do, *lektz nisht di finger*, don't lick your fingers!" Keep in mind, he was telling them, no matter what, no matter how bad it is, no matter what you must do to stay alive, *anshei kodesh tihyun li*. That will protect you from fatal *timtum halev*, even if you are forced to consume *maachalos assuros* to stay alive.

The extra plural *nun* – actually *two* such double plural *nuns* in this *pasuk* – warns us, I suggest, about the particular risks involved here: the potential loss, in families, not just of individuals, or even many individuals of a particular time or place, but the loss, *chas v'chalilah*, of *all* future generations, until the end of time; devastating, final, irrevocable. Family after family, each one a continuous line of unbroken connection to God and Klal Yisrael since the very beginning, since the Avos and since Matan Torah, now cut off and lost forever.

Those who, in effect, cut themselves and their children off didn't even realize what they were doing. They didn't get it. They mostly still don't get it. They weren't thinking strategically about their families, and certainly not about the Jewish People. Unprepared, unprotected, uneducated, they just...fell away, and carried *doros* and *doros* away with them. *Timtum halev*. May Hashem protect us.

V'anshei kodesh tihyun li: be holy people, all of you, each and every one of you, so that you and your generations to follow will not be cut off. The mandate to be *kodesh* is for *every* Jew, not just rabbis and scholars (the extra plural *nun*).

U'vasar ba'sadeh treifah lo socheilu: guard your inner purity as well, whether it's literally the food you eat and absorb or any of the myriad *treif* influences of all kinds that are all around and waiting to pounce and take you over – indeed, to take you *under* – to clog up your pure Jewish heart and soul and to separate it from your Creator. Be careful what goes into your mouth (*and what comes out of it*). Be careful about what goes into your ears. Be ever so careful about what you look at: that's the portal the yetzer hara uses to gain access to your heart.

La'kelev tashlichun oso: discard the *treif*, brush off those harmful influences, throw them to the dogs. They're not for you. They will ruin you and they will ruin your children, and their children after them.

It's not just about you. It's about all the generations of your forebears who struggled and suffered to make you a Jew and to keep you connected to God. It's about all the generations that will follow who need to have that same connection. Spare them the *timtum halev* that is so destructive. Live. Truly live, the life of purity and holiness and Godliness that is our heritage and our birthright, as well as our obligation: *V'anshei kodesh tihyun li.*

How? *V'eleh hamishpatim.*

Parashas Mishpatim 5771

Finders Keepers, Losers Weepers

I must have been six or seven years old at the time. I was playing on the stoop in front of the four-family house we lived in, one of a row of nine such houses, on Eastern Parkway. Some little toy fell out of my pocket. In a moment, Laurie, a neighbor child of a different background, had it in her hand. When I asked for it, she told me that it was now hers. I lost it, she found it, and *finders keepers, losers weepers. That's the law. Too bad on me.*

I couldn't believe she meant it. But she did. Her mother had told her so.

I knew that that couldn't be right. It was mine. No one disputed that it had been mine. While I was leaping boxes in the street game we were playing, it had fallen out of my pocket. How could picking it up make it hers, when it was mine?

I might have been too young to quote from Parashas Mishpatim, or from Ki Setzei, or from *Shulchan Aruch*, or from the Gemara. But I knew, with every bit of intelligence, instinct, and knowledge that I could muster, that she was wrong and I was right – not that the Torah meant anything to her.

The problem, of course, was not what six-year-old Laurie thought about what was right, but the civilization, the culture that formed her.

It's interesting that my very wise mother, on another occasion, when I wanted to do something the kids on the street wanted to do, but that was out of keeping with what I should want to do, said to me, with a healthy dose of irony in her voice, "You want to do that? Why, because *Laurie* thinks that's a good thing to do? That makes it right? What Laurie wants and does is not what *we* do." I got the point. My mother had a great sense of mission, a sense she made sure to instill in her children. (Amazing that, of all the children she could have named for her example, she chose Laurie.)

Laurie, and the culture that taught her "finders keepers, losers weepers," did not stand alongside us at the foot of Mount Sinai as we were swept away into a separate spiritual realm by the very voice of God proclaiming *Anochi Hashem Elokecha, I am "Hashem," your God, Who took you out of the land of Egypt, from the house of bondage,* a pronouncement that changed everything, forever.

The nine commandments that follow the first all derive their power and their absolute validity from that first commandment. Do not steal, because God has instructed us that it is wrong, and forbidden. Do not murder, do not live licentiously, do not bear false witness, do not covet what belongs to others, because God has instructed us that it is wrong and forbidden. The same applies for the other commandments as well.

Ask a typical young European today – liberal, post-Christian, intellectually self-satisfied – what standard defines what is objectively right and what is wrong, challenge their moral relativism, and they will be hard pressed to give you a coherent answer. They might try to muddle in something about not harming other people, but ultimately, if you press them, the answer typically comes down to "if it *feels* right," it's right. Sadly, this is a moral infection that is affecting a growing number of young Americans too, a disorder contracted on college campuses, where shallow groupthink and slogans have replaced traditional values.

There is a very good reason that the sublime and exalted scene at Sinai, with its religious and moral pronouncements, is followed immediately by a deluge of what appears to be mundane, "civil" law. The ox that gored, loans, torts, property, things lost and found. And that is because to a Jew, there is ultimately no moral difference between "You shall serve no other god" and the laws governing the responsibility of a man who negligently digs a pit in a public place and causes harm to someone else's property, between "I am Hashem, your God" and the laws governing the return of a lost object to its rightful owner. Because God is holy, and, in His immeasurable kindness, He offers us the opportunity to aspire to holiness as well. And that holiness is achieved as much by how we relate to each other as by how we observe religious ritual. They are both important, and they both derive from the same source.

I don't know what became of my neighbor Laurie, but I am grateful for the important lesson I learned because of her way back then while playing stoopball on Eastern Parkway. The potential for utter Godlessness in the mindset that proclaims "finders keepers, losers weepers, too bad for you," struck me, even then, as profoundly different from the values in the moral safe haven I was raised in, where it was He Who proclaimed *"Anochi Hashem Elokecha"* Who defined what is right and what is wrong, what is just and what is not, a truth transmitted by parents who, whatever ups and downs in life there were, whatever the challenges, setbacks, bumps, and glitches, understood their mission in raising their children, and the mission of our family, and of our people, in this world.

Parashas Mishpatim 5776

Hadras Panim

They would appear at the door, those wonderful young men, some more experienced at this and some less, totally unprepared for my...caprice. Sort of. Smart, accomplished fellows, excellent at their Torah studies, of good families, resplendent in their dark suits and regulation Borsalinos with the proper brim diameter, they were also well prepped by their mothers that they were the very best *schoireh*, truly ideal, exactly what the doctor ordered (Dr. Reich, that is), or should have ordered.

Yes, they were coming to meet my daughters. But I admit, I have a weakness. I can't always help myself. And so they wound up "meeting" me too, to the squirming discomfort of my daughters. No, I wasn't trying to sabotage anything. Of course I wanted my girls to get married. But as I said, I couldn't help myself.

So after the usual pleasantries, I would sometimes ask first-timers a question they were not used to. I asked it in all friendliness, in true curiosity, and out of a genuine desire to know.

Here they were, serious Jewish young men, immersed in full-time advanced Torah study. And contrary to the entire weight of all of Jewish history and tradition right up to recent times, they were all clean-shaven. Not one beard among them. Yes, I know, had they been in *chassidishe* yeshivas, they would have had proper beards. But these fellows, even if they had some *chassidishe* background, were in what we call Litvish-type yeshivas, where the boys all shaved. Why? I asked them. You're a religious, learned Jew. Where's your beard? That is, after all, the classic sign of the Jew.

Typically, this was greeted with a blank, uncomprehending stare. At first, they didn't even understand the question. When I laid it out for them, they did seem to get it (sort of). They were, after all, top boys. They might have been prepared to say, or perhaps to hear, a *shtickel* Torah, or field questions about future plans. But for this they were unprepared.

It soon became apparent to me that they by and large had no clear idea why they, and their fellows, didn't have beards. But what bothered me really was not so much that they shaved; they did, after all, have authorities upon whom to rely that permit them to shave. Rather, it was that they thought it *normal and expected* that *bnei Torah* should shave off their beards. They were really clueless on this. And, it appeared to me, my very question made them suspicious of my *frumkeit*. Like I'm not religious enough to understand that they're *supposed* to shave.

That the classic image of a Jew, consistent throughout the ages and across the world, was absent in them, that volumes based on *nigleh* and *nistar* stress the importance of the beard (and *peyos*) adorning the face of the Jew was set aside by them, that in shaving they were utilizing a *heter* and bypassing what had always been the Jewish norm, they seemed entirely oblivious to.

Some would refer to photos from early twentieth-century Lithuanian yeshivos, with the young men clean-shaven, as proof that this was the ideal. They did not realize that that was the unfortunate reality of that period, and not the ideal.

Adding to this equation is the attitude of many of the young girls that these boys were meeting in their quest for a wife. Even girls from excellent homes – *and even girls whose own fathers wore beards* – frequently would not want a boy with a beard.

What's wrong with their chinuch?

I am sure that the *roshei yeshivos* have their *cheshbonos* as to why they permit this. I myself can think of an excellent rationale why this should be permitted. But what I do not understand is why it should be considered normal and expected.

Judaism does not have a separate set of laws, rules, and regulations for *rabbonim* or for men older than thirty-five, whereby a beard suddenly becomes necessary, or desirable, or – sorry, girls – *tolerable.*

I realize that in today's society there are a great many men who must, or believe they must, utilize the *heter* to shave in a permissible manner for the sake of their livelihood. *Please understand that this is not at all about them.*

I also believe that it can be preferable for a young man to wait to see where life will lead him before making the decision to grow a beard, as it is far better to grow it later if possible, than to grow it first and then face having to shave it off. That would be bad indeed. And that, I believe, is the one logical rationale for those boys who might go out into the job market, to wait. For those who know they never will, I can see no such rationale. Shaving the beard, for a Jew, may have a *heter*, but *it is not normal.*

European Jews in the twentieth century were accustomed to seeing Jews with shaved faces. Perhaps the majority did so. But it was still shocking to many to come to America and encounter clean-shaven *rabbis*. Of course there were historical and sociological reasons for it. But their surprised reaction, even of those Jews who were themselves clean-shaven, was kind of funny: *a bruch tzu Columbus! What kind of country is this?*

From the time of David Hamelech, cutting off a Jew's beard has been a sport among gentiles who wish to humiliate Jews. One of the cruel humiliations, calculated to demoralize, inflicted by the Germans upon the Jews was to force them to cut off their beards. The beard, for the Jew, is no trivial matter. It is part of his identity as a Jew.

So why this discussion now? Parashas Mishpatim, of course.

V'anshei kodesh tihyun li, u'vasar ba'sadeh treifah lo socheilu; la'kelev tashlichun oso. You shall be holy people unto Me; do not eat *treif meat; throw that to the dogs.*

The Ateres Yeshuah ties that mandate to the opening words of the *parashah.*

V'eleh hamishpatim asher tasim lifneihem. Rashi asks the classic question: Why are the many judicial laws in this *parashah* discussed immediately after a reference to the Mizbe'ach, the Altar in the Mikdash? Rashi quotes a midrash that places the two together as instruction to seat the Sanhedrin, the supreme Torah court, in the vicinity of the Mizbe'ach. Furthermore, the Torah makes a point that the *mishpatim,* the virtual torrent of laws governing various relations between Jews that fill Parashas Mishpatim, are meant specifically for the Jewish People. And these laws, God tells Moshe, should be laid out in an orderly fashion for the people, *k'shulchan ha'aruch,* like a set table.

Homiletically, the Ateres Yeshuah connects these concepts and offers a rationale.

An important concept throughout history has been that *a Jew appear as a Jew.*

Remember that this was one of the redeeming practices of the Jews in Egypt that made them worthy of redemption. And so maintaining one's appearance as a Jew – classically, by mode of dress, the beard and the *peyos* – is, historically, key to maintaining continuity of the nation.

People worry, and not without cause, that looking *too* parochially Jewish, or acting *too* Jewish, will interfere with their ability to make a living. Thus, the message implied by the proximity of the Sanhedrin, representing the spiritual sustenance of the nation, to the Mizbe'ach, which represents, among other things, the physical sustenance of the nation, its *gematria* (numerical equivalent) being equal to *zan* (*parnassah* or sustenance): together, there is *Torah u'gedulah b'makom echad*; let Yiddishkeit and material success flourish together.

And so the mandate *v'anshei kodesh tihyun li,* you shall be holy people unto Me, aside from the literal meaning regarding not eating *treif,* also refers to our daily business dealings with others, that we conduct ourselves at all times honestly and honorably, distance ourselves from any form of dishonesty or theft, as befitting a holy people. But beyond that, it also refers to our own commitment to be holy Jews in every aspect of our lives, that we not shed our Yiddishkeit in the mundane sphere of making a living, that we remain who we are meant to be, unashamed, obvious members of God's holy congregation of Israel. *Basar ba'sadeh treifah lo socheilu,* when you are out "in the field" doing your daily pursuit of a livelihood, remain *anshei kodesh,* holy people; do not go "*treif*" to this ideal by acting or appearing non-Jewish in the expectation that you will do better that way.

The Midrash tells us that the *treif* meat that is to be thrown to the dogs is the dog's reward for not barking when the Jews left Egypt, in deference to our triumphant upper hand at that time. God does not forget the needs of – and what is due – every creature He created. And so the Gemara (*Bava Basra* 8a) describes a hungry man asking to be sustained, as God, in nature, sustains the dog and the raven. Ultimately, it is God Who provides our sustenance. Thus, says the Psalmist (Tehillim 55:23): *"Hashlech al Hashem yehovcha v'Hu yechalkelecha"* (Cast your burden upon God, and He will sustain you).

It's easy to preach from a position of security. I am not preaching, but raising a subject.

There are very many people out in the workforce who feel less than fully secure in their positions, and therefore vulnerable. They feel they must conform to societal modes, and within the parameters of halachah, they do so with the sanction of our authorities. There are halachically permissible ways to shave. But not everyone is bound by those external pressures.

Years ago in America, even the *frumest* doctor worked bareheaded. And he certainly had no beard. That was then. My generation was really the first to assert itself in this regard. We felt secure enough as Americans, as Jews, as American Jews and as Jewish Americans to follow our consciences and present ourselves to the medical world and to the public as obvious, practicing Jews. That we could do so was a function of America's growth and development in this regard, but also that of the American Jewish community. It was a coincidence of a more tolerant America with a more self-confident and self-assertive American Jewish community.

In my training, and in practice, I have felt free to present myself as I am, as who I am. Let whoever doesn't like it go somewhere else. And let God take care of me. I have been blessed that it has never been an issue.

I realize very well that not everyone is in a position to behave independently this way. But I suspect that, in our wonderful America, many more can. *Hashlech al Hashem yehovcha v'Hu yechalkelecha*. That is part of the mandate *v'anshei kodesh tihyun li.*

For a Jew, an important part of being *kodesh*, being holy unto God, is presenting oneself to the world, to each other, and really importantly, to *oneself*, as a visible and obvious Jew. It is our uniform. Even more so than the Borsalino.

A *ben Torah* who learns exceptionally well, or who davens exceptionally well, is not being a *shvitzer*, a show-off; he is just doing what a Jew is supposed to do. The beard, it seems to me, is no different. It is what a Jew is supposed to do.

Parashas Mishpatim 5772

Terumah

A Healthy Life

"There are no atheists in foxholes."

That old adage about human nature has much truth in it. When things are tough, when one is afraid, in grave danger, and feeling powerless, when all one can do is pray, even those who do not normally bother themselves with God, much less spend any energy on serving Him, are likely to remember Him in their desperate appeal for life.

Especially in times of serious illness, *lo aleinu*, with all that medical science has to offer, man is, in the end, helpless. He prays that the treatment will work. He prays that after failed treatments, the doctors will find another strategy that works. He prays that the pain will be relieved. He prays that the suffering will be alleviated.

Less likely, unless he is religious, is that man will pray that he or his loved ones not become sick in the first place. A religious person prays for health even when he is not sick. And in life, with all its vulnerabilities, there is a far broader concept to "sickness" than medical malady alone.

The Jew understands that the focus of prayer is that the Ribbono shel Olam extend a *refuah shleimah* to all the sick of Israel, and to all the *sicknesses* of Israel, both physical and spiritual.

Illness, thus, includes not just medical malady, and not just spiritual malady, but also the absence of the entities in life that make for a happy and fulfilled existence. Poverty, for example, or the personal miseries of the heart, or the pain of having disappointing children, or bad luck in life, are a form of illness, even as coronary heart disease is. And relief from these hurts is a form of *refuah*, even as a coronary bypass is.

Ateres Yeshuah cites the Midrash on *v'yikchu Li terumah*, they shall take for Me *terumah*, "*l'romem osi b'tefillaschem*," that they shall elevate Me (*k'v'yachol*) with their prayer. And the focus of prayer is to ask for *refuah shleimah* for all the sick of Israel, and all the sicknesses of Israel, whether physical or spiritual.

Our inherited prime mediators, he continues, for the blessing of this *refuah*, are the Avos: Avraham, Yitzchak, and Yaakov. And it is known that each of the Avos represents a facet of this blessing: Avraham (ה' ברך את אברהם בכל, Bereishis 24:1), Yitzchak (הברכה אחת היא לך, Bereishis 27:38), Yaakov (גם ברוך יהיה, Bereishis 27:33). This is part of their bequest to their descendants.

Add up ברך, ברכה, ברוך and you get the same (677) as *refuah shleimah* (רפואה שלימה). This power, this blessing, is *ezras Avoseinu* (עזרת אבותינו), also 677. Bring Me *terumah*, Hashem says, *v'yikchu Li terumah*, dedicate your resources to Heaven – *give tzedakah* – as Rashi says, *Li, l'shmi*: for the sake of My Name. Add up *terumah* (תרומה) and God's Name (הוי"ה) and you get the same, 677.

The blessings bequeathed to us by the Avos, *refuah shleimah* for all that ails us, physically, materially, and spiritually, individually and as a nation, tzedakah given for the sake of Heaven – are all interwoven and draw their power from the same supernal source.

There is an expression, in philanthropy, "Give until it hurts." While that certainly has validity, the real power of tzedakah lies in giving *before* it hurts, that we may merit that it does not come to hurt. The atheist cowering in the foxhole has no clue about this. It is foreign to his way of thinking. He only now gives God a thought, and a "chance," because it already hurts.

We, the children of Avraham, Yitzchak, and Yaakov, of Sarah, Rivkah, Rachel, and Leah, of the hundreds of generations of holy souls who came before us, know better.

God rules the world according to His divine plan, to which we are not privy, except in the broadest outlines. We cannot see every connection, every precise cause and effect. But we do know what God wants of us, how He expects us to spend these limited years we are in the world and the resources that He put in our trust. He wants us to be "healthy," and to do the things we are supposed to do to acquire and maintain that "health."

My father, *a"h*, liked to say that in order to write a check to tzedakah, you need to have the money in the bank account, and you need *az di hant zol nisht tzitterin*, that your hand not shake so badly that you are unable to write.

It takes courage and understanding to be able to give your money away, especially if it is hard-earned money. For most of us, our money is, in fact, hard-earned. That is the way of the world. It is also the way of the world, it is human nature, to want to hold on to it. That is entirely understandable. It is only through a far deeper and wiser understanding that we can have that courage, that we can write that generous check.

When we understand that, when we have the will to be *metzaref* (to bind) our *terumah* to שם הוי"ה, we also have the power to invoke *ezras Avoseinu*, to draw upon the blessings of ברכה, ברוך, ברך of Avraham, Yitzchak, and Yaakov, and thus have the greatest opportunity and the greatest hope for a true and thorough and lasting *refuah shleimah* in every meaning of the word, in every aspect of our lives.

In this world, in this life, there is no better way to enrich every aspect of that life than to give, for the sake of Heaven, with an open hand. We have no greater power in our hands than this. It is the key that God has put into our hands, and indeed, is surely one of the reasons God gave us hands.

Parashas Terumah 5774

A Tale of Two *Terumahs*

Inspired, excited, and united, the Children of Israel, standing at the foot of Mount Sinai, proclaim *"naaseh v'nishma,"* we will do and we will listen. So God throws a little test into the flow of commandments that follow. *"V'yikchu Li terumah,"* they shall take for Me *terumah*, an offering. Gold, silver, textiles, etc.

Rashi emphasizes that this is an offering borne of the good-heartedness of the donor, for the sake of Heaven. *Asher yidvenu libo.*

We *have* to give, but how, and when, and how much, in what spirit and in what manner, makes a big difference. Sometimes it's very much in keeping with God's stipulation that it be given *"Li,"* for His sake, and of which He is, *k'v'yachol*, proud, and sometimes a donation is given in a manner that cannot be described in any manner as elevating the Name of God. And while this particular *pasuk* relates to the building of the Mishkan in the Midbar, it really applies to charitable giving in general.

So let me tell you two brief stories. The first is about my late cousin Jesse, described by everyone in the family as *a goldene ying*, a young man with a heart made of gold. Jesse was the first member of our family to be born on these shores, while my parents and everyone were still in Europe, the Holocaust looming their way. He served in the US Army in World War II, and later opened a clothing store in Williamsburg with his brother-in-law Julie, another fine and kind young man.

When the surviving refugees arrived, among them my parents with my brother, my aunt and uncle with their daughter, and another uncle and aunt with their daughter and son, they were all, of course, dirt poor. The apartment I was born in had no toilet, no heat, and no hot water. It was an old tenement house, built in the mid-1800s. For them, of course, it was a safe haven in a safe country. They understood that with time they would, with God's help, build themselves up to a better standard of living. But meanwhile, they, and the others, had no resources – other than their own strengths and resourcefulness.

Enter Jesse and Julie. Julie was not our relative but in his heart he surely was, as Jessie, with Julie's full agreement, made sure that all the arriving relatives and their children were adequately clothed. This went on for years. And we never, *ever*, felt that we were receiving charity. My father always paid for what we bought, but we knew that the prices charged reflected not the retail value of the clothing, but the priceless value of Jesse's Jewish heart. *Asher yidvenu libo.*

Sadly, Jesse died much too young. And with him, the world lost *a goldene ying* who understood, even with his limited book learning, but very much in his spirit and in what his parents instilled in him, the concept of *terumah* given with a full heart, "*Li*," for the sake of Heaven, to the delight of our Father in Heaven.

I have described, elsewhere in these pages, the story of another survivor, a remarkable man named Naftuli Saleschutz, later Americanized to Norman Salsitz. He was one of the rare Jews who actually survived while remaining in Poland under German control for nearly the entire war. This is not the place to review his entire story. He chronicled much of that in his several books. God chose to save him, but in human terms, his remarkable strengths, his resourcefulness and resilience kept him alive where most others succumbed. His story is absolutely astounding, and his personal strength of will and character and determination were extraordinary. He was not someone who would ever seek or take a handout. He would never have needed to. He knew how to take care of himself.

Arriving in America, brokenhearted from the suffering and the loss of his people, he was personally bereft, his father having been murdered before his very eyes, and the rest, his beloved mother and sisters, all killed. As he lay dying, his father had called out to him, "*Nekumeh!*" – that he avenge Jewish blood. And he did.

He had in his pocket one name, relatives who arrived in America years before the war and had done well for themselves. Desperate to connect with family, he looked them up.

He entered his cousin Charlie's office, where the young man sat, barely looking up at him. Finally, clearly unhappy, he looked at Naftuli and shoved a $100 check on the desk toward him, saying, "Here, and don't bother me anymore."

Naftuli thought he was brokenhearted before. At this he was utterly shattered. His feelings then were indescribable. He left the check untouched (he had come for *family*, not for money) and fled. It was something he could never forget.

Naftuli's relative did write a check. But can it in any way be described as *"Li,"* for the sake of God, in honor of Heaven?

And so, as we face the challenge of parting with our hard-earned money – and for most of us, it *is* a challenge – as we do our own *terumah*, we should remember that as we do so, we have the additional choice and challenge: shall we be a Jesse, of blessed memory, or a Charlie?

You might think the choice is easy or obvious. But the Satan knows very well how to obscure things, confuse us, mix us up. We must *always* see the big picture, and *always* aspire to be the one others recognize, and God recognizes, as *a goldene ying*.

That is really the gold God wants of us.

Parashas Terumah 5775

Face to Face

In the moment, the only Turkish word I could think of, *bulanik*, meaning "blurry" (a term I learned from my patients), was not going to help me find a public toilet.

I was in the marketplace in Kusadasi, a port town on the Aegean coast of Turkey. It is not far from the ruins of the ancient Greek city of Ephesus, which we had visited that day. Ephesus was once a thriving metropolis, with a significant Jewish population (we saw the ruins of an old shul). Interestingly, the ancient public toilets that have been uncovered there helped me understand references to such public facilities in the Talmud.

Later, in Kusadasi's bazaar, it seemed like a good idea to find the modern, and hopefully clean, successor to such a facility. I did not know the Turkish word *tuvalet*, and the place was so foreign and exotic that I wondered if anyone there would understand if I asked in English.

The faces around me were very foreign. Turkey has a large population of mixed ethnicities and appearances, some more Western and others not, but the predominant appearance is that of the ethnic Turk. These people did not look like me.

I spied a local fellow, a young man whose face and eyes were, to me, not foreign at all. He did not look like a Goldberg, but he did not look like a Mustafa either. On an impulse I addressed him in Hebrew. He promptly and without hesitation responded in the same language. A merchant in the market, he took me to the place I was seeking, waited for me, and brought me back to his rug shop.

We had a long talk. We drank apple tea. He told me about his hopes to marry and to move to Israel. We exchanged contact information. I bought a small rug (which now sits in my *tuvalet* in New York). About two years later he called me when he was in New York and we had dinner together.

David was from Izmir, not far away. Izmir, whose old Greek name is Smyrna, is home to an ancient Jewish community, now much reduced in numbers. It was where, in 1665, the notorious Shabtai Tzvi, a native of that town, proclaimed himself the Messiah.

Although he learned from Sephardic *rabbanim*, Shabtai Tzvi was himself not a Sephardi. He was a son of the original Romaniote community.

It should be obvious to you, of course, that not every Jew of the East is a Sephardi.

When the Jews of Spain (Sepharad) were expelled from that accursed peninsula, they sought refuge wherever they could find it. From Bavel, through Syria, Greece, Turkey, the Balkans, Italy, and all along North Africa, there were already existing ancient Jewish communities, which the Sephardim joined. The Jews there had their own histories, languages, and traditions. Often they remained separate, but it was not unusual for the Sephardim, with their energy and their learning, to predominate and to set the tone for the community in general.

The Romaniotes were (and there still are around fifty thousand identifiable in the world today) the ancient Jews of the Greek world, once very numerous, who spoke Yavanic (Judeo Greek – essentially, Greek Yiddish). They have their own *siddur* and *nusach*. Along with their Sephardic Greek brethren, primarily from Salonica, the Romaniotes were dragged off by the Germans and murdered in Auschwitz.

I do not know or recall if David was Sephardic or Romaniote. But his face was definitely Jewish. His face spoke to me, quite clearly, in that exotic Turkish marketplace.

In his eyes, before a word was exchanged between us, I saw a brother.

I have written previously about the impact of familiar Jewish faces in quite a different context, this one painfully close to home. I had been at an exhibit of recovered photographs of prewar Polish Jews. Virtually all of them having been murdered, I never actually met any of them. But I knew virtually all their faces. They were faces, and eyes, familiar to all of us. They are the children of our own gene pool. I have seen and known, in my life among Jews – especially Ashkenazi Jews – alternate versions of those cheeks, that chin, that nose, those lips, those eyes.

It drove me crazy.

How could I look at those doomed faces, the faces of my loved ones, and remain sane?

Of all the remarkable things fashioned for the Mikdash, as enumerated in these *parashiyos*, the *keruvim*, the "cherubs," golden, winged structures with the faces of children, mounted above the Ark containing the two tablets of stone of the Aseres Hadibros, are perhaps the most remarkable.

How strange, for a religion that eschews all such imagery, to have these golden structures at all, let alone placed so centrally, literally covering the very tablets that forbid our making an idol or an image of any kind. What's more, images of the *keruvim* appeared woven into the walls of the Mishkan.

Much has been said about the nature and the role of the *keruvim*. Go look that up, if you wish. It is the faces that speak to me just now. The golden, beautiful, childlike faces of the *keruvim*, face to face, in holy embrace – indeed, in intimate embrace.

Those faces in the physical Mikdash correspond to the metaphysical faces on the very throne of God. They represent the undying love and eternal embrace between Israel and their Father in Heaven. But they represent more, I believe. They represent, as well, the undying love and eternal embrace between Jew and Jew, a bond that is, I think, a necessary precondition for that heavenly embrace. If we want God to bond lovingly with us, surely we must bond lovingly with each other as well.

The Torah here lists the various structures to be built for the Mishkan and how to build them. For the *keruvim*, however, an extra declaration of purpose is made, aside from the physical description. *V'no'adeti lecha sham: There is where I will encounter with you*, God tells Moshe (Shemos 25:22). *I will speak with you from atop the Cover, from between the two keruvim that are upon the Ark. From that place I will communicate My mitzvos to the Children of Israel.* Moshe would enter the Ohel Mo'ed, and the voice of God would descend from the Heavens, enter the space between the two *keruvim*, and from there communicate with Moshe.

From there. From between the two faces wrapped in intimate embrace. That is the designated channel for God's communication with His Chosen People.

Face to face. Of the many assaults on medical care in the US over the past years, one particularly troublesome one relates to this directly. The soulless big government bureaucracy mindset that believes that only they know what is good for everyone else, that it is their mandate and their right to control everything, including the relationship between you and your doctor, *requires* the doctor to keep your records electronically.

No more private paper records, just between you and the doctor. Big Brother wants in, and Big Brother wants control. Big Brother now stands between you and your doctor.

Whatever else that involves, one of the biggest complaints about this system, more from doctors than from patients, but very much about the patients, is that the doctor must now turn his face away from the patient for much of the encounter and peer into a computer screen. For those minutes of that important encounter, when the patient has come to put his life and health in the doctor's hands, when the doctor and patient need, *really need*, to encounter each other face to face, eye to eye, heart to heart, the doctor is forced to look away from the patient, even if his mind is very much on him. It's not fair to that patient. He *needs* the doctor's face, and the doctor needs the patient's.

The soulless bureaucracy cares nothing for this, but the doctors and the patents do.

Great effort is made, certainly in this doctor's practice, to overcome that. But the point of this aside is the critical human connection for which the face is the medium, whatever the context.

The faces of our loved ones, of our kin, of our tribe, evoke the deepest sense of connection, belonging, and commitment. And showing a good face, a caring face, a kind face, a loving face, to a fellow human being is so central to what God put us on this earth for, that it is the same medium through which God, at a time and place where His direct communication with us was at its highest form in all of history, chose to channel that communication, the unparalleled prophecy of Moshe Rabbenu, through the pure faces of the *keruvim*.

There is, I believe, an important lesson there. God put aside His aversion to our having sacred physical images of any kind, I suggest, to drive home the point to us that the path to our connection with Him also involves our connection to our fellow human beings, and in particular, to our fellow Jews, whose hearts are our hearts, whose fate is our fate, whose pain is our pain, whose needs are our needs, whose hunger is our hunger, whose joy is our joy, whose triumphs are our triumphs, whose disappointments and tragedies are our disappointments and tragedies, whose *nachas* is our *nachas*, whose lives and souls are so intimately bound to ours that their faces are also our faces, as together we also seek the very Face of God.

The worst things in history have happened to us when God turned His Face away from us, *Rachmana litzlan*, the *hester panim* the Torah warns us about. The best things in our history happened when, with full faith and love, we evoked God shining His countenance upon us with our own corresponding full hearts. And that is how God wants us to face each other as well. Heart to heart, face to face.

Parashas Terumah 5777

Said the Schnorrer, "I Don't Take Charity!"

I don't like the term *schnorrer*. Not that schnorrers don't schnorr. Sadly, they do.

All too often, however, the term is applied to someone in need who really doesn't deserve it. He may need help, he may in fact accept that help, he may even solicit that help, but he is not, by disposition or by intent, really a schnorrer. He's just in need and must resort to a bit of schnorring (so to speak), but he really hates doing so. And he will stop as soon as he can. He's not *really* schnorring – he is not, in fact, a schnorrer – and most of us are happy to help him. Sadly, however, there are those who just don't want to give, and they use that pejorative term to justify their not giving. And that's really objectionable.

Some years ago, in a community near New York that had no yeshiva, a new yeshiva prepared to establish itself. It was reasonable to expect that the Jews living there would be happy to have their community enhanced in this important way. There were many people, however, among them people of considerable financial resources and influence, who were not at all happy about it. The excuses they came up with to oppose the yeshiva would be funny if the whole thing were not so sad.

"They'll ruin the neighborhood! Sure, I'd like there to be a nice yeshiva here, but before you know it, the *kollel* wives will set up discount stores in their basements! It will bring down the whole quality of the community, along with the real estate values!"

"They'll ruin the neighborhood! Sure, I'd like there to be a nice yeshiva here, but they'll go schnorring door to door! What a *shande* it will be! Besides, they've probably got plenty of money, but they just want more from us!"

"They'll ruin the neighborhood! They'll hang around all day, not doing anything! I don't believe in that! They should go out and work!" (The yeshiva students were to be high school boys ages thirteen to fourteen.)

Etc., etc., etc. These comments were really made, as were others, by Jews who consider themselves good Jews, shul-goers, generous, and Jewish-minded. Giving was a problem for them. *Nebech*, they just didn't get it. And they were probably a little rusty on Parashas Terumah.

"*Daber el Bnei Yisrael v'yikchu Li terumah, me'es kol ish asher yidvenu libo tikchu es terumasi*" (Shemos 25:2). *Tikchu* is a mandate to take. Do take money from the Jewish people for a holy cause. They need to give it, and they need you (those in charge of such things) to take it from them. Encourage them to give. BUT: *asher yidvenu libo*: Rashi famously teaches, take it only from those who willingly give it. Otherwise, says Hashem, I don't want it.

An amazing scene played itself out in our own shul one morning, years ago. A collector – yes, he was probably a schnorrer, but a different kind of schnorrer, a schnorrer with an unusually high degree of self-respect, along with various other personality quirks – approached one of the *mispallelim* who himself had no short-age of personality quirks. The latter fellow took out some coins, but rather than place them in the hand of the collector, he dropped them on the table. I believe he simply was uncomfortable touching other people. The collector, however, saw red. He blew up. Deeply insulted, he swept the coins to the floor and ranted and raved, ending his tirade with the immortal words, "I don't take charity!"

I am certain that he actually meant it. A fellow who went from shul to shul collecting money from people somehow did not see what he did as taking char-ity. Perhaps he thought it was just allowing a friend to help a friend. Perhaps he thought people or society owed it to him. Perhaps he didn't think about it at all, but when it was not done in a manner to his liking, he would not accept it. I believe that if it had been a stack of bills instead of coins, he would have done the same, sweeping it to the floor in an angry, grand gesture.

In a strange way, it *was* a grand gesture, undignified in its execution, and yet, bespeaking a formidable dignity. I know the man to be a *tipesh*, and he spoke and acted foolishly. At the same time, I was awed by the grandeur of what he did.

A Jewish court does not accept the testimony of professional gamblers. Such a gambler always goes into a given wager with the expectation of winning. He may, in fact, lose and be forced to pay. But he is not, *in his heart*, relinquishing that which he pays upon losing. And the gambler who takes that payment as his winning is taking something that is not his, rendering him a *goniv*; the first fellow never really gave up ownership.

The Torah says, *v'yikchu Li terumah*. It's interesting that the Gemara (*Kiddushin*, *Ha'isha Nikneis*) draws a parallel and infers great significance from the Torah's use of the same root, *kicha* (acquiring), regarding marriage and regarding Avraham Avinu's purchase of Me'aras Hamachpelah ("*kicha kicha mi'sdeh Ephron*"). A pur-chase requires a real and true acquisition, with the seller giving up all power of ownership, fully in his heart, along with taking the money, in order to make that sale and the transfer of ownership valid. A marriage too requires a real and true change of status as well, a real *kinyan*, fully in the heart, along with the money (i.e., the ring), to make that marriage valid.

I would suggest that the same principle applies here as well, with the use of the same root, *kicha*. God wants us to give to *hekdesh*. We *must* give money. He wants us to work, and to sacrifice, to increase sanctity in the world. But He doesn't want it from us unless we really mean it: *asher yidvenu libo*. Without meaning it, we're not really giving it.

Our job is not just to give, but to really mean it. Our job is to *want* to give, in addition to actually giving. Our job is to see a person in need and to want to help him – and not blow him off with the excuse that he is a schnorrer, or that *mosad haTorah* is back schnorring again. They are the opportunities God blesses us with, to buy life. And if our hearts somehow don't let us see it that way, we must fix our hearts.

Chazal have taught us an important principle, *Rachmana liba ba'i*. God wants our hearts. Our hearts make our donations kosher and acceptable. Our hearts allow us to transform mundane money into heavenly scrip. What an opportunity! But to be valid, for God to find it pleasing, we must train our hearts to allow us to give wholeheartedly.

And so, when the Torah says in our *parashah*, "*V'asu Li Mikdash v'shachanti b'socham*," one lesson that is clearly derived is that this is all a self-potentiating equation: our hearts make our donations and our works acceptable, and our donations and our works help make our hearts acceptable, so that God may enter: *v'shachanti b'socham*.

Parashas Terumah 5771

On Being Elevated

Terumah. Rhymes with *tekumah*.

A charitable donation, in Jewish society, is often referred to as a *terumah*.

Thus, in this week's *parashah*, the people are called upon to give terumah to the Mikdash.

Actually, the language, *v'yikchu*, suggests "taking," rather than simply "giving."

And so, while there is a mandate for each of us to give, there is also a mandate for society to assure that we give, by taking, in a prescribed manner.

Tzedakah is so important that the body politic is empowered to enforce its being given (see *Bava Basra* 8b; Rambam, Hilchos Matanos Aniyim, chapter 9, *Yoreh De'ah* 256). It is treated like a communal tax. Even one's private property can be held in escrow against the communal tzedakah debt.

In life, virtually everyone needs the occasional hand up of some kind. It is a great blessing to be in the position of being the one giving the hand up to someone else in need. But the circle of life, and the circle of need, touches everybody in some way. And, as they say, what goes around comes around. And, apart from the certainty that every one of us will need someone to help us in some way (not just monetarily, but in any sphere of life), the reward for *chesed* is very great, *and itself raises us up.*

While the word *terumah* is understood to mean a charitable gift, the etymology of the word clearly relates to the word *l'harim*, to lift up. And so one who gives tzedakah lifts up not only the recipient, but, in the process, *oneself.*

L'harim, in turn, is similar to *l'hakim. Lakum* is to stand up. *L'hakim* is to cause something to stand up, or to be established. The word *tekumah*, a standing up, is commonly used in the context of causing to stand again – revival, renewal, reestablishment. Thus, the word is often used in describing the miraculous revival, in our time, of an independent Jewish commonwealth in the Land of Israel, the State of Israel. *Tekumah.*

"*L'harim*," to raise. Raise up others through tzedakah, through a *terumah*, and thereby raise oneself. "*L'hakim*," to cause someone or something to stand up and be established, typically through devoted effort, and thereby raise oneself.

Terumah. Rhymes with *tekumah.*

Parashas Terumah 5772

Pure

I don't know what his name was. He left his native Galitzia as a young man to try his luck in America. Where many others struggled and remained poor, he did well. Twenty years later, perhaps in 1910 or so, he returned to visit his old mother and the haunts of his youth.

He went to visit the great Dzhikover Rebbe, the Ateres Yeshuah, to receive the tzaddik's blessing before returning to America. As was customary, he placed a *pidyon*, a charitable donation, on the Rebbe's table. It was a generous sum.

The Rebbe looked at it very briefly and then looked away. He would not touch it.

"How did you get this money?" the Rebbe asked. "What do you do in America?"

"I have real estate. I own buildings, and my *parnassah* is from the rent people pay me," he stammered.

"This is not rent money," the Rebbe declared. "What is your business?"

"Real estate! I own buildings! I earn my money honestly!"

The Rebbe remained unmoved. That the money on the table was unclean, that it was defiling his room, was obvious to his holy eyes. "I insist that you tell me. For the sake of your worthy ancestors who were Chassidim and *anshei maaseh*, now tell me!"

The man finally broke down. Yes, he owned buildings. But no families lived there. The rooms were not rented by the month, but by the hour. They were places of *zimah*, of the lowest sinful behavior. "Take this filthy money out of here," the Rebbe told him. "I can't abide it another minute."

I remember, in my childhood, a man giving a *sefer Torah* to one of the shuls in the neighborhood. I knew that he was a *mechallel Shabbos*, and that the money that paid for that *sefer Torah* was generated from the man's business activity on Shabbos. I wondered about that. Was it really OK for the shul to accept it? I don't know if they even knew. And I understood that within the context of how this man lived his life, he was trying to do a good thing. But it seemed to me problematic.

It is a common practice for people to try to "kosherize" their religiously illicit behavior by donating part of what they earned illicitly to charity. There are various passages in the Torah that make it clear that God wants no part of it. Parashas Terumah addresses this question.

V'yikchu Li terumah: Rashi spells out *yafrishu Li mi'mamonam nedavah*. They shall separate for Me a gift *from their own money*. *Mi'mamonam*. The Reishe Rov, H"yd, in his *Haderash V'ha'iyun*, zeroes in on Rashi's language as a clue and a hint about the great care we must exert to ensure that monies we dedicate to *hekdesh* be utterly clean of any possible improper source. However great the mitzvah of tzedakah is, so great that its value is immeasurable, it is only great and only acceptable if it is itself pure and free of any sinful source. It must have come into the possession of the donor in an honest, honorable, and righteous way. *Mimamonam*. Anything else is an abomination and an affront to God.

Yeshayahu Hanavi (56: 1) declares, *shimru mishpat v'asu tzedakah*: purity of *mishpat* must precede tzedakah. Tzedakah money, to be proper tzedakah, must be honestly and halachically come by. And further (61:8), "*ki Ani Hashem ohev mishpat sonei gozel b'olah*" (I, God, love justice and hate robbery in an *olah* [in My service]). You can serve Me, says God, only through honesty and justice and fulfillment of My Torah.

And the wisest king, Shlomo, wrote (Mishlei 22:9), "*Tov ayin hu yevorach, ki nosan mi'lachmo la'dol*," for he has given *of his own*, honestly earned bread to the needy.

So, what's all this about? Why such a big deal? Isn't it reasonable for a sinner to try to atone, to some degree, with such a fine and generous gesture? After all, charity is charity! And in the end, the poor are fed and the institutions (the Mikdash, etc.) are financed.

Certainly, on its face, it makes sense that allowing someone to do so is, in fact, an invitation to make money through sin, and then giving some away becomes the acceptable cost of doing business that way. Remind you of another religion, where a brisk business was done in the sale of indulgences? Do whatever you want, confess, say some formulaic recitation, pay some money (on a sliding scale, of course), be forgiven, and happily continue your wicked ways? That's not us.

Beyond that, what respect is it for God and His words, if they are, *wink wink*, so cynically and deviously circumvented? And is God's Law negotiable?

But beyond that, the Reishe Rov touches on a key element of the very nature of the relationship between God and His people, the nature of human beings as opposed to all other creatures, and the ultimate nature of what we possess in this world, what we *appear* to possess, and what we *actually* possess.

Bava Basra 9b: *He who gives to the poor merits seeing the Shechinah.*

Man, alone among all the creatures, possesses the capacity and the nature to seek to do good, to be altruistic. Sure, animals have certain instincts to protect their own young; some even are capable of some measure of loyalty, but that too is instinctive. Only man *chooses* to do good, reasons to be selfless, willingly sacrifices for the sake of others.

And that is because man was created in God's image, because, in the creation of man, God "blew" of His own supernal Spirit into him, to make man what he is (*va'yipach b'apav nishmas ruach chaim*). Man's capacity to choose to do good derives from the holy repository of Godliness with which man was created and given life. And so, when he *does* choose to do good, that choice, that goodness, is only good if it is pure, if it derives from and reflects its holy source.

And thus, a remarkable statement in the Midrash: *V'yikchu Li terumah: hada hu dichsiv, Shema Yisrael Hashem Elokeinu Hashem Echad*. Giving for the purpose of holiness is a function of the ultimate expression of the Jew's faith, Shema Yisrael.

And it can only be holy, as it needs to be, if it is conceived in holiness and in purity.

And so, if a man, in goodness and in purity and in altruism and for the sake of Heaven, gives of what he possesses as a *terumah*, it highlights the ultimate question of what a man has, in this world, and what he does not. For after all, whatever possessions he has, whatever he thinks he has, he does not have at all. For none of it accompanies him when he leaves this world. He is accompanied into the next world not by what he has accumulated, but by what he has *given away*, in tzedakah and *terumah*. That can never be taken from him. *Avos* 6: "*Ein melavin lo l'adam lo kesef v'lo zahav v'lo avanim tovos u'margolios, ela Torah u'maasim tovim bilvad.*"

And the result of this imperative to purity of purpose? *V'asu Li Mikdash v'shachanti b'socham.* They shall make Me a Mikdash, and I will dwell *within them.* Not within *it*, but within *them.* God's reward to Klal Yisrael for infusing all we do with purity of purpose, for performing His commandments in the spirit of those commandments, for not defiling what we do in His Name by debasing it with improper means or motives, thereby keeping it pure and holy, is that the very Source of holiness comes to rest *within us*, and gives us *life.*

And that, for the Jew, is the ultimate achievement in this life.

Parashas Terumah 5773

Tetzaveh

All the Same, All the Same

We saw it coming, about eighteen hours in advance.

We were in a hotel on a *yom tov*, part of a large Jewish crowd. We saw them "casing" us. They appeared to be a nice family: father, mother, and young daughter. We still had an unmarried son.

To be clear, they were doing the right thing. And we learned that they were indeed a very nice family.

We knew it was coming soon when the mother, quite casually, struck up a conversation with my wife, in the course of which she managed to ascertain intelligence that was apparently of paramount importance in considering a *shidduch*: whether my wife "wore long" on Friday night, tablecloth habits, and other similar important information necessary to ensure that one's child marry an appropriate life partner. Right out of the stereotype textbook. She spoke with that odd, yet familiar accent that makes you want to ask someone where they were born, which foreign country, even though you know that it is the peculiar accent of people born and raised in New York but whose speech inflections are strongly influenced by Hungarian American-style Yiddish (even if English is their primary language).

My wife – the devil made her do this – gave all the "right" answers. Very soon thereafter, within minutes really, having passed muster, we were approached by an intermediary. The two young people did meet, right there at the hotel. We could not really do otherwise. She was a lovely girl. The *shidduch*, though, did not happen.

There are many paths in Judaism. To a greater or lesser degree, to practice Orthodox Judaism, a certain amount of conformity is necessary. But that conformity can range from the basics of Jewish lifestyle to the utter conformity, in every aspect and nuance of life and style, that was apparently so important to that young girl's family.

Do you have to be an utter conformist, in every little detail of life, to be a good Jew? A good Chassid? A good Yekke? A good *yeshivishe* Litvack? Can you get into Heaven if you are, to some degree, your own man?

I remember when they apparently changed the rules of entry into Heaven. It seemed to happen quite suddenly. The yarmulke section of Judaica stores (aka *seforim* stores) used to have one section of knitted yarmulkes, and then for the velvet ones (for serious Jews), three separate bins of more or less equal size: black, blue, and brown. One day all the blue and brown yarmulkes disappeared. Apparently, one could no longer get into Heaven in one of those, so they stopped carrying them. It was interesting to note which store owners just shrugged when asked about it, and which denied they had *ever* sold blue or brown velvet yarmulkes.

Parashas Tetzaveh spells out in detail how the vestments of the Kohanim were to be made. They were identical to each other – a uniform. But were they *absolutely* identical in every little non-critical detail? Apparently, not necessarily. There was some room for variation, as long as the biblically mandated outlines were met. (See *Yoma* 35b – or should I call it *Yuma*, even though that's incorrect, to sound more acceptably *frum/yeshivish/charedi/*religiously correct? Maybe I don't need to; I can hide behind Artscroll, who use *Yoma* and get away with it.) They were a very specific uniform, and uniforms do tend to be…uniform. But even apparently identical uniforms, on close examination, may each have their own subtle characteristics. And yet they are still uniforms. That which is the same – the important points – is indeed the same. And the minor variations are fine points that do not take away from the whole, but may indeed enhance the whole.

So too, in daily Jewish life, we find uniforms useful. A yarmulke is a uniform. A hat and jacket is a uniform. Modest clothing is a uniform. And so, too, are *shtreimels* and *bekeshes*, dark suits and white shirts, black fedoras, long skirts, *sheitels* and snoods, etc., etc., etc.

But that yarmulke might be leather or knitted wool or velvet. Uniforms! The black hat might be *chassidish* or…non-*chassidish*. Now, if the hat is *chassidish*, is the ribbon knotted on the right side or the left side? A uniform! How many inches is that yeshiva boy's hat brim? A uniform! Is it worn up or down? A uniform!

So how detailed, how comprehensive, does the uniform have to be in contemporary Jewish life? How all-encompassing, how minute the detail? How flawed, how unacceptable is it, to deviate even a little bit?

And who decides? WHO DECIDES?

There was an interesting question discussed in the *Yated* of January 24, 2014 (oops! 23 Shevat 5774), which is really what prompted this discussion. We all know that in Eretz Yisrael (oops! Eretz Yisroel, if I want to be considered properly linguistically *frum*), *frumkeit*, the politics of *frumkeit*, and the politics of identity based on *frumkeit* are very serious business. More so than here in the USA.

It seems that the latest and the greatest test of whether you are properly *frum*, whether you belong, whether you are in or out of uniform in the yeshiva world in Israel is whether your yarmulke has a *seret* (a banded rim around the edge). If you are *really* frum, you have a *seret*. If you don't, no matter how big that yarmulke is, no matter now black that velvet is, no matter how well or devotedly you learn and daven, *you are out of uniform. You are an outsider. You don't belong. You are not quite frum. You might even be "moderne"! Or (gevalt!) a Zionist!*

Maybe the truth is that you are just a shnook, unaware, not *yeshivish* cool, not hip to the *yeshivishe* insider thinking. Or maybe you are something of an individual, not interested in herd groupthink, and maybe unwilling to have every last little bit of your personal prerogatives dictated by others.

Who decides this stuff?

The article goes on to relate that one young boy had to leave his yeshiva because he refused to be dictated to on the *seret*. Apparently, he was considered rebellious on that basis. We do not know, of course, if he was, in fact, otherwise rebellious. When his father showed one of the senior *roshei yeshiva* in Israel two yarmulkes, one with a *seret* and one without, the *rosh yeshiva* saw no difference between them. The father told the *rosh yeshiva* what happened, and asked why it's so important. "If it's not important," the *rosh yeshiva* replied, "why not just do it? Why insist on *not* doing it?"

That *rosh yeshiva* carried the yeshiva world on his shoulders.

He was utterly given over to the learning, teaching, and propagation of Torah. He had no time for such issues, and no energy to waste on them. To him, any issue that distracts from learning is just not worth it. But not everyone can be like the *rosh yeshiva*. Most people are just regular people. And regular people, when unduly impinged upon, will not accept or will at least resist the tyranny of those who try to impose, absolutely unnecessarily, the sentence of sameness – utter, mindless sameness – on everyone else.

Back in the 1960s, it was hip to be a nonconformist. It was, in fact, so hip, so cool to be a nonconformist, to rant about the conformity of society, that they stood apart, those rebels, all in *exactly the same way*. Long, unkempt, greasy hair. Ripped jeans. Tie-dyed T-shirts. They all looked exactly the same, they talked exactly the same. In their protest against sameness, they themselves were all exactly the same. It was funny.

The late Pete Seeger sang a song then about people, "all the same, all the same," who lived in ticky tacky houses that were all the same, who behaved all the same, who thought all the same, who raised their children all the same, and so on. It was ironic that those who protested against the majority society's alleged sameness themselves by and large slavishly followed their own gurus' dictates, their own counterculture groupthink. They were, it seemed, all the same, all the same.

Is it different today? Is college campus groupthink and groupspeech any different?

It seems not, for so many students. Elites decide what the right opinion is, what the right mindset is, what the right words are, and the rest parrot that.

Our own world, the world of Torah and *avodah*, is not immune to the vagaries of human nature, or to the predilection of some people to the herd mentality and the aversion of other people to it. The problem and the challenge is one of judgment and of normalcy.

You can't judge a book by its cover, but you can make judgments about people by how they present themselves to the world. It is a decision that they make. But that is not the whole story, and there is certainly a limit to how regimented, how uniform they can reasonably be expected to be.

The choice of a type of yarmulke shouldn't make too big a statement of self-identification, but it has come to be so. OK, that's how it is. We have allowed that to happen. Is a fellow who wears a velvet yarmulke ipso facto a *charedi l'dvar Hashem*, and someone who wears the same size yarmulke, but it's made of knitted wool, ipso facto not *charedi l'dvar Hashem*? You know that's not so.

Does wearing a velvet yarmulke with a *seret* make you religiously OK, but by wearing one without that little *seret* do you reveal yourself to be not a serious Jew, not a serious yeshiva student, not properly *charedi*? Does not submitting to that pressure (created by whom? for what divine purpose?) make one a rebel against God, religion, or proper religious authority?

You know it does not. If the *rosh yeshiva* asks it of you, he undoubtedly has a purpose, and you should do what he asks. But just *stam azoy*, because the "frum street" will judge you?

Are silly criteria a proper basis for *shidduch* decisions? Is slavish devotion to arbitrary convention that signifies nothing a good *shidduch* credential? On the same page as the story in *Yated* noted above, there was a report about a mother who cancelled her son's date because she heard that the young lady in question, a fine girl of good family, had been seen wearing pointy shoes. Now follow this: pointy shoes were once in, then they were out, and now they're in again. This mother didn't know that they are in again, so she thought the girl must be a nerd, so she cancelled the already agreed to and scheduled date. *Help!*

The Torah spells out much detail in the requirements for the vestments of the Kohanim and for the various utensils in the Mikdash. But not every last little possible detail. There is room for – *there is need for* – uniforms in life. They serve an important function. There are various types of Jewish uniforms in our various communities, and wearing those uniforms helps people understand who they are and what is properly expected of them.

The uniform may be minimal – such as just wearing a yarmulke – or far more elaborate, such as full Chassidic garb. The Torah specifies *arba begadim* and *shmoneh begadim* for Kohanim. But it also leaves room for a person to be an individual.

Forcing people to fall into line by imposing arbitrary and unnecessary formulaic demands of style may sometimes be more about rigidity and power than anything else.

Too much is *too much*. Some people, fearing being left out, will indeed fall into line. Some people don't care enough about it to give it much thought, and just do what everybody else does. Some people may really believe it. And some people may be so repelled by this arbitrary invasion into their personal prerogatives that they go elsewhere – sometimes with tragic consequences.

If God wanted us all to be perfect carbon copies of each other, He probably would have created us that way. But He did not. What He does want of us, I believe, is that we each harness our own individual strengths and abilities in His service. He wants us, I believe, to respect and to appreciate each other, even if we do our striving somewhat differently.

And, as everyone understands, the most beautiful music is not monotonal, but finds its richness in that blending of sound we call harmony.

Parashas Tetzaveh 5774

Feeling Loved

It is a good thing to be loved. It is a much better thing to also *feel* that love, to *know*, really know, that one is loved.

It is a good thing to be safe. It is a much better thing to also *feel* safe, to *know*, really know, that one is safe.

And it is a measure of one's love for someone else to make that someone truly *feel* loved, truly feel safe. That's what you do if you really love someone. That is part of the gift of love. You make sure they know it and they feel it.

Sadly, there are clueless people who just don't get it, who don't understand that, and who fail, in a fundamental way, to provide the full measure of love that they would be happy or willing to provide, if they weren't so insensitive or so thick headed.

Parashas Tetzaveh continues with prescribed rituals and requirements to create a proper Mikdash, one medium through which Israel is to serve its God, and in the merit of which God will express His love.

In the midst of this extensive series of ritual commandments, God declares: "*v'no'adeti shamah li'vnei Yisrael v'nikdash bi'chvodi.... V'shachanti b'soch Bnei Yisrael v'hayisi lahem l'Elokim. V'yadu ki Ani Hashem Elokeihem asher hotzeisi osam me'eretz Mitzrayim l'shachni b'socham; Ani Hashem Elokeihem*" (Shemos 29:43, 45–46).

Rabbi Akiva (*Avos* 3:18) famously stated it most eloquently in his *chavivin Yisrael* Mishnah. Beloved are the Children of Israel to God, as He considers them His own children. *As an extra measure of His love, He made sure that they know that they are so beloved, and that He considers them His own children.*

How much more meaningful to us is our faith and our service, knowing that, come what may, we are in His embrace? That He is our God, and that all He does, He does for our sake?

The world can be a very harsh place, and it has largely been so for the Jew. For whatever reason, for a variety of reasons (subject of another essay!), we have been widely despised and mistreated. One *nechamah*, a life vest, an anchor for those Jews who have been able to hang on, is the understanding that for the Jew it is the past and the future that are normative, that the God of our fathers, however hidden in the mystery of His ways, is with us, and always will be with us, that our chosenness is as real today when it is harder to discern as when it was obvious to all.

And as it goes nationally, so it goes individually. *Banim atem l'Hashem Elokeichem* (Devarim 14:1).

A small child believes that his father is all powerful, until he learns, in life, that he is not.

But a wise child understands and appreciates that father's efforts, and that he has done his best. Our Father in Heaven *is* all powerful, and we, His faithful children, understand that it is His omniscient wisdom and judgment and goodness that directs our fate, and that is beyond our own limited understanding. That limited understanding can sorely test one's faith – please God, may we *not* be tested! – but that is the reality.

But knowing, and feeling – *truly feeling* – that the Creator is our God, that He has chosen us, that He has placed Himself *k'v'yachol* in our midst, *that he has made sure to let us know, time and again, that He is our loving Father who has placed Himself in our midst*, is the ultimate safety, the ultimate security, the ultimate expression of Godly love.

As a nation, we *know*, because He has has made sure to let us know, that we are truly His. And that He is truly ours.

But of course, there is another dimension to these passages. *V'shachanti b'soch Bnei Yisrael*, I will "dwell" among Bnei Yisrael, and I will be their God. And they will *know* that I am Hashem, their God, Who took them out of the land of Egypt *l'shachni b'socham*, in order to dwell among them. I am Hashem, their God.

Rashi, Ramban, Ibn Ezra, and others cite the quid pro quo: I took them out of Egypt, says God, for the purpose of, *and on the condition of*, My dwelling among them. I want to dwell among them, I have moved history and have made miracles to bring that about, and now it is up to them: invite Me to "dwell" among you, within you – make a Mishkan for Me and receive Me, as your God, into your midst – and I will indeed dwell among you and you will experience My love and protection. You will *know* that you have it. You will be loved by your all-powerful God, and you will know it. You will be protected by your omnipotent God, you will be safe, and you will know it.

And if you do not enter into this covenant with Me, if you do not make a place for Me to "dwell," to "rest My Presence" among you, if you do not live your lives in the unique manner that I have prescribed for you in the Torah, then you are negating the entire purpose of My having brought you out of bondage in Egypt.

And if that were, *chalilah*, the case, what purpose would there be for the very existence of the People of Israel, or for that matter, of the world?

On Purim, our covenant with God was renewed. *Kiyemu v'kiblu b'ahavah* (Megillas Esther 9:27).

That is a relationship that, for all our shortcomings – and there are many – we have "paid for" with blood, toil, sweat, and tears, with sacrifice and with pain. With fire and with water. With hunger and with thirst, with fear and with humiliation, with expulsions and with poverty, with terror and with loss, with murder and with mayhem, with autos-da-fé and with mounds of corpses, with steel and with lead. With gas.

It is, in the end, a relationship that will never be broken. Come what may – *oh, God!* Ribbono shel Olam! *Come what may!* – it is a relationship, an embrace, a union that will never be broken.

Parashas Tetzaveh, Purim 5773

I've Fallen and I Can't Get Up!

Life can be a pressure cooker, even for those without the terrible challenges other people do face. And those pressures can affect people in terrible, often unpredictable ways.

God has high expectations of us, but it is the same God, our loving Father in Heaven, Who created us, and created within us the very heart, the mind, the frailties, the complexity, the strengths and the weaknesses that make us human beings.

And so as human beings we sometimes rise high, and sometimes we fall. Rising high can be a trial. Falling low tends to be a much worse trial, as it vitiates our strength, our will, our ability to pick ourselves up and overcome.

The Torah can be understood on multiple levels and often sends us important messages encrypted within passages that appear, in their literal sense, to be addressing another context altogether.

We are commanded, in Parashas Tetzaveh, to use only the purest clear olive oil for the Menorah in the Mikdash. The olive is to be pressed (*kassis*), but not crushed.

There have been many homiletical analyses and lessons drawn from this requirement and the fact that it is spelled out in the Torah.

The literal reading states that the Children of Israel should bring pure, pressed olive oil, for the purpose of lighting the Menorah. The Ateres Yeshuah attaches the words *kassis la'maor* (pressed and light): it is pressed, squeezed, *for the* purpose *of producing light*.

Sometimes, in the ups and downs of life, in a way that is beyond our vision and our understanding, the very purpose of the downs imposed upon us is that we may rise to the occasion, draw upon our innermost strengths, and turn those "downs" into "ups" that are higher than we would have ever risen had we not fallen first.

Life is not a game of hooks and ladders, but sometimes it may seem so. It is said that God does not give us tests that we are unable to withstand, although that is often far from obvious to the one being tested, *lo aleinu*. To the one who is falling, the likeliest path, the path of least resistance, is to fall further still. And the more one falls – the more one falters – the more difficult it is to climb back up. There are trials and tests in this life and in this world that are so terrible, and so difficult, the fall so profound, that it would seem impossible, especially to the one who has fallen, to get back up.

And yet God is telling us here that people are sometimes pressed and squeezed for the very purpose of having the opportunity of overcoming, of getting back up. And that it is, in fact, possible to do so, that *kassis* happens for the purpose of lama'or, that the ensuing light is brighter than it could have ever been before, and even purer.

And the result of this terrible effort, this triumph of the human spirit, is l'haalos ner tamid, to bring joy, nachas, k'v'yachol, to the Eternal One, to increase the light in the universe, and indeed even to elevate the very act of falling into but a necessary step, indeed a holy step, in the process of rising ever higher.

We pray that we never be tested. But this is life. At its best it has its ups and downs. And so we must pray also that whatever those tests might be, whatever the ups and the downs, we have the strength, the vision, the resolve, and the help from Heaven that we need to overcome, to elevate, to stand higher, to transform the darkness in this world and within ourselves into light.

And if fall we must, when we falter, as we surely will, to remember what God has taught us: that the squeezed olive produces the purest oil, the brightest, purest light; that we *can*, indeed, stand up.

Parashas Tetzaveh 5776

Hubris: Caveat Praeceptor!

You're probably ready to criticize my mixing of Greek with Latin.

I know, I know. But it's done all the time. Especially by the intellectually arrogant and overly proud, which I am, of course, not.

Human nature is such an interesting thing. There are traits that we need to succeed, even to survive. Those very traits, however, can lead us directly to the pit, *chalilah*, if we are not careful.

We all know that as a people, for all our wonderful qualities, we are not so easy.

To say the least. (Antisemites, don't read this.) Says the Gemara (*Beitzah* 25b): Why was the Torah given to Israel? Because they are *azim*, hard (*tough!* and strongly implicit: *azei panim*). The qualities and the nature given to them, which make possible their survival in the face of so much persecution from generation to generation, would, if unchecked, allow them to dominate completely the other nations of the world. Hashem gave us the Torah, the absorption of which softens us, makes us kind and considerate, and turns our predisposition to *azus panim* into a defining nature of *baishanim, rachmanim,* and *gomlei chasadim,* the very antithesis of *azus panim,* a *middah* that Hashem abhors.

Parashas Tetzaveh details instructions regarding the vestments of the Kohanim, including the Kohen Gadol. The various articles of clothing, we are taught, provide *kapparah* (penance) – or prevention, hopefully – for various sinful acts, each according to that particular vestment (see *Zevachim* 88b).

The hallmark of the Kohen Gadol's special uniform is the Tzitz, the golden plate with Hashem's Name on it, worn on the Kohen Gadol's forehead. It provides *kapparah* for *azus metzach* (brazenness). The Chasam Sofer cites the above Gemara in *Beitzah*, and explains that while we need that strength to withstand the constant attacks upon us by the other nations, we must always remember that, as Chazal taught, *az panim l'Gehinnom*.

Azus panim, sometimes referred to as *azus metzach*, is deadly; the Tzitz, worn on the forehead (*metzach*) of the Kohen Gadol, is a protective reminder to us to be ever so careful and to sanctify the *azus* that Hashem endowed us with for holy purposes only, *Kodesh la'Shem* – just as is engraved on the Tzitz, the words "*Kodesh la'Shem*." And so, if we are worthy, the strength of the *azus metzach* will be sublimated by the strength of the tefillin, worn in that same location, which will make our enemies see that the Name of God is upon us, and they will be frightened.

The Kesav Sofer, on this *pasuk*, cites his father's explanation (above) and takes it a step further, with remarkable insight into human nature – including, and perhaps especially, the human nature of leaders.

The Mishnah (*Avos* 5) recounts: Rabbi Yehudah ben Teima says, *havei az ka'namer*: for the sake of Heaven, to do God's will, be as bold and as strong and as aggressive as a leopard. He follows this immediately with *az panim l'Gehinnom*. And he follows that, in turn, as an apparent non sequitur, with a prayer for the rebuilding of the Beis Hamikdash.

Explains the Kesav Sofer: Having given a green light to *azus*, to bold strength and aggressive assertiveness – for the sake of Heaven, *of course* – the Mishnah is telling us: STOP! WAIT! REALITY CHECK! You, especially you leaders: yes, you rabbis, you lay leaders, you *gevirim*, you people with power and influence, you *roshei yeshiva*, you donors whose opinion "counts," you teachers, you school principals, you parents, you whom the people tend to follow: be careful! The *azus* that you righteously employ to fight the external *and the internal* enemies of Torah can easily lead to a *gasus ruach*, which may seduce you, even – indeed, *especially* – unknowingly, to deal with the people in an improper manner, with the wrong attitude, with *azus metzach*. (See *Sanhedrin* 7b regarding the admonition to those in authority "not to step on the heads of the holy nation," i.e., Klal Yisrael. Whatever the specific intent of this dictum, in context, the choice of language was no accident.)

It may also lead you, *chalilah*, to sin privately. People in authority, people accustomed to having their way, people accustomed to being treated with deference, people unaccustomed to being challenged, are at risk. After all, it's easy to convince oneself, if you're fighting the good fight, if you're *leading* the good fight, then *whatever* you fight for, *whatever* you do, must be good and must be right.

Power can do that, *Rachmana litzlan*. And so power over the people is dangerous. The remedy for *azus* that is not *l'shem Shamayim* is the Tzitz Hazahav. But without the Beis Hamikdash, we lack this remedy. So the logic of the Mishnah is *not* a non sequitur, but very much in order: *Az panim l'Gehinnom* – and since it's such an easy slide, *lo aleinu*, we need the Beis Hamikdash and the Tzitz on the Kohen Gadol for *kapparah* and for protection. Hence, says the Kesav Sofer, their juxtaposition in the Mishnah, with the prayer that the Mikdash be rebuilt.

Nearly everyone has some kind of power over someone else. Men, be so careful with your wives and children. It can be a hard world out there. We go out daily and do battle to provide for our families. It's easy to forget, when we come home, to take off the armor many of us must wear in that battle and leave it by the door before we enter.

We have the God-given capacity to harden ourselves as a way of coping with the world.

We have the God-given mandate to soften ourselves for our wives (and husbands), our children, our fellow Jews, our fellow human beings. Indeed, for ourselves.

One lesson of the Tzitz Hazahav is that each of us be, always, a safe place for those who depend upon us.

Parashas Tetzvveh 5771

Ki Sisa

Exultation

Pardon the wild generalization, but look around you. Don't you get the impression that the average non-Jew out there seems to be less "bothered" than the typical Jew? Don't you get the sense that Tony is happier in the moment, less worried about everything, than is Mendel?

Don't misunderstand. I'm not talking about overall satisfaction with life, or contentment with one's position in the universe. A Jew understands where he is in God's overall plan, and that is a comforting, reassuring, fundamental awareness, the travails of life aside. He is quite happy to be who he is. But what about just relaxed, happy, in-the-moment contentment, no worries (as long as he is in a generally OK position with regard to basic life and health)? Does a Jew, however happy he is in life, ever have that utterly happy-go-lucky, devil-may-care kind of unfettered happiness that our non-Jewish neighbors seem to be so capable of?

There is a well-known concept that having divided the world between them, *olam hazeh* belonging to Esav and *olam haba* belonging to Yaakov, despite Yaakov's better cosmic situation, Esav still tends to walk around happier than Yaakov.

Yaakov can't really enjoy *olam hazeh* too much, because not only is he not in control and subject to Esav's depredations, he can't even enjoy the prospect of *olam haba* too much either because, Yaakov that he is, tzaddik that he is, he is constantly worrying about his every action in *olam hazeh* lest he do something that will keep him from meriting *olam haba*.

Esav, on the other hand, doesn't even think about *olam haba*, much less fret about it, so he can do whatever he wants and fully enjoy *olam hazeh*.

"Poor" Yaakov. Even when he sins (God forbid) in some juicy manner, he can't really enjoy it, whether he fully realizes it or not.

When the Israelites sinned with the Golden Calf, they undertook to rejoice and exult in their wrongdoing. They violated the most fundamental laws of

Judaism, including the three "cardinal sins" no Jew should ever allow himself, no matter what, for the irreparable harm done to his *neshamah*. At the moment of excitement, however, the sinner does not think of that. He thinks only of his exultation and excitement. He is fixated on his excitement of the moment. Unless...

Targum Yonasan describes their joy with a remarkable choice of words: *meyabvin b'chedva*. "*Chedva*" describes a state of joy. "*Meyabvin*" is derived from the term for wailing lamentation.

Yehoshua, waiting at the foot of the mountain for his teacher Moshe to descend with the *Luchos*, hears the sound of shouting exultation coming from the camp of Israel. "*Va'yishma Yehoshua es kol ha'am b're'oh*" (Shemos 32:17). Yehoshua hears them shouting in their excitement. He thinks perhaps it is the sound of war – *kol milchamah ba'machaneh*. Moshe replies that it is not the sound of war at all, neither military strength nor weakness. The Gemara (Yerushalmi, *Taanis* 4:5) relates that Moshe criticized Yehoshua here: the future leader of the nation (as Yehoshua was destined to be) should be able to distinguish and discern the nature of the noise emanating from the nation he is leading.

There are those who defend Yehoshua in his perception of that terrible shouting noise. "*B're'oh*" indicates that he perceived a kind of confusion, an unnatural mixture of joy and lament – hence, his thought that it was the sound of war. It was, in fact, a kind of war. It was an internal war, a war within the sinners themselves: *Meyabvin b'chedva*.

In their exultation, in the excitement of their sins, there was embedded, and expressed, the internal contradiction of simultaneous joy and lament. Esav can have unbridled joy in his sins; Yaakov cannot.

A Jew who has heard, with his own ears, *Anochi Hashem Elokecha*, as did the revelers with the Golden Calf, might well fall into sin, but he can never fully enjoy his sin. A Jew who has learned *Bereishis bara Elokim*, who has pored over *amar Rava, amar Abaye,* may for some reason fall away, but he cannot really be joyful in that place he has fallen to, even if he thinks he enjoys what he is doing there. On some level he knows that he is not where he should be, even as he willfully resists returning to where he belongs.

But even then, that door remains open for him.

That is our legacy. That is what Yaakov Avinu, with the help of his courageous and far-seeing mother, Rivkah Imenu, fought for, on our behalf. That is part of what sustains us as a nation, as God's Chosen Nation, despite whatever failings and shortcomings our frail human nature allows to get in the way. They are an impediment, often a very painful one, but not a roadblock.

Our enjoyment of the beauties of this world is a gift from God, Who bestowed it upon all of mankind. The particular way we as a people enjoy this world is its role and place in the much bigger picture of existence. It is a pathway. We pray that the road we travel in this world be a pleasant one. But we are also aware, constantly, that it is, for us, a road whose purpose is to lead us somewhere beyond this mundane existence, a place so welcoming and so brilliant that it will illuminate that road, if we will let it, if we open our eyes to it, if we set our eyes on the goal and the nature of true happiness, that is God's gift to each and every one of us.

Parashas Ki Sisa 5777, Yerushalayim Ir Hakodesh

Making Shabbos

Bella, Rela, and Gabriella were three devoted sisters who lived parallel but different lives.

They were raised on the Lower East Side of New York, where their mother, Sadie, was a homemaker and their father, Bernie, worked hard in the needle trades. The best day of the week was Shabbos, when they spent the day in close company with each other as they observed the holy day. Sadie was a great *balabusta*.

The girls grew up, married, and moved away. Bella married a plumber and settled in Brooklyn, where they raised a nice, *frum* Jewish family. To help make ends meet, she worked as a school secretary. Rela became an accountant. She married an accountant, and her children grew up to be accountants. They lived in Staten Island, where they were active in local Jewish affairs. Gabriella, who did not allow anyone to call her "Gabby," or any name other than "Gabriella," was an artist (in her mind, an "*artiste*"). She married a successful businessman and lived in a fancy part of Long Island. Her husband was generous with his tzedakah. She had, and frequently used, a "studio" her husband built for her in their house.

Although they lived different lives, the sisters remained close. They made a point to go food shopping together on Thursdays for their Shabbos needs, along with a nice tête-à-tête in an area restaurant. All three considered themselves working women, but none of them had heard of Rosie the Riveter, who was in large measure responsible for their careers.

It is commonplace today for women who are wives and mothers to work outside the home as well. Very often this is due to economic necessity. Years ago, before World War II, this phenomenon was much less common, even in economic hard times. Society had changed, and Rosie was part of that.

With millions of American men away in the military, and America in a war economy, the millions of jobs that needed to be filled were occupied by women, many working for the first time. And they were doing "man's work" very well, building the tanks and the aircraft and the ships needed for war. And so, Rosie the Riveter, dressed in overalls and carrying a workman's lunch pail, became the symbol of this new segment of the American labor force. They kept America running, even as they kept the home fires burning.

After the war, many women returned to their domestic lives. And others continued to be part of the workforce. Two paychecks in the family certainly increased disposable income and prosperity. Some argue, however, that the increased cash in the economy drove up prices, the resulting inflation causing two wage earners in the family to become a necessity rather than a luxury. Thus, many families found themselves essentially back where they started, but now two incomes were needed to stay afloat, rather than one. And the rising expectations of society, the notional inflation of what an American family can expect its standard of living to be, contributed to this trend as well. It became quite common, if not the norm, for women, even with children, to be out in the workforce.

Of course, some women need those jobs, economically speaking, more than others. And the great challenge of the working mother and homemaker is to balance her outside job with the important work she does in running a home and raising children. A challenge indeed.

Our friends Bella, Rela, and Gabriella each fell in a different part of that spectrum. But the difference between them was more than economic. Raised all the same, they nevertheless, as life went on, did not all have the same attitudes.

Bella was down to earth. Although a good and reliable office worker, she really worked to make ends meet. Together, she and her husband did OK, and raised their family in a nice "balabatish" way. First and foremost, Bella was a wife and mother.

Rela was a professional. Also a good wife and mother, she nevertheless had professional duties and obligations that were also part of her life and her self-identity. Her handsome paycheck reflected her success. She learned how to balance the two, and they did OK as a family. The children grew up normal.

Gabriella (don't call her Gabby!) was a fancy lady. She generally got what she wanted, and her children, raised in a certain milieu, certainly got more than they needed, and often got even more than they wanted (and they wanted, and expected, a lot).

And so the sisters shopped together for Shabbos. But they did not shop identically. While Bella and Rela bought the ingredients with which to prepare the

Shabbos necessities, Gabriella went straight to the takeout department, where they had her order packed and waiting for her. Everything she bought was ready-made. The artiste did not have time to bother with cooking. And besides, the pre-cooked food wasn't bad. On some occasions, when necessity dictated, Bella and Rela would buy some ready-made things as well, but that was not usual, nor was it their preference to do so. It made them feel guilty when they did, but their families realized that they were hardworking women who did as much as they could, and were fine with it.

As Bais Yaakov graduates, the sisters certainly were familiar with much of Scripture, especially those passages that have become part of our ritual – the words of Kiddush, for example. And they certainly knew, by heart, a *pasuk* from Parashas Ki Sisa: *V'shamru Bnei Yisrael es haShabbos, laasos es haShabbos l'dorosam bris olam.* But they did not all understand or interpret those words quite the same.

Taught well by their plain but devoted parents, the girls loved Shabbos and made it a really special day in their homes. But just as *kol Yisrael yesh lahem chelek ba'olam haba* does not mean that all Jews have an *equal* portion in the world to come, so too, not all Jews who observe the laws of Shabbos have an equal portion in *making* Shabbos. And that *pasuk* from Ki Sisa tells us that it is up to *us* to actually *make* Shabbos: *laasos es haShabbos.*

There is a famous Midrash on this *pasuk* (*Mechilta*): Rabbi Elazar ben Prata says, *V'shamru Bnei Yisrael es haShabbos laasos es haShabbos* – whoever is *meshamer* Shabbos, it is as if he (or she) *made* Shabbos.

Notice the grammar. *Meshamer* is a much more powerful form than *shomer*. It denotes not just observing but *causing* it to be observed, not just obeying the laws but actively and powerfully observing the holy day, creating it, in a human sense, by actively and attitudinally making it as special as it can be, by exerting oneself to the extent possible to vouchsafe it as the holy day of Shabbos for one's own generation and for generations to come.

The Torah Temimah offers the observation that other mitzvos are self-evident as mitzvos – tzitzis, tefillin, *sukkah*, etc. But Saturday already exists for all the people of the world, a day like any other. It is evident as Shabbos only through our actions. It is, in Heaven, a holy day. On earth, in this world, it is evident as a holy day only because we undertake to make its holiness manifest, through our observance. And that is by virtue of what we do *not* do on the holy day, i.e., labor that is forbidden, and by virtue of what we *do* do on that day, i.e., the physical and the spiritual things that we do *li'chvod Shabbos Kodesh*. And that includes what we do in the days preceding Shabbos to prepare for its blessed arrival.

By thinking of Sunday as Yom Rishon l'Shabbos, and Monday as Yom Sheni, we are making Shabbos holy. By planning our Shabbos meals, or perhaps our guests as the week progresses, we are making Shabbos holy. By working to earn enough to provide for a nice Shabbos, we are making Shabbos holy. By anticipating our *shiurim* or *sedorim* in learning for Shabbos, we are making it holy. By stopping to pick up some Shabbos treats, we are making it holy. By letting our children see us do these things, by having them experience these things, we are making Shabbos holy. By talking about it, in happy anticipation, we are making Shabbos holy. By planning our working lives to allow for its observance, whatever the apparent cost, we are making Shabbos holy.

And, especially, it is through our toil that we make Shabbos holy. Shopping and cleaning and organizing. By cooking and baking, by filling the house with the aromas of approaching Shabbos, by letting our children see and smell and absorb the excitement of Shabbos preparation, our joy and excitement in this weekly endeavor, we make Shabbos holy, and we make its holiness immortal through our children and theirs to come.

But what of the new paradigm, the working mother? It is certainly difficult for them. But the great women of Israel have always been our strength. They can, it seems, do anything. They are strong and capable and dedicated, and they make our world possible. We owe them. The men do their part, but a large measure of *laasos es haShabbos*, of *kol hameshamer es haShabbos*, our ladies of Jewish valor accomplish. But they do not necessarily all do so equally.

There are Bellas and there are Relas, and there are also Gabriellas. There are women who are overwhelmed by the demands of life. Let them buy Shabbos when they need to, *gezinterheit*, as long as their children are not shortchanged in their Shabbos *chinuch*. And there are women, and men, for whom some of the more mundane tasks that are part of making Shabbos are too much of a chore. Sometimes the shortcuts that they take have a price tag that if known in advance would be deemed much too high and not worth it.

Music is an extremely powerful medium that can move the spirit deeply. Hence its use in prayer. The other senses can be similarly powerful. When I was about thirteen years old, my mother served me a dish of some kind of porridge that she had never served me before. She sat with a wistful look on her face and watched me closely as I tasted it. I saw a tear in her eye.

"Bubby," I blurted out, without prompting. "Bubby made this." My mother burst out crying. Bubby passed away when I was two years old. The aroma and the taste of what my grandmother made with her loving, Holocaust-withered hands and had served me, perhaps once or twice when I was no more than two years old, were embedded somewhere deep within me, and now came forth and moved me deeply. I joined my mother in her tears of loving longing.

My memory and my overwhelming emotion, evoked by a smell and a taste, were not triggered in me because I am unusual, but because I am human. That is how God made us. It is a tool and a capacity that can be employed to great effect.

Think of the beautiful aromas emanating from the Jewish kitchen on Erev Shabbos. Think of the warmth. Think what that does to, and for, the spirit, for the Jewish *neshamah*. Think what awareness of the toil – happily undertaken – by the family, by the father and the mother, in every sphere of endeavor, for the sake of being *meshamer es haShabbos*, does for the developing and the enduring *neshamah* of Yiddishkeit and holiness in our children. It lasts forever.

Let us teach our children that not just by observing Shabbos, not just by obeying the laws, but by being *meshamer es haShabbos*, we are also being *osim es haShabbos*.

And by *making* Shabbos, we are also making life, true life, for ourselves and our future generations. It lasts forever.

Parashas Ki Sisa 5774

Mommy Will Buy Me a New One

In their naïveté and innocence, not understanding what it takes to provide for a family, not being aware of the pain and struggle of most people to put food on the table, and to make possible the necessities of daily life, small children in our society naturally don't worry too much about where things come from, where money comes from, and just assume that if they lose or abuse something they have, "Mommy will buy me a new one."

Children who say that are lucky enough to live in homes where Mommy is, in fact, in a position to buy them a new one. They are rather unlucky, however, if Mommy in fact routinely buys them a new one when they carelessly lose or abuse something they have.

A spoiled child is set up to become a spoiled, dysfunctional adult.

In my office, to my horror and amusement, the following scene used to be quite common, and still would be if I had not taken steps to stop it. One worker is warm, so she turns on the air conditioning. Another worker, now cold from the air conditioning, doesn't turn off the air conditioner; she turns on the heat. And as the temperature varies up and down, each one counters the change with burning vast amounts of additional energy in an effort to move the temperature up or down.

Nobody thinks or cares enough to do it rationally. Why? Why run both the heat and the air conditioning simultaneously? You know why.

Because neither is paying for either. What do they care? *Mommy will buy me a new one.*

I am frequently the first one to arrive in shul in the morning. It's not at all unusual for me to find the lights were on all night, or that the heat or the air conditioning were blasting all night, or the door unlocked all night, or the door actually ajar all night, or any combination of the above. Of course no one does this intentionally. But I cannot believe that someone who participates in the costs of keeping up the shul would act irresponsibly this way, as he certainly would not do so in his own home, where *he* has to pay for it. But when it comes out of *yenem's* pocket? Who cares? *Mommy will buy me a new one.*

How about washing one's hands in shul and using six or eight paper towels to dry them, when one or two will do? How about using ten of the shul's tissues for a two-tissue nose blow? How about opening a new two-liter bottle of soda when there is an identical bottle right next to it, practically still full? Now both will go flat. Who cares? No cost to me. *Mommy will buy me a new one.*

The *parashah* declares that all must participate, on one level, in the upkeep of the Mikdash, equally. On another level, of course, those with more are expected to give more, and those with less give less, each according to his ability. But on the basic level, *"he'ashir lo yarbeh v'hadal lo yamit"* (The rich shall not give more, and the poor shall not give less; Shemos 30:15). On a basic level we all need to have a similar, personal, caring vested interest in our shul. It's not all about money, and it's not always about money.

We all need to work for the benefit of our *mikdash* in a caring manner. We are all *baalabatim.* We all need to have a stake in it, and we all need to care.

On a fundamental level, however, the issue goes deeper. I believe it is hinted at in the *pasuk* as well. If one person's contribution to the shul is frittered away and wasted by another person's thoughtless carelessness, then the one who does contribute has to contribute even more, needlessly, to make up for the loss. *He'ashir lo yarbeh v'hadal lo yamit:* he who does contribute should not be forced to be needlessly *marbeh* as a result of the irresponsible actions of others who, by their thoughtless actions, are *mamit* the resources contributed by others who have generously shared with the congregation the fruits of their labors.

And the fundamental consideration, the driving force behind what should be so obvious, is itself a fundamental mitzvah stated elsewhere, but that applies here very well: *v'ahavta l're'acha ka'mocha.*

Parashas Ki Sisa 5771

The Heart of the Matter

Sam was always an energetic fellow, light on his feet. So when he noticed that his legs were just not carrying him the way they used to, he made an appointment with an orthopedist to check things out. What happened to the legs that had carried him so well until now?

Dr. Gold, an experienced physician, did what a doctor does. He assessed the patient as a whole, listening to the complaint while considering the whole medical picture. He was not a "leg technician" (or, as Obamacare and other forces in the healthcare insurance industry will likely impose upon us, a non-physician "health care provider"), but a real medical doctor, educated and trained to be, first and foremost, a doctor, capable of making a proper medical diagnosis. He carefully examined the patient and came to the conclusion that there was nothing wrong with Sam's legs. He suspected Sam might have coronary artery disease as a basis for this problem, and urged him to visit the internist to check this out, and also to rule out a blood disorder.

In the end, Sam turned out to have a "tight stenosis" of his left anterior descending artery, the main vessel that feeds blood, with its life-sustaining oxygen, to the heart muscle. A stent was emplaced, and, with wide-open circulation restored to the heart, Sam's old energy returned. His legs worked fine. And his life was saved.

Sometimes, in life, we seek to treat a symptom that is not really the primary problem, but unless we address that primary problem, we cannot effectively treat the symptom. This principle applies spiritually just as it does physically.

On Ki Sisa, the Imrei Noam cites the Algazi (*Ahavas Olam*), who, in turn, cites the classic words of Shir Hashirim, "*Ki cholas ahavah ani*" (I am sick with love). This metaphor illustrates that very point, that someone may feel sick everywhere in the body, and even the mind, but it may all stem from the heart. So too, in our long and bitter exile, we may cry out about *parnassah*, about having children and seeing them follow the proper path in life, about the heavy boot of oppressors on our necks, all of which are real problems. But the underlying source of all those problems is the same: the exile itself, the loss of the Beis Hamikdash and its attendant abundance of blessing for all of Israel, the loss of *kapparah*, the loss of spirituality, the loss of protection, the loss of a major aspect of the Divine Presence among us. Prayer for the various specific needs and blessings in life is certainly in order. But certainly prayer and hope for the ultimate cure is even more to the point.

Thus, in *Nachamu, nachamu ami*, the classic prophecy of consolation for Israel, Yeshayahu Hanavi (40:2) says *Dabru al lev Yerushalayim*, speak to the *heart of Yerushalayim* (referring to the entire congregation of Israel): you will, in the end, be consoled, you will be redeemed, *your heart will be cured and all of you will be made well. Those who put their hope in God will renew their vigor, they shall raise wings as eagles, they shall run and not be weary, they shall walk and not tire.* Because their hearts – *the heart of the Jewish People* – will be repaired.

The Imrei Noam homiletically applies this lesson to our *parashah. Ki sisa*: here it means to count, as in a census. Depending on the context, however, it can mean to carry, to lift, to appoint (as in a promotion), to tolerate (as a burden), to consider. *Lifkod* also refers to counting, but it can also refer to something being missing – as in the notation in the Torah that after the war against Midian, *lo nifkad mimenu ish*, not one man (Jewish soldier) was missing.

Thus, "*Ki sisa es rosh Bnei Yisrael li'fkudeihem v'nasnu ish kofer nafsho laShem bi'fkod osam v'lo yihyeh ba'hem negef bi'fkod osam*" (Shemos 30:12). When we consider, assess, make an accounting of the primary (*rosh*) failing, the missing element (*pekudeihem*) for the *cholas hanefesh* which brings about the *cholas haguf*, then let each one give an atonement for his soul to Hashem, *v'nasnu ish kofer nafsho laShem.* Look for the spiritual failing of the heart and repair it.

Speaking nationally, the various physical malaises of the Jewish People arise from primary *spiritual* causes. When the Beis Hamikdash stood and functioned as it should, when the people lived as they should, we were blessed, protected, and provided for. The Torah lists the many *berachos* that result from our keeping our side of the "bargain" we made with God at the foot of Mount Sinai. They are blessing without end. And they are ours, if we only do as we are supposed to do, as we have already promised to do, as we have been rewarded immeasurably in the past for doing.

And yet, somehow, the obvious eludes enough of us so that we are not, in fact, where we need to be. When you think about it, it's shocking but true. God imbued the human being with free choice, so that he can earn merit. Sadly, that freedom so often results in bad choices and bad consequences. And the connection between those bad choices and those bad consequences all too often eludes those who chose poorly in the first place.

Tehillim 2:8 relates a remarkable, fundamental promise to the Jewish People: *She'al mimeni v'etnah goyim nachalasecha, v'achuzascha afsei aretz.* Ask it of me, says God, and I will grant you, I will vouchsafe your inheritance from the nations. You will be free and independent and safe in your own land, and those who were your enemies will fear you and leave you in peace, for they will know that I, God, am with you. It is yours. *But you have to ask it of Me.* And that means *actually asking* Him, prayer, and the actions of the believing Jew: Torah and mitzvos.

A recent quote from one of Israel's current political and military leaders underscores this problem and this paradox. He is reputed to be brilliant. We have already seen in the past how not brilliant he really is. This time, if the quote is correct, he said that the Iranian mullahs look up and they see Allah, and they know what they want to do.

We, he says of the Israelis, look up and we see nothing.

Gevalt. And he is said to be the *einikel* of very *choshuve Yidden*.

It seems so simple and so obvious. And yet there exists within the human heart an ailment, a spiritual malaise, a *klippah*, that stands between a Jew and his Father in Heaven, that blinds him to the truth and causes him to choose poorly, unless he tears that *klippah*, that obstructing flesh, away.

In the context of our national Jewish life, as well as the personal, we need competent doctoring to diagnose and treat the afflictions of the heart, so that the entire organism can function in a healthy and robust manner. That is something each Jew can and should do for himself, and something that we should allow our spiritual leadership to help us do as well. And if we do turn to He Who has proclaimed, for all time, *Ani Hashem Rofecha* (I am Hashem, Who heals you), we will surely find that *lo yihyeh ba'hem negef bi'fkod osam* (there will be no ailment among them).

Parashas Ki Sisa 5772

The Mixed Multitude

"The Jews are taking what's rightfully ours! They're chiselers and cheats!"

Just ask Yishmael and Esav. Ask Lavan and his sons and generations of Jew haters to this day.

"The Jews are getting rich off our backs!"

Just ask Avimelech's servants, and generations of envious, deluded Jew haters to this day.

Ask the race baiters; ask Sharpton.

"The Jews are a disloyal fifth column!"

Just ask Pharaoh, and generations of paranoid Jew haters and antisemitic politicians to this day.

"The Jews are multiplying like vermin!"

Just ask the Egyptians, and generations of Jew haters to this day. Ask the Germans.

"The Jews are smart and crafty. We need to outsmart them!"

Just ask Pharaoh, and generations of Jew haters to this day.

(We insiders know there are lots of foolish, stupid Jews, but...shhhhh! Don't tell! More on that later.)

"The Jews all worship money. That's all they really care about!"

Just ask the Erev Rav, and generations of Jew haters to this day.

Ask Karl Marx, Jew hater par excellence. (But wasn't he a Jew? More on that to come.)

A quote from Marx's *A World without Jews*:

> Money is the jealous One God of Israel, beside which no other God may stand.
> What is the object of the Jew's worship in this world? Usury.
> What is his worldly god? Money....
> It is the circumvention of law that makes the religious Jew a religious Jew.

Time and again, the Torah reveals patterns that will be repeated over and over again down through the ages. It is almost as if those who hate us are reading from a script.

Well, are Jews smart? Many are, of course. Others are not. But how stupid does one have to be to have seen and experienced the hand of God, to be openly and clearly freed by Him from bondage in Egypt, to have witnessed the Ten Plagues, the miraculous splitting of the sea, saving the Jews and drowning their pursuers, with their massive enrichment from the spoils, to have heard the very voice of God at Sinai, to have clearly seen that Moshe was God's chosen and loyal servant, His instrument in effecting all this, and then to turn around and, while still encamped at the foot of Mount Sinai, to cast their gold into an idol, a golden calf, and to proclaim, "This is your god, oh Israel, who has taken you out of Egypt"?

Does that make any sense? Could they have been that stupid? Do you suppose they had among them a disproportionate number of future Nobel Prize winners?

Egypt, before the Exodus, was a tightly closed place. Part of the wonder of the Exodus is the wholesale departure of several million people, where nary a single slave could escape before.

And once the floodgates opened for the Jews, many others left as well. The Torah refers to them as the Erev Rav, a "mixed multitude" of an unknown number. Non-Jewish escapees, of various types and backgrounds, who left on the Jews' coattails. What I have never understood is why they were permitted to travel along with the Jews. Perhaps Moshe's compassion affected his judgment on this issue. But they were not a good influence. And in the end, what happened to them, and where did they go? Did they enter the Land of Israel along with the Jews?

The Torah and the Neviim are silent on this, but there has been a fair amount of discussion in various sources. Particularly striking is the view held by the Vilna Gaon, based on the *Zohar*, that they persist among us today, and have been, down through the generations, the sowers of discord and damage to the Nation of Israel. They are those who thrive on strife and *lashon hara*.

They are those who pursue base desires. They are those who pretend to be tzaddikim, but at heart they are rotten. They may build shuls, but are motivated to do so solely by the desire for honor. They pursue money and pleasure. They may become rabbis and leaders, but for the sake of *kavod*, with no thought for the welfare of the people. They may wear the uniform, and play the role, but they have no *yiras Shamayim*. They whisper in our ears, they give us advice, but they are misleading us.

How terribly frightening, and how vulnerable that leaves us. We are, it seems, not safe, even from those who appear to be in our own camp.

The Erev Rav are those who turn against their "own" people (the Jews) for the sake of currying favor with the enemies who persecute us. These people, abundantly in evidence today, viciously and libelously attacking Israel at every opportunity, writing hateful, slanted news stories and op-eds in the nasty *New York Times*, have been aptly labeled by playwright David Mamet as "race traitors." It's hard to understand their actions unless one understands that their real race, their true spiritual background, is that of the Erev Rav, those who actually instigated the creation of the Golden Calf and induced the Jewish People to sin.

And so the Kesav Sofer, in this light, offers a novel approach to understanding the bizarre, inexplicable declaration regarding the Golden Calf, "This is your god, Oh Israel, who has taken you out of Egypt!"

As do other commentators, he wonders how the same nation that declared "*naaseh v'nishma!*" – we will unquestioningly follow God – could make such a foolish declaration.

He answers that in fact, they did not: "God gave the [Jewish] people favor in the eyes of the [Egyptian] people, they gave them [everything], and they emptied Egypt [of wealth]. The Children of Israel journeyed from Raamses to Sukkos, about six hundred thousand men on foot, aside from the children [and women]. Also a *mixed multitude* [the Erev Rav] went up with them, with sheep and cattle, a great herd of livestock" (Shemos 12:36–38).

The Children of Israel left Egypt with a great load of riches, headed to Sinai and the Promised Land. The rabble of the mixed multitude had no interest in Sinai or the word of God, but they did like the riches that went along with the rest of the package.

Later, during a weak moment, when the Jews were confused by Moshe's unexplained absence, the Erev Rav struck: Ha! We know you did not leave Egypt to pursue the spiritual life! You did it for the riches, just like us! You think you're so holy, so pure? No way! Here! Look at this golden calf – *this* is your real god! This is the true object of your worship. You Jews worship money while you pretend to worship God. The desire for riches is what made you leave Egypt.

"This is your god, oh Israel, who [*the pursuit of which*] has taken you out of Egypt!"

Some things, it seems, don't change down through the generations. History, in this regard, repeats itself over and over. But particularly frightening is that aside from surrounding us, our enemies include those who hide among us, who have become part of us, but who retain the base and seditious attributes of the rabble, the mixed multitude who have latched on and won't let go, it seems, until Moshiach comes and liberates us from them as well as from the external oppressors.

Until then we must choose very carefully whom we allow to influence us, whose example we follow, whose pure heart beats with us and for us, who aspires with us and for us, for the holiness and the goodness of Sinai and the Promised Land, rejecting utterly the Golden Calf in favor of the faith and the dedication, the love and the devotion of *naaseh v'nishma*.

Parashas Ki Sisa 5776

Vayakhel-Pekudei

E Pluribus Unum

The refugee came running into Avraham's encampment to tell him that his nephew, Lot, had been captured in the war between the four kings and the five kings, and had been carried off toward Mesopotamia. Avraham marshaled his resources and headed north to rescue Lot. He reached the Mesopotamian outpost at Dan, from where he was able to launch the attack that brought back Lot, as well as the other captives and the booty that had been taken.

Stand at the excavated ancient gates of Dan, and you will be struck, as I was, at how different this city gate and wall look compared to the ancient walls and gates elsewhere in Israel. We are accustomed, in Israel, to see old stone walls and fortifications. Here it is mud and brick, classically Mesopotamian, with a starkly different look from the rest of Israel further to the south.

It was at this point, at the gates of Dan, that Avraham's initial military thrust at first ran out of steam. It was not because he himself was originally Mesopotamian. Rather, something about the place, nothing physically present at the time, sapped his strength, *tashash kocho* (*Sanhedrin* 96a).

Sometime in the 1700s, the two great brothers Chassidic masters Rebbe Zusia of Hanipol and Rebbe Elimelech of Lizhensk, in the quest to perfect themselves, wandered about as itinerant beggars, that the hunger and deprivation they suffered help cleanse them and purify them. They spent many a night cold and hungry. One night, exhausted, they stopped to rest in a small town. They were famished, but found they could not eat. They were fatigued, but found they could not rest. They were overcome with a profound sadness, in that place, a dreadful fear and revulsion. In the middle of the night they fled the place, unable to explain their dread and their horror, but they could stay there no longer. The name of the town was Oswieciem, known to most of us today by its German name, Auschwitz.

Many hundreds of years after Avraham arrived at Dan, his descendants, led by the wicked Yeravam ben Nevat, set up an idol, a golden calf, in that place.

Politically motivated, it was designed to give the Jews of the northern tribes of the breakaway Kingdom of Israel an alternate religious focus, to keep them from making the traditional and Torah-mandated triannual pilgrimage to the Temple in Jerusalem. Guards were posted along the roads to prevent such travel. The people were redirected to the two new temples, at Beit El to the south and in Dan to the north. In many ways, though a depraved distortion, these places were set up to otherwise mimic the service in Jerusalem. To this day, significant structures of that abomination can be seen, and visited, a short walk from the ancient Mesopotamian gate.

Avraham arrived at Dan and the very place filled him with dread and revulsion, sapping his strength. He managed to free Lot, but he found the place, future site of his descendants' idolatry, intolerable. And Dan was apparently worse than Beit El, near Shechem, because of the apparent preexisting penchant of the tribe of Dan for idolatry, as described in Navi and rabbinic sources.

Despite the greatness of Dan the son of Yaakov, the tribe of Dan, historically, was the least prestigious among the tribes. And yet, strangely, there is a special place in history, and in the future, for this tribe of Israel.

In Parashas Vayakhel we are told of the building of the Mishkan and its intricate, complex components and instruments of divine service. Famously, the Heaven-inspired artisan who put it all together was the young Betzalel ben Uri ben Chur, son of a highly prestigious family in the prestigious tribe of Yehudah. But Betzalel was not alone in his work. God also chose, and imbued with ability and wisdom, Oholiav ben Achisamach of the tribe of Dan. Together these two designed and fabricated the Mishkan, an interesting and clearly intended joining in holy effort of these two somewhat contrasting tribes in building the vehicle that unified all of Israel in serving and entreating God.

Fast-forward to an even more fantastic building project, the Beis Hamikdash in Jerusalem 480 years later. It was undertaken by Shlomo Hamelech, the wisest man who ever lived, son of King David, royal scion of the royal tribe of Yehudah. And chosen to assist Shlomo, in charge of the actual execution of the project, was Chiram of Tzor, a descendant of the tribe of Dan, an artisan and the son of an artisan, who was filled with the God-imbued knowledge of how to make and assemble everything.

That these two tribes were put together for these two endeavors, the most revered elements of our past, is no accident. That the tribe that represents the greatest and the tribe that represents something lesser come together for this great project symbolizes the unification of all of Israel and the actual equality of all Jews before God, and, hopefully, before each other (see *Midrash Rabbah* and *Tanchuma*). Let no Jew abuse another because of his position, for all are equal before God.

Sealing the deal is the midrashic tradition that Moshiach himself, the ultimate redeemer, the future king of Israel, will be of the tribe of Yehudah, but his mother will be a daughter of the tribe of Dan.

The Torah was given at Sinai, God revealed Himself to us there, when we stood together, as one. *Va'yichan sham Yisrael: k'ish echad, b'lev echad*. As one. That was an essential part of our strength and our merit.

This lesson of unity among our people, accentuated by the greatest and the least coming together in holy purpose, gives us not only the strength we need to carry us through, but also the hope that this unity, and the love and the mutual respect that it engenders, will serve to cleanse whatever we need to have cleansed, to purify whatever we need to have purified, so that no one and no place in Israel will ever again embody fear or darkness or revulsion, but rather light, love, holiness, joy, and divine fulfillment, for all of Israel together, forever.

Parashas Vayakhel 5776

Getting It Done...Right

If you want something done right, do it yourself.

It sounds like a cliché, but it certainly is not. And it is not always the case. But it's terribly frustrating in life when people we rely on to do something do it halfway. Doing something halfway right also means it's halfway wrong. It means that it was done unenthusiastically, carelessly, half-heartedly. Foolishly. And, as anyone who asks anyone else to do something knows, it happens all the time. And some people do it that way all the time. It makes you wonder how they get through life.

The past several *parashiyos*, culminating in Pekudei, involve a great many instructions, with lots of exacting detail, regarding the fabrication of the Mishkan and its accoutrements. The Torah makes very clear that our forebears not only carried out the instructions, but they did so exactly, faithfully, and enthusiastically.

In fact, three times in rapid succession the Torah certifies that Bnei Yisrael did everything as commanded, "*ken asa*." Simply translated, in this context, the phrase would mean that as commanded, so did they do. But *ken* has a deeper meaning too. Yosef's brothers, having been accused of being spies, protested "*kenim anachnu*" (Bereishis 42:11) – we are truthful, we are faithful, we are honest, we are reliable, we are upright. I think all those concepts are implicit in the Torah's repeated testament to the fact that *"ken asa."*

Told to do something, they did it right. They did it faithfully, they did it reliably. They did it in a way that pleased He Who commanded them to do it.

And so it says, *"Va'yar Moshe es kol hamelachah v'hineh asu osah ka'asher tziva Hashem ken asu"* – Moshe inspected their work, and found that they fulfilled Hashem's will exactly, and as a result, he was moved to bless them: *"va'yevarech osam Moshe"* (Shemos 39:43).

Rashi quotes the *berachah*: *"Yehi ratzon she'tishreh Shechinah b'maaseh yedeichem."*

May the Shechinah rest upon your efforts. Notice that it doesn't say that the Shechinah should rest upon the Mishkan, which they just completed. It says *"maaseh yedeichem,"* the efforts of your hand, the fruit of your labor. That is, "you should be successful."

When they finished working on the Mishkan, the Jews returned to their regular pursuits, such as they were. Moshe's blessing is thus twofold: that having succeeded at faithfully carrying out Hashem's will, and thus pleasing Him, they should now also succeed at whatever else they do in their everyday lives, *and* that what they do in their everyday lives should indeed also be pleasing to Hashem.

This is a very great *berachah* indeed, and is the result of their faithfully carrying out their mission. There is an important lesson here as well. *"Ken asu"* should be a model for how we undertake to accomplish something – indeed, anything. It will always serve us well.

There is another associated lesson in this story as well. Moshe delegated the labor to others. They fabricated the Mishkan, but, because of its great mass, they could not erect it. This Hashem assigned to Moshe himself. Rashi quotes *Tanchuma*: "How can I lift it?" Moshe asks. "No man can do so." Hashem tells him to just go ahead and lift it.

It's true that no man on his own can. But unless he extends the effort to do so, it will remain on its side. Go through the motions of lifting it, Hashem says, and it will rise – leave that to Me.

In life, there are many important goals. Sometimes these goals seem so far out of reach that many people make no effort to attain them, giving up in advance. This is not the way the Torah teaches. Out of a defeatist attitude comes only defeat. But for human striving, sometimes for what seems unattainable, nothing would be built, nothing accomplished.

Sefer Shemos begins and ends with this lesson. Baby Moshe is floating in a basket on the Nile. Pharaoh's daughter sees him. It is this good woman's destiny to save him and mother him for a while. Although his basket is beyond reach, she reaches out anyway – and, by an act of God, her arm indeed reaches him, he is rescued to become the prince of Egypt, and the rest is history.

Now Moshe himself, having in turn rescued his people, de facto king of the Jews and the humble servant of God, having internalized that lesson, shares it with us in Toras Moshe: lift that Mishkan and it will rise; establish that *makom Torah* and it will be built; start that *mesechta* and you can complete it; strive for your goals, whatever they are, in purity, honesty, and goodness, and you may very well accomplish them, no matter how daunting it seems in the beginning. Because when you do it right, when you do it in a caring manner, when you do it *l'shem Shamayim*, when you really try for all the right reasons, when it's *"ken asu,"* nothing is beyond reach.

Parashas Pekudei 5771

Kumaz

There is a classic lesson in the Flood story, in which the Torah describes how many of the various species were to be brought onto Noach's Ark. Of the *tahor* ("clean") animals, seven were accepted; of the *tamei* ("unclean") species, two. But the Torah, ever streamlined of language, uses extra words, referring to *those that are not tahor*, rather than say simply saying *"tamei,"* to teach us that we should always be careful to express ourselves in a clean and nice way.

And so in Parashas Vayakhel, it seems surprising to find, among the categories of gems donated by the Jewish women, something called *kumaz*, the earthy purpose of which Rashi points out circumspectly but, in effect, explicitly. Why would the Torah specify, needlessly it seems, the nature of that particular type of "adornment"?

And further, it seems especially odd since we know that Moshe Rabbenu had grave concerns about constructing the Kiyor, the laver for ritually cleansing the hands of the Kohanim, from the *maros tzovos*, the shiny copper mirrors that the Jewish women used in Egypt to beautify themselves, to entice their husbands, who were weary from slave labor. How much *more* questionable is the use of *kumaz* to make the holy vessels?

Remember God's answer to Moshe's hesitation about the mirrors. Au contraire, God tells him, that makes me like it even more. I like that the best. With that, the Jewish wives kept up their oppressed husbands' spirits, their zest for life, and brought about the phenomenal increase in the Jewish population, until they were a large nation, ready for the establishment of our national identity and our national mission.

Some, like Ramban, explain that the *kumaz* could also be used to safeguard virtue, depending upon how, and with what intent, it was employed.

And so, the point: the world is a complex place, and the path of life is full of choices.

Sometimes it may appear to be just a matter of nuance that distinguishes good from bad, pure from impure, virtue from vice. Of course, it is never really mere "nuance," but that is how it may superficially appear.

We are all given essentially the same raw materials with which to build our lives.

We can choose to use that material for evil, or that very same material, those same resources, for good. People may use mirrors, or adornments, or art, or words, or sentiment, and debase themselves and those resources by their actions and their choices. And people may use mirrors, or adornments, or art, or words, or sentiment, to achieve the loftiest goals.

In times of trouble, our ancestresses, the *nashim tzidkanios* in Mitzrayim, used those mirrors, and perhaps that *kumaz*, to build up their husbands and to build a holy nation. They understood how to harness the powerful forces of nature that the Creator imbued into humanity in order to elevate and to sanctify and to build, even as others used those same tools for the lowest purposes.

But still, why spell it out so starkly? Because it is a lesson in life that we need to understand, and we need to learn to control. Because sometimes it takes a hint of the explicit to reveal the true power of the implicit. Because we need to understand that God put it in our power to elevate the mundane into the sublime. Because a people that can transform the baser applications of *maros tzovos* and *kumaz* into holy work can also march, in the forty-nine days from Yetzias Mitzrayim to Har Sinai, from the forty-ninth *shaar hatumah* to the very highest level of *kedushah*.

And thus, the Mikdash in the *midbar* was built. Just as God wanted it.

Parashas Vayakhel-Pekudei 5773

They Also Serve Who Only Stand and Wait

I had a *rebbi* who was brilliant. In the world in general this is not unusual. There are many smart people in the world, brilliant people among all the nations. In our Jewish world, in our Torah world, it is, it seems, especially common. This is,

I believe, not just because our people are bred to be smart, but because brilliance itself, particularly in Torah, has always been recognized and valued, has always been prized, and has always served as a stepping stone to success, regardless of the circumstances of birth. This particular *rebbi*, however, was particularly brilliant.

I have always found it fascinating that babies, who we think don't know very much, somehow know to recognize other babies as similar to themselves. You can see it in how they interact, even if they are too young to interact in what we would otherwise consider a meaningful way. Genius tends to recognize genius as well. This particular *rebbi*, a master of Shas and *poskim*, who had *kol haTorah kulah* at his fingertips, who lived Torah, was also intellectually broad enough to recognize and to appreciate brilliance wherever it was to be found, including in the non-Jewish world. He was in awe of God's gift of genius bestowed on select human beings, and he respected that genius.

This *rebbi* once remarked to me that he envied anyone who had not yet read Milton's *Paradise Lost* for the first time, because he had yet before him the absolute wonder and awe of discovering genius and beauty of such magnitude that one encounters but rarely in a lifetime, for the first time.

John Milton himself struggled with impending and then actual blindness. One of his most famous and oft-quoted lines, "They also serve who only stand and wait," is from his poem "When I Consider How My Light Is Spent," written in contemplation of the darkness – and the helplessness – coming his way. This is commonly understood to mean that it is possible to serve God, or society, just by "being there," with good intentions.

There is much truth and justification to this, depending, of course, upon the circumstances. May we never be tested, *chalilah*, by an inability to act, by being forced to "only stand and wait."

In the "outside" world, the non-Torah world, people of genius, people of art, are often given a kind of free pass. It is enough for them just to be clever in their special way in order to discharge their obligations in life. This is mirrored, and perhaps finds its basis, in Christian theology, which maintains that the burden of the Law (i.e., the Torah and its mitzvos) has been removed from the shoulders of Christians, who need only believe in Christianity, and do nothing else, in order to be "saved."

In our Jewish world, except under the most trying and terrible circumstances, a Jew is expected to act. There are 365 *lo saaseh* commandments; there are 248 *aseh*. And for the most part they apply to everyone, equally. Beyond that, a Jew cannot be passive in his or her Judaism. We are expected to perform, even if it's difficult, even if it's inconvenient, even if it's expensive, even if we're not in the mood, even if we can find some excuse.

In Parashas Vayakhel, there are repeated references that support this notion. Interestingly, there are *pesukim* that address the men, and those that address the women, about doing: giving, donating, and physically doing the work that it takes to build a *mikdash* for Klal Yisrael. *V'chol chacham lev ba'chem yavo'u v'yaasu.* Literally, those with talent are called upon to use their talents to fashion the holy objects. In a broader sense, this is also a call to Jews who are smart enough – *chacham lev* – to really get it, to understand, to indeed do, in every possible sense, the will of God. *V'chol ishah chochmas lev b'yadeha tavu* – for the women as well, a call to physically *do.*

The *meforshim* emphasize here that it is not enough for those with clever ideas just to offer their ideas for others to act upon, and thereby fulfill their obligation. They must pick themselves up and come and actually do. They must work. They must give of themselves.

The story is told of Rav Yitzchak Elchanan, the great Rav of Kovno, who approached a certain man who was a *talmid chacham* for a donation to tzedakah. The man said that he contributes by learning Torah and is therefore exempt from giving much money. Rav Yitzchak Elchanan told him that he can't hide behind his Gemara. "You can't excuse youself from tzedakah by opening a Chumash. Right now, open your pocket instead."

"*Eleh hadevarim asher tzivah Hashem laasos osam*" (Shemos 35:1). There are those who can only stand and wait, and may Hashem's blessings be upon them if that's all they can do. For the rest of us, who *baruch Hashem* can do, we must always remember that we *must* do. We must give of our financial resources. But that alone is not enough. We must give of our intellectual resources. But that alone is not enough. We must give of ourselves – our time, our energy, our physical effort, our kindness and consideration, our caring, our love, our good words, the very work of our lives.

With our giving truly of ourselves, we build holiness in this world; and for ourselves and for our families, we buy life.

Parashas Vayakhel 5771

Veritas et Alius Balonius

Modern academia prides itself on – indeed defines itself by – the unbiased quest for the unvarnished, objective truth. Bulloney!

We all know that what passes for the truth in these places is only the PC-approved version of any issue. Let's take the example of the world-renowned university in Massachusetts whose motto is the Latin word for "truth."

Right.

Science can advance when the truth is looked at objectively, when observed phenomena are noted and evaluated, and all logical conclusions are considered, until facts are established and the truth can emerge.

Galileo observed the heavenly bodies and came to the inescapable conclusion that the earth revolves around the sun, as had Copernicus some years before. But the Church taught the Aristotelian dictum that the sun revolves around the earth. It had taken the astronomic model of a pagan and turned it into a doctrine of Christian faith. And even if Galileo could demonstrate quite clearly that the opposite holds true, he is a heretic and must die for his false teaching. And so Galileo recanted rather than die. *Veritas.*

Why are there more male physicists than female physicists? This is a question of significant societal interest. The feminist orthodoxy – indeed, a matter of political feminist faith – is that this is the result of anti-female discrimination and the intentional, institutionalized holding back of women. If true, that would certainly be an injustice that needs to be corrected. But is that really so? And if it was so, to whatever degree, in the past, it is certainly not currently so. What about the possibility that there is something about the XX chromosome set that renders women as a whole somewhat less inclined to math and physics than the XY set? It's certainly possible. After all, XX is XX, and XY is XY. There is no reason to assume that they are functionally identical. We know that they are not in other areas. Why should they be?

An honest scientific assessment would certainly be in order, as for any question of science and knowledge. It would be a worthwhile fact to ascertain in the quest for scientific truth, and would also provide important avenues of exploration in one of the frontiers of scientific knowledge.

So when the president of the above-mentioned institution dedicated to *"veritas"* raised this possibility at an academic symposium, an especially obnoxious but influential strident (so called "feminazi") type in the audience got up and announced that even mentioning such a possibility made her nauseated and sick, and she loudly and ostentatiously walked out of the hall.

So did he laugh off that dogmatic fool as she deserved? Well, at Veritas U, you cannot dismiss a feminist's rant, no matter how stupid. Shades of Galileo and the Inquisition!

He recanted! But that wasn't enough. He apologized! But that wasn't enough. He tried to placate and buy off the PC forces. But that wasn't enough. The Inquisition let Galileo live, but the university senate, in the name of the great god of feminism and all things politically correct, decreed his death. And so they killed him, professionally speaking.

He lost his position. For seeking truth at Veritas University.

It is absolutely contrary to liberal and feminist dogma to suggest what is obviously true: that men and women are not exactly identical. There can be no endeavor for which men might be better or more appropriately suited than women. And this is so not because it is truly so, but because it is to them a matter of faith, of their religion.

Indeed, their politics is their religion.

A central tenet of that "religion" is that in the "vast right-wing conspiracy" out there, there is a constant, unremitting, premeditated, and eternal *war on women*. All social phenomena that relate to women are the result of that cruel war, and it is the duty of every enlightened person do battle against it, *by any means necessary*. To seek, or even discover, a truth that does not conform to that view, or that explains phenomena outside that framework, is an act of heresy – primitive, know-nothing evil, in league with the devil, and certainly undeserving of consideration. It may not be heard. It must be suppressed. For it there is no freedom of thought, opinion, or expression. To question that orthodoxy is to be part of the problem, to be a participant in the war on women, and, while we're at it, to be against all decent human ideals.

It has become a standard weapon, *quite cynically employed*, of a segment of the political world, to hurl upon its opponents the characterization that they are engaged in *"the war on women"* in order to delegitimize them. Such accusations often originate with those who know better, but for whom it is a useful tool, as it is mindlessly accepted and vociferously, evenly religiously repeated by their ignorant "useful idiots," their army of "true believers."

(This is a process used endlessly, and with increasing success, by the enemies of Jews and of Israel who have their own minions, ignorant, uneducated, unsophisticated in these matters, but who, seeking a sense of virtue, mindlessly and falsely hurl accusations of "apartheid," "racism," "occupier," "torture," "suppression," and so on, ad nauseum, against our people.)

Every other set of chromosomes may be objectively examined. But not the X and the Y.

Understanding the biological workings of life must be suppressed to fit the politically correct model. Discovering that X and Y are different, if they indeed are in this regard, would never justify the stupidity of gender discrimination. It is obvious to all that women make just as fine mathematicians and physicists as men do. But that's not really the point. Understanding biology is the point. The objective search for the truth is the point.

The politically motivated suppression of the search for truth, especially at an academic institution whose motto is "truth," is the point.

Conventional religious views are, of course, laughed off at these places, dismissed as primitive and not worthy of consideration. The only religion given credence is that of political liberalism; feminist ideology, however radical or ridiculous, is unchallengeable. Many of these same searchers for *veritas* give the same credence to the Arab narrative in its dispute with the Jews. That too has become part of their unthinking "faith."

So, according to the Torah, is XX exactly the same as XY?

Of course not. How can it be? That is not a value judgment. It is just stating the obvious: men are men, and women are women. Thank God for that!

Let us confine our little analysis to the sphere mentioned above, that of work.

This is not about fairness, or equal pay for equal work product, or equal opportunity, or any of the parameters that normal, fair-minded people should consider obvious. Lack of fairness to women, denial of opportunity, in this day and age, is just primitive, stupid, and wrong. But simply stated, in the realm of work that people do, are there roles generally more suited to women, and other roles generally more suited to men? The contemporary PC will tell you No! No! No! But history, biology, the experience of thousands of years of civilization, and plain common sense tell you…of course!

In forbidding labor on Shabbos, the Torah says, in various places, "six days shall work be performed." But the language of those statements, while quite similar, is not identical.

Sheishes yamim te'aseh melachah (Shemos 35:2) is almost the same, but not quite the same, as *sheishes yamim ye'aseh melachah* (31:16). Notice the subtle difference? One letter. But that one letter says a great deal.

Work – the work of life, the work of the world – is sometimes referred to in masculine form and sometimes in feminine form. *Ye'aseh* and *te'aseh*. Now, why do you think the Torah would do that? The nauseated professor and her ilk at Veritas U should take note, though they won't. But we can.

We can learn that the Torah is telling us that there is a nature and a system in the world, instilled by its Creator, that allows the world to run the way its Designer ordained. Sure, there is room, in normal life, for much overlap. But men are men and women are women because God made men men and women women. And even as men and women, as free, capable people, should, in a just society, be free to pursue their goals and aspirations, to work and to create and to accomplish in this world according to their individual abilities, to be paid according to their worth and not according to their gender, so too should it be recognized and respected that *as a whole*, there are, in fact, differences between men and women that predispose them to potentially differing roles, differences that complement each other and result in the harmonious and successful running of the world. In a happy, fulfilling life. In the joining of two differing strengths that result in a powerful whole. In mutual respect and admiration. In awe.

Different is not lesser. It's better. Ask any happy couple.

The strident PC crowd will never find peace or satisfaction. How can they, when they are trying to impose their warped ideology on the beauty of creation?

There is a brouhaha going on now in Israel over the role of women in the IDF.

There are political forces demanding that girls should not only be deployed in combat roles equally with men (even if that means lowering the rigorous physical standards required for such roles, so that they can pass, and without regard for the unthinkable fate that would undoubtedly await them, God forbid, in case of capture), but that troops should be assigned, in unbelievably close-quarter physical intimacy, to tanks, without regard to gender. And no one, even the yeshiva students who represent such a high percentage of tank crews, or their *rebbeim*, should have the right to object. Those who have done so, or even expressed their grave reservation, have been declared haters, misogynists, primitive fanatics, execrable bigots engaged in the war on women.

It's all over the media. It is written of, and spoken of, as if there is no room for, need for, or purpose to discussion. No one, it seems, has the right to disagree with this politically driven foolishness. There are, of course, brave souls of principle who do speak up, *very cautiously*, very gingerly, but they can expect to be marginalized as religious extremists. One prominent person who spoke up forcefully has been nearly universally excoriated, with calls for his dismissal and defunding of his IDF-related institution. And halachic Judaism is itself portrayed by the political and media class as extremist at best, and really, fanatical.

In Parashas Haazinu, Moshe invokes the heavens and the earth as entities that are constant, with their defined functions, as varied as their functions may be, as compared to human society, especially Jewish society, which may or may not be constant, but which may renege on its mandate. Nature does not do that. Unlike human beings, it has no reward or punishment, no incentive, no choice. It does what it was created to do. People, on the other hand, are a wonderful amalgam of nature and mankind's unique ability to exercise its intellect and its free will to manipulate the world. As part of nature, we are imprinted with the natural ways of the world, with its varied yet fixed expressions of creation.

As the one creature with *nishmas chayim* (as opposed to the *nefesh chayah of* the animals), humans are also directly infused by God with elements of the supernal along with the mundane elements of nature that govern everything else.

And so we have our basic natures, and we have the God-given ability to make moral choices regarding how we act in this world. We have the option, indeed the mandate, to stretch our abilities to the limit. If you can do it, and want to do it, and it serves your purposes in life to do it, well – *go for it*. And society should not, within reason, hold you back. But we also cannot escape, nor should we escape, the basic realities of our nature. And to live harmoniously, one must live in sympathy with nature.

So anyone can and should achieve the most he or she can. That is our mandate and the fulfillment of our purpose in this world. That applies to every human being, regardless of gender, or race, or any other factor that defines differences between human beings. The concepts of fairness and opportunity for *all* are a wonderful gift of the intellectual and social development of modern mankind. Discrimination, racism, bigotry, and unfairness are just plain stupid and primitive. But that does not negate the basic truth and the reality that not everyone is the same. They are not.

Why are some people smarter than others? Because they are. You think it's not fair? That's the reality. That's life. There are functions in this world that are not suited to people who are not smart. There are functions in this world that almost anyone can do, although some will do them better than others, or will have greater inclination to them than others. That is the normal flow of life, and that is how the world works.

God has told us, through the Torah, that this is so. There's nothing wrong or politically incorrect about awareness of this reality. To insist, stridently and mindlessly, that it is otherwise is intellectually dishonest and can lead only to dysfunction, distress, and profound dissatisfaction.

The truth, the *honest* truth, not a politicized version of it, is true *veritas*.

And that is a noble end, worth striving for.

Parashas Vayakhel-Pekudei 5777, Yerushalayim Ir Hakodesh

ספר ויקרא

Vayikra

I

There was a sad and resigned look on the man's intelligent face as he told me about his son.

A brilliant, dedicated professional, he moved to Israel from America years ago and raised his family there. He was a *talmid chacham* from a fine family, and, with his similarly accomplished wife, in a good marriage, raised a beautiful family.

One son had walked away from Torah observance. It was terribly painful, and he could not understand or explain it. The son told the father, "Abba, *zeh lo medaber elai*" (It [Judaism, religion] doesn't speak to me).

How terribly sad for that family. How terribly sad for that young man.

How does that happen? Is it faulty education? Faulty upbringing? Problematic home life? It certainly could be those things, but just as certainly may not be those things at all.

There are no guarantees in life. Just ask anyone who's been around in life.

That's a lesson most people learn sooner or later. We can't always make things happen the way we want them to, however earnestly we try; we can't always make others see things our way, no matter how earnestly we believe it, or want them to believe it, no matter how true it is.

And not everyone is built the same. We don't all have the same sensibilities and sensitivities. What most people will find moving or convincing does not, in fact, move or convince everybody. That's the way God made human beings. What is obvious to most of us is not obvious to all of us. And that is the problem with the quest for spirituality. It is not smooth sailing for everyone.

Being "hard of hearing" in this regard does not excuse a Jew from his obligations, but it does make it harder for some than for others.

Parashas Vayikra famously begins with the final letter of the word *va'yikra* (ויקרא) written with a small *aleph* (א). God called (ויקרא) to Moshe. Many homiletical interpretations have been offered to explain that. Most commonly, it is said to be a manifestation of Moshe's great humility. Later on, the same word is used

297

to indicate that God called to the wicked Bilaam, but there the spelling is different. The *aleph* is missing altogether, to diminish Bilaam's importance as the recipient of God's call. Spelled that way, it is suggestive of happenstance rather than intent, even of something unclean and impure – going to the very character of that villain.

Moshe, in his modesty, would have spelled it the same way for himself, as if he were unworthy of being called, personally, by God. Of course, he could not, as it was not up to him. Every letter in the Torah was directly dictated by God Himself. And so Moshe included the *aleph*, but he wrote it a little smaller than the other letters.

If I may, I would offer another view of that small *aleph*.

God indeed called to Moshe, but He, in fact, calls to each and every one of us, in every generation. As Jews we cannot possibly propagate our nation and our faith from generation to generation unless we hear His call. He calls to us, but how well do we hear Him?

I suggest that with that small *aleph*, we are being taught a valuable lesson in how to understand how the millions of individuals who comprise our nation, different each one of us, hear that call, feel that spirit, perceive that kinship offered by God. We are not all the same. We do not all have that sensitivity, and those whose constitutions are simply not as receptive or as responsive as others, those who do not readily feel it, are burdened by a terrible test of faith. It is simply harder for them; and the rest of us, in love and empathy, should have the wisdom to understand that.

No Jew is beyond reach. Every Jew has the spiritual capacity, an inheritance from our holy forebears, to connect with God. The *klippah*, the hard shell of this worldly existence that separates all of us from God, from Godliness, which it is our mandate to break through in our journey through life, is harder and tougher in some people than in others. But it *can* be broken through. It is our duty, indeed our calling in life, to do so. It is also our duty in life to recognize that struggle in others, and, with love and understanding, to do what we can to help them break through as well.

ויקרא. God calls to us all equally. But we don't hear Him equally, and in His desire to have us understand each other, to help each other, to love each other, He made that *aleph* – which denotes "one," the individual – small and different to teach us that we are, in fact, individuals, that we are not automatons, that each of us is a world unto himself, that each of us has strengths, weaknesses, and needs different from everyone else, *and that's how God Himself made us*, by His divine design.

There is nothing the Creator requires of us, individually and as a nation, that we cannot do. After all, He designed us, and He knows our nature. But He chose, in His wisdom, to design challenges into the system He created, so that we may earn merit in this world. The individual who is spiritually challenged is indeed challenged, but like other impediments in life, or perhaps more than other impediments in life, it is a challenge that can, and must, be overcome. It is the particular burden of those individuals.

It is also the obligation of the rest of us to recognize and to appreciate the burdens other individuals must face in life, spiritual as well as mundane, to reach out, to support, to love, to bear, to understand, to care. To hear, as God calls to us, not just the large sound of the large letters, but the small, still voice, the haunting sound of that little *aleph*.

Parashas Vayikra 5776

Let's Eat

There is a joke about the Yamim Tovim, Shabbos, and other calendar occasions in Jewish life, typically told by people who have no understanding of the significance of any of those occasions. According to this witticism, in each instance, the observance boils down to "such and such happened, now let's eat." For sad days, "it was bad, now it's over, let's eat." Bad joke. Bad ignorance. Good observation about eating. We use *seudos* to mark these occasions and to honor them. Eating a *seudas mitzvah* is a recognition and an elevation of human nature, taking a mundane action and making it sacred, for the sake of Heaven.

All animals eat. Carnivores kill and devour. Jews eat too – they eat meat, if they choose to, but they sublimate their animal function by elevating it through a God-given formula designed to make life and its everyday functions holy. One of God's great gifts to human beings in general, and to Jews in particular, is that we can elevate virtually any of our life functions –which often parallel closely similar ones in the animal world – or the most mundane, even the most inelegant activity, by channeling our actions to reflect the will of God and dedicating them to His service.

And so we observe three *seudos* on Shabbos, we consume wine and spirits *li'chvod Shabbos*, and we hold *yom tov* meals, Pesach *sedorim*, meals before fasts, meals after fasts, meals at life cycle events (bris, *pidyon haben*, mourning, *lo aleinu*), etc. All are considered *seudos mitzvah*.

If indeed these are mitzvos, however, why is it that some people, indeed some people who are very scrupulous in their observance of the mitzvos, seem to be lax in this regard?

I will take the liberty, for Parashas Vayikra, of using Vayikra as a *kol koreh* to remedy a condition alluded to in Parashas Ekev and hinted at in the *haftarah* of Parashas Ki Sisa.

Rashi, in Ekev, plays on the word *ekev* to describe *mitzvos kalos*, mitzvos that a person *thinks* are light, *she'adam dash b'ikvav*, that a person tramples underfoot.

The Maharal explains that these are mitzvos that a person thinks, for some reason, are not that important, and thus not too rewarding. We know, of course, that only God knows the true reward for any mitzvah, and Chazal have warned us not to make this mistake.

One example of such a mitzvah, as cited in Ekev, is *simchas yom tov*, which would include holding a proper *seudas yom tov*.

There are many people who are not careful with Shalosh Seudos of Shabbos. Specifically, the third meal, while technically Seudah Shlishis, the third meal, is typically referred to as Shalosh Seudos, literally "three meals," even though it's actually only one meal, the third, but which is assigned the importance of all three.

What, then, about the fourth *seudah* of Shabbos, after Havdalah, the Melave Malka, inaugurated *li'chvod Shabbos Kodesh* by David Hamelech, and which bears his name?

And what of Rosh Chodesh? A special *seudah* is called for in halachah for this important day as well.

Well-meaning people, good Jews, careful *medakdekim b'mitzvos*, somehow often forget that these two mitzvos are mandated in *Shulchan Aruch*, alongside other mitzvos, but they have somehow been relegated to the category of "*mitzvos kalos she'adam dash b'ikvav.*" Mitzvos kalos? Says who? Does any of us really know God's mind, or understand fully what His *cheshbonos* are?

For Parashas Ki Sisa I was blessed to be in Yerushalayim. During Shalosh Seudos in Kehal Chassidim in Shaarei Chesed, the rebbe addressed this very topic. In the *haftarah*, Eliahu Hanavi, on Har Hacarmel, confronts the prophets of the Baal, and the people who give them credence: "*Ad masai atem poschim al shtei hase'ipim?*" he asks. How long will you jump between both ideas (i.e., that of God and that of the Baal)?

The rebbe extended this phrase homiletically, quoting a *maamar* that applies this challenge to those who ignore or skip over (*poschim*) the two important mitzvos and age-old Jewish customs of Melave Malka and *seudas* Rosh Chodesh. For each of these mitzvos has its own *siman* in *Shulchan Aruch*, with only one *se'if*, with that observance as the only mitzvah in the *se'if*: *shtei hase'ipim* (300 and 419).

We all love Shabbos. We can demonstrate that love not just by observing the strict laws governing it, but by symbolically escorting the Shabbos Queen upon her departure. How reluctant we are to have her depart! And so we "escort" her, right after Havdalah.

Melave Malka is a beautiful affair, with candles, wine, *hamotzi*, wonderful prayers and *zemiros*, accompanied by David Hamelech and Eliahu Hanavi.

The cycle of our year and the determination of our holidays is set by Rosh Chodesh. David Hamelech's independent course to kingship was set on that day's special *seudah*, as described in Tanach. This *seudah* is an ancient and important Jewish practice. And it honors a system of tracking time that is not only classically Jewish, but whose arcane astronomical facts were divinely revealed to our people thousands of years before NASA could derive the same data by satellite observation.

As Jews we have the opportunity to sanctify every mundane act that we do. Eating is often not just a mundane act, but, in its execution, at least by some, it can be a rather gross act. By holding a *seudah l'shem Shamayim* even when we're not hungry, we demonstrate not just *kavod* for the mitzvah, but that when we eat other times it's not necessarily just to satisfy our animal desires, but that we are capable of a higher purpose.

And to serve a higher purpose is why we are here.

Parashas Vayikra, Rosh Chodesh Adar II 5771

Oyfgeklert

There is more than one way to understand that fine Yiddish word, *oyfgeklert*. It can refer, simply and benignly, to explaining something to someone, clarifying it, so that he understands it. In its best (and most devilish) application, an *oyfgeklerter* is someone so clever, so sophisticated, so full of knowledge and understanding, so enlightened, that he is, in his own estimation, wiser than the wise men of Israel. He knows how things really are and how they ought to be.

For many years, yeshivas in New York were under periodic pressure from the educational authorities to teach general studies ("English") in the morning, when children's minds are fresh, and Jewish studies ("Hebrew") in the afternoon. The yeshivas resisted, understanding that the premise was true, but their priorities were reversed.

This was the case for virtually all yeshivas and day schools that were traditionally Orthodox, wherever in the spectrum of Orthodoxy they fell. In those days there were also many "Talmud Torahs" in New York, after-hours classes attended by public school children whose parents wanted them to get at least a little Jewish content in their education. While there were very likely some success stories in the Talmud Torahs, many children hated going to them. They resented being cooped up and drilled with "useless" and "meaningless" stuff they were not interested in, while their friends were out playing and enjoying their freedom. And, by this time of the day, many had had it.

And so it was somewhat shocking to me when an *oyfgeklerter* fellow I know, a real intellectual, told me about a yeshiva day school he and his friends were designing to provide a contemporary education for contemporary Jewish children. They understood how things should be. They intended to alternate days when "Hebrew" would be first and when "English" would be first. Triumphantly, he explained that this would show the children that both are of equal importance.

Equal importance? If our people had historically treated them with equal importance, we would have long ago disappeared as a people.

I should point out that this fellow was a *shomer Torah u'mitzvos*, who would not be *mechallel Shabbos* or eat *treif*. Only his *oyfgeklerter* mindset was *treif*. He had it all figured out, much better than the rabbis who, unlike him, lacked the benefit of a PhD.

Now, don't misunderstand. There's nothing wrong with a PhD. It is a very great achievement and an excellent credential. Yes, I too have a doctorate, in medicine, and I have studied history and philosophy and literature and languages. But I like to think those endeavors, broadening as they are, serve primarily a fundamental purpose in helping me be who I should be.

For mankind in general, the pursuit of knowledge is part of the mandate God gave at the time of creation: use the faculties and the abilities that the Creator has given you to discover, dominate, and govern the world. *Chochmah*, knowledge, wisdom, is out there in the world, available to all humans. *Chochmah ba'goyim taamin.* For the Jew, however, those other forms of knowledge, while they may be important and useful, are secondary to the knowledge of God's will: *ki hi chochmaschem. This*, the Torah, is *your chochmah.* For the Jew, the primary source and repository of wisdom and knowledge is Torah. A Jew who is wise in the general knowledge of the world but not in Torah is not really a wise Jew, qua Jew.

And so, while there are rabbis who also have doctorates, with all respect to their achievements, it is the rabbi title that really counts, that really has primacy. For therein lies the wisdom and the intellectual accomplishment of the Jew. And a congregation that seeks a rabbi who *must also* have a PhD is, I believe, unaware of what a rabbi is, and what the accomplishment of Torah knowledge is. It makes me think of the *oyfgeklerter* fellow who designed a "yeshiva" day school to teach the children that *limudei kodesh* and *limudei chol* are of equal importance.

The Baal Haturim teaches that in writing the word *va'yikra* with a small *aleph*, Moshe modestly sought to downplay his own importance with language similar to that used regarding Bilaam, the wise man of the gentile world at that time.

The Ateres Yeshuah relates the *aleph* to *chochmah* (knowledge), citing a reference to Iyov (33:33). Here, Moshe and Bilaam, both the wise men of their generation, are vastly different in what their wisdoms represent. Moshe's is pure and holy. Bilaam's may be entirely impure and unholy, such as his sorcery, or, like general knowledge, essentially neutral but easily misdirected and led to impropriety. Bilaam hoped to lead the Jews to ruin by introducing alien concepts in the guise of "knowledge."

But to function in this world we must acquire knowledge. Nearly all the mitzvos require some knowledge and mastery of how the world works. Astronomy and agronomy and art and music and architecture and animal husbandry and medicine and virtually all such endeavors in life are necessary to fulfill the mitzvos. So it is clear that we must acquire such knowledge in addition to straightforward Torah learning.

And it is not only permissible things that we must learn about, we must also gain some knowledge of even the impermissible. On *lo silmad laasos*, do not learn from the other nations to do the bad things they do (Devarim 18:9), the Gemara (*Sanhedrin* 65) says, don't learn it to do it, but learn it enough to understand it so that you may avoid it.

And so the small *aleph* comes to teach us attitude and proportion. There is some element of "outside" knowledge that we must acquire. That is the world. That knowledge is represented by the *aleph*. But it is a *small aleph*. Depending upon who you are, learn what you must, learn what you should, but keep it in perspective. In the overall picture, in the totality of your existence as a Jew, keep that *aleph* small. Keep it in its place.

Historically we see how true and important it is. I myself remember, many years ago, people – mostly ignorant of real Torah *hashkafah*, people who had been exposed to *haskalathink* – talking about serious Torah learners as "bench kvetchers" who do nothing "practical." Those same critics would look upon a PhD candidate in medieval French literature with admiration. Those same critics were, no surprise, often rather loose and liberal with halachah when away from home. Those same critics were embarrassed by the perceived "ignorance" of *bnei Torah*. Those same critics had children who turned out OK if they were exceptionally lucky, but by and large had children who did not, in fact, turn out OK.

Those same *oyfgeklerter* critics had no understanding at all of what Judaism is really about.

The Talmud Yerushalmi (*Peah* 1:1, 5b) asks, may one teach Greek to one's son? For our purposes, we can understand this to mean not just the Greek language, but general knowledge of the world. The Gemara's initial answer is yes, but only when it is neither day nor night, for we are obligated to study Torah day and night (ergo, the answer is *never*). But, the Gemara counters, we are commanded *u'vacharta ba'chaim*, you shall choose life: we must engage in, and teach our children, pursuit of a livelihood! Does the obligation to study Torah day and night also render it impermissible to pursue a livelihood? Clearly, the Torah *commands* us to pursue a livelihood. So it must mean that we should study Torah day and night as much as possible, and give it a position of primacy in our lives, even as we also pursue our livelihoods and, in the course of making our lives, pursue the knowledge and the skills that allow us to make our way in the world, i.e., *studying Greek*.

Well, then, the Gemara observes further, is it permissible to teach one's daughter Greek? Yes, *because it is a tachshit, an adornment, for her*. Thus, the Gemara tells us that there is nothing inherently harmful in general knowledge, if done right, for if there were, it would not be permissible for a woman, who historically had neither the obligation to study Torah nor to earn a livelihood. But it is not only permissible, it is considered an adornment.

There is an old tradition that the first time a small boy is brought to the *cheder* to learn Torah, he is wrapped in a tallis, given sweet things to eat, and taught the first *pasuk* in Vayikra. The spiritual struggle that he will inevitably face in life, balancing the mundane needs of this world with the pursuit of the spiritual, which must override the physical and the mundane, is placed before him even at that very moment, with the word *va'yikra*.

There is so much knowledge in the world, so much to know, so much to learn, so much to master. For the outside world, that pursuit of knowledge is an end unto itself. For the Jew, it is a far more treacherous path. Unbridled from the pursuit of Heaven, it can lead to ruin. Harnessed for the sake of Heaven, it leads to the sublime. For as much as there is to know, for the Jew secular knowledge is but a tool in the far greater endeavor of knowing the will of God, the highest and the greatest form of knowledge a human being can attain.

Ki hi chochmaschem. This, the Torah, is *your* wisdom, the culmination of knowledge.

As much as there is to know in the outside world – and much of it is important and beautiful – for the Jew it is but a little *aleph* appended to an infinitely greater concept, as limited as the human capacity to do so is: knowing God.

Parashas Vayikra 5774

That Little Aleph

The small *aleph* in Vayikra represents Moshe Rabbenu's great modesty. To minimize the grandeur of God calling upon him and transmitting all the details of the Torah through him, Moshe took it upon himself to make the *aleph* small, so that the word comes closer to saying God "happened upon" Moshe rather than that God came calling on him.

Tanchuma quotes a *pasuk* in Mishlei, "*Gaavas adam tashpilenu, u'shphal ruach yismoch kavod*" (29:23), to illustrate that whoever runs after *serarah* (authority or dominion) will find that *serarah* runs away from him. And whoever runs away from *serarah* will find that *serarah* runs after him. This is similar to the concept that whoever runs after *kavod* (honor) will find that *kavod* has a way of running away from him; and whoever runs away from *kavod* will find that *kavod* has a way of finding him.

Thus, the famous quip, when someone complained that he always runs away from *kavod* and yet *kavod* never seems to catch up with him, that the reason is that as he "flees" from *kavod*, he is always looking over his shoulder to see where it is, and if it is finally catching up with him.

The first king of Israel, Shaul, was a very modest man and a great tzaddik. His was a tragic story, with a very short reign (two years) and marred by depression, melancholy, irrational acts, and a violent end. The Shaul at the end was very different from the man who was anointed by Shmuel Hanavi. That Shaul stood head and shoulders over the rest of Israel, in spirit as well as physically.

Shaul fled from *serarah*, as well as from *kavod*. That's part of what made him head and shoulders above the rest, and made him worthy to be king. Shaul kept quiet about Shmuel's revelation to him that he would in the future be king. And when Shmuel wanted to present him to the nation as the anointed leader, Shaul hid and had to be searched for and brought out from his hiding spot. He insisted that before being appointed, the Urim v'Tumim be consulted to make sure he was worthy – "if not, leave me alone." Thus, the tragedy of Shaul's downfall is greater still, given his inherent greatness.

At the Burning Bush, through seven days of arguing, Moshe resisted God's command to go to Egypt and become the leader who would redeem Israel. In the end, God forced him to go. But once he stated to Pharaoh God's demand, "Let My people go," Moshe withdrew, reasoning that he had already fulfilled his mission. So God had to command Moshe time and again, for each encounter with Pharaoh: "*Lech el Paroh*," "*Hisyatzev lifnei Paroh*," "*Bo daber el Paroh*," and so on. Each was a new command and a new mission, because Moshe kept insisting that he had fulfilled his mission, and he wanted to withdraw from *serarah* and *kavod*. In the end he led them out of Egypt, he separated the waters of the Yam Suf, he got them the *mon* (food from Heaven), he produced water from a rock in the desert, he encountered God on Mount Sinai and received the Torah, and he built for them the Mishkan. And still he insisted, "that's enough, what else do they need me for?"

To this God replied, "I have a mission for you greater still. You will teach them of *tumah* and *taharah*, of *korbonos*, of how to encounter God." What greater *serarah*, and what greater *kavod*, is there than that? The great men of previous generations were typically the only ones in their *dor* who were worthy to lead. Moshe's generation had other great men and potential candidates. But *serarah* and *kavod* pursued him, because none fled from those honors more than did Moshe.

And so, a story. It's a true story, so it will be disguised somewhat. But the lesson is so powerful that it should be told.

A young man witnessed something quite disturbing. A venerable tzaddik, a well-known and well-respected rebbe, behaved in what appeared to be a most unbecoming manner, courting *kavod*, peeved when he did not get it, and childishly and unashamedly happy when he did.

Shocked, horrified, and disappointed, the young man could not keep it to himself.

This young fellow is an excellent, moral *yerei Shamayim*, certainly not given to *lashon hara*, but the spectacle was too disturbing for him, the lesson too cutting, and he couldn't keep it to himself.

Someone from the yeshiva world once explained to me that some people in that world do enjoy the *kavod* they derive from it, because, being human, and all too often being poor, that is one of the few "worldly" things available to them. Maybe he thought this was an example of that. But this case was too glaring, too public, and unbecoming of a Torah leader so many people look up to.

Some time later this young man entered into a hellish nightmare of personal problems.

Nebech, he and his family suffered for years. On one occasion he happened to be talking with a *rosh yeshiva*. The subject of *rodef achar hakavod* came up, and the fellow mentioned the story of the rebbe, and how the embarrassing result was that *kavod* ran away from him instead.

The *rosh yeshiva* was shocked. "I was there!" he exclaimed. "That's not what happened at all!" In fact, the *rosh yeshiva* had been very much involved in the incident in question. He then went on to explain the rebbe's actions as entirely the opposite of what the young man thought. The rebbe had been *fleeing from kavod*, but it caught up with him, and he laughed when it did. The young man had altogether misread that event and the rebbe.

Filled with dread and remorse, the young man wanted to ask *mechilah* of the rebbe.

But that tzaddik had already gone from this world. Desperate, he gathered a minyan of friends and went to the *kever*, where he tearfully begged forgiveness.

Not long after that, the young man's troubles were resolved.

The lure of *kavod* is very great, being driven by that lowest form of self-adulation, *gaavah*. The quest for dominion, power, *serarah*, is, ultimately, but an expression of *gaavah*, and the desire for *kavod*. Every human being has within himself a natural desire for *kavod*. It is part of our makeup. And yet, God wants us to do otherwise.

To do otherwise is to show that we are not, after all, the sole center of the universe.

Yes, the world was created for my sake, but not only for me, and not that I should approach it selfishly and hedonistically. It's my opportunity to appreciate what God has given me, and to use that opportunity to fulfill the role God has assigned me by putting me in this beautiful world. But He has not put me here to seek aggrandizement at the cost of others, dominion over others, or to place my *kavod* above that of others.

He also did not put me here to judge others. What a lesson that young man's story is! All is not always as it seems, and such judgments can be deadly wrong. And how often do people seek *kavod* by putting other people down? It is our own *kavod* that we must not seek. The *kavod* of others is something that we should constantly seek, especially if those others have earned our *kavod*. And while not all people may be equally deserving of *kavod*, just being here in this world, created in the image of God, deserves at least some *kavod*.

Sadly, there are people who through their actions disqualify themselves from being worthy of respect. Those actions may be gross and obvious, such as in an evil person.

And they can be far more subtle. They may be no more obvious than being driven by the quest for *kavod*, as that says much about a person's character.

Kavod, and even *serarah*, are not inherently bad. They are a necessary part of this world, and can be good and pure and correct. It is the *quest* for them that can be the problem. Moshe had *kavod* and he had *serarah*, but not because he pursued them. We do honor our parents. We do honor our proper civil leaders, our Torah scholars, our *rebbeim*. They should have that honor, and they should have the *serarah* that they have. And the surest way to deserve and to achieve that *kavod* and that *serarah* was taught to us by one who was slated to be king, who stood head and shoulders over all of Israel, but who, in his modesty, hid from it, and by the one, the Raya Mehemna, who for seven days, beside the Burning Bush, resisted being appointed, and who could not bring himself to write in the Torah that the Ribbono shel Olam sought him out to be the teacher, for all time, of how to relate to God.

And in the process, he taught us a very big lesson vested in a very small *aleph*.

Parashas Vayikra 5772

Tzav

Vemen tzu Nemen, Nisht tzu Farshemen

Most of us have experienced the annoyance of davening Shemoneh Esrei near someone who davens out loud, carefully enunciating each word. His *kavanah* is great; ours, as a result, is disturbed. Everybody knows you're supposed to recite the silent Shemoneh Esrei silently, including the loud davener. They're just oblivious.

We also know, however, that prayer – including the type of prayer that we would never recite out loud, especially in the presence of others – wasn't always said silently.

When Chana, the future mother of Shmuel Hanavi, heartbroken over her own barrenness, pours out her heart in silent prayer at the Mishkan at Shiloh, Eli the Cohen Gadol thinks she's drunk. People, it seems, used to pray loudly, regardless of the subject matter. Moving her lips but making no sound struck him as odd behavior, perhaps drunkenness.

At a later point, Chazal made a *takkanah* that prayer should be recited silently. The basis for this ruling is found in our *parashah*.

We know that the Torah has no extra words. And so each word has its own significance, and typically what appears to be an extra word, or an extra letter, is there to teach something. This is the basis for much of the Talmud.

There are times, however, when the Torah indeed uses more words than appears necessary. There is always a lesson to be learned from those instances.

Early in the Torah, in the Flood narrative, a lesson regarding refinement in speech is learned from the fact that the Torah mentions animals that are *tahor*, and then, in an uncharacteristically wordy manner, refers to those that are not *tahor* (rather than spelling out more succinctly, but in a less refined manner, that they are *tamei*). The lesson: always try to express yourself in as refined a manner as possible. That refinement will rub off on your general behavior as well.

In Parashas Tzav, the specific requirements for the processing of various *korbonos* are laid down. The *chatas*, a sin offering, is to be *shechted* in the northern area. But it doesn't say that. We only know it because it says to *shecht* it "in the same place that the *olah* is *shechted*" – and that is in the north. Why the roundabout and extra verbiage? To teach a lesson, of course. In human relations, an extremely important lesson.

The Gemara (*Sotah* 32b) and Yerushalmi (*Yevamos* 8:3) tells us: in order not to embarrass the sinners. When they bring their *korban chatas* (similarly with *asham* – these are the only two *korbonos* treated this way, with this roundabout language), the repentant sinners are indistinguishable from other people, who are bringing an *olah*.

In terms of how the Torah is written, this deviation, this choice of language, constitutes going to great lengths to make this point, to teach this lesson. And Chazal seized upon it to establish that the Amidah, the essence of prayer, should be recited virtually silently, like the prayer of Chana. *Al chet* is recited silently. No one should hear, or witness, another's repentance. No one should be "busy" with the next person's personal sins. No one should be in a position to "enjoy" the next person's personal embarrassment.

No one's repentance should be hindered by fear of public embarrassment.

Now, if all this is true of the *inadvertent* embarrassment of simple *awareness* of someone's sins (prayer) or even the fact that someone has sinned (*korban chatas*), with so much emphasis on avoidance, what can be said about God forbid actually embarrassing someone else? Or worse, intentionally embarrassing someone else?

Or worse still, embarrassing someone else in public? *Rachmana litzlan!*

Publicly embarrassing someone is akin to murder, we are taught, and it is preferable to jump into a fiery furnace than to do so.

Most of us, on reflection, would not do so. And yet, unthinkingly, it is done all the time.

The Torah has taught us about sensitivity. If we are sensitive about language regarding animals (*tahor* and *not tahor*), what shall we say about human beings, created in God's image, who think and feel?

Sometimes we must criticize a child, a spouse, an employee, a neighbor. We may indeed do so, preferably with sensitivity. But never in public. *Never.* Our mouths are created to speak holy words. They should never be used as instruments of personal destruction. The sin is very great, and the price unbearable, *lo aleinu.*

Let us, in our relationships, stop and think. Let us condition ourselves, always, to absorb the lessons we have been so richly taught, to think carefully before we speak in any negative way to anyone or regarding anyone. For the Jew, there's much work in this life as we toil, from birth until we are gone, to earn our place in Heaven. How easy it is, and what a pity it would be, to ruin it with a careless word.

Parashas Tzav 5771

Shemini

Chai Chai

"What are your final words before sentencing?"

In the bizarre world of the evil totalitarian regime, those were the *opening words* of the trial, uttered by the judge.

Sick, barely able to stand, the prisoner, Chana, retorted *"Final words?* I haven't even said my *first* word yet!"

"You are guilty of parasitism, and sentenced to five years in prison! Take the prisoner away!" That was the entire "trial."

And she was led away to prison. Lacking the strength to walk, she held on to the chains that bound her and managed to drag herself along. On the way, she witnessed something astounding, but entirely consistent with the perverse, surreal world she found herself in. Somehow, one of her fellow prisoners managed to break free, and fled.

Realizing that they could not catch him, the guards simply grabbed someone randomly chosen off the street and bound him up, to take the place of the escapee. They needed to deliver ten prisoners, and ten prisoners they would deliver. That was the universe created by the "worker's paradise," the Soviet Union, and its god, Josef Stalin, *yemach shemo*.

The charge of parasitism was the result of an intestinal malady so severe that she could not perform the slave labor she was condemned to, as an enemy alien Polish refugee.

And so, doubled over with pain and cramps, bleeding, febrile, dehydrated, she was led off to prison. A criminal. A parasite.

In prison, she became sicker still. Ultimately, when it was nearly too late, she was transferred to a "hospital," a small, provincial place. She lay there day after day, her life in the balance. It didn't take long for her to come to know the entire small staff of nurses, doctors, and orderlies. After several weeks, with no improvement, she was told that it would be necessary to operate on her, and the surgery was scheduled.

The night before the surgery, in the middle of the night, sensing someone at her bedside, she opened her eyes and saw someone she had never seen before.

A man with white hair and a kindly face, in a doctor's uniform, stood beside her, staring at her. Quietly he asked her, in Yiddish, *"Mein shvester, vus tist di du?"* (My sister, what are you doing here?). His exact words.

"I'm to have surgery on my intestines tomorrow," she replied. He looked at her intently and asked, *"Di vilst leben?* [Do you want to live?] Don't let them operate on you! Whoever they operate on dies!"

"How do I get out of it? They do what they want!"

He told her to tell them, in the morning when they came for her, that it was that time of the month and she could not have surgery. They would defer it.

That is what she did. They canceled the surgery. She never did have that operation.

In the days and weeks afterward, she slowly improved.

And she never saw that "doctor" again.

When she asked about him, no one at the hospital knew whom she was talking about.

There was no such doctor or other staff member. *But you can guess who it was.*

Eventually they returned my mother to prison. How she ultimately emerged and was found by, and reunited with my father, who was a slave, is its own story.

When God reaches down and plucks us out of mortal danger and restores us to life and safety, we Jews utter a blessing, *birkas hagomel*. Our actual obligation, in fact, is to bring a *korban todah* (Vayikra 7:12 in Tzav; see Rashi there). The four categories of danger, escape from which specifically carries this obligation, are classically noted in Tehillim 107, *"Hodu la'Shem ki tov, ki l'olam chasdo,"* and halachically stated in *Berachos* (44b): *Amar Rabbi Yehudah amar Rav: Arba tzrichin l'hodos.* Four are required to give thanks (i.e., a *korban todah* or *birkas hagomel*): those who survive an ocean crossing, those who survive a desert, those who survive serious illness and are cured, and those who survive imprisonment and are released.

Interestingly, Tosafos remarks on the order of the four categories being different in Tehillim and in the Gemara, while the Lubavitcher Rebbe notes that Rashi, in the Chumash, lists them in yet a different order. Each has a novel explanation (outside the scope of this essay, and worth looking into).

When King Chizkiyahu was critically ill, he was informed by the prophet Yeshayahu that by God's decree he would not survive. He turned his face to the wall and prayed. God accepted his prayer and rescinded the decree. Chizkiyahu then composed his famous, immortal prayer of thanksgiving (Yeshayahu 38:19): *"Chai, chai hu yodecha, ka'moni hayom,"* he declares, *"av l'vanim yodia el amitecha"*

(A living person, a living person shall thank You, as I do today; a father who remains alive can then transmit his faith to his children).

Chai, and the repeated *chai*, are an acronym: the letters *ches* and *yud* and *ches* and *yud* are *roshei teivos* for the four categories of survivors who are obligated to bring a *todah*.

So someone who, by the grace of God, survives a desert – "*va'yitzaku el Hashem ba'tzar lahem, mi'mtzukoseihem yatzilem*" (Tehillim 107:6) – must bring a *todah*.

Someone who, by the grace of God, survives imprisonment – "*va'yizaku el Hashem ba'tzar lahem, mi'mtzukoseihem yoshiem*" (107:13) – must bring a *todah*.

Someone who, by the grace of God, survives serious illness – "*va'yizaku el Hashem ba'tzar lahem, mi'mtzukoseihem yoshiem*" (107:19) – must bring a *todah*.

And someone who, by the grace of God, survives the danger of an ocean crossing – "*va'yitzaku el Hashem ba'tzar lahem, u'mi'mtzukoseihem yotziem*" (107:28) – must bring a *todah*.

What about someone who, by the decree of God, was subjected to all four, and worse, and by His grace, survived them all (to the extent that it is possible for a human being to undergo such experiences, and to truly "survive")? What does such a person bring?

And how do you bring a *todah*, a thanksgiving offering, for having survived, when nearly everyone else – parents, children, siblings, family, loved ones, an entire civilization, one's people – did not? When the suffering of innocents was unspeakable?

When one has passed through the *emek habacha*, the vale of tears, and has become familiar, *while still alive*, with the three gates of Gehinnom?

And yet, when the Germans had my mother in their grasp, when she survived an encounter with the Gestapo while all around her there was beating and torture and mutilation and shooting, but she outsmarted them, when she escaped eastward and the Soviets did their best to harm her, but she bested them, when she and my father each and both together were subjected to all four of the above ordeals and worse, and finally made it to these blessed shores, they looked at the cold-water flat they were in (a nineteenth-century tenement, with no heat, no hot water, no toilet; I remember it), they looked at the two little red-headed sons God had sent them, they looked at their new birth of freedom, they looked at the opportunity to work honestly for a living (no welfare payments for sitting at home!), and as surviving Jews have done in the face of trouble and loss and sorrow since time immemorial, they uttered, "*Todah*." Thank You, God, for preserving our lives, and allowing us to continue life, to raise another generation of Jews, as You have mandated.

Did they ask, "Why us? Why did we live, when so many did not?" I am sure they did.

Being a survivor is nothing new for the Jew. Elazar and Isamar were *"bnei Aharon hanosarim,"* Aharon's surviving sons. There is nothing in the Torah that makes clear that they were better or otherwise more deserving of life than their two brothers, Nadav and Avihu, who were consumed by a fire that emanated from God. What their offense of *esh zarah* was we do not know exactly, but it is apparent that they were great men, pious and holy, worthy sons of Aharon Hakohen. But they died – they were killed – while their brothers survived.

When the Mishkan was being inaugurated and all was made ready, the sacrifice waiting on the Mizbe'ach (Altar), the Torah says, *Va'tetze esh mi'lifnei Hashem va'tochal*, a holy fire emanated from before God and consumed the sacrifice. The people saw, they praised God, and they bowed in prayer. And two *pesukim* later, the Torah says, *Va'tetze esh mi'lifnei Hashem*, a holy fire emanated from before God and consumed Nadav and Avihu. The identical language cannot be an accident. Clearly, there is a lesson intended. We are not told what the people did in response to this latter emanation of Godly fire, this terrible display of His power and His judgment, but one can reasonably conclude that they were in shock. We do know of Aharon's timeless response, its holy eloquence vested in his silence: *va'yidom Aharon*. "*Lecha dumiyah tehillah*" (for You silence is praise; Tehillim 65:2).

Why me? *Cheshbonei Shamayim*. God's calculations are unknown to us, and, in truth, are unknowable. We who survive can only draw the necessary and logical conclusions.

We must recognize that we have been chosen to survive, and to consider having been so chosen in making our own choices in life.

Why me? *We are all survivors. Every Jew alive today is a survivor.* Certainly, my parents and those of their generation, and their children after them, and our children after us, are survivors in a very direct sense. But given Jewish history, with all the depredations from without – and sadly, from within – every identifiable Jew in the world is, in fact, a survivor, and carries the mandate, as a survivor plucked from the flames, to do God's work on this earth, to fulfill the role set out for the People of Israel in human civilization.

Why me? What interactions will I have in life, what effect on others, on this world, that will fulfill the Creator's will for this world? What are the ramifications of every deed I do that will somehow justify my having survived? *Cheshbonei Shamayim*. Only God can really know. But what we can know is that He has chosen us to survive through history to play our role in *lesaken olam b'malchus Sha-dai*, to do our part in doing right in the world.

Nadav and Avihu fulfilled their role, somehow, *b'krovai akadesh*, and were taken from the world as young men, in a dramatic burst of flame that emanated from before God.

The millions upon millions who were cruelly taken from this world, in a very different sort of fire, but one which we have to believe was also, in some unknowable way, God's will, also fulfilled their role, somehow, and became *kedoshim*. *B'krovai akadesh*.

Why me?

Except for where He reveals it clearly, we cannot know the mind of God. As *maaminim bnei maaminim*, as His faithful children, we know that His judgments are for the ultimate good. But it should certainly be clear to us that we have been chosen to survive as part of God's plan. And as human beings with free will, it is up to us to choose to be His instruments for good in this world. Clearly, that is our obligation as it is our privilege.

It was the same Godly source of fire that inaugurated the Mikdash and that consumed Nadav and Avihu. God is telling us that it is *not* random in His world. And it is a measure of our faith to understand and to accept that.

Why me? Because God has chosen me, for His own unknowable reasons. He has indeed chosen each and every one of us. And in the exercise of our free will, it is our mandate to live our lives in justification for having been chosen.

And for that privilege, even in the face of all the pain, to be grateful. To say, "*Todah.*"

Parashas Shemini 5773

Kiri Ram

It was a lovely summer afternoon when Rabbi Luttwak came face to face with a billy goat.

The odd thing was that Rabbi Luttwak recognized the goat. Out for his afternoon constitutional on the quiet country road, he saw it standing not ten feet away, on the other side of a low stone wall. The two eyeballed each other. It wasn't by the goat's beard (*its goatee*), that he knew it, but by the trademark red bow tie around its neck. It clearly belonged to Finkelstein, proprietor of Phinkelstein's Phantastical Phun Pharm, situated nearby, a local attraction for kids (*human* children) and their families in the various summer bungalow colonies (yes, and the fancy summer homes). Somehow it had gotten away and wandered off.

The obvious thing would be to grab it and lead it back to Finkelstein, thereby fulfilling an important mitzvah. But Rabbi Luttwak was a *talmid chacham* and a *rosh yeshiva*. Dressed in his *rosh yeshiva* frock, and crowned in his *rosh yeshiva* hat, he was visibly identifiable as a *rosh yeshiva*, and climbing over the stone wall, getting his pants and shoes muddy, catching it, and walking down the road leading a goat in a red bow tie would be beneath his dignity. Knowing the Gemara (*Bava Metzia* 30a) and the *Shulchan Aruch* (Choshen Mishpat 263:1–3), he realized that he was exempt in this case from the commandment of *lo suchal l'hisalem*, you may not look away from your neighbor's lost animal, but you must, in fact, get hold of it and return it to him (Devarim 22:1–3). *Kavod haTorah* is important not only for its own sake, but reverential regard for those who represent it also safeguards it and preserves it.

Too bad, he thought, my friend Asher isn't walking with me today. He could have done it. An intelligent and learned fellow, Asher had chosen a different career path (too bad about that, his *yeshivishe* friends mused: *he coulda been somebody*), and thus would have readily, and happily, clambered over that wall and gotten hold of the goat, fulfilling the important mitzvah of *hashavas aveidah. I feel bad for poor Finkelstein. I'll call him when I get back, but who knows if he'll ever be able to find his goat by then.*

The fact is that there may have been other options for Rabbi Luttwak; there is often a subjective element to such questions, different legitimate approaches, allowing for a variety of expressions in halachah and in practice, all within the framework of Torah.

This is a delicate issue. Deference to Torah scholars must also be tempered with great care that it not engender the opposite of reverence. *Talmidei chachamim* are warned not to "step on the heads" of the people, because they represent Torah and its way of life. Rabbi Akiva famously relates (*Pesachim* 49b) that before he became learned, when he was an *am haaretz*, an ignoramus, his resentment (and that of his class) toward the rabbis was so great that he would have bitten them as viciously as a donkey bites. And it was the thousands of Rabbi Akiva's students who perished during the Sefirah period because they did not deal respectfully with each other, often interpreted as behaving haughtily.

The existential fistfight between Chassidim and Misnagdim is over. They may, in fact, squabble over various things, they may even playfully mock each other over this or that, but in the end what they have in common is much more than what separates them, and there are so many of each other's practices that they have so thoroughly adopted that it is not always obvious that they have done so, that it wasn't always their practice. But even so, differences of approach may be so striking that they may even *seem* irreconcilable in one people. And this applies not just in modern times to Chassidim and Misnagdim, but, central to human nature, it is a conflict in approach to religion that is as old as organized religion itself.

There are people whose seriousness about religion requires them to be of serious demeanor, even dour, at all times that they are occupied with things religious. For some people, their elevated and enhanced constant awareness of *yiras Shamayim* makes them also appear serious and even subdued at all times. And then there are others, also fine Jews, also quite serious about Judaism, whose religious fervor is expressed differently. Their joyousness is obvious. And they can, of course, both be correct.

So too, different people, equally observant, may have different spiritual sensitivities to the intangibles of the spiritual universe. The same thing may affect one person considerably, for better or worse, and another person not at all. An example would be seeing a symbol of *avodah zarah*, or even more striking, seeing something only *suggestive* of a symbol of *avodah zarah*, even unintentional. I submit that those who are sensitive to such things are susceptible to being affected by them in some spiritual but real way, while those who are not, are not, or if they are, to a very small extent.

In the waning days of the leadership and the life of Eli Hakohen, Israel found itself yet again in violent conflict with the warlike Philistines. Locked in struggle, stymied, battered, they resorted to removing the Aron Hakodesh from its resting place in the Tabernacle at Shiloh and carrying it into battle with them. They should not have done so.

The Philistines, at first, were frightened and intimidated by its presence. But, true to their warlike nature, they "girded their loins," redoubled their efforts, and won the day. There was a mass slaughter of Jews, the two sons of Eli were killed, and the Ark was captured.

Capturing the Ark turned out to be no blessing for the Philistines. They brought it to Ashdod, where the people were afflicted with terrible suffering: not only did they get severe, painful hemorrhoids, they were bitten in their hemorrhoids by savage mice. Ashdod sent the Ark to Gat, where the same thing happened. Gat sent it to Ekron. The Ekronites fared no better. The only solution for them was to send the Ark back to the Jews. They placed it in a new, clean, never-used wagon (out of respect), along with a peace offering of five golden hemorrhoids and five golden mice (!). They let the cows pulling the wagon find their own way. They headed straight to the Jewish settlement of Beit Shemesh.

Beit Shemesh rejoiced, but when they behaved somewhat irreverently, many died. So off they sent it to Kiryat Ye'arim, and it finally sat twenty years in the home of Avinadav in Givah.

Now under Shmuel's leadership, the people repented and went on to defeat the Philistines.

Fast-forward to David Hamelech, who, having established his capital in Jerusalem, undertook to bring the Ark there, in anticipation of the building of the Beis Hamikdash. David had the Ark placed in a new, clean wagon (as had the Philistines). He was seriously faulted for this, as the Ark must be carried on the shoulders of the Levites (and even then, it really carries itself).

Along the way, Uzza, a righteous man, saw the oxen falter, and he reached out his hand to support the Ark, perhaps instinctively, to keep it from falling. He should not have done so. The Ark would not fall, and Uzza had no right to touch it. For this he was struck down dead.

This scene is described in the *haftarah* of Parashas Shemini. The obvious connection, and the striking parallel, lies in the sudden death, from Heaven, of otherwise righteous people who made a fatal miscalculation at the moment of the exalted celebration of the initiation of a holy Sanctuary (Uzza here and Nadav and Avihu at the consecration of the Mishkan in the desert).

David was sorely vexed. Rather than continue to Jerusalem, the Ark was deposited in the home of Oved Edom. In the three months it was there, Oved Edom's home and family were greatly blessed. David then brought it, with great celebration and fanfare, to Jerusalem.

The joy was very great. David wore his most festive robes. He danced and sang with all his might, *mefazez u'mecharker* (II Shmuel 6:16). He hopped and stomped and shouted and sang. He kicked up his heels. He clapped his hands and shouted, *"Kiri Ram! Kiri Ram!"*

Midrash Rabbah (Bamidbar 4:20): Come and see how much David made little his own personal honor in order to honor God. It would have been normal for him to march sedately before the Ark, dressed in his royal robes. Rather, he donned festive robes and rejoiced merrily before it, with all his strength, to do it honor. He danced mightily, and with each clap of his hands he called out, *"Kiri Ram!"* meaning "I am a servant [כירי – see *Eruvin* 53b] of God the Most High! [רם]." And in response, all of Israel sang out and shouted and blew rams horns and played all manner of musical instruments.

When the procession entered Jerusalem, all the women peered down from the balconies and the rooftops to watch David dance and celebrate. The king had no qualms about his *kavod* in this, and he worried not at all about his dignity. His wife, Michal, the daughter of the late King Saul, whom David replaced on the throne of Israel, was sorely displeased and ashamed of him.

She came out to taunt him. "How honored is this day, O king of Israel! You exposed yourself before the handmaids of your servants, as would a low idler expose himself!" David had raised the hem of his garment while dancing, so that his ankles had been visible. She was mortified at his lack of hauteur, of royal dignity.

David shot back: I rejoiced thus before the Lord Who chose me over your father and all his house, to appoint me prince over His nation, Israel. And, in His honor, I would readily debase myself even more, yes, even before those maidservants before whom you think I should act haughty.

Poor Michal did very poorly in life after that.

Citing this episode, Rambam, in Hilchos Lulav and Esrog (8:15), writes that active rejoicing in the performance of a mitzvah is a high order of worship, and one who holds back will pay for that. Whosoever arrogantly stands on his own dignity at such times and imagines that he is, in so doing, enhancing his own honor is a sinner and a fool. But one who humbles and even demeans himself on such occasions achieves greatness and honor, for he serves God from love. For King David taught us that true greatness and honor derive from rejoicing before the Lord, even as David hopped and whirled before the Lord.

Why did Uzza die for reaching out to steady the Ark, when quite apparently the heathen Philistines were able to handle it as they moved it from place to place, without being struck down? Why did Nadav and Avihu die for their halachic misstep? Exactly *because* of their exalted spiritual status. The greater the spiritual sensitivity, the greater the vulnerability.

In a similar vein, people who are sensitive to the spiritual negativity of symbols of *avodah zarah* are, in fact, affected by it, even in the physical realm, in a way that others are not.

There are various, parallel paths to God. Not everyone is built the same. There are those who rejoice in Him in a manner that anyone would recognize as rejoicing, and there are those whose love of God and His mitzvos is no less, but who externally exhibit it less obviously. And even then, it is less obvious mainly to those who don't really understand them.

You can buy those silly pictures of "dancing Chassidim," whirling figures in *shtreimels* and flying *gartels*, in any tourist shop in Israel. You are not likely to find even one picture of "dancing Misnagdim." And yet Misnagdim do dance (at least a little), and (in their own way) do rejoice fully in the Lord and in His service. That David Hamelech was obviously *chassidish* (!) doesn't take away from anyone else's rejoicing with all his might before the Lord, in whatever form that takes.

Rabbi Luttwak, a very fine man, who felt for Finkelstein and his loss, nevertheless did what he had to do to serve God in the way he understood, and was taught, by upholding the dignity of Torah scholarship. It was not his own honor he was safeguarding, but the image of the Torah scholar, the repository of God's teaching. He could not allow himself to be seen chasing a goat in the fields. He did what was for him the right thing. (By the way, in the end Finkelstein got his goat back. Asher, only a doctor, came across it in the fields, gave chase, and brought it home to Phinkelstein's Phantastical Phun Pharm.)

Haughtiness is diametrically opposed to Godliness. There are those, unfortunately, who seek honor in this world more than they seek God, and even hide behind a cloak of religion in their quest for honor and power. There are those who are so busy safeguarding their own *kavod* that there is no room in their hearts and in their actions for *kavod habrios*, the honor of their fellow human beings, or for *kavod Shamayim*, the honor of God.

Haughtiness closes one's heart off and turns it cold. It is altogether removed from what the Jewish heart should be. The true Jewish heart pulses with love of God, love of His Torah, love of one's fellow Jew, love of one's fellow human being. The true Jewish heart serves God with unbridled and unselfconscious joy, whatever form that might take. The true Jewish heart, in the service of our Father in Heaven, dances and jumps and whirls, kicks up its heels, claps its hands, and calls out to Him, *"Kiri Ram! Kiri Ram!"* I am your servant, O God Most High.

Parashas Shemini 5776

Latching On

My father's was more or less the last generation to take up smoking without knowing how unhealthy that practice is. He was about twelve years old when he started, as were most of his peers.

My brother and I worked hard to get him to stop, making it our key demand before returning the afikomen to him. He did, indeed, stop. But I don't really know if it was our efforts that did it, or his visiting his older brother, who had just come home after a major heart attack, and finding him smoking in his sickbed.

"Kein yinger vell ich shoyn nisht shtarben," my uncle told him. I won't die young anymore, he said. Uncle Mendek (Menachem Mendel) thought it was funny. Father did not.

What my uncle was saying, of course, was that at that point it would no longer make any difference if he smoked or not. So why be deprived of the comfort of a lifelong, addictive habit? He was wrong in his case, but there is a logic to that perspective that can, indeed, hold true in more appropriate cases.

Every sick person with a loving family knows what it is like to be hounded by worried, caring relatives not to engage in practices that cause further deterioration of their health.

We've all seen relatives who sneak that piece of cake, that salty herring, that cigarette, grown men fearful of being caught – and upbraided – by their loving, concerned, and exasperated kin. It is only when someone is so far gone that nothing makes a difference anymore that they are freed of their restrictions, for the short time they have left.

Parashas Shemini contains a long list of the types and categories and specifics of what a Jew may eat and what he may not. God gave mankind broad latitude in eating essentially anything on earth that he desires, whether vegetable or animal, with the exception of the limb torn from a still living animal (*ever min hachai*). For the Jew it is quite different. For him the stakes are much higher, and thus the requirements placed upon him are far more stringent.

Thus, says Rabbi Tanchuma in *Midrash Rabbah*, the spiritual purity that a Jew must attain in order to achieve what he, as a Jew and as one who serves the Creator through His Torah and mitzvos, can and should achieve, is different from that expected of the rest of mankind, however decent and upright those others might be. It is our unique legacy, and our unique burden of privilege. What may be perfectly appropriate for others can be entirely inappropriate, spiritually unhealthy, and forbidden for us. What is harmless for others may be utterly devastating for us. What makes no difference for others makes for us all the difference in the world.

Comes the Sforno and raises the stakes even further: what would eventually become the laws of *kashrus*, and other mitzvos that acquire and safeguard holiness for Israel, existed in the mind and the will of God long before Israel or the world existed. They would have been commandments to us even had we not sinned so grievously with the Golden Calf. But our forefathers did sin, and in so doing, lost something irretrievable.

At their most glorious moment at Sinai, our forebears famously proclaimed *naaseh v'nishma*. Specifically declaring their commitment *to obey and to do* even before undertaking to hear and to learn what it was God required of them, it was an act of utter faith and devotion. Upon that declaration, each Jew received two crowns upon his head, one for *naaseh*, and one for *nishma*. *Pesachim* 88a tells us that when our forefathers placed *naaseh* before *nishma*, six hundred thousand angels, *malachei hashares*, descended from Heaven and placed two such crowns, referred to as *edyom*, upon each Jew's head. They were not made of gold or jewels, Rashi tells us: they were made from the Ziv Hashechinah (the glow emanating from the Shechinah itself). They were a bond of absolute connection to God, attached to each and every person in Israel, requiring no intermediary and no device to maintain that connection. The Shechinah would rest on each Jew directly.

After their frightful sin, their downfall with the Golden Calf, that was lost. The Gemara goes on to relate that 1.2 million angels of destruction, *malachei chabalah*, descended and snatched those crowns away: *Va'yisnatzlu Bnei Yisrael es edyom* (Shemos 33:6), they lost their crowns. Upon Moshe's entreaties, God forgave them, but it would no longer be quite the same. He would still bring them safely to the Promised Land, but He would distance Himself from them: *ki lo e'eleh b'kirbecha* (Shemos 33:3), I will not go up there in your midst. *Lo sigal nafshi eschem* (Vayikra 26:11); God was much put off by them.

But, ever their champion, Moshe fought to find some way to bring them back into God's Presence, in whatever way possible. And so, the very mitzvos that would have been, that *should* have been, a *product* of that intimate bond with God's holiness, a celebration of it, became the *means* by which they could somehow still connect to it, although at a much lower level than it could have been, had they not sinned and thrown that bond away.

By clinging to *taharah*, to purity, and eschewing *tumah*, through what we choose to eat; by not ingesting foods that, in a metaphysical way, *metamim es hanefesh*, that contaminate the Jewish soul within us; by a Torah-infused life, by the myriad of choices we make in daily life, we can still, even shorn of our crowns, bereft of the Ziv Hashechinah that for a shining brief moment glowed upon our heads, we can still latch on to Him. By holding fast to the Torah and mitzvos, through the *taharah* we can achieve thereby, we also hold fast to our Father in Heaven, Who, although, by our own doing, is to a degree withdrawn, is also, by His own promise, never too far away.

Parashas Shemini 5775

Use It or Lose It: Don't Abuse It

Gaavah – haughtiness, pride – is considered one of the lowest character traits.

The Torah makes a point of informing us that Moshe Rabbenu, our greatest leader ever, the greatest prophet ever, was exactly the opposite: *anav* – the humblest man on the face of the earth.

And yet, we are taught that a *talmid chacham* should have a *sheminis she'b'sheminis*, "an eighth of an eighth" of a measure of *gaavah*. This is often explained as the need to stand up for what he represents, Torah and the Jewish way of life.

Our *parashah* hints at another perspective on humility, its greatness, *and its inherent risks.*

The *parashah*, aptly called Shemini, opens on the eighth day of the inauguration of the Mishkan. For the first seven days, Moshe set up the Mishkan each day and did the daily service, functioning as the Kohen Gadol. On the eighth day, Aharon was to replace Moshe as Kohen Gadol, with his sons as the Kohanim, that function remaining with Aharon and his descendants forever.

Moshe sets everything up, and now it's Aharon's turn to step up and take over as Kohen Gadol. Aharon stands there with his prepared *korban* and doesn't move. What's wrong?

Rashi explains what happened. *She'haya Aharon bosh.* Aharon was too shy, modest, and humble to assume so monumental a position. He was a very great man, self-effacing, happy to let others have the glory. He considered himself unworthy to be Kohen Gadol. Indeed, his very modesty concerning his being chosen indicates what an appropriate choice he was.

Remember that Moshe, back when his mission first began, at the Burning Bush, was concerned that as the younger brother, he was stepping on his big brother Aharon's toes by assuming the leadership. Hashem told him that Aharon was coming to greet him, genuinely *happy in his heart* at Moshe's elevation, with no jealousy or secret resentment.

So total self-effacement is always a good thing, right? Not necessarily. Remembering his own sad predicament, Moshe had words of advice for his brother: *Lama ata bosh? L'chach nivcharta!* Why are you so shy and reluctant? *For this you were chosen!*

This eighth day was a terribly sad day for Moshe. He was, in fact, "supposed to be" the Kohen Gadol himself, with his children following forever after. But he lost that opportunity back at the Burning Bush, when Hashem gave him his mandate to be the leader and redeemer, and when, in his great modesty, he resisted and argued with God for a full week. Finally, Hashem said to him, with some anger, *Enough! I am God, I made you, I made you for this purpose, now go and do what I require of you. Aharon will help you.*

Moshe went. But his resistance, his extreme reluctance, to the point of "fighting off" Hashem for the sake of his own modesty, cost Moshe a great deal. He was Kohen Gadol for seven days, the same time period he spent trying to deny his own mission. And then he was replaced by Aharon on the eighth day.

The loss of the opportunity to serve Hashem this way was a great blow to Moshe. And the cost extended way beyond Moshe himself. Aharon the Kohen Gadol lives on forever as Kohen Gadol through the continuing *kehunah* of all his subsequent generations. We know of the many Kohanim Gedolim, generations who followed Aharon. Every Kohen alive today knows he is Aharon's *einikel* and carries his holy mission in him and which will remain in his line forever. But who ever heard anything of Moshe's descendants after another generation?

I Divrei Hayamim (23:13) cites Aharon and his great generations of Kohanim performing the holy service. Moshe's generations, while numerous, disappear anonymously into the general tribe of Levi, without a discernible trace. Excessive self-effacement brought to its logical conclusion.

Moshe says to Aharon: *Now is not the time to be overly shy! Look what happened to me! Go! Do it! You were chosen for this! Don't let what happened to me happen to you.*

My father, a"h, used to teach me that too much of anything is no good. "*Afilu tzi git iz oych nisht git.*" Even too good is also not good. It's possible for too modest to be no good. We each have a mission in life. God put each of us here for a purpose. We must honor God by fulfilling that purpose. We must do what we can and what it takes to fulfill that purpose. A leader must lead. A prophet must prophesy. We soldiers must…soldier on. We usually know what we should do. The trick is to have the backbone and the determination and the honesty to do it.

Each of us is "it" for some important role in this world. The Creator implanted within us the wherewithal to fulfill that role. That's part of the "it" that constitutes our core strength and our potential. One lesson of Shemini, the day that Moshe and all his subsequent generations lost the *kehunah*, is that Hashem expects us to be the "it" He made us to be, that He gave us the strength to be, each according to his own abilities. And not to use that strength is to lose it. And to abuse it. And pity, pity for the loss.

Parashas Shemini 5771

Uzza

What did Uzza do that was so bad?

When David Hamelech, with great fanfare, was bringing the Aron Kodesh back from its "exile" of having been captured and then returned by the Plishtim, the two sons of Avinadav – the man in whose house it had rested for months, bringing much blessing to that house – led and walked along with the wagon carrying the ark, Achyo in front and Uzza by the side. At one point the oxen stumbled and the Ark appeared to be falling off the wagon. Uzza reached out to support it and was struck down dead, an act of God. He had had no right to do so. No one other than a designated Levi may touch the Ark, and the Ark does not need to be supported. Indeed, it supports, it carries those who "carry" it. It carries itself. And so by reaching out to support it, Uzza in effect publicly denigrated it. And for that he paid with his life in a public spectacle (II Shmuel 6). A very grave lesson in reverence for things holy was taught.

Wow. The Aron Kodesh was to all appearances about to fall off the wagon onto the ground. What was Uzza supposed to do? Even if in the *midbar* the legal protocol was very specific and very strict about the handling of the Aron, more than four hundred years had passed and a lot of mundane handling, without any recorded thunderbolts, had taken place since. Perhaps those original rules applied only in the *midbar*. Why should Uzza have concluded that the original rules in the *midbar* applied right now? It was falling! Should he have stood by and let it fall? If it had been captured and carried off by the Philistines, why should it now be immune from falling? Would he have been honoring it more if he just let it fall to the ground? How could he know for sure that it would not?

We know, after the fact, that it would not, in the end, have fallen to the ground. We know, after the fact, that David Hamelech was wrong to place it onto a cart rather than have the Leviim carry it. But Uzza was, in fact, following the instructions of his master, King David. Should he have been *moreh halachah bi'fnei rabbo*? Doing that is one of the sins that have been offered as explanation for the deaths of Nadav and Avihu.

The Plishtim apparently carried the Ark without being struck down. They later suffered for keeping it in their domain, so they were ultimately compelled to return it. But Scripture says nothing about anything happening to those who picked it up and made off with it. Indeed, how would it have gotten to Philistia had they not picked it up?

And further, the Aron Kodesh that Uzza touched, according to the Midrash, may not have even contained the *luchos* (the Tablets of the Law from Mount Sinai) at all! According to this view, just as the Plishtim were making off with it, a very brave and mighty man of the tribe of Binyamin, identified as Shaul, who would later be king, swept down and rescued the *luchos* themselves from the Ark as it was being carried off, and returned them to Eli Hakohen in Shiloh. Shaul was not struck down for grabbing the *luchos* themselves. Why should Uzza have been struck down for supporting what might have in fact been a holy but empty ark?

And so, it seems, what happened to Uzza was an extraordinary event, outside the realm of our usual sense of justice. And we read this portion of the Navi as the *haftarah* for Parashas Shemini, in which another similar extraordinary event occurs, the sudden striking down dead of Nadav and Avihu, the two older sons of Aharon Hakohen, for the ill-defined offense of *"esh zarah."*

We don't really have a precise understanding of *esh zarah*, and what their offense actually was. There are a number of explanations offered by Chazal, which vary widely in the nature and degree of apparent offense. In some renditions Nadav and Avihu are serious cads; in others they are wholly righteous. We just don't really know. But there is a natural inclination, given our God-given sense of justice, and our God-given mandate to judge judiciously, to find some serious fault in their behavior that makes sense of their shocking fiery demise.

One might conjecture that the story of Uzza, and its reading at the same time as the story of Nadav and Avihu, comes for the very purpose of being *melamed zechus* on behalf of Aharon's sons. They erred, and they paid with their lives for it. But perhaps their error should be judged kindly by *us*, even as it appears that Uzza should be judged kindly by us. That they each paid with their lives for what we would normally not consider a capital offense serves to teach us yet another critical lesson, one which I believe we need to learn if we are to maintain our sanity and our religious balance as we consider this world we live in.

God is just, and He demands that we be just in our lives and in our civilization. But we need to understand that there is a realm of justice that is beyond our under-standing, a realm in which all of the past, present, and future, opaque to us but all perfectly clear to God, are simultaneously in focus before Him as He makes His divine judgments in the world. The terrible mystery of *tzaddik v'ra lo* is no mystery to Him. The seemingly small infractions for which tzaddikim may pay with their lives, but which serve as a lesson and a lifesaving warning to the rest of us about proper reverence before God, is no mystery to Him.

It is for us to recognize and to learn those lessons, not only to be zealous and careful in our own reverence, not only to understand and accept that there is much that we cannot understand even as we carry on faithfully, but also to accept those bewildering lessons in the way Aharon taught us, with his great faith, the only possible response to the unknowables of divine justice, to the unanswerable ques-tions that we cannot allow to weaken our faith: *va'yidom Aharon*, the dignified acquiescence of faithful silence.

Parashas Shemini 5777

Who Will Dedicate His Heart to Be Close to Me?

"Ki mi hu zeh arav es libo lageshes Elai?" (Who is he who will devote himself, dedicate his heart, to be close to Me? Yirmiyahu 30:21).

Esav came in from the fields, well satisfied with his day's work.

The Torah does not spell it out, but we know what he had been up to.

On that day he turned his back on everything his parents, Yitzchak and Rivkah, stood for, everything his holy grandfather Avraham Avinu represented. In a fit of spiritual Schadenfreude, he broke with God and with everything holy that he had been taught, and willfully committed the most grievous cardinal sins. And he established himself, forever, as the antithesis of everything holy, the complete opposite of his brother Yaakov.

Esav encountered Yaakov preparing lentils. "What's this?" From the earliest times, he knew, such a lentil dish was prepared specifically for mourners. "Who died?"

Midrash Rabbah (Bereishis 63:13) describes Esav's reaction to the news that his grandfather Avraham had passed away. "Can it be that that tzaddik is also susceptible to the *malach hamaves* like anyone else? Hah! I knew it! *Leis din v'leis dayan!* There is no Judge and no justice in the universe! If there were, a perfect tzaddik like Avraham would never have died!"

Like many self-absorbed and self-centered people, Esav was oblivious and indifferent to the consequences of his own actions, and it never occurred to him that the very reason Avraham passed away that day – five years earlier than he would have – was because God wanted to spare him the sight of his own grandchild, Esav, rebelling against God and everything holy and good.

And how convenient for Esav that Avraham's death provided him with a "justification," however specious (and after the fact), for his own malfeasance.

The death of a tzaddik, it seems, is in fact different and has its own special considerations.

There is a tradition that on Yom Kippur, when we read in the Torah about the death of the two sons of Aharon, Nadav and Avihu, whoever sheds heartfelt tears over that tragedy will be protected against losing his own sons in his lifetime.

There are those who interpret their deaths as the result of a flaw in their behavior or even their character. Others see it more in terms of an error on their part. Virtually all commentators understand that their deaths resulted from a basis of judgment far removed from normal standards of justice. It's as if they were struck down more to make a point than because they deserved it. They were, in fact, great tzaddikim, and it was in that fact that Aharon found solace.

So why did they have to die, burned from the inside out?

Moshe tells the horrified Aharon that God had revealed to him in advance that when He would come to rest His presence among the Jews (with the establishment of the Mishkan), the occasion would be "sanctified" with the death of those close to Him: "B'krovai akadesh." Moshe had not known, however, who it would be.

Do you understand that? I don't.

Yes, I have seen the *meforshim*. Yes, I understand that sometimes the death of tzaddikim can be a *kapparah* for that generation. Yes, the various commentators talk matter of factly about the death of these two great young men largely because *someone close to God had to die*. Yes, after the *egel* and God's forgiveness for it, after their seeming to have "gotten away with it," it was necessary to teach a strict lesson about treating God and the Mikdash with the utmost care and reverence. But in truth, I don't really get it. I never have, and I suspect that most people, even the most learned, also don't. The words of explanation are easily mouthed. But they are not easily understood.

I am not so learned. But I do have a pretty good understanding of Judaism, and how our system works, how God has ordained for us a system of life and beliefs based on His goodness and His immutable law. It always makes sense. Even the laws whose reasons are unknown to us still make sense within that overall system.

And so the idea that somebody holy *had* to die to mark the establishment of the Mishkan, and its matter-of-fact acceptance by the commentators, *explained as if it makes sense to us*, is something I have never really understood. I suppose it's my own shortcoming. But I suspect I am far from alone in this.

There is much we do not understand about life. The age-old problem of "theodicy," the existence and the allowance by an all knowing, all-benevolent God of evil, often gratuitous evil, in the world – *tzaddik v'ra lo*, the suffering of innocents – remains a challenge we can deal with only through faith. The Big One – the Holocaust – remains an unanswerable mystery to mortal man.

What happened to Nadav and Avihu is not as altogether unimaginable as the classic case of *tzaddik v'ra lo*. They were, after all, culpable. Their punishment was harsh by usual standards, but the occasion of their fatal encounter was anything but usual.

But why a tzaddik, or tzaddikim, *had* to die upon the inauguration of the Mishkan remains, I believe, a mystery understood only by God.

"*Hatzaddik avad, v'ein ish sam al lev v'anshei chesed ne'esafim b'ein mevin ki mi'fnei haraah ne'esaf hatzaddik*" (The tzaddik dies and people do not contemplate why; they do not understand that it is because of the impending evil that the tzaddik is taken away; Yeshayahu 57:1).

This apparently has two meanings. The tzaddik dies as a result of the evil done by others in his generation – part of the package, the burden of being a tzaddik, rendering him different from other people. And sometimes the tzaddik dies to spare him from the evil that is about to befall his generation. Thus, Avraham Avinu died five years early to spare him the sight of his grandson Esav becoming a total *rasha*.

A few years ago, I had the opportunity to visit one of the great tzaddikim of our generation. Like the others present, I sought his blessing. The room was crowded, so people bent over to whisper their stories to him privately. As the man just before me straightened up, I could see the anguish on his face as he exclaimed, "*Lamah? Lamah?* Why? Why?!" It was heartbreaking. The tzaddik looked at him with compassionate eyes and said the only thing he could say, which was the only truth and the only consolation that he could offer: "*Cheshbonei Shamayim.*" This is the will of God, according to His understanding and His judgment.

As children of God, as people of faith, it is something we must accept. And if we accept it, accept it with the full strength of that faith.

To the person of faith, this is the ultimate challenge. May we never be tested.

Please, Ribbono shel Olam, please, please, may we never be tested. The Torah, God's blueprint for a Jew's journey through this life, offers a formula to help us cope: *Tamim tihyeh im Hashem Elokecha.* Be wholehearted with your God. Rashi, who himself suffered through the depredations of the murderous Crusaders, explains: *Walk with Him (God) wholeheartedly, look to Him, cling to Him; whatever He ordains for you accept wholeheartedly and with perfect faith. Then you will be with Him; you will be His (and He will be yours).*

What was God's reasoning for ordaining the deaths associated with *b'krovai akadesh*?

I don't know. But I believe it does serve as a vehicle to help us understand this matter of wholehearted faith.

Most of us know people who lived through the hellish nightmare of the Holocaust, whose suffering and loss are unimaginable. Among them are those who, after all that God allowed to happen to them and their loved ones, still get up each morning and say *modeh ani, thank You, God*. How do they do that? And there are those who have been at war with God, or at least divorced from Him, since then. And it is not for us to judge them. *How can we?*

And so, when a Jew is sorely tested, *lo aleinu*, as were the murdered victims of the Holocaust and the thousands of other such tragedies in our turbulent history, and those close to them who witnessed, experienced, but survived those deaths, the defining moment for *b'krovai akadesh* becomes manifest. What camp will they fall into?

Are they so wholeheartedly and completely tied to God that they can withstand the natural and utterly normal inclination, at the very least, to rethink their relationship with Him?

These are the "krovai," those who are close to God, those who are unalterably and irrevocably bound to God, whose wholehearted connection and devotion to Him are such that they will never let go, no matter what. That is what makes them "krovai," says God. That is what makes them Mine. And through them, says God, through that kind of devotion, "akadesh": My holiness becomes manifest in the world.

As to the others, I have to say that their suffering makes them His as well, but in a different way. And that difference is between them and God.

Aharon's reaction to the sudden burning up of his sons had to be one of shock and horror. But his response, the Torah tells us, as he gained understanding of what happened, was silence. Va'yidom Aharon.

Much is made of that famous silence. He is praised for it, and he is rewarded for it.

The point of that silence is not only, I believe, because he accepted God's judgment, or because he came to understand that his lost sons were tzaddikim after all.

Aharon's silence teaches us much about how a human being, whom God created to be a normal person, can serve God in extraordinary, abnormal circumstances.

Would it be normal to witness the burning death of one's two sons and then shout out jubilantly, "Hallelujah! Praise the Lord!"? There are people who might do that, but don't count on them for a sound, sane opinion on anything.

Sometimes, the silence of acceptance speaks more eloquently and profoundly than any words.

Aharon's dignified, sane silence – not complaining, not rebelling, not ranting against God, and not an inappropriate, bizarre ebullience over his sons' tzidkus and their role in the fulfillment of the divine will – was the only appropriate response from a man of his stature, and an eternal lesson to us.

Chazal tell us that that silence was rewarded with a portion of the Torah being transmitted directly from God to Aharon rather than through Moshe. There is yet another reward, related by the Midrash. There are various words that could have been used to describe Aharon's silence. The word va'yidom derives from domem, a term typically applied to an inanimate object, such as a stone. The High Priest of Israel, a man of great honor, respect, and importance, held himself as humbly as if he were but a stone.

And va'yidom is numerically sixty, the number of letters in the Birkas Kohanim, the divine blessing Aharon and his descendants were later privileged to become the conduits for, as, for all generations, God bestows His blessing of peace upon His children, Israel.

Aharon, the *ohev shalom v'rodef shalom* among his fellow men, made his peace with God in such a superlative way that he and his children after him were chosen to become the vessels through which God blesses His people with the ultimate blessing in life, *peace*.

Life can be very sweet. Life can be painful and turbulent. For most of us, there is some of both. We pray, of course, for more of the former. The reality for each of us is as God, in His beneficent wisdom, ordains. But even the good things in life cannot be enjoyed without the blessing of peace, which makes that enjoyment possible.

The story of Nadav and Avihu, and their bereft father Aharon, is for us a lesson and a metaphor for what people experience in life, and how a person can cope. The Torah is teaching us how to hold on tight, to cling to God with wholehearted faith, to understand what our role is when the events that engulf us are not understandable. Indeed, please God, may we never be so tested. But those who, in the storms of life, make of themselves "*krovai*" cause God to declare that through them "*akadesh*," His Name is sanctified. And *Harofeh l'shvurei lev u'mechabesh l'atzvosam*, He is the Healer of the brokenhearted, the One Who binds up their sorrows.

And in the end, they come to know and appreciate and deserve *shalom* as no one else ever could.

Parashas Shemini 5772

Tazria-Metzora

Goodness Gracious, Gracious Goodness

We all know how it works: *white is pure and good*.

The good guy cowboy is the one in the white hat.

The pure, virtuous bride wears a white wedding gown.

The white dove symbolizes peace, purity, and promise.

When a Jew is dressed, after 120, to meet his Maker, it is in a white kittel.

The red wool strip tied to the *azazel* goat on Yom Kippur turned pure white as a sign of God's forgiveness, *white as the [pure] snow* (see Yeshayahu 1:18 and *Yoma* 67a).

There are innumerable allusions in Jewish and general literature to white in this way.

White is pure and good. *White good, dark bad!*

And so it's interesting that the determining factor in whether a skin lesion is the type that causes serious *tzaraas tumah*, a profound spiritual uncleanliness, is its *whiteness* (Vayikra 13:3). *Dark good, white bad!* Why, in this particular instance, is it the opposite of the usual?

The Itturei Torah asks this great question. And the answer he quotes is even better than the question.

It's Sunday afternoon, and you're trying to get some work done, or you're in the middle of something with your family, and the doorbell rings. For the umpteenth time that day, it's a collector. It's seven o'clock on a weeknight, you're tired and tense from the day's work, you need to relax, you just sat down to a dinner that is only good if you eat it fresh and hot straight from the oven, and there's the doorbell: another collector. Doesn't he know this is when working people eat dinner? *Of course he does! That's when he'll find you at home! That's exactly why he's here now!*

You just finished with one collector, and you realize that the one at your door was in the same car as the previous one, but was lurking nearby, waiting for his turn as the driver kept his car out of sight. This latter one complains when you give him less than you gave his colleague.

You're at the Kotel trying to concentrate on your prayers when a hand is shoved under your nose: another "pro" collector working the crowd, indifferent to what you came there for. You're walking along purposefully, headed to an appointment. Walking in the opposite direction is someone who is also obviously purposefully headed somewhere. But then you see that person look at you, size you up, and veer toward you with his hand out, an opportunistic collector who never misses an opportunity.

These scenarios wouldn't be so bad if we really knew that those people are truly needy and deserving. Sadly, we don't really know for sure. And even if they are, that doesn't stop them from being annoying.

So do you chase away the poor wretch at your door? Of course you don't. A Jew would never do that. And if someone were to do so, check his *yichus*. A Jew just doesn't do that. You would give him at least something. But *how* would you give it to him?

How would you address him? As an annoyance? Would either your words, your face, or your manner reveal to him just what an annoying nudnik his presence makes him?

Let's assume he really is legitimate. He really is needy. He knows that he has been unable to provide for his family. It may well have been beyond his control, but many men in such a circumstance would see themselves as failures. How can this fellow feel, standing at your door, asking for a handout? How we deal with these people in a non-monetary way reveals much more about us than the actual amount we give them reveals about our finances or our financial generosity.

A mean-spirited person might make the poor fellow feel like dirt even as he gives him a handout. Instead of a kind word, which itself is part of the mitzvah of tzedakah, he humiliates or embarrasses the poor person. That is evil, that is a grave sin, that is akin to murder, that is *tzoras ayin*, a mean-spirited indifference to the suffering of others, and its punishment in the Torah is *tzaraas* (see *Arachin* 16a and *Chagigah* 5a). The *middah k'neged middah* is that instead of bringing whiteness as purity into the world, which he could have done and should have done, he has brought whiteness as *tumas tzaraas*. What is usually the universal sign of purity becomes, for him, the badge of *tumah*.

There is a sin called *onaas devarim*, oppressing someone with words (or, I would suggest, even attitude): "*V'lo sonu ish es amiso v'yareisa me'Elokecha*" (Vayikra 25:17).

It's apparent from the *pesukim* that our ability to stay secure in the land depends on our observing this mitzvah. The Gemara (*Bava Metzia* 58a, b) concludes that one who publicly shames someone, who causes him to blanche, to turn *white*, as, in his humiliation, the blood drains from his face, is one of the rare sinners who loses his portion in *olam haba*. He has, in a sense, "killed" that person (who turned white, like a corpse), but he has done so in a way that is, in a sense, beyond murder.

To humiliate the poor person, who is already humiliated enough because he must beg, is indeed beyond any excuse. Like the speaker of *lashon hara*, he damages his victim callously in a way that only a human being is capable of, and which God cannot abide.

He is marked by *tzaraas*. And the sign of that *tzaraas* is a white lesion, reminiscent of what he did to his victim.

Now, remember, what was this guilty person doing that brought about his guilt? He was doing a good deed! He was giving tzedakah! The Gemara (*Chagigah* 5a) relates that Rabbi Yochanan would weep upon reciting the *pasuk* in Koheles (12:14, the final verse): "God will judge every deed, every hidden thing, whether it be good or evil." Why weep about *good* deeds? Because even when we do good, we may God forbid spoil it by doing it in a negative way, perhaps in the end doing more harm than good. Rav Yannai offers an example: one who gives charity to a poor person but embarrasses him in the process. It would be better for both of them, Rav Yannai asserts, if he had not given the charity at all.

The Satan is such a devil. He tries to get us to do bad things. If he fails at that, he tries to get us not to do good things. And if he fails at that, he tries to get us to *regret* having done the good thing we did.

Chazal describe what the Satan did to try to stop Avraham from bringing Yitzchak to the Akeidah. In the end, when Avraham performed faithfully as commanded by God, the Satan used the death of Sarah immediately afterward to try to make Avraham feel sorry he did it. Fortunately for us, Avraham was Avraham.

And so each night we pray, *v'hoser Satan mi'l'faneinu u'me'achareinu*. Ribbono shel Olam, please remove the Satan from before us and from *behind* us, for this very reason: that we never be deterred from doing the right thing, that we never regret having done it, and that we don't spoil it with some foolish or thoughtless word or deed.

It's actually easy to spoil something good done with basically good intentions. Just ask any husband who tried to say or do something good and then got himself into deep trouble by slipping up in some silly way that not only ruined it all but left him in much worse shape than when he started.

My mother, *a"h*, taught me that if you are going to do something for someone, even reluctantly, make sure you do it graciously. You're doing it anyway. Make the most of it by doing it with a smile, with a nice disposition.

When that miserable poor person has his hand out – and he *has* to be miserable, to a greater or lesser degree – you know that as a child of our Avos and Imahos, as a person with *chesed* imprinted in his DNA, you will give. It may be more, it may be less, but you will not say no. And when you do say yes, when you do connect with that recipient by giving him what he needs, give it to him *in the way that he needs*, and in so doing, get what you need.

Be good in your graciousness by being gracious in your goodness.

Dispel the darkness of this world with the light of that goodness.

And that light will keep the "white" in our lives pure and bright, as it was meant to be. *Make white right: keep white white.*

It's always, always better to be the good guy. And it's always worth it.

Parashas Tazria-Metzora 5772

IwantwhatIwantwhenIwantitandIwantitNOW

NowgimmeititsMINEMINEMINEMINEMINE!

Most doctors, and certainly most surgeons, will tell you that that they spend their working lives at war, doing battle, fighting the good fight, often getting maimed and scarred along the way. Those who are not in their shoes, however wise and understanding of life and the world, cannot understand what it's really like. Even when things go well and easy, it's never really easy, it's always fraught, the stakes are so high, the pressure is so great.

It's the most wonderful thing to do, but there's a price.

Certainly, anyone who deals with the daily challenges of life, with *parnassah*, with family relationships, with health, with bosses and with coworkers, with employees, with the stress of business, with nature, with their own *mazal*, must do battle every day. In medicine all those challenges exist, and then the monumental challenges of the unique responsibility one bears sit on top of that.

Recently, after a long and challenging day in surgery, having completed a particularly difficult case that, thank God, went well, I was in the recovery area, telling the patient and his wife that he was fine, that the difficulties were overcome, and what time to come see me the next morning.

Now, *I* don't need them to say "thank you," although it is, of course, nice to be appreciated. I do think, however, that *they* need to say it, as an expression of common decency. Thank you for going to war on our behalf. And that is what most people indeed do.

The wife's actual response (spoken to the patient in the language of her original country before she came to America a few years ago): "Tell him [meaning me, the doctor] not to be late tomorrow. I don't want to have to wait for him." Lips moving in a cold, "*unsympatish*" face. Icy eyes. I'm certain that I had given her no reason to say such a thing.

It was so outrageous that I was amused. You have to laugh at that. 'Tude! Big-time attitude. This same person, whose husband that very morning could not see at all, and who could now see perfectly, just had her husband's sophisticated eye surgery performed totally for free. The surgical suite was free..All their medications are free. Transportation is free. Rent is subsidized. Food is subsidized. The Mercedes and the condo in Florida, of course, are registered in the daughter's name.

Gimme, gimme, you pay, *and make it snappy.*

Actually, some of the most patriotic and appreciative Americans I know were in fact born abroad, including many from that same woman's original homeland. Someone of that particular background that I work with told me of an amazing insight she had when she came here. In America, she said, if John sees that Joe has a nice car, he's likely to say to himself, "Joe has a nice car. I'm going to work hard, and I'll get one too." Where she comes from, John is much more likely to say, "I don't have a car, I don't want that bum Joe to have one either." How wonderful, how good, she concluded, this country is.

God bless America. Everything good is possible. Those who have tasted life elsewhere particularly appreciate what we have here. And some, native and immigrant, cynically abuse the great blessing of this country and what its good people offer.

Parashas Metzora continues the rather lengthy treatment of *nega tzaraas* in its various forms and manifestations. Why so much? Not a word in the Torah is extra or wasted.

Why so many *pesukim*, so many words, so much detail, on this apparently arcane subject?

We all know that the principal sin for which *tzaraas* occurs is *lashon hara*.

The main character faults that lead to *tzaraas* and the sins that result in it are *gaavah* and its own underlying defect, *tzoras ayin*, the inability or the unwillingness to look upon someone else kindly.

Anyone familiar with Torah and with Judaism knows that if there is one underlying principle upon which everything else in practical Yiddishkeit is based, it is the mitzvah *v'ahavta l're'acha ka'mocha*. Hillel and Rabbi Akiva are both well known for their famous dicta on the subject.

V'ahavta l're'acha ka'mocha is indeed a difficult mitzvah to understand, if taken literally. Who can really love someone else as well as himself? What normal, non-self-loathing person can do that? Is that what Hashem really requires? Hashem does not give us impossible mitzvos or require us to behave contrary to the very nature He endowed us with.

Much has been written on the subject. Most people understand that in practical terms it means "do unto others what you would have them do unto you; don't do unto others what you would not have them do to you." The Torah Temimah offers a remarkable insight that goes to the very heart of human nature and brings us right up against our nasty culprit, *tzoras ayin*. And we all recognize this aspect of human nature when we encounter it. Says the Torah Temimah, to fulfill *v'ahavta l're'acha ka'mocha*, one must *fargin* someone else what they have. It sounds simple, but it's not. Jealousy and the potential for mean-spiritedness run deep in human nature, and it is the spiritual duty of each of us to root them out.

Tzoras ayin involves a morbid and spiritually pathological self-absorption that begets every bad *middah* that human beings are capable of. Haughtiness, snobbery, slander, dismissive disregard for others, stinginess, indifference to the pain of others, jealousy, vindictiveness, the propensity to callously use others, insincerity, lack of appreciation of others, approaching the world with a cynical "I'll take what I want" attitude, are all functions of *tzoras ayin*. Gimme gimme and the heck with you is *tzoras ayin*.

It is a mindset that is morally bankrupt and brings every form of *tzarah* – and yes, *tzaraas* – into the world.

The Torah invests a great deal in discussing *tzaraas*, because it represents a moral failure of great magnitude. That moral failure stands between a human being and God. It stands between a Jew and *v'asisa hayashar v'hatov*, between a Jew and *v'davka Bo*.

And clinging to God and His ways is what makes the life we live meaningful and truly worth living.

Parashas Metzora 5771

Measure for Measure

A daughter of the tribe of Ephraim, she lived in the heartland of the Shomron, in a place called Naaron. Perhaps she was out walking or playing near her parents' home when she was nabbed, or perhaps the house was attacked and, a survivor, the young girl was carried off into slavery. The Aramean raiding party brought her back to Syria, where she became the servant of the wife of the king's great warlord, Naaman.

Naaman was a haughty man, the most feared and respected of the king's generals.

Haughty and arrogant as he was, he was stricken by *tzaraas*. Great supplications were made on his behalf to the various deities of that nation. Naaman, of course, remained smitten with his disfiguring disease.

The little Jewish house servant knew what every Jewish child would have known, that there was a prophet of God in Israel, Elisha, who could, without a doubt, cure her master. This she told her mistress, who told her husband, who told the king, who then sent a message, along with gifts, to Yehoram the king of Israel that Naaman was coming to him to be cured, and that a cure was the expected outcome.

Yehoram rent his clothes. "What is this?" he asked. "Do I have such powers? The King of Aram cannot be serious about my curing Naaman. It is a pretext to attack me and my kingdom!" He was beside himself with dread.

Elisha told the king, "Let him come to me, and he will know that there is a prophet in Israel." *Let the Name of God be sanctified in the world.*

Naaman came, behaved in his usual haughty and arrogant manner, but in the end was put in his place and ultimately cured by the prophet, who had him immerse in the River Jordan seven times, after which he was miraculously healed. Let the haughty Naaman, and his king, know that there is a prophet in Israel, and that its God is Master of the universe. Chastised, Naaman was totally won over. He offered Elisha a large reward, which the prophet humbly refused, in the Name of God. Naaman returned to Aram, vowing never to sacrifice to any deity but to the God of Israel.

Elisha's attendant Geichazi sensed an opportunity and ran after Naaman, concocting a story that there were some poor students who had arrived, and that they needed the money that Naaman had offered. Geichazi took it home. The prophet Elisha knew, of course, what Geichazi had done, and informed him that, having desecrated God's Name, he and his three sons who had joined him in his perfidy would now be afflicted with the *tzaraas* that had left Naaman. And so they were stricken with *tzaraas*.

Some time afterward, Ben Hadad, the king of Aram, made war on Israel. A terrible famine ensued, and starvation was rampant. After seven years of desperate hunger, the head of a donkey sold for eighty pieces of silver, and a quarter of a *kav* of dove's dung sold for five pieces. In their desperation, women spoke of eating their own children.

And then Elisha pronounced the word of God: at this time tomorrow, a measure of fine flour, or two measures of barley, will sell for a shekel, a pittance, at the gates of Shomron. The king's officer scoffed: "Even if God were to make windows in the sky, this thing will not come about!"

Elisha told that scoffer, "You will see it come about with your own eyes, but you yourself will not get to eat of it."

Four men suffering from *tzaraas* (Geichazi and his three sons), desperate with hunger, came to the conclusion that they were about to die of starvation and had nothing to lose by going to the camp of the invading Arameans and throwing themselves upon their mercy. The invaders had food and stores aplenty. They arrived to find the Aramean camp empty. God had caused them to hear the sounds of an overwhelmingly large and powerful army attacking them, and they had fled in panic, leaving their food and treasures behind. The four ate and drank and carried off all the gold and goods they could and hid the loot away. Eventually they were conscience stricken, and went to inform the starving Jews at Shomron that the enemy had fled, the siege was broken, and there was a glut of food available.

The people of Shomron went out and brought back so much food that on that day, a measure of the finest flour, or two measures of barley, were available for sale at the gates of the city for a mere shekel, a pittance.

The king's officer who had scoffed, saying that even if God had opened a window in Heaven for food to pour through, it would not and could not happen, indeed saw it happen. But he was trampled in the rush of the crowd, and he died there, still hungry.

We read of these matters in the book of Melachim as the *haftarah* for the *parashiyos* of Tazria and Metzora. The *haftarah* typically mirrors a major topic in the weekly Torah portion.

Much of Tazria concerns the subject of *tzaraas*. Thus, the story of Naaman's *tzaraas*, and the *kiddush Shem Shamayim* that ensued when Elisha cured him, fits right in. But *tzaraas* is a physical malady with a spiritual basis. Most famously, it is punishment for the grave sin of *lashon hara*. But there are other sins that bring it about as well, chief among them haughtiness and arrogance. Naaman was guilty of both (they do usually go together). Elisha, who brought about Naaman's cure, was of the very opposite character, a man of holiness and humility, kindness and *chesed*.

It is striking that it took a man with those elevated *middos* to cure Naaman's *tzaraas* and to bring him down from his warlord's high horse and his haughtiness.

Another profound lesson from this story is insight into the manner in which God usually deals with those who sin against Him: *middah k'neged middah*, measure for measure. The Mishnah (*Sanhedrin* 11, 90a) states that whoever scoffs at and denies belief in *techiyas hameisim*, the eventual quickening of the dead when God wills it in the future, will be punished by losing his portion in *olam haba*, the world to come. The Gemara explains further that because he scoffed at the teaching of the awakening of the dead, he himself will have no portion in the awakening of the dead, *middah k'neged middah*. The source the Gemara cites is the incident of the officer who scoffed at the prophecy of God's deliverance of the people from starvation, who mocked the possibility, "even if God were to open up windows in Heaven," and who then was punished by seeing God's deliverance but never benefitting from it.

These *parashiyos* are usually read shortly after Pesach. The haughtiest of men and the haughtiest of nations, Pharaoh and his Egyptian empire, were brought down low, and to eventual utter destruction, by a nation of humble runaway slaves, by the might of their God. The Jews marched out of Egypt *b'yad ramah*, as God laid the mighty Egyptians low *b'yad chazakah* and *bi'zroa netuyah*: with a mighty hand and with an outstretched arm.

I, and I suppose most everybody else, have always taken that language as the poetic expression of God's might in redeeming His People and in smiting their oppressors.

I recently came across an essay (in the *Wall Street Journal*!) that, in light of the above, casts a profound new dimension on my understanding of that language and its significance to the defeated Egyptians and to my ancestors as they made their triumphant exodus from bondage in Egypt.

I cannot vouch for the precise historicity of the essay I read, or its precise timing relative to the Exodus, but the language referred to makes it a virtual certainty, and it is a profound one indeed.

The pharaoh who kept our forefathers in bitter slavery was also a mighty emperor. There is much archeological evidence that Egypt's influence extended well north of Egypt itself. Apparently, during the time the Jews were in Egypt, a large Egyptian army fought a terrible battle with powerful foes somewhere in what is today Syria.

The odds were against the Egyptians, but they won a great and resounding victory. In his haughtiness, typical of potentates of those times, Pharaoh had statues proclaiming his greatness and prowess at arms set up all over the empire. There are archeological remnants of this.

And the language on those proclamations was the same, all over the empire, trumpeting to the Egyptian people and to its captive and enslaved subjects: mighty Pharaoh, divine master of the world, defeats his enemies *with a mighty hand and with an outstretched arm!*

Wow. I would never have guessed, assuming this is true (and I have no reason to doubt that it is), that the language so famous and so familiar to us, and immortalized in the Torah through all the ages, used to describe God's defeat of the Egyptians, *b'yad chazakah u'vi'zroa netuyah*, was itself part of the punishment meted out to them, turning their own haughty, boastful language back upon them, a wonderful morale booster for the despised slaves now set free to laugh at their former taskmasters.

Middah k'neged middah. Measure for measure.

The haughty, the wicked, the arrogant, the cruel are the villains of history and the enemies of the civilization that it is our mandate to create and to maintain. They are associated with *tzaraas*, the ultimate *uncleanness*.

It is for God Almighty to sit in judgment, and to mete out, as He sees fit, punishment of the wicked measure for measure, *middah k'neged middah*. It is for us to live our lives as the antidote, as Elisha was the antidote, with holiness and humility, with kindness and with *chesed*. And thus we can hope to earn, in all our many times of trouble, God's deliverance, *b'yad chazakah u'vi'zroa netuyah*.

This parashah coincides with the observance of Yom Ha'atzmaut, 5 Iyar, marking the miraculous establishment in our times of the State of Israel. All politics aside (and there is much of that) and all criticisms aside (and there is much of that), we are, all of us, in Israel and in the Diaspora, besieged by implacable foes whose hatred, arrogance, haughtiness, and power seem greater than ever. Let us then stand together, pray together, and act together in the manner that God desires, so that He may treat these enemies of today as He did our enemies and oppressors of old, unmask their corruption, their *tumah*, break their haughtiness, and lead us to our Redemption, indeed, *b'yad chazakah u'vi'zroa netuyah*.

Parashas Tazria-Metzora 5775

The Deep, Secret Heart of Man

Who knows what dark secrets lurk in the heart of man?

Sinners walk among us, and no one knows. There are those who pose as pious but whose impiety is carefully and deeply hidden. That's part of the way the world works. Sometimes you find out, sometimes you don't. And it's not always your business.

We have discussed the placement of the *korban chatas* in the same spot as the *korban olah* for the very purpose of keeping the sin and the sinner hidden.

We have discussed the silent recital of *al chet* and Shemoneh Esrei for the same reason.

We should not know. Parashas Tazria is mostly about a sin that, for expiation to become possible, must become so public that the sinner himself, to his shame, must announce it to anyone who has not noticed.

When Balak enlisted Bilaam against Israel, evil, clever Bilaam told him that the power of the Jews resides in their mouths. Other nations live by the sword. The Jew lives with prayer, with Torah study, with the Name of God on his lips, with a kind word, with a kind look, with modest, clean speech. Bilaam's plan was to curse them using their own tool – speech – thereby negating its power. In that he failed. His backup plan, to get them to behave immorally, sadly had more success.

Ein kocham ela ba'peh. This is very clear from all of Scripture. And yet, people being what they are, Jews sometimes foolishly undo their own power, their own ability to cope with and to master life, by sinning with their mouths – *lashon hara.* And the classic punishment for *lashon hara* is *tzaraas.*

In rabbinic parlance, the chief distinguishing characteristic of humans as compared to animals is that man is a *"medaber,"* one who speaks. The power of the *lashon* is very great. The tongue can bring man to great heights or to depravity. It is a matter of free choice.

The rituals prescribed in the Torah upon the clearing of *tzaraas* involve shaving the various body parts implicated in the genesis of that disorder: the head (*gaavah,* arrogant haughtiness), the eyebrows (*tzoras ayin,* looking unkindly on one's fellow), and the beard – especially the mustache (which should have guarded the mouth from speaking *lashon hara*).

The final common pathway for these failings is the mouth. *Lashon hara* is so vile, so low, so odious, so destructive that its penance stands apart. *V'hatzarua asher bo hanega* (Vayikra 13:45): no secrets here. We may not know who otherwise is a sinner, or what deep, dark secrets lurk in someone's heart. But if he's got *tzaraas,* the Torah is testifying: *bo hanega;* you know what he's done.

But that's not enough. He must dress as a mourner, with torn clothing, a wrapped-up head, and his mouth covered (*al safam yateh* – the mustache that should have covered and guarded the mouth from sin but did not must now be covered over in shame), and call out wherever he goes: "Unclean! Unclean!" Beware, he warns the world, to his shame, do not become *tamei* like me; *do not become disgusting like me* (see Onkelos's rendition).

The Gemara (*Bava Kama* 92b) cites this latter requirement to support the popular saying that "poverty follows the poor." Misery tends to follow misery. A miserable person spreads misery around him. Rashi explains further: it's not enough for him that he is miserable; he must publicly embarrass himself with regard to his misery.

Why is this sin different? Why so public? Not just because the sin is so grave that it requires an extra measure of punishment to clean it up. In fact, he has *tzaraas*. He can't hide it. Whereas other forms of sinfulness may indeed remain hidden deep in the heart of man, this is not. He sinned publicly. He spoke *lashon hara*. He publicly harmed others, and he publicly damaged himself.

At the root of such a sin is *gaavah* (haughtiness), which makes possible nasty behavior toward others, of the type that puts people in this category. This punishment breaks his *gaavah* and makes redemption possible. But further, this poor miserable *tzarua*, dressed in a *tzaraas* uniform, head wrapped, mouth covered, calling out wherever he goes, "*Tamei! Tamei!*" arouses the sympathy of those who see him, who then pray for his recovery.

Some may even sympathize with him for the same reason. It is said that historically it was difficult to get a jury to convict someone of driving while under the influence of alcohol. That practice was so common that every jury had several people on it who also drank and drove, and were loath to convict and condemn someone for doing what they themselves do. How many among us, even those who know better, are never guilty of *lashon hara*?

The *tzarua* must sit alone: *badad yeshev*. The Gemara (*Erchin* 16b) explains that his bad behavior, *lashon hara*, caused a bad separation between people, between man and wife, between friends. His words tore asunder peace from between people who should have only peace between them. For his tearing people apart, he must now sit apart, alone, *chutz la'machaneh*.

Without peace, without each other's love and support, life can be rather nasty.

The Torah makes a special case of one who does this to people. The best remedy of all is to learn the lesson of the laws of *tzaraas*, so that we need know them only as a holy academic exercise, and never in practice. The power to hurt and to embarrass is not real power. It's just stupid and mean. *Never* to do so is real power. Jewish power. God's formula for power.

Parashas Tazria 5771

Acharei Mos-Kedoshim

Choosing Life

Most people who know me are aware of the horror with which I view smoking, and the even greater horror with which I view its tolerance in Jewish society. It's clearly an act that is forbidden by the Torah, as determined by many of the great *poskim* of our generation, based on indisputable medical information now available. And yet, for a variety of reasons I will not go into here, it is treated with remarkably more tolerance than one could imagine for an act so outrageously destructive, and, by all criteria used to make such judgments, clearly *assur min haTorah*.

Human nature is such that people often do not heed warnings unless the bloody evidence stares them in the face. People who drive too fast or too close usually continue to do so until they are involved in or witness some gory, bloody accident.

In my practice, confirmed smokers who do not yet have lung cancer or emphysema or heart disease or the inability to walk due to peripheral vascular disease – or, in the context of my practice, macular degeneration – listen politely but often remain largely unmoved. It's only when their vision starts to go that they get scared enough to really listen and maybe do something to try to break their addiction.

Parashas Acharei Mos begins with a warning to Aharon regarding the sanctity of the Kodesh Hakodashim, lest he die. The Torah spells out that he was given this warning after his own sons died for that very offense. Rashi, quoting the Midrash, explains that a warning accompanied by the concrete evidence of someone who suffered and died as a result of a given behavior is much more effective than just a warning alone.

The *parashah* then goes on to discuss the Yom Kippur service, which saves us from death, and which is the Torah reading for the Yom Kippur davening. This is followed by warnings about several other practices that may bring about the death of the violator. The *parashah* then concludes with our nation's key to life itself. And because of its importance to our continued existence, it too is read on Yom Kippur.

This portion concerns morality. In the ancient world, Jews were unique for their moral practices. In today's corrupt, amoral society, where anything goes, where shameful acts are engaged in openly and shamelessly, Torah Jews are again virtually unique for their moral practices.

K'maasei eretz Mitzrayim – the disgusting immoral practices of Mitzrayim, which you left, and Canaan, where you are headed, are to be avoided at all costs. Do not do it, and do not follow their mores – *u'v'chukoseihem lo selechu* (Vayikra 18:3). Follow My ways, says Hashem, and you, as a nation, will live. Otherwise, you are lost.

These immoral practices cost the nations that occupied the Land of Israel – Canaan – their land and their lives. "Do not become contaminated by these [immoral practices], because through these practices those nations became contaminated and I will expel them before you" (Vayikra 18:24). They contaminated the land, which then vomited them out. Do not yourselves fall prey to these practices – no matter how attractive, no matter how enticing, *no matter how socially acceptable*, lest the land vomit you out as well. Do not become, in the Targum's translation, *disgusting*. It will not be tolerated, and you will not survive in this holy land.

We know all too well that we lost the land for this very reason and have been suffering ever since. Not that we weren't warned, not that we shouldn't have known better, not that we didn't see the seven Canaanite nations expelled for those very same sins.

Aharon was warned with a gory and tragic example still before his eyes. Klal Yisrael was warned with an example before their eyes, but they chose to forget. Smokers know very well what the truth is, but they choose to look away. We miserable sinners know the truth, but we tend to look away as well. How else can we explain our foolish behavior, time and time again?

There is a charismatic speaker in Israel named Amnon Yitzchak. He is something of a character, but he has a lot to offer. He has been rather effective in bringing alienated Jews back to their roots, particularly among the Sephardim, with whom he has a common background. Like many of them, he himself was not raised religious, his parents having been members of that generation of Sephardic immigrants torn away from Yiddishkeit by the socialist/secularist (Ashkenazi!) Establishment that tried to recreate the Jew, and Israel, in a Godless image.

He has an interesting and novel approach. Nonobservant childless women often ask for his blessing and help. (Typically, I think, Sephardim who "wander off" tend to wander off less far than their Ashkenazi counterparts. They are rarely truly very far off. They know where to turn in times of trouble.)

Amnon Yitzchak counsels them to cover their hair. Considering everything else they do, it seems an odd suggestion. These women often hesitate, fearing resistance from their husbands and ridicule from their friends. He counters with the question, do they prefer to have a child, or to avoid their foolish friends' ridicule? He claims that many of these women do as he suggests, and are often blessed with children.

Why does he insist on covering the hair? For one thing, a Jewish woman who covers her hair ultimately will not eat *treif*, will not dress immodestly, and will likely, bit by bit, find her way, and that of her family, to full observance.

More fundamental, I believe, is the inherent power of *tznius* in guaranteeing Jewish continuity. *Tznius* is the polar opposite of *k'maasei eretz Mitzrayim*, and of the abhorrent practices of the nations that inhabited the Land of Israel before we inherited it. Before the land vomited them out for their disgusting, amoral lifestyle. For their total lack of *tznius*.

The passage in our *parashah* that commands decency, morality, and modesty attests: You, who observe My laws, who live according to My teaching, who fulfill My will, who live morally and modestly and decently, *shall live*. I am Hashem.

Tznius, for the Jew, as an individual and as a nation, begets life. The Torah, in our *parashah*, defines the opposite of *tznius* as *tumah*, for which Onkelos uses the word *disgusting*.

A prominent characteristic that distinguishes the way of life of the Torah Jew is that it is the very opposite of disgusting. Our mores and our standards are not defined by popular society and culture, not by TV or by "talking heads" or by the PC. The Ribbono shel Olam, the Creator of life, through His holy Torah, has given us an eternal formula for continued life.

Goodness and decency and morality are our God-given portion. Let us hold on to that portion, and we shall live.

Parashas Acharei 5771

Dust in the Wind: A Love Story

The blitzkrieg burst with terrible power and effect into the stunned and utterly defeated Polish town. German soldiers strutted about, menacing, drunk with their own invincibility, everything they had come to believe about their own superiority and the inferiority of others clearly proven.

Terrorizing, intimidating, demoralizing the local population – especially the Jews – was policy. The heroes of the Wehrmacht needed no goading to carry out their patriotic German duty.

There had already been a number of random shootings.

A group of hapless Jews was randomly plucked off the street and herded into the synagogue, among them the town rabbi. The German officer pulled a Torah scroll from the ark, tore off its satin mantle, and threw it onto the floor, where it unrolled. He then ordered a Jew to trample upon it.

Horrified, the Jew tried to explain. "I can't! Please don't – " That was as far as he got before the German blew his brains out, splattering the blood and tissue in the others' faces. He turned to the next Jew, pistol at the ready, and ordered him to trample on the Torah. Defeated, utterly panicked, the poor Jew did what he had to do to stay alive. So did the next one, and the one after, to the German's great satisfaction. It's hard to blame them. Little did they know how little extra life it bought them.

The monster – an ordinary, law-abiding German, never a criminal, who was doing, in his estimation, his national duty – then turned to "Mendel" (alas, in this true story, I do not know his actual name) and ordered him to trample upon the Torah.

Mendel was the town lowlife, a man of low moral habits. He openly smoked on Shabbos. He never appeared in *shul*. He was a gambler, a swindler, and a seducer. He flouted every convention.

The German relished his victory over the cowardly Jews. Impatiently he waved his pistol at the man, to get on with it. And so he was surprised when Mendel spoke. "I have done many things in my life that I should not have. *This I will not do.*"

He hadn't realized it until that last moment in his life, just before he too had his brains blown out, before knowingly choosing that fate. Mendel was in love. The dissipation of his day-to-day life belied what was at his Jewish core. In the end he could not break the bond of love with the God of his fathers. It was all he had left of that primal connection to his source, and he would not let go, at any price.

One of the great themes of the Passover holiday is the eternal bond of love between God and Israel. God rescued our forefathers from bondage in Egypt despite their low spiritual state after so many years in slavery, because they nevertheless held tight to their identity as the children of the Avos, and through them, the children of God.

This lesson and this history is reviewed and reinforced in the joyous drill we know as the Seder.

It is capped, on the seventh day of Pesach, with the *shirah*, the triumphant song our forefathers sang at the Yam Suf upon the final destruction of our tormentors. And in between, we recite in shul the greatest and most intense expression of yearning love of all, Shir Hashirim, the Song of Songs.

And yet, it is not always so easy to reconcile the idea of that love with the realities of life.

Ask most people who have been around in life and you will be told that it isn't…and it is.

And they're both true.

The same wise king who composed Shir Hashirim, Shlomo Hamelech, the wisest man ever, also composed Koheles, a far more sobering analysis of life than the heady Shir Hashirim.

Sobering, and disturbing indeed.

For the fate of man and the fate of beasts is the same, says Koheles, and they all have the same spirit. Man is not superior to the beasts, for it is all futile: all go to the same place, all are dust, and all become dust.

For the living know that they will die, while the dead know nothing – their memory is forgotten: their love, their hate, their jealousies – all are lost, and no longer do they have a share in this world, in what happens under the sun.

All we are is dust.

Or so it seems. Shlomo Hamelech is telling us what a thinking man might conclude from observing life, but for the reality of God's ongoing presence, His inscrutable plan, His *hashgachah*, His Revelation, His love.

The true reality, which Shlomo expresses in his incomparable Shir Hashirim, is that on the deepest level, God and Israel are inseparable.

Intellectually, that is expressed in the conclusion to Koheles, that *sof davar*, the final sum of the matter, when all has been considered, when all is said and done, that one should fear God and keep His commandments, for that is man's purpose in this world. For God is not indifferent to who we are and what we do: God will judge every deed, even everything hidden, every intention, whether it be good or evil.

Emotionally (and what an emotion!), Shlomo Hamelech describes, in Shir Hashirim, the nature and the strength of that bond, its durability, no matter what else might happen, no matter what other reality may appear, on the surface, to be operational.

Think of the words in their purely spiritual context, while cleverly couched in terms a person can understand and relate to deeply: "His left hand supports my head, and His right embraces me."

I have loved you, O Israel, from the very beginning.

Place me like a seal upon your heart, like a seal upon your arm.

For our love is stronger even than death, its intensity more profound even than the grave.

Its flashes are the very flame of God.

The deepest waters cannot extinguish that flame of love, nor can rivers drown it.

Nothing in this world can compare to it.

I am a wall – ani chomah – my faith is as firm, as enduring, as resistant, as determined as a wall.

There is much that is deeply moving in the Hoshanos prayers. To me, perhaps the most intense and the most moving is the set that begins with אום אני חומה: Hoshana! The nation that declares, "I am a wall!" Come what may, be it exile, slaughter, degradation, dispersion among our tormentors, storm-tossed, given over to beating and battery, our beards ripped from our faces, subject to every form of degradation and torture because we are Your people, we continue to hug and to cleave to You, to bear Your yoke, unique in the world in steadfastly declaring Your oneness, Your sacred sheep, who identify only with You. Hoshana!

How can anyone utter those words and not be swept away?

How can anyone utter those words without thinking of the full range of our people, the saints, the dedicated plain folks, and yes, the Mendels who are also part of our nation, indeed part of its strength, who have played their roles in the long, glorious, and tortured history of Am Yisrael?

Mendel and his six million coreligionists who were swept away (and indeed, his twenty million – or was it fifty million – fellow human beings who perished at that terrible time), who were, and then were not, who were erased without an apparent trace, what were they? Nothing? Dust in the wind?

God created the world ex nihilo, *yesh me'ayin*, "something from nothing."

And He is not, as the seventeenth-century philosophers portrayed Him, a great Watchmaker in the sky, who created the watch, wound it up, set it running, and left it to its own devices. He created the world, and He continues to run it, intimately, in every detail, connecting past, present, and future, with a plan, and with absolute justice, far beyond the ken of mortal man.

Everything counts, and everyone counts. Certainly, we believe that the Jewish People occupy a special and unique place in God's plan for the world, indeed in His rationale for its creation. But He also created many millions of others, and they too are His creatures, and their existence and their toil in this world are part of that plan.

He expects goodness of human beings; of Jews, He requires it. Of Jews He also requires love, for Him, and for each other. It is central to what gives meaning to life.

On Shabbos erev Rosh Chodesh, we read the specially designated *haftarah*, Machar Chodesh. It too contains a love story, a lesson for all generations.

One of the most tragic figures in Tanach is Shaul, the first king of Israel.

He was chosen because he stood head and shoulders above all others, spiritually as well as physically. He was good and wise and modest and did not seek to be king. Indeed, he tried to avoid it. But it was his destiny. An error in judgment cost him his kingship. Part of the tragedy is the painful way in which he lost it. He became afflicted with a severe melancholia that utterly robbed him of peace. He turned on David and pursued him relentlessly. He also understood, correctly, that David's success would mean his own son Yehonasan's undoing.

Yehonasan understood that reality too. And yet he loved David with all his heart.

He recognized David as the pure soul that he was, *ne'im zemiros Yisrael*, the sweet singer of Israel. He understood that the Ribbono shel Olam runs the world according to His divine plan; individuals must operate according to the human agenda of choosing to do what's right. Yehonasan intervened in his father's plot to eliminate David; in so doing he undermined his own chances for the future. David and Yehonasan each knew full well what this meant.

David emerged from his hiding place and fell to his knees before Yehonasan, bowing three times. They embraced and kissed each other, and they wept. David in particular was overcome with weeping, in love and gratitude for his friend's love, devotion, and sacrifice. Yehonasan sent David off with blessings of peace, and the oath of love binding them, with their God, together forever.

There is much cruelty in this world. Indeed, it often looks as if all is in vain, empty futility, *hevel havalim*. It looks as if there is no point, no purpose, no hope. It looks as if we leave nothing behind us when we make our exit from the world. It looks as if we are but dust in the wind.

But we know that that is, in fact, far from the truth. We know that we are imbued by our Creator with the power and the ability to learn, to grow, to build, to love. and to care, to touch other people in the world in such a way that in so doing, we create worlds of lasting goodness.

And we, Bnei Yisrael, also know that the Creator, who is our loving Father and whose special beloved children we are, runs His great big world, with all its various agendas, with us in mind. We know that our relationship with Him is a unique love story, from both sides.

And we know, in the face of whatever confronts us, that *sof davar*, the final sum of the matter, when all has been considered, when all is said and done, one must fear God and keep His commandments, for that is man's purpose in this world. For God is not indifferent to who we are and what we do. God will judge every deed and every intention. And that is because God loves us so profoundly, and it is His desire that we love Him. Because His left hand supports our head, and His right embraces us. He has loved us from the very beginning. *Place me like a seal upon your heart, like a seal upon your arm!* For our love is stronger than even death, its intensity more profound even than the grave. Its flashes are the very flame of God. The deepest waters cannot extinguish that flame of love, nor can rivers drown it. Nothing in this world can compare to it.

Ani chomah. I am a wall: my faith is firm, as enduring, as resistant, as determined, as a wall. Come what may.

Even Mendel, as estranged as he appeared to be, understood that.

How much more so should we.

Parashas Acharei 5776

Oxygen

One of the most painful and difficult things a person can witness is to watch someone desperately struggling for breath. It is a terrifying spectacle. It's scary not just because the victim is suffering badly, but because the fear, the panic, the potential vulnerability of *oneself* being unable to breathe goes to the very core of the instinct for life.

In my naïveté, as a young medical student, I thought that fear was so potent that it could be harnessed to change people's lives for the better. I thought that young smokers could be cured of their stupidity (with regard to smoking, at least) by being brought to the emphysema ward, there to see the "pink puffers" (and their chronic bronchitic brethren, the "blue bloaters") sitting with their oxygen tanks, with that frightened look permanently etched on their faces. It was quite apparent that they spent every waking minute laboring at and in a near panic over getting that next breath of air into the remnants of their lungs. I wasn't a smoker, but it scared me terribly.

And so the thought that the *neshamos* of our departed loved ones, who can no longer accomplish anything for themselves, may well be spiritually "struggling for breath," as it were, to reach some spiritual plateau and need *us* to accomplish it for them through tzedakah and Torah and *chesed* done on their behalf, has been, for me, a powerful and effective motivator.

Society in general does have an interesting tendency to speak of those who have died as if they never had the various flaws that so annoyed us when they were alive.

That is often referred to as *acharei mos…kedoshim!* They become "holy" or great *after* they have died.

Well, it's not really necessary to wait until someone has died to be nice to him, or even to think well of him, or to *fargin* him.

These *parashiyos* are replete with especially lofty concepts. One in particular stands out as the gold standard for human behavior, the Golden Rule: *v'ahavta l're'acha ka'mocha*.

There are many discussions and *derashos* about how to understand that.

The one that I will mention here is that of the Torah Temimah. His simple and elegant point is that of course it is impossible for someone to actually love others quite as oneself. That is contrary to human nature. And when it comes down to it, *chayecha kodmim*: one's own life, legally and morally, has precedence. Rather, it is an imperative to *fargin* someone else the same good things in life that one wishes for oneself. As simple and as obvious as it sounds, when you reflect on human nature, it is often quite a challenge.

There are all kinds of people and all kinds of personalities. Some people are naturally kind and warm and openly loving. Others are by nature colder and more reserved, even if they are basically good and caring people. The quality of life of those who share their lives with loved ones is defined and profoundly affected by that particular aspect of the nature of those loved ones.

A normal person needs to feel loved and appreciated. Some have that need more than others. It is a core, basic human need. If it is unmet, can a person be happy, at peace, or truly fulfilled in life?

There is a stereotype in literature of the cold WASP who is uncomfortable openly expressing love. "He *knows* that I love him! Why do I have to *say* it?" That comment, in the story, is often followed by some desperate, tragic action on the part of the emotionally love-starved "loved one."

There are people who are starved for the simple joy of hearing, from those close to them, words of love, of appreciation, of thanks for what they do, a compliment for something well done, or perhaps just a compliment, words of praise that they may well deserve, or perhaps just words of praise. They may be as desperate as the chronic lunger is for breath, as that yearning *neshamah* is for a helping mitzvah by a surviving relative. And they live their lives in quiet desperation and bewilderment, unable to understand why it should be so hard for the people who do love them to sweeten their lives with a simple word or gesture. And if they express that need, will it be met with clueless incomprehension, or even ridicule for being an "adulation addict"? And will anything change?

And where is *v'ahavta l're'acha ka'mocha*?

Where is *fargining* someone, especially a loved one, that "breath of air" that he or she so desperately needs, and which should not be so hard to provide?

And isn't it so much better to provide those loving, kind, and complimentary words to someone one cares about while he or she is still alive? How often do people miss the chance to do it when they can, and then forever regret that they did not? Posthumous words of love and praise are very nice, but they're too late. *Acharei mos...kedoshim!* as described above is a joke. *Acharei mos, kedoshim* in this context is a tragedy.

Different people do indeed have different natures. But that does not absolve the naturally stingy person from giving tzedakah, or people with inappropriate predilections of all types from acting as they should. There are people who, by nature, do have a hard time uttering words of love or praise. The lofty moral teachings of these *parashiyos* demand of us that we model ourselves on God, our Creator. Time and again the imperative is stated, "Be holy, for I, God, am holy." God is the Essence of Goodness, and so must we be altogether good, and giving, even if it is hard or somehow awkward for us. There are many aspects of "giving." Words of praise and love are a uniquely human form of giving, which, as human beings created in the image of God, it is our mandate to provide to other human beings, especially to those who are close to us.

In my life as a doctor, a husband, a parent, a friend, in the many thousands of meaningful interpersonal encounters in which I have impacted in a serious way on the lives of others, I do believe I have never gone wrong in paying someone a compliment, saying something nice about them, making them feel good about themselves. *Never.* Most often, I can detect a kind of lightening of the spirit in that person. And sometimes, it's almost as if I can hear the relief of that proverbial deep breath being drawn, that intake of desperately needed "oxygen." Take it from this doctor: this is real.

The world is full of people who appear OK, who function and work and laugh and have great families, and who carry on their lives in what appears to be a normal, happy way. And they may in fact be happy. And they may also, at the same time, be desperate, or perhaps less than desperate but in pain, yearning for that kind and loving and praising word and gesture that is for them the very sweetness of life, but which remains out of reach, like that full breath of air for the emphysemic. It's just not there, when it could be and should be. And even those closest to them, who do love them and care for them and who would never harm them, who would sacrifice for them, just don't get it, and just don't respond, even if asked.

Those caring loved ones can, if they would only heighten their own awareness, infuse that potent, life-giving "oxygen." And why wait for "*Acharei mos, kedoshim*"? *Do it now. Do it today. Do it every day. Do it all day.*

And every time you do, you will be *zocheh* to fulfill that most challenging and all-important mitzvah, *v'ahavta l're'acha ka'mocha.* You will be a life giver. And it will bring blessing and happiness and sweetness into your own life.

Parashas Acharei-Kedoshim 5772

Stoppuhr

A hollow tooth.

A hollowed-out belt.

Where do you hide some small thing that may stand between you and your death, or the death of your family? Something you absolutely cannot afford to lose, or to have stolen from you?

How do you get by, how do you keep body and soul together, when, even if no one is actively trying to murder you, it's almost impossible to keep from starving or from succumbing to typhus or myriad other such diseases?

How, when all private commerce – any attempt to buy, sell, or trade – is a high crime, punishable by years of slave labor, a virtual death sentence, and without such activity, there cannot be enough food, does one keep one's family alive?

What if honestly buying some commodity, such as a bolt of cloth, results in a ten-year sentence as a capitalist speculator, so if caught, you have to say you *stole* it, because theft will only get you a five-year sentence?

And what if, while trying to cope with all this, one can barely speak the local language, in a foreign country?

At what point, how utterly desperate would you have to be to part with the last vestige of a safety net, that little diamond held as a last resort, hidden in a hollow tooth, or that US twenty-dollar bill, payable in gold, hidden in a hollowed belt, when you had had much but could carry with you very little, as you fled the German onslaught, keeping barely a day ahead of them?

And what if you're afraid, but you see around you those who cannot cope, lying bloated with hunger in the streets? What if you have elderly family members, or little children, who cannot possibly survive without your efforts?

You do what you have to do. You get hold, somehow, of some small commodity, and trade with someone who needs it, for something somebody else needs, and hope, somehow, that you will survive the process and perhaps turn a small profit that will allow you to continue. And so, day after day, for an eternity. Perhaps you will get hold of some dried leaves that some people smoke because there is no actual tobacco to be had, something vile called *makhorke* that a soldier in a passing troop train might trade for an extra army-issue shirt he is carrying, which is a rich return on investment and might feed the family for a week. Or might result in disappearing into the Gulag. Or the soldier might trade an extra pair of pants he is carrying for a piece of smoked fatback, a commodity that might then be sold for rubles to send to starving elderly parents in another province.

And so, if one is blessed, one survives. And after the war, one must smuggle oneself out of there. From Asia to Europe. From Russia to Poland. From Poland to

Soviet-occupied Germany. From Soviet-occupied Germany to the Soviet sector of Berlin. From the Soviet sector to the American sector. And there, in the DP camp, to hope, and to wait.

Every passage, every step expensive as it is illegal and dangerous. Everything dependent on the ability to *hondel*, to trade, to painstakingly parlay every possible item into something else that makes life possible.

Over the years, A has been painstakingly traded for B, B for C, C for D and E, D and E for... Over and over again. And now, as the end approaches, as the visa has finally been approved, what does one do with the pitiful few Deutschmarks one has accumulated?

How do you parlay that into something of value that one can transport to the new land? Perhaps to trade again?

You look, naturally, for the best trade, the best deal you can get in portable "wealth."

Miraculously, you still have the little diamond, the last resort, hidden in the hollow tooth. You still have that twenty-dollar bill hidden in that same, hollowed out belt. And with the bit of currency you have accumulated, with the net result of that long, tortured pathway, you find someone, perhaps a defeated German desperate for some cash, willing to part with a gold watch at an advantageous price.

What is the story of that beautiful gold stopwatch, that *Stoppuhr*, in the accursed language, that you managed, along with the shirt on your back, to bring to America? Is it that German's family heirloom? Or was it a different family's family heirloom, taken from a Jew before murdering him? Who can know?

Who can know? We can only guess what it took to get to that point.

Who can know? Who can understand, really, how all your efforts, all your struggle, all your fear and your danger, all your desperation, were, in the end, translated to the survival of your wife and child, and that *Stoppuhr*, that gold stopwatch?

Who can assess its preciousness, its value? Who can put a price tag upon it?

Who can even imagine it?

Who can speculate on its origin and remain sane?

We are commanded, in Parashas Kedoshim, to hold our parents in fearful reverence. That mandate is, indeed, the very first pronouncement that follows on the overall commandment to be holy, *Kedoshim tihyu*. Absent that reverence, that awe, that appreciation, we cannot even begin to be a holy nation.

Not every generation of parents faces the terrible tests and challenges my parents did in providing life and sustenance for their children. Thank God for that. But in whatever form it takes, in whatever severity, the challenges of giving and sustaining life are always great, in *every* generation. And one mandate in life, for those so sustained by the efforts and the sacrifices of their parents, is to understand

and appreciate that effort, and to recognize that a portion of the reverence due the Creator is reassigned, by Him, to parents, who are His agents in this world.

Be a holy nation, God declares, for I, God, am holy: let every person hold his parents in fearful awe. Without that you cannot aspire to holiness.

There is much travail in this life. Without the efforts of our parents, we could not survive. Without their example, we would not know how.

There is a beautiful, lyrical passage in the *haftarah* (Amos 9:13–15) that softens the prospect of the ceaseless travail that is the human condition, and in particular, the historical Jewish condition, come "the end of days": *Hineh yamim ba'im.*

> Behold, the days are coming, declares the Lord, when the harvest will be so bountiful that the harvesters of the crop will still be busy gathering while the plowman is already preparing the field for the next season, when he who treads upon the grapes will have so many grapes to crush that he will encounter, in the vineyards, the preparer of the next crop. The mountains will drip sweet wine, and the hard hills will soften to yield crops.
>
> And I will return the captivity of My people Israel, and they shall rebuild the desolate, destroyed cities and inhabit them. They will plant vineyards and drink their wine; they will make gardens and eat their fruit.
>
> And I will plant them on their land. They will no longer be uprooted from their land, which I have given them, declares the Lord, your God.

This is God's promise. In the end, He will lighten our burden, and the suffering of so many generations in providing sustenance will be replaced with the blessing of ease and plenty.

And it will be in our own, restored Land of Israel.

Meanwhile, we look at that stopwatch earned with blood and tears, that little diamond finally released from its hiding place in a hollow tooth, that old twenty-dollar gold certificate issued by the US Treasury in 1922; we marvel at how unspeakably precious they are; we tremble with fearful awe and reverence for parents who somehow found the strength and partnered with God Almighty to give us life, to sustain us, and to bring us to this day.

Parashas Kedoshim (תשע"ו), Yom Hazikaron, Erev Chag Ha'atzmaut 5776, Yerushalayim Ir Hakodesh

Bald

They look at me with that "Huh?" look on their faces.

They understand the words I said, but don't understand, really, what I said.

As people live, and can remain active longer, and as the social safety net for people of retirement age applies to the many people who retire from work (often government jobs) while they are young enough and well enough to remain active for years, there are more and more people out there with not much to do, and plenty of time to do it in. There are many, of course, who keep themselves busy with good, productive things of all kinds. Torah-observant people often spend their time with *shiurim* and *maasim tovim*. And then there are those whose days are empty and boring, largely spent in front of the TV set. There are many like that. I see them in my office.

When I suggest that they volunteer in a hospital or in a nursing home, easing the pain and loneliness of the sick and the aged, thus filling their own time with purpose and meaning beyond the daytime TV soap operas that fill their lives, for some, I can see the lightbulb of realization turn on. Many others say, "Uh, yeah," but their faces tell me – clearly – what they really mean is "Huh? What? Me? Huh?" They don't get it at all.

Our Sages were well aware of the risks of not occupying one's time and energies in a full and balanced way. In *Avos* 2:2, Rabban Gamliel, son of Rabbi Yehudah Hanasi, teaches that the effort of filling and balancing one's life with a healthy mix of Torah study and work (*derech eretz*) keeps sin (which, we know, is always crouching at the doorstep) away. One needs both.

On the subject of the potential nefarious effect of TV, Rabbi Akiva (*Avos* 2:17) warns that *sechok* and *kalus rosh* (excessive levity and lack of seriousness – the stuff entertainment TV is made of) accustom and predispose a person to immorality. That so obviously applies to television, especially if it fills one's time. No matter that there was no TV in Rabbi Akiva's time. There have always been TV equivalents. But television provides these noxious influences beyond all previous bounds of decency, in unprecedented intensity, abundance, and ubiquitous availability.

The Imrei Noam cites the Rambam, whose *Sefer Kedushah* (Book of Holiness) contains many hundreds of *halachos* and teachings regarding the challenging goal of maintaining the holiness of the Jew in this world. It opens with the prerequisite, given human nature, of morality and decency in our intimate relationships. After *twenty-two chapters* devoted to this personal purity, Rambam – physician and philosopher as well as Torah giant – shares a critical lesson on this sensitive subject.

Nothing in all the Torah is as difficult for most people, he teaches, nothing has quite the power to seduce or is as difficult to resist as immorality, together with avarice (theft) and the draw of *lashon hara*. Stay away from excessive levity and lack of seriousness, he teaches, from lewd influences (did he just describe most of what television has to offer?). Rather, one should fill one's mind with thoughts of Torah and wisdom, for there is no better antidote to immorality. These and honest work and good deeds save us from the pit.

The Imrei Noam teaches that it is idleness – mental as well as physical – that is a prime culprit in predisposing people to fall in this way. And the commandment in Parashas Emor, "*Lo yikrechu korcha b'rosham*" (They shall not make a bald spot on their heads; Vayikra 21:5), can be said to allude, homiletically, to this very problem. It is an admonition: Do not leave your heads and your minds "bald," empty of the wisdom derived from Torah, and from Torah together with *derech eretz*. That will only lead to trouble.

The subject of avoiding the ubiquitous, terrible influences that open a person to sinfulness and immorality is a far broader subject than can readily be treated here.

It serves, however, in the context of this discussion, as a segue into the challenge faced by so many today, the challenge of having, in effect, nothing to do.

For most of history, people have had little opportunity for idleness. Most people toiled until they were essentially used up, physically and mentally. We now are blessed with a new reality in the world. People often are able to stop work while they are still young and strong and active enough to live a different kind of life than they had for years. They can do so productively, if they are wise enough, or foolishly and wastefully if they don't know better.

There is much to be done in this world, for Jew and non-Jew alike, each according to his place. What a resource the senior population can be, with their wealth of experience and wisdom and empathy, in doing good, in building the world, in supporting and nurturing our civilization, in alleviating suffering and loneliness in the less fortunate.

There are lotions and there are pills against baldness. Sometimes they help, but so what? Moral "baldness," spiritual "baldness," as understood in this context, can be prevented, and if need be, cured. We can fill our heads and our hearts and our time with wisdom and with goodness, with compassion and with caring, enriching and enhancing life for ourselves by enhancing life for others.

Parashas Emor 5777

Don't Let Me Down

I heard a terrible story. I hope it's not true, but who knows? It might be.

A man was balancing his checkbook and noticed that he was short $900. Further investigation revealed that $1000 was paid on a $100 check. He called the bank, who confirmed that they paid $1000 on that check. It then emerged that someone had added a zero to the 100 and managed to cash in $1000.

When he told the bank clerk that the check had been cashed in Israel, the non-Jewish bank clerk said, "Yeah, we get this sort of thing very often from there."

Gevalt! We get this sort of thing very often from there? How embarrassing!

I hope it's not true, but I know that it might be true: it has happened to me too, although in my case the bank representative made no observation about Israel. In the end the bank had to make up the loss, as they are supposed to pay what the *words* on the check say, rather than the numbers. And so the non-Jew gets ripped off by the...*non-non-Jew.*

Chillul Hashem, anyone?

In Parashas Emor there is an interesting admonition. The Kohanim are warned not to desecrate God's name: "They shall be holy before God, and they shall not desecrate the Name of their God, for they are the ones who offer the *korbonos* (*lechem Elokeihem hem makrivim*) and they are [and must be] holy" (Vayikra 21:6).

Why single out the Kohanim not to desecrate God's Name? None of us may desecrate God's holy Name. Indeed, why single out *the* holy group, the Kohanim, the very people whose training, whose lives and careers are specifically dedicated to His service and to sanctifying His Name, and warn *them* against desecrating it? It's the rest of us who need that warning! Such an admonition seems insulting to the Kohanim. Would you be comfortable reminding your *rosh yeshiva* not to be a *ganiv*? (Don't try it.)

In my office, the more Jewish you look – the more obvious the uniform, the bigger the beard and *peyos*, the blacker and rounder the hat, *the frockier the frock* – the less likely it is that I can sneak you in out of turn. It's obvious why, and those holy and wise Jews in that uniform understand it very well. To avoid the resentment of others about being treated unfairly. To avoid *chillul Hashem*.

We all know the famous statement in *Shabbos* 114a: a *talmid chacham* who goes out in a grease-stained coat is *mischayev b'nafsho*. He is liable for his very life, for by doing so, by appearing unkempt and unclean, he may bring about loss of respect for Torah, for Judaism, for the Jewish People, for God.

In this admonition not to be *mechallel Shem Shamayim*, the Kohanim represent Judaism, Jews, Torah, holiness. They represent God before the world. The world perceives the God of Israel through the actions of those people who are in His camp.

That is true as gentiles see the behavior of Jews of all stripes, and that is true as non-*frum* Jews see the behavior of their *frum* brethren.

Like it or not, we bear the responsibility of representing God and His Torah before the world, and before other Jews who have wandered far from Torah. In our *pasuk*, it says "*kedoshim yihyu*": they shall be holy. Rashi quotes the Midrash: *al korchachem*, whether you like it or not, whether you want it or not, this is who you are, and this is your responsibility. You cannot avoid it or escape it.

It is specifically those identified as *kedoshim*, those who are, by their way of life, the "holy ones," who have to be especially vigilant here. All Jews are holy. All *bnei Torah* are holy. But those who are the obvious public face of Judaism are especially responsible, and especially vulnerable. *Rabbonim, roshei yeshiva*, rebbes, *kollel yungeleit*, people who dress *yeshivish* or *chassidish*, are in the forefront and bear the greatest responsibility, and, the Torah is telling us, are held to the highest standard and the greatest strictness. But beyond that, all of us – people who wear yarmulkes, women whose mode of dress identifies their affiliation, people who are known to be Orthodox – in short, every identifiable *frum* Jew is on the line. And perhaps the biggest risk is not *intentional* bad behavior, but *careless* bad behavior. The result can be just as devastating.

My father, a"h, who taught me much, made a point, once, when I was quite young, of telling me about his recent haircut. Back then a haircut cost 75 cents. "*Ich hob ihm gegeben a dollar*" (I gave him a dollar), he said, with a twinkle in his eye. (That's a 33.3 percent tip.) "*Luz er vissen az Shimon Reich iz geven!*" (*Let him know that Shimon Reich was there!*). My father was being playful, but the lesson was that when you look like a Jew, make sure you also look generous and considerate, not stingy.

It's not easy, unless you make a habit of it, to be careful all the time. It's not easy, unless you make a habit of it, to be vigilant about everything you do. It's not easy, unless you make a habit of it, to be constantly concerned about every interaction, however trivial, with everyone you come in contact with, or even pass in the street or on the subway.

It's not easy, unless you make a lifelong habit of it, to avoid giving offense, or being annoying to someone, or appearing careless or insensitive toward others, *all the time.*

But that is exactly what God expects of us. For He has designated us His special, holy nation, and when people look at us, they see the God of Israel and His Torah. We are linked to Him. And, in His great, compassionate mercy, in His boundless love, He has bestowed upon us the greatest gift of all: He has linked Himself to us.

And for that, we must be always vigilant to never let Him down.

Parashas Emor 5773

Flesh of My Flesh

She didn't realize that her feet were torn and bleeding until much later in the day.

She ran through the fields and the brambles, infant on her arm, half panicked but totally clear and rational, determined to get to the next town without being stopped or detected by the patrols that were even then laying down a dragnet around the town. In fact, she was shot at and chased, but she managed to elude them. Nothing would stop her. She had to save her husband. And she did.

Having escaped the Germans in Poland, having survived prison and slave labor in the Gulag, having survived typhus lying, delirious, alongside unknown bedmates in the "hospital" who did not, they wound up, along with thousands of others in similar circumstances, struggling for survival in the Asian lands of the Soviet empire. Weaker, older people lay starving in the streets. The only way to survive was to somehow acquire a commodity that was in demand somewhere else, go there and sell it, and with the proceeds, buy food and shelter, and with what was left, to start the process over. In the insane world, the dark universe that was the Soviet Union, this was highly illegal and severely punished. A long prison sentence could well be a death sentence for the captive as well as for the family that depended upon him. But it was a widespread practice, there being no other way to survive.

Shimon had gone to the next town hoping to sell the few odds and ends he had managed to put together, items he kept hidden under his coat until he might find people he could safely sell to. Back home, Chana overheard a conversation that revealed that the KGB or the militia was, on that day, about to surround the black market area in the adjoining town and cart everyone caught with goods off to prison. Unable to use the road, she raced through the fields and the wild to get in the back way in the hope of finding him and getting him out of there before the net fell over him.

She did find him, and she did get him safely back home. As hard and as self-lessly, uncomplainingly, as he toiled in life on her behalf and on behalf of their family, it was also always her job, and her mandate in life, to protect him.

He was strong and kind and good, and he devoted those attributes to care for her and the family. She was, as a result of hardship, sickly, but her strength, borne of character and determination, was boundless. And as much as it was later expended on behalf of her children, it was always primarily for him. For, as God designed this relationship in the Garden of Eden, they were of one flesh. And that was as it should be. And it was from them, my parents, of blessed memory, that I learned what such a relationship can be, and to what I could, if blessed, aspire.

Some years ago I attended a wedding that was, in its strict ritual, halachic. But the (Ashkenazi) bride did not circle the groom seven times (or even once), as is traditional. She, like many other ill-informed but strongly opinionated people, parroting "feminist" dogma steeped in secular "values," refused to show "subser-vience" to her husband and would not do it.

How utterly clueless. I feared, instinctively, that those young people, so given over to the need to appear PC, might not make it in their marriage. I felt sorry for the young man, who, despite his foolishness, was otherwise a nice fellow and who, I thought, otherwise deserved to have a wife who would devote herself to him (as he would to her), and, in circling him under the chuppah, would be spinning her magical web of protection all around him. That special power is something God endowed women with.

Not to comment on what happens in other cultures, we, in our Jewish world, recognize this: every Jewish man blessed with a really good marriage understands the utterly determined power with which his wife spends her life protecting him, to the best of her ability and beyond, from the dangers and the hurts of this world.

There is nothing like it in this life. A woman may be fiercely protective of her children; they are, after all, the fruit of her womb. The anticipated life of her children, however, is ultimately apart from her and beyond the years of her own life. A husband, her choice, her lot in life, is also her responsibility and her charge for life.

In Parashas Emor the Kohanim are commanded, given their elevated spiritual state, not to expose themselves to *tumas hames* by having contact with or even being under the same roof as a corpse. The exceptions to that restriction, close blood relatives, are specified: mother, father, son, daughter, brother, unmarried sister. The word *wife* does not appear. And yet we do know that the wife is, indeed, included. She is, in fact, mentioned first. Rather than *wife*, a different, and most telling, term is used.

In rabbinic correspondence literature, when the recipient of the letter is a blood relative of the author, he is typically addressed not just by name, but by the descriptive *"she'er besari,"* literally "remnant of my flesh." The shared blood, the shared genes, the shared common roots are acknowledged, to honor that person. The source of that term to describe a close relative is Scriptural (see Yeshayahu 14:22).

The Midrash (*Toras Kohanim*) takes it a step further: *there is no she'er other than a wife.* How interesting that the very term that denotes an actual blood relationship is what defines this relationship by choice. They are of one blood, of one flesh, by *choice* rather than by accident of birth, and by the instinct and the nature instilled in them by their Creator. And that imperative, that drive, that power, is part of what God implanted in woman to protect and envelop her man, and keep him safe to live out his years with her.

Ishto gufeih hava'i: they are of one flesh.

It is not necessary, in our *parashah*, for the Torah to specifically mention the Kohen's wife as a close relative, for that is so obvious as to be redundant. But beyond that, it uses, for her, the term *she'er*, a "remnant" of his own flesh, to highlight that the nature of that relationship, when things are as they should be, is, in a sense, closer and more binding than any of the others.

The Kohen's parents give him life. His wife keeps him alive – as do our wives keep us alive. They are the warmth and the refuge in this world without which real quality of life is not possible.

They circle us not just under the chuppah but throughout life, continuously spinning that magical, mystical web around us, keeping us safe, keeping us *alive*, with a strength that is so profound that it defies the imagination, unless one understands that it derives from the very Source of strength and of life itself, the Creator, Almighty God, may His Name be blessed.

Parashas Emor 5775

For Heaven's Sake

The young woman, heavy with child, pushed the twin stroller with the crying toddlers in front of her as she approached the clerk. There was a mix-up with her paperwork that she had to straighten out in person. Hesitating briefly, she checked off "single" where the form asked her legal marital status, and handed it to the clerk. She tried to shush her children as she turned to leave. "Chaim! Moishie! Be quiet and Mommy will give you a candy. Daddy is waiting outside." A bit frazzled, Ms. Goldberg adjusted her *sheitel* as she walked out.

The clerk took it in, expressionless, but inwardly delighted.

The young couple approached the official in City Hall. "Where do we get married?" The bride was wearing maternity clothes. The groom was wearing a black hat and a dark suit, white shirt, and dangling tzitzis.

The official took it in, expressionless, but inwardly delighted.

Events like these have become commonplace in recent years. Years ago we would never see such a thing. Sure, I understand that these people, who have been properly, halachically married for some time, completely *b'kedushah, al pi haTorah*, might not legally register their marriages initially. Let's skip the whys and wherefores for now. There is often a reason they do it this way. But: *How do you think this looks? Is this how people who, in the eyes of the world, represent the Torah, and the God of Israel, should present themselves?*

I can readily imagine the gentiles' conversation at the bar, or in the living room. "Those Orthodox Jews? They act so religious. But they're no different from anybody else these days. I see their paperwork. Do you know how many unmarried mothers there are among them? No morals, no shame."

And yet we are the people who are supposed to be the very models of morality.

There are, in these *parashiyos*, repeated admonitions for us to be, and to act, holy, for, says God, "I am holy." In Emor, the Torah has a specific admonition for the Kohanim: "*Kedoshim yihyu l'Elokeihem v'lo yechallelu shem Elokeihem*" (Vayikra 21:6). They shall be holy unto God, and they shall not desecrate His Name, for they (the Kohanim) are involved with His holy service.

The *meforshim* ask, why are the Kohanim specifically singled out here?

It is, we are told, because the *avodas hakodesh* described here, the holy service, is specifically performed by them, and thus, they represent those who "do God's work."

Thus, the same standard may be applied to all those who "do God's work" – Torah scholars, yeshiva students, *kollel* fellows, and their wives, all those people who by their dress and lifestyle are visibly and obviously identifiable to all the world as Torah Jews, those who are the public and communal face of *ovdei Hashem*.

For better or worse, whether they want to or not, in the eyes of the non-*frum* Jews and the world at large, *they represent the God of Israel and His Torah*. And that must be reflected in their actions, real or apparent.

Thus, the Gemara's assertion (*Shabbos* 114a) that a *talmid chacham* – who, in the eyes of the world, represents God and His Torah – who goes in public with a grease-stained, dirty garment is deserving of the death penalty. That's how careful one has to be. That's the level of responsibility a visibly *frum* Jew bears.

The Gemara above cites a *pasuk* in Mishlei (8:36): *kol mesanai ahavu maves*. Literally that means that those who hate God in effect love death. The Gemara *darshans* that *mesanai* can be read as *masniai*: those who cause God to be "hated," or looked upon scornfully, because of the negative behavior of those who represent Him, such as a *talmid chacham* who presents himself publicly in dirty clothing. They have shown themselves to "love death" – as God offers us the choice between life and good on the one hand, and death and bad on the other, and commands us, as His People, to choose life, and good (Devarim 30:15, 19). By choosing "bad," they have also chosen "death," and deserve death for the *chillul Hashem* that they cause.

"*V'lo sechallelu es Shem kodshi v'nikdashti b'soch Bnei Yisrael; Ani Hashem mekadishchem*" (Vayikra 22:32). Do not desecrate My Holy Name, says God, but rather, it is your responsibility to make My Name holy, for I am God, Who makes *you* holy.

Years ago, in Europe, there were times and places where getting married in the government offices was mandatory in order to have the marriage registered as legal.

But those same offices presented what was, for some, an insurmountable problem: they were required to appear bareheaded, and sometimes to do so under an image of *avodah zarah*. That they would not do, and they paid a penalty for their refusal. But it was known and understood by all that they were, in the eyes of God and Man, actually married all along.

In this wonderful America, chuppah and *kiddushin* are fully recognized and accepted vehicles for legal marriage, requiring only that the marriage be properly registered.

I suppose these young people have their rationale. I will not delve into that question here. I suspect, however, that they do not take into account what impression their decision makes on the outside observer, *and the implications for themselves in being responsible for creating that impression*. And whatever they think they gain by not bothering to make their marriage "legal" is, I believe, more than offset by the negative.

Some years ago, I was visiting a resort area in Switzerland popular among Swiss Jews, mainly from Zurich. I was shocked to see a sign prominently placed in the lobby of the Jewish hotel, in Hebrew and Yiddish, exhorting the guests to be ever so circumspect while walking in the street. Don't talk loudly. Don't be raucous. Walk no more than two abreast. Keep a low profile: *they are looking at us.*

As an American, feeling free and as much a *baalabos* in the United States as anyone else, I was shocked. This exhortation was aimed at Swiss-born Jews, Swiss citizens.

Well, that's Europe, and that's Switzerland. God bless America.

But the reality is that even here they are, in fact, looking at us. Not like in Europe, thank God. But even here we stand apart; we are different. People – Jews who are far from Torah, as well as the sea of gentiles among whom we live – look at us and they see the Jewish God and His Torah. Willy-nilly, we are, *k'v'yachol*, the guardians of His reputation.

This holds true for all aspects of behavior: honesty, decency, kindness, courtesy, and everything else. But even people who are kind and honest and courteous and sincere and moral in every way can betray that trust if they are careless how they appear in public – if, in the realm of the most fundamental form of morality, their garments appear to be stained dirty.

Parashas Emor 5772

In Uniform

You've no doubt seen them in your travels. They may think they're anonymous, or nearly so, but not to you, or even to anyone who lives around Jews who are obvious Jews. The *peyos* are more or less hidden under the baseball cap. But the beard, the physiognomy, the white shirt over a pot belly and dark pants over scuffed shoes, accompanied by a wife dressed for Thirteenth Avenue, make it quite obvious to all but the most oblivious who this guy is.

There is nothing at all wrong with this attempt at anonymity. Who says, if you're tramping through the wilds of the Canadian Rockies, that you have to trumpet your whole ethnic and religious identity? You're not harming anyone or anything, ipso facto, if you just want to go about your vacation quietly and be yourself. It would help, of course, not to say too much, lest your manner of speech, your sometimes bizarre sentence construction, your vague accent give you away.

Other times, however, in the course of real life, the uniform is, in fact, an important part of one's self-identification. For the Jew, it is part of what helps define and enforce the parameters of appropriate behavior. When you look like that, you cannot – you ought not, you *must* not – shame the God and the people you represent by engaging in bad behavior. Too bad that imperative isn't always remembered, or respected, by some people in "uniform." And that bad behavior is thus doubly harmful, to the good name of God, the Torah, and the Nation of Israel, as well as to the individual (not to mention any victims of said behavior). By and large, people who present themselves to the world as obvious, identifiable Jews are cognizant of this and behave accordingly.

Likewise, the admonition (in Vayikra 21:6) singling out the Kohanim with a warning to display holy behavior. It may be true that they are the *least* likely to misbehave, but the vulnerability, the potential for harm, is greater than for others. It is *davka* the "holy ones" – not just the Kohen but the rabbi, the *talmid chacham*, the *yeshivaleit*, the *chassidish*, indeed every identifiable *frum* Jew – who need to be the most careful not to be, *chalilah, mechallel Shem Shamayim* by bad or even unintended, *careless* behavior.

And so perhaps this helps explain a huge enigma in the *haftarah* for this *parashah*, in the book of Yechezkel (44). In defining what is expected of a Kohen, certain discrepancies are listed that don't coincide exactly with the halachah we know from the Torah. Much has been written on this subject. Perhaps most glaring is the admonition that Kohanim not eat *neveilos* and *treifos*.

Kohanim should not eat *treif*? Good morning! What is he saying? How about Rabbi Goldberg? Can *he* eat *treif*? Or Henry Goldberg, barber. Can he eat *treif*? Why are the Kohanim singled out here, not to eat *treif*?

Hold that thought. Further in Emor (chapter 23), in the midst of the listing of the holidays of the year, and the various observances of those holidays, is the admonition to leave the corners of the fields, and any dropped produce, for the poor. Do this because *I am Hashem, your God.*

Nice law. *Leket, shichechah, peah* to be left for the poor.

But wait, weren't you paying attention just last week, in Parashas Kedoshim (19:9), *where the exact same law is stated*?

Why the repeat? And why in the middle of the various laws of *yom tov*, including the associated *korbonos*? It is interposed between Pesach and Shavuos on one side, and Rosh Hashanah, Yom Kippur, and Sukkos on the other side of this repeated mitzvah.

Rashi, quoting Rav Avdimi in (Midrash) *Toras Kohanim*, teaches that in so doing, the Torah is telling us that whoever fully fulfills the mitzvos of *leket, shichechah,* and *peah* (i.e., gives tzedakah wholeheartedly, the way he is supposed to), *it is as if he personally built the Beis Hamikdash and brought all the prescribed sacrifices as mandated in the Torah.* And one who fails to do so, it is as if the Beis Hamikdash exists, but he ignores it and brings nothing.

The Torah Temimah adds that one reason for the holidays as prescribed is to ensure that the Kohanim and the poor are properly taken care of by the rest of the nation; and that obligation, we see from here, exists all year round.

Now let's go back to the admonition in Yechezkel that the Kohanim not eat *neveilos* and *treifos*.

Because you are astute, you have no doubt already remarked that our own current Parashas Emor says something very similar regarding the Kohanim: "*Neveilah u'treifah lo yochal l'tamah bah; Ani Hashem* (He [the Kohen] shall not eat *neveilah* or *treifah* to become *tamei*; I am Hashem; Vayikra 22:8).

The actual explanation gets kind of technical (see *Chullin* 100b), involving various aspects of *tumah*, ritual uncleanness, and under what circumstances certain ritually unclean items impart *tumah* to a person. There is also a special ritual form of slaughter for birds (*melikah*) that under other circumstances would result in the bird being a *neveilah*. The Kohanim may eat these birds when they are brought as *korbonos*, but otherwise they would be strictly forbidden to them as *neveilah*. Perhaps this is an extra admonition to them to be careful and strict with something they are sometimes permitted.

But the real lesson, it appears, is that of *tosefes kedushah*: an *extra* measure of holiness that is expected of Kohanim, those who do "God's work," and who are habitually present in the holy precincts of the Mikdash. There are other restrictions placed on Kohanim in this portion of Yechezkel that appear to exceed that which is required by the Torah, as if they *each* were the Kohen Gadol. And that is because the rest of the people look to the Kohanim as teachers and role models. Kohanim are reputed to be *zerizim*, extra diligent in seeking holiness. Here, they are being *taught* to be *zerizim*.

The *tafkid*, the mission of the Kohen is not just to do the work in the Mikdash. It is also to teach the rest of the Jewish People the difference between *kodesh* and *chol*, between the holy and the profane, between *tahor* and *tamei* (Yechezkel 44:23), between the exalted existence of the spirit and the mundane, the difference between Israel and the rest of the nations. To push, in one's daily existence, for that extra measure of moral and religious rectitude that sets us apart as a nation (and which, alas, is often so resented by others).

Yechezkel Hanavi is preparing the people, and the Kohanim, for the rebuilding of the Beis Hamikdash and the resumption of the divine service. The best way to keep it, this time, is to be ever cognizant of what God expects of us. To be *zerizim*. To be eager. To be good examples and role models for those who look at us and who look to us.

And this applies, clearly, to all those who are identifiably in the camp of Israel, and certainly to those who are in its leadership.

It's great to be a *zariz*, to be zealous in one's personal piety, to quake and to shake, immersed in prayer and study. But the objective measure of authentic zealotry for the sake of Heaven, we are taught, lies less in the corners of your beard than in the corners of your field: How zealous are you in providing for the poor? It's hard to part with your hard-earned money. *Now do it anyway.*

Do it, zealously, as a testament to who you really are. Do it, zealously, for the sake of Heaven, as that is your faith. Do it, zealously, because the uniform you are wearing, whatever form that takes, is serving its true purpose, reminding you, and testifying to the world, that you are privileged to have been chosen, by the Creator Himself, to be an exemplar for the world in how a human being, by his actions, can be an expression of God's Will in this world, how a Jew can be, in his everyday actions, a living expression of God's holiness in this world.

L'chach notzarta: for this you were created.

Parashas Emor (חז"ל) 5776, Yerushalayim Ir Hakodesh

My Shiny *Gartel*

The world is divided into two groups of people: those who prefer a shiny *gartel* and those who do not. I'm a shiny *gartel* kind of guy.

Parashas Emor contains a major section outlining Shabbos and the *yamim tovim*. We honor those holy days: we observe the rules, we involve ourselves with Torah, we have special prayers, special meals, special clothing. Indeed, special *begadim* for Shabbos and *yom tov* have always been an essential part of the Jewish wardrobe. Permit me, then, to take the liberty of using this *parashah* to tell my shiny *gartel* story.

Some months ago, while in Israel, excited and enthusiastic about being there, I bought a really beautiful tallis for use in Israel. It has a beautiful, dense weave, it's nicely striped, with the most *mehudar* tzitzis, and is, in fact, the kind of tallis – a *Terkishe tallis* – that my *zeides* wore in their own enthusiastic service of the Ribbono shel Olam in the Chassidic world of Galitzia that was.

With my new Shabbos tallis, and my Shabbos *begadim*, I needed a new Shabbos *gartel*. It had to be wide enough, not thin, and, of course, shiny. I went in search.

It came as a big surprise that I could not find one. In Yerushalayim Ir Hakodesh, of all places. Naturally, I expected to find it readily in Meah Shearim or Geulah. I tried several stores. In each, all I got was a shrug: "This is what we have." No shiny *gartel*.

I'm old enough to remember Rechov Meah Shearim as it used to be.

The dusty old *tashmishei kodesh* shops that used to line the street have largely been replaced by sleek tourist emporiums, "Judaica" stores that have lots of stuff, sometimes even a *gartel*, but no shiny *gartel*. I know enough to look where the locals shop.

Still no shiny *gartel*.

There's one little place on Rechov Meah Shearim where I've bought little things from time to time over the years that is still very much like it must have been 100 or 120 years ago when the neighborhood was built. With confident expectation, I went in.

The shop is tiny, although there is a back room of undetermined size and function.

Behind the counter stood a little old man whom I recognized from years ago. He had a white beard and flowing, curly white *peyos*. There were a few *seforim* out for sale, apparently randomly chosen, and one or two small sets of *seforim*, not all of them complete. It was a bit dusty. There were no other customers. I asked him if he had a shiny *gartel*. He opened a little drawer, where there were a few yarmulkes and a few *gartel*s. There was no shiny *gartel*. I thanked him and walked out.

At the door, something stopped me. It was as if a hand grabbed hold of my heart and made me turn around. I told him I'd buy what he had.

He pulled out his widest *gartel*, and a piece of paper, and he started writing.

The cost of a *gartel* depends on its width, *x* number of shekels for each of the braided black strings that constitute the fringed ends of the *gartel*.

He was writing a multiplication, calculating the cost. He went through it several times and then asked me to check his arithmetic to see if it was right. It was very endearing.

I confirmed his calculation and handed him 100 shekels. He went into the back room to look for change.

It was then that I noticed a man sitting in the corner, behind a pile of – stuff.

He said to me, "You don't know what you just accomplished. That man – the owner – has been standing here all day. Not one customer had walked in, and he was discouraged. It's now three in the afternoon and you were the first customer to walk in. And then you walked out. But now you're buying something. You are *mamesh mechayeh nefashos*."

Just then the *baal habayis* returned with the change. He calculated on paper how much change to give me and asked me to check it. He asked me to count the money to make sure it was right. It was then that I realized that all his calculations were not a function of arithmetic dysfunction, or the act of a simpleton. It was his way of being scrupulously honest in his business and making sure I was comfortable with the transaction.

He also engaged me in very pleasant conversation in down-home Yiddish. His demeanor was soft and sweet. He spoke to me as he would to a close relative. "Where are you from? Don't misunderstand: it doesn't matter to me really where you're from. But when I wish you a safe journey back, it helps to know where you're going."

There was something about the old-time *temimus* of this Jew that moved me very deeply.

I was not only in an old-time Meah Shearim shop. I was experiencing a Jew and a Jewish civilization that the crush of modernity was sweeping away. I connected with him in a way that one rarely does with a stranger. This Yid, and what he represents, was anything but a stranger.

I didn't take the change. Instead, I bought every *sefer* he had available.

The next day I went back and bought whatever else he had. I suppose he was happy with that. He was too fine to show it. But I certainly was happy.

And when I opened the little bag and took out the *gartel*, in my hand was the shiniest *gartel* I ever saw.

Parashas Emor 5771

Behar

Proclaim Liberty throughout the Land

The secular Zionists, years ago, used to present a silly argument. While we were in the Diaspora, they argued, keeping the Torah and the mitzvos served to keep us apart from the surrounding cultures, which would otherwise overwhelm us, possibly to the point of disappearance. The Torah thus preserved us while we were in exile. In Israel, however, they said, where "everybody" is Jewish, it's no longer necessary.

Of course, they fail to take into account at all such inconvenient considerations as the fact that the Torah is not a human invention, but the living word of the Living God, the revealed expression of His will, eternally binding on each Jew and upon all Jews, our blueprint for life, and, by the way, our very deed to the land. Imagine that: supposedly Zionists, they would do away with our very justification for being there.

Strangely enough, despite their wrongness, their wrongheadedness and their ignorance, in a way, there is, remotely, perversely, something to what they say, although not at all in the way they think.

The Torah, in Parashas Behar, prescribes the seven-year Shemittah cycle, with the seventh cycle, culminating in the fiftieth year as the Yovel (Jubilee). On that Yom Kippur, the Shofar is sounded throughout the land, and *dror* (liberty) is proclaimed. Servants are released from servitude; land that has been sold returns to its ancestral hands. For the second successive year, the land is not cultivated, yet there is plenty. It's kind of like Shemittah squared.

The ringing theme, known to virtually all, enshrined on the Liberty Bell in Philadelphia as the epitome and the inspiration of the new nation that arose on these shores as conceived in liberty, declares, in the words of the Torah: "Proclaim liberty throughout the land, and unto all the inhabitants thereof" (Vayikra 25:10).

It is a moving declaration of human liberty. Ibn Ezra, on the meaning of *dror*, cites a small songbird that sings beautifully when it is free. If captured, it withers, stops eating, and dies.

It also has specific legal meaning. Beyond that, like much else in the Torah, each word has meaning specific to the choice of that very word. Thus, from the words "l'chol yoshveihah" (all its inhabitants), we know that it only applies when all the tribes of Israel are dwelling in the land (see *Erchin* 32b; *Yerushalmi, Shviis* 10:2; and *Gittin* 4:3). For only when we are *all* free and dwelling peacefully upon our own land, specifically the Land of Israel, are we truly free. That is *dror*.

On this concept of *dror*, the Baal Haturim presents a striking *gematria*. *Dror* = 410, the exact number of years that the first Beis Hamikdash stood.

The problem with that, of course, is that for many of those years that the Beis Hamikdash existed, most of the tribes of Israel had already been exiled, and there had been much foreign dominion over the land and over the Jewish People. In fact, the Baal Haturim's reference only highlights that sad history, which stands in stark contrast to the very concept of *dror*.

One might answer, simply, that he was evoking the *concept* of *dror*, *what it could be like, what it should have been like*, had we not, by our sins, brought upon our heads the very exile and punishments that put our national *dror* to an end.

Allow me to offer an alternate insight into the juxtaposed words *dror* and *aretz*, and revisit that Baal Haturim, taking aim directly at those silly secularists cited above.

The secular Zionists had argued that the Torah and mitzvos should apply only in the Diaspora, where they are needed to keep the people whole, and are not needed in the land itself, living in which is, they maintained, sufficient Jewish fulfillment.

In fact, the dilemma and the challenge facing the leadership of our people when we went *into* exile was just the opposite: there were those who argued that the Torah was given for living in Israel, but would no longer apply in the Diaspora.

Both arguments are, of course, silly and ignorant. The Torah was given not *in* the Land of Israel, but in the Sinai Desert, at least in part to demonstrate that it applies at all times and in all places. Moshe Rabbenu pined to enter the land, at least in part, in order to be able to fulfill those specific mitzvos, largely agricultural, that apply uniquely to Israel. He wanted to fulfill *all* 613 commandments, not just the vast majority that could be fulfilled everywhere else.

But the defeated and depressed exiles had been living, as a nation, in the Land of Israel for 890 years when the first Beis Hamikdash was destroyed. They might well have assumed that the whole thing was over, that the old rules no longer applied, that God had rescinded (*chalilah!*) His relationship with us. A parallel situation existed years later when the second Beis Hamikdash was destroyed.

The spiritual leadership of our people, with a steady hand, made sure to keep us true to our eternal calling as the Torah nation. The land is itself holy, but it needs the Torah in order to bloom. Our long and dedicated history demonstrates quite clearly that while its *full* fruition is in the land, the Torah exists, functions, applies, and is totally binding quite independent of the land.

And so, as we faced exile, the two needed to be, in a sense, uncoupled. In order to preserve the Torah in the exile, it had to be freed of its bond to the land, however important the land is, however bound up with the Torah it is.

And so even as the 410 years of *dror* as cited by the Baal Haturim included years that were good and years that were bad, years when all the Jews were in the land and years when they were not, we can look at "*v'karasem dror ba'aretz l'chol yoshveihah*" and understand it in its primary meaning, to proclaim liberty throughout the land and to all its inhabitants (the People of Israel), and we can also see in it a subtle and less happy message: the history of our people will include the sad requirement that the Torah and the nation whose code of life it is must be "liberated" *from* the land, insofar as Torah observance and Torah life are concerned, so that the Torah and the People of Israel might survive wherever they are. And they have indeed been dispersed all over the globe.

As we approach Shavuos, the holiday that marks our being given the Torah, it is well to remember *where* we received it (in the wilderness, in exile) and where we were headed when we received it (the holy Land of Israel, where the life of Torah can be complete). God, the Torah, the People of Israel, the Land of Israel, are, by the Ribbono shel Olam's grand design, all bound up together. We pray that the flowering of Israel, and the flowering of Torah in Israel, is, in our day, a harbinger of Redemption, of true and complete *dror* in its most wonderful sense, with all of us free, all of us there, rejoicing in the Lord God Who made us what we are, Who made possible what we can be, Who will emplace us permanently in that holy and beautiful land, and bless us permanently and eternally with *dror*.

Parashas Behar-Bechukosai 5775

Ready to Help

Several years ago there was, reportedly, a fool of a zealot in Israel who, upon seeing a little (Orthodox) girl in a dress he judged too skimpy, spat at her and yelled terrible things. It was all over the media. It was terrible. It resulted in open season on the *frumer*, even by the *stam* Orthodox.

I don't know what actually happened, but I know that, sadly, it might have happened as reported. There are hotheaded fools among us who, with their misplaced zealotry, bring about the opposite of the desired effect. Some of the most important lessons in Jewish teaching somehow never reached them.

One of the greatest lessons in the power of tzedakah is to be found in Parashas Behar, in the classic commentary on *"Ki yamuch achicha,"* if your brother falls low. Do not let him fall, the Torah commands, but reach out to him and lift him up, that he should live beside you.

Toras Kohanim, cited by Rashi, compares the situation to a heavy load (*life!*) balanced precariously on a donkey's back. If it starts to tip over, it is usually easy for just one person to reach over and adjust it so that it doesn't fall. Once it actually falls, it takes the efforts of many to pick up the fallen load and put things right.

So too, the unfortunate fellow who is faltering in life can often be readily helped, before he actually falls. Once his situation actually collapses, it is far more difficult to put him back on his feet. And that applies to his psyche as well as to his finances.

The *Midrash Rabbah* on this verse cites Tehillim 41, *"Ashrei maskil el dol,"* happy is he, blessed is he, who is clever enough to know what to do with a poor person. The Midrash offers a variety of homiletical interpretations. Classically, understood in terms of charity, the lesson is taught that one who is clever enough to sustain the poor, and who thus *k'v'yachol* does God's work for Him, who thus becomes, in a manner of speaking, God's creditor, puts himself in a most enviable position.

There are, however, other interpretations of *"maskil el dol"* in the Midrash. One, the teaching of Abba bar Yirmiyah in the name of Rabbi Meir, posits that this refers to one who is *mamlich yetzer tov al yetzer hara*, who helps defeat the common human trait of temptation to do wrong, not only in himself, but by knowing, cleverly, how to exert a good influence on others.

We know that even a good person, sorely tempted, may sin, but he may well be horrified by what he has done, even as he continues to be drawn to it. But once he becomes accustomed, by repeated behavior, to a particular misdeed, he quickly loses that aversion, the sin now having become normal behavior to him. He becomes blinded to what he is doing. And he may well resent and resist the efforts of others, however well intentioned, to correct his behavior.

And so the "correcter" must be clever indeed to effect that correction.

On this Ateres Yeshuah cites the example in *Bava Basra* 15b: when the defendant, the sinner, is told to "remove the splinter from between his teeth" (i.e., refrain from some infraction, possibly a minor one), he may retort to the judge, "Remove the beam from between your eyes!" (i.e., don't criticize me, you do much worse!).

We have all seen people do that. I remember, years ago, when a certain (nice) young teenage fellow in shul was sitting in the back and carrying on a loud and animated conversation with his friend during davening, a well-meaning neighbor, a concerned father himself, trying to be helpful, very tactfully pointed that out to the boy's father, who, instead of saying thank you, angrily retorted, "Your son does worse!"

You need to be clever in offering constructive criticism, and you need to know your audience.

And it's best to do it before the bad behavior is ingrained. Do it without embarrassing anyone, and do it, if you can, without even spelling out what the person did wrong. It can easily backfire, making everything worse.

Shlomo Hamelech says (Mishlei 9:8), don't correct a *letz*, a non-serious person, lest he hate you; correct a *chacham*, a wise person, and he will love you. The Imrei Noam explains: don't criticize someone's actions by telling him he is a *letz*, that he is not a serious person. He will hate you for it and will not accept your criticism, however well intended it is. Rather, help him, lovingly, to understand how pleasant are the ways and the deeds of the *chacham*, the wise and the good, encouraging him to emulate those pleasant ways. It will make him love you and accept your advice.

Ki yamuch achicha – if your brother falls low, if he becomes poor in judgment, help him before he falls too low, lest it become so much more difficult to lift him up, before his bad behavior becomes too ingrained. Do it because, as the *pasuk* continues, *v'chai imach*, he will live alongside you, because we are all in this together, but *al tikach mi'menu neshech v'sarbis*, don't take from him excessively, don't take from him his dignity and his self-respect, don't cause him pain; rather, do it lovingly, kindly, wisely, pleasantly. *V'chai imach*. It will accomplish what nasty criticism never can.

My mother, as wise a parent as anyone could want, used to advise me, when I had to criticize my own children, "*nur mit gitten*," do it only in a good and pleasant way. How well she knew.

Life is full of situations in which one needs to remind others about the right thing. Often one prefers not to, and indeed often it is not one's place to. But sometimes it is, and it would be cruel not to, assuming it is done the right way, gently, lovingly, caringly, respectfully.

Arrogance and anger have no place in this scenario and never produce anything good.

We are all aware of the damaged people in our midst, victims of bad parenting or bad teaching. Even those who grow up to lead normal, productive lives, are not what they could or should have been. But in all our relationships, really, as friends, neighbors, employers, and coworkers, even in casual encounters with people we don't know, the same holds true.

All of us are sometimes off base. We are the *dol*, the "poor person" who needs a bit of help, a little guidance, when it is in place. It takes humility and openness to successfully receive that help, and talent, patience, and kindness to successfully extend it. Doing what we should on behalf of our fellow Jews, doing it right, doing it cleverly, doing it kindly, not only helps them, but evokes, for us, the prospect of the rest of that *pasuk*: "*Ashrei maskil el dol; b'yom raah yemaltehu Hashem*" (On the day of evil, God will rescue him; Tehillim 41:2).

Parashas Behar (חו״ל) 5776, Yerushalayim Ir Hakodesh

Render unto Meilech

Do animals have rights?

Are the beneficiaries of the various "entitlement acts" enacted by Congress really "entitled" to the largesse that is being bestowed upon them?

Can you rob someone who has nothing?

Many people, myself included, have always taken serious exception to the idea that animals, like people, have "rights," or that the recipients of government programs (usually hugely wasteful and abused programs) are actually "entitled" (except by government fiat) to what they receive. Rather, it is really about *us*. *We* are obligated to treat animals decently. *We* are obligated to care for and support the poor. It's not their individual entitlement, it's our individual and communal obligation.

Years ago there was a fellow who used to come around our shul in the morning, asking for a handout. I don't know if he was really in need, but I used to put fifty cents in his hand each morning. He seemed content with that. Once, after he didn't show up for four days, he told me that I *owed* him two dollars.

It was like he pushed my irk button. I didn't like that at all, and I told him so. And he heard me not at all as I explained to him, in a civil but annoyed way, what was wrong with his thinking. He moved on, but I realized that I had indulged *myself* with my tirade rather than make him understand anything.

And I may have been dead wrong.

Can you rob someone who has nothing? Yes, you can.

Parashas Behar has a number of commandments that begin with the phrase "*Ki yamuch achicha*," when your brother (fellow Jew) falls down low, is down on his luck. On one of these (25:25), *Tanchuma* cites a verse from Mishlei (22:22), "*Al tigzal dal ki dal hu, v'al tedakeh oni ba'shaar*" (Do not rob a poor man because he is poor, and do not crush the poor man in the gate).

Don't start up with a poor person, says God, *because I, God, made him poor, for My own reasons, and thus you're starting up with Me.* And what can you rob from someone who has nothing? If you have been in the habit of supporting him, if you have been giving him money, you might one day say, "Whoa! How long will I continue to support him? Why is it up to me? How about somebody else? Does it have to be forever? And if I keep giving to him, I'm only perpetuating the cycle of poverty! Enough!"

And if you do this, says *Tanchuma*, know that *you are robbing that poor man, because he has no place else to turn. You are his parnassah.* I made you rich (i.e., you can give), and I made him poor, says God. I can just as easily reverse the roles, as the next *pasuk* in Mishlei says, "*Ki Hashem yariv rivam v'kava es koveihem nafesh,*" for Hashem will argue for them, and rob those who rob them, even of their lives.

Why? Because by withholding what he has come to count on from you, you are robbing him of his very life, and your very life is at stake. And God does listen to the poor: "*Ki shome'a el evyonim Hashem*" (Tehillim 69:34).

Wow. That's a hard situation. It's *almost* a *disincentive* to support a poor person or a poor family! One can get stuck with them. And yet...

My late father-in-law, Zalman Aryeh Hilsenrad, *a"h*, started and operated an incredible *keren hachesed* in which families in the United States "adopt" desperately poor families in Israel, sending them checks every month, year after year. Once in a while there is a family whose circumstances change for the better, and they no longer need help. More often than not, the grinding poverty goes on. The poor keep on needing, and the adopters keep on sending. The loyalty of the needy to the program is sadly understandable. The loyalty of the adopters is fine and noble beyond words.

Years ago my wife and I started with a poor scholar and his children. We established a close personal relationship with them. Little did we realize then that by today we would be sending money *to the third generation.* How tragic is that? And lest you think that they like it that way, I assure you they do not. I cannot repeat here what some of the men of that family – *talmidei chachamim* all, in full Yerushalmi uniform – said of the architects of the system that keeps them and their children mired hopelessly in poverty ad infinitum. They are, *nebech*, miserable, but to feed their children they must continue to take, even as we must continue to send, all the while thankful for being on the giving end.

So if supporting a particular poor person or poor family creates such an ongoing obligation, why get started?

The other major theme in Behar, *Shemittah*, clues us in. *Six years shall you work the land. On the seventh, it is Shabbos unto God; the land shall rest and not be worked.*

Sound familiar? Of course. *Six days shall you work. On the seventh, it is Shabbos unto God; you shall rest and do no work.*

The Jew who ritually rests on Shabbos attests by doing so to the fact that it is God Who created the world. We exist to serve His will. See the first Rashi in Bereishis: God created it, God owns it, and God apportions it according to His will. Hence, our perpetual title to the Land of Israel.

The Jew who rests his land (in Israel) during the Shemittah year, by doing so, attests to the fact that God created it, God owns it, and God apportions it according to His will.

We, who may have deeds and title documents and *chazakahs*, are, in fact, only trustees. We are on the land by His blessing, to serve His will.

Thus, as the Sfas Emes points out, if we rest the land during Shemittah for the sake of Heaven, when we do work the land, we thereby elevate that working of the land to be a holy act, and the land itself becomes sanctified.

So too, when we rest on Shabbos for the sake of Heaven, we elevate all the other days of the week, and the work we do on those days becomes sanctified as it relates to Shabbos. Thus, the very names of the days are defined by Shabbos: Rishon, Sheni, etc.

As God gives us the land to work during those six years of the cycle, and as God gives us commerce and *parnasssah* during those six days of the week, and as God gives us the wherewithal to share our bounty with the poor, He does so for a purpose: that we may do good, *that we may strive to be like Him in our doing good*, that we may earn merit.

We are entrusted, by God, with the things that we have, so that with them we may serve His will. The first order of business is to acknowledge Him. When we practice *shamor* and *zachor* on Shabbos, when we refrain from *melachah*, we are attesting to the fact that God created the world and everything in it, and what we have, we have from Him.

And in so doing, we justify His giving us what we have.

When we refrain from working the land during Shemittah, we are attesting to the fact that God created the world and everything in it, and what we have, we have from Him. And in so doing, we justify His giving us what we have.

When we prop up the poor, *ki yamuch achicha*, when we give to them generously and wholeheartedly from what God has given us, we are attesting to the fact that God created the world and everything in it, and what we have, we have from Him. And in so doing, we justify His giving us what we have.

Given the centrality of these principles to our core beliefs, it is no surprise that the two mitzvos famously known for carrying an openly promised reward,

Shemittah (guaranteed bountiful produce for the sixth, seventh, eighth, and even the ninth year) and tzedakah (*u'v'chanuni na b'zos*, etc.) appear together in this *parashah*.

And Shabbos, which is so central to Jewish life, which so blesses and enriches and warms Jewish life, which defines our relationship with our Father in Heaven, is truly its own reward.

So, do animals have rights? Nah. We humans have obligations.

Are the poor entitled? Superficial human logic says no, but we have obligations.

But if we understand where whatever wealth we have comes from – why, by what justification, and for what purpose we have it, and how tenuous our hold upon it really is – when we come to realize that you *can* rob someone who has nothing, we also come to understand that the same Creator who entitled us to what we have also entitles the poor to a portion of what we have.

P.S. Please forgive that title. I couldn't help myself.

Parashas Behar-Bechukosai 5772

The Courage to Be Poor

There is an old Scottish song extolling the virtue of those with "the courage to be poor." In that world, many people who were poor turned to highway robbery (taking the low road on the high road!) to relieve their situation. And therefore someone who remained honest despite his poverty was a rare, morally courageous person.

We like to think that such a distinction is not really relevant in God-fearing Jews. Of course our poor do *not* steal. Sure, anyone can be tempted (rich as well as poor!), but it is assumed that one is honest, and stealing is so egregious an offense that a *yerei Shamayim* – even a poor man – will not do it. Even so, there is a real temptation that the poor man must deal with, which is alluded to in Parashas Behar.

The Kesav Sofer offers a novel interpretation of passages that are usually understood in quite the opposite way, lending depth and insight to a fundamental principle of Jewish existence.

V'chi yamuch achicha (if your brother falls low, becomes impoverished), *u'matah yado imach* (and his hand becomes weak and incapable, and you are in his vicinity), *v'hechezakta bo, ger v'toshav* (you shall strengthen him, support him, hold him up), *va'chai imach* (so that your brother may live with you, that he may coexist with you; Vayikra 25:35).

And even though we are not permitted to test God, *in this one instance we are permitted to do so*. Indeed, God *invites* us to do so: *b'chanuni na b'zos* (in this instance, in the giving of charity to the poor, you *may* test Me; *please test Me*), promising to open up for us the very windows of Heaven and to pour down upon us His bounty in reward (Malachi 3:10).

In a startling reversal of this usual understanding, the Kesav Sofer provides a novel view of these passages from the other side. It is not such a big deal, he says, for the rich man to share a bit of his riches with the poor; he won't miss it. (The Kesav Sofer judges the haves very kindly here, I think!) But if the donor is himself a poor man, and he *will* miss it, then he really is identifying with the poor man; he really does feel his pain; he really does love him. *B'chanuni na b'zos*, please test Me *b'zos, when you are yourself in this low circumstance*, and see how I will reward you!

Now applying this approach to the *pasuk* in Behar, *u'matah yado imach*, understand it to mean that the poor man fallen low is weakened *imach*, alongside you (who are also poor).

And then the challenge: *V'hechezakta*. Strengthen *yourself*. Strengthen *your own* resolve and determination. Overcome the natural and understandable inclination to help yourself instead of looking out for others. Reach out and strengthen your poor brother even when you yourself are in need, and then of you it will truly be said, *Ashrei maskil el dol b'yom raah* (lucky, happy, blessed, fortunate is he who is wise enough to know what to do with the poor man) *b'yom raah* (when things are bad for himself). *Yemaltehu Hashem!* God will rescue him from his own poverty, for the power of this kind of tzedakah is very great indeed. *B'chanuni na b'zos*. Test Me in this circumstance, God says.

The Midrash portrays a poor man, faint with hunger, standing in the market with nine pennies in his hand, unable to buy a piece of bread because it costs ten pennies. His life is hanging in the balance; his soul is nearly ready to depart. The lucky fellow who gives him the one penny that it takes for him to buy a piece of bread to keep himself alive has saved his life – at the cost of a penny. God then says to that savior, when *your* life hangs in the balance – when, like that poor man, *your* soul is nearly ready to depart – I will step in and save *you*.

Ashrei maskil el dol b'yom raah yemaltehu Hashem.

Lucky, happy, blessed, fortunate is he who is wise enough to know what to do with a poor man.

He may be poor himself, but he has the courage to do what he should, despite his poverty.

He may be rich, but he has the courage to do what he should, despite human nature.

What he can surely count on, what he will never lose, is God's promise and his guarantee: in this you may test Me, in this *please* test Me, for I will open up for you the very windows of Heaven and pour down upon you blessing without measure.

In the manner best known and best understood by God, when that courageous person's very soul is most at risk, *yemaltehu Hashem*.

Parashas Behar 5774

Whose Is It, Really?

Why keep Shabbos?

Obviously, first and foremost, we keep Shabbos because our Creator requires it of us.

It is God's Law. But there is also much else that is at play.

God created the world, and everything in it, in *sheshes yemei hamaaseh*, the six days of creation. He then created Shabbos. In a divine sense, He "rested" on Shabbos, so that we may also rest on that day, that we may devote ourselves solely to matters of the spirit on that day, a gift of inestimable value.

From our perspective, however, by observing Shabbos, we are making a statement.

In the face of all who scoff, by keeping Shabbos we are clearly affirming that Hakodosh Baruch Hu in fact created the world, that on the seventh day we "rest" as, *k'v'yachol*, He did, and as He has commanded us to do. It is an unequivocal statement of faith.

The first Rashi in Bereishis quotes Rabbi Yitzchak, stating that the Torah begins with the story of creation, to establish and to clarify that it is God Who brought the world into being; He is its Master, He is its Owner, and He apportions it in any way He wishes. Thus, those who would accuse us of stealing the Land of Israel are divinely refuted.

The Jew, therefore, should very well be careful to keep Shabbos, because it is his deed to the Land of Israel. To deny Shabbos would be to deny God's act of creation, which in turn would deny the rest of the divine narrative that constitutes our title to the land.

Parashas Behar begins with the law of Shemittah. We are to work the land for six years and to rest it on the seventh. The rationale here, it seems, is very similar. By resting the land in the seventh year, we affirm that God, Who created the world, created this land, He is its Master, He is its Owner, He apportioned it to us, and we serve Him in this way. The land is really His, we are affirming, and we are there by His leave.

The Sfas Emes points out that thus, during the six permitted years when we do work the land, having observed Shemittah now elevates that work in the non-Shemittah years to a holier plane. So too, when we count the days of the week, Yom Sheni l'Shabbos, Yom Shlishi l'Shabbos, etc., we infuse the *kedushah* of Shabbos into all the work we do during the rest of the week.

Our *parashah* has an additional parallel to Shabbos and Shemittah. *V'chi yamuch achicha*: should your fellow Jew be brought low, should he be in need of help, *should he need tzedakah*. The Torah's instruction is clear: *v'hechezakta bo*, you shall strengthen him, you shall help him. Do not allow him to fall, for then it's ever so much harder to get him up than it would have been to keep him from falling.

Hashem gives us things – the opportunity to work, the Land of Israel, financial resources – for a purpose. They represent an opportunity to do good. Foolish would be the person who is thus given the opportunity to do good with what he has, but fails to do so, thus erasing the very reason he was given those things.

Shabbos, Shemittah, tzedakah. In each case we affirm: God created the world. He is Master of all that is in it, He apportions its resources as He chooses, what we have we have from Him and only from Him, and He expects us to behave in a certain way with what He has given us.

It is interesting that the two of these mitzvos that are in in our *parashah*, Shemittah and tzedakah, come with objective guarantees, *v'tzivisi es birchasi* for Shemittah, and (in Malachi) *b'chanuni na b'zos* for tzedakah. Do as commanded and you will be rewarded.

Guaranteed.

What about Shabbos?

Certainly there is divine reward for keeping Shabbos, as for any mitzvah.

Rather than a stated guarantee, however, there is something else.

Shabbos defines our relationship with our Father in Heaven. It is an act of mutual love between Hakodosh Baruch Hu and ourselves, and indeed it is ushered in, classically, with the ultimate declaration of such love, Shir Hashirim.

The beauty, the light, the warmth, the spirituality, our bonding with our families and our fellows, our bonding with Avinu she'ba'Shamayim and the very palpable sense of His bonding with us: for the Jew, Shabbos is its own reward. Guaranteed.

Parashas Behar 5771

Bechukosai

Komemiyus

"Ata mag'il et nafshi!"

You disgust me.

It was a disturbing, emotionally charged scene, during Shacharis services at the Kotel.

A young man, perhaps thirty-five, was yelling at a somewhat older man. He was in tallis and tefillin, in the midst of davening. He had been saying something to the object of his criticism, and now it had suddenly escalated into a shouting match. It was upsetting to witness.

It was a busy morning at the Kotel, with lots of minyanim going, and lots of non-Jewish tourists walking around and taking pictures. The older man, a professional Kotel beggar, in obvious Jewish attire (and not especially clean and neat) was badgering gentile tourists for money. Horrified, the younger man had urged him to stop. It was a *chillul Hashem*. The schnorrer (I hate that term, but it appeared justified here) was ignoring the criticism and told the young man to butt out of his business. The young man persisted, saying that it was clearly contrary to halachah, not to mention harmful to the dignity of that holy place, of the Jewish religion, and of the Jewish People.

The "pro" would have none of it. He knew his rights. Who was this fellow to interfere with his business? "My rabbi told me I can do this!" he retorted, as he approached his next mark, a blond German tourist with a camera, snapping away.

That was too much for the young critic. It's bad enough to turn the Kotel into some Third World site with beggar boys running after the visitors, hands outstretched. Wading into a group of Germans, wheedling and begging, was too much. He lost it, and started yelling, *"Ata mag'il et nafshi!"* (You disgust me!).

Parashas Bechukosai presents a choice for the People of Israel. Choose Me, says God, and I will bless you in every way. I will dwell among you; you will be Mine and I will be yours. You can count on it, for I am the God Who took you, miraculously, out of bondage in Egypt. I destroyed the yoke with which you were harnessed, and freeing you, I have caused you *to walk upright*: *"komemiyus"* (Vayikra 26:13).

And if you don't choose Me, says God, if you rebel, and reject My mitzvos, terrible things will happen. And we know, sadly, that in time, they did. That is part of the long, hard story of Jewish history.

There is an interesting use of the same word on both sides of this choice, this historic equation.

If Israel chooses to follow God's path, *"v'nasati mishkani b'sochchem,"* I will emplace Myself among you, *"v'lo sig'al nafshi eschem"* (Vayikra 26:11), as Rashi elucidates, I will be tolerant, patient with you. Literally, of course, those words mean *"I will not be disgusted by you."* Strange blessing, isn't it?

Ramban explains: the body cleanses, purges itself of something disgusting by vomiting it out.

The act of purifying a utensil by immersing it in boiling water is called *hagalah*, purging the impurities, the same basic root. The blessing here is that God will accept and purify us, *without* requiring any such drastic measures.

The other side of the equation is introduced by depicting Israel making a very bad choice. If you (Israel) are put off by My mitzvos, if you make yourselves as if *disgusted* by My laws, *"v'im es mishpatai tig'al nafshechem"* (26:15), and you violate our covenant, then all the bad things will happen.

Indeed, terrible things will happen. But even then, says God, even when Israel is in the land of its oppressors, when all appears lost, I will not forget them, I will not altogether be put off or disgusted by them, *"lo me'astim v'lo ge'altim...l'hafer brisi itam"* (26:44), I will not abandon My covenant with them, but will, in the end redeem them, for I am their God. Therein lies our hope.

The Reisher Rav, Harav Aharon Lewin, was a man of great insight and sophistication in addition to great learning. He lived in Poland during a period when there was much falling away from Orthodox practice, and died, with his wife, הי"ד, the terrible death of a martyr at the hands of the accursed Germans.

The Rav understood human nature, and how a people so historically bound to God and to Torah could be seduced away. In his *Hadrash v'Ha'iyun* on the Torah (written down in large part while commuting on the train between his home and his duties in Warsaw as a member of parliament, where he stood up bravely and eloquently for Jewish interests), he analyzes how a person proceeds, stepwise, to throw off the yoke of the Torah.

Im b'chukosai timasu, if you are put off by My statutes, My *chukim*, laws for which no explanation is given, but which must be obeyed because it is God's will, and you turn away from them with the excuse that you cannot find a rational explanation for them, well, that is typically a pretext, an excuse, allowing one to take the next rebellious step and turn away altogether from God's commandments, even those whose rationale is given or obvious, to escape all obligation, to seek "freedom and emancipation," as the bond of perceived legitimacy has been broken. *Im b'chukosai timasu*, then the next step is *es mishpatai tig'al nafshechem*, you will behave as if you are altogether disgusted by the whole thing. Because the real truth is you have gone through this process *l'vilti asos es kol mitzvosai*, because what you really want is to escape from the mitzvos.

Well, with the stakes so high, why would anyone want to defy God, Who sets the rules?

Ah, human nature! If it were so obvious to everybody, there would be no contest, and then how would one earn credit for choosing to be good?

But let's get back to that key word, *komemiyus*, upright.

Even with all the miracles that accompanied our forefathers' exodus from Egypt, God did not lead them to the Land of Israel by the shortest route, straight from the Nile delta (the presumed site of the land of Goshen) along the northern Sinai and directly into Israel, as they would have to face the Plishtim, the mighty and warlike Philistines, before they were ready. They were free, but in their heads, not quite. They were not yet quite *upright*. They did not stand straight and tall. They did not stand like free men, unafraid.

Many of my friends and acquaintances who were born in Russia and who, years later, returned to Russia as Americans for a visit, have told me that they are usually identified immediately as Americans, despite their perfect Russian. Years ago it may have been their clothing that gave them away, but in recent years, that is no longer the case. I believe that there is something far more subtle, but far more fundamental at play. During their years in America, they have changed. They are free. They are unafraid. They stand upright. Their body language gives them away.

The concept of *komemiyus*, standing upright, evokes the concept of *hadar*, held so dear by Ze'ev Jabotinsky and his incomparable disciple, the great Menachem Begin, as a goal for the exiled, downtrodden Jewish People as it emerges from that lowly state. It encompasses dignity, honor, splendor, courage, strength, beauty, self-respect, being proudly faithful to Judaism and its glorious heritage. We do not exist to mirror or mimic other nations and their foibles. We stand up straight, with debt or apology owed to no one. We are the nation that God Himself led out of slavery in Egypt, having shattered the bonds which had fettered them, that they 'v return, free, upright, *komemiyus*, to the Land of Israel.

entry, is that in your life you have learned, and you have done according to what you have learned.

My late father-in-law, Zalman Aryeh Hilsenrad, *a"h*, had a chapter in his *sefer My Soul Thirsts* in which he depicts the life of a typical contemporary fellow.

In his youth, he knows he must learn Torah, but he is busy pursuing a professional course of study, or establishing a business, and he rationalizes that when he is more settled in a career, he will do what he should. We next encounter him as a young married, with children, busy building his professional business. He wants to go out to learn, he knows he ought to, but he's so busy with securing his position that he has no time left for regular *sedorim* in learning. And after all, he needs to relax sometimes too. When he's older and well established, and presumably has more time, he also no longer has the energy. And after all, he also needs to relax sometimes as well. When he's older still, when he reaches the point in his life when he was sure that he would be able to devote himself to Talmud Torah, he just no longer has the drive, or the patience, or the mental agility. And then he's old and sick, and it's over.

Rabbi Yisroel Bergstein, *a"h*, the founding *rav* of our shul, once commented to me that the biggest *chesed* a father can do for his children is to let them see him learning.

It is an ideal and an example that will serve them their whole lives, as well as for the lives of their children.

We're all busy. We all have obligations. We all get tired. Modern life can be incredibly stressful and demanding. We all have reasons to do "learning lite" rather than to really accomplish through real *toil* in our learning.

Whether we are of average intelligence, superior, or even inferior, there is no end to what we can accomplish, each on our own level, if we set ourselves to work, if we are determined and are truly *ameilim ba'Torah*.

How wonderful that would be, to really know, to know how to do, to do with far greater meaning, to be truly enlightened, to fulfill the will of our Creator, to serve Him *b'chassidus*, to give Him *nachas ruach*, to experience the true joy in life that is possible for a Jew, to inspire our children to strive for the same, to earn His blessing for ourselves, our families, and for the greater family of Israel.

Who said it's easy?

It's not. But it's so very good.

And God assures us it's so worth it.

Parashas Bechukosai 5771

Komemiyus, standing upright as Jews, the Chosen of God, *hadar*, if you will, is the very antithesis of the concept of *ge'ilah*, of being disgusting. I suspect that is why these terms are used here, in our *parashah*, to give further context to the nature and the implications of the choice that God has placed before the Jewish People.

It seems so obvious how we should choose. That it has been so often – and remains to so many – not so obvious is one of the great, dark realities of human nature.

"*Ata mag'il et nafshi*" is something no Jew should ever have to say to another Jew. I do not know the actual circumstances of that collector at the Kotel, and I'd best not judge him, even if I do have an opinion about the propriety of his behavior. But God forbid, oh dear God forbid, that we should ever again evoke such a response from the Ribbono shel Olam, or ever again face those terrible consequences described in Bechukosai that have left us shattered, dispirited, and desolate. It would be too, too much to bear. "*Ki im maos me'astanu, katzafta aleinu ad me'od*" (For even if You have utterly rejected us, have been disgusted by us, You have already raged against us so much; Eichah 5:22).

Parashas Bechukosai (חז"ל) 5776, Yerushalayim Ir Hakodesh,
Shechunas Komemiyus

Who Said It's Easy?

What worthwhile thing doesn't take work?

Very few things that we hope to accomplish in life come easy. Even things that are given to us as "free gifts" take work – typically, hard work – to properly take advantage of them.

Thus, the student who is not so brilliant can usually learn whatever he needs to know, as long as he works hard at it, and while the more brilliant student can learn it more quickly, he also needs to work hard if he wants to really master the subject brilliantly.

Anyone who is years into a really good marriage can tell you that it requires work – years of work – on the part of both partners to learn how to do it right, how to live happily and successfully with each other. The same goes for parenting, and virtually any other worthwhile endeavor. It is true of one's job or business, finances, sports skills, interpersonal relations, character traits.

Clearly, the more important something is in one's life, the more one is – or should be – willing to work to accomplish what is necessary. We all know people who do seem unwilling or psychologically unable to do what it takes, to really work hard at what they need to do. They are effectively dysfunctional. Let's confine our discussion to the normal, typical person.

The challenges of daily life sometimes make it difficult for some of us to properly prioritize how we should spend our energies. For the Jew, this itself – proper prioritizing – is a major challenge.

Parashas Bechukosai presents a straightforward quid pro quo. Do as I require of you, says the Ribbono shel Olam, and you will be blessed. Do otherwise, and *chalilah* the opposite will occur. That is the substance of the *tochachah*.

Rashi clarifies what is meant by *"Im b'chukosai telechu"*: *she'tihyu ameilim ba'Torah*. You must toil in Torah. But it also says *"v'es mitzvosai tishmeru v'asisem osam."*

Rashi continues, *"hevu ameilim al menas lishmor u'l'kayem,"* work hard that you may know *and* that you may do.

Work hard that you may come to know the divine will.

Work hard and know the divine will that you may, in fact, properly fulfill God's commands, and thus draw closer to Him.

It's not enough just to listen to the occasional *shiur*; you must toil and study hard, *on a regular basis*, that you may really come to know something of Torah. If you're brilliant and you learn quickly, then the challenge to really toil and to excel is that much greater.

It's not enough just to know, or to work hard just to know. You must work hard to know that you will indeed do. There have been times and there have been people who are essentially detached from the God aspect of Torah study, pursuing it intellectually but not spiritually, who "know" but do not "do." This is an abomination.

To learn and to do, to toil, to work really hard, *to labor*, not just to know God's word, but also to fulfill it, to observe the mitzvos energetically and enthusiastically – that is to be a *chassid*. And that, we are told in our *parashah*, will result in God's blessing.

Pasuk 26:14 tells us the other side of the equation: If you do not toil in this way, if you are not *ameilim*, both to know and to do, you are lost.

There is a well-known and oft-quoted Mishnah in *Avos* (2:5): Never say I will learn when I have the time: *you may never have the time (shema lo tipaneh)*. To my understanding, *shema lo tipaneh* implies that not only may you *always* find yourself too busy to learn, with too many other distractions at all the various stages of life, *you also run the risk of having that option taken away from you. Life does that. Too late; missed the boat.*

The Gemara (*Pesachim* 50a) tells us that there is an announcement at the gates ˙eaven: *Ashrei mi she'ba l'kan v'talmudo b'yado*. Your key to entry, or to enhanced